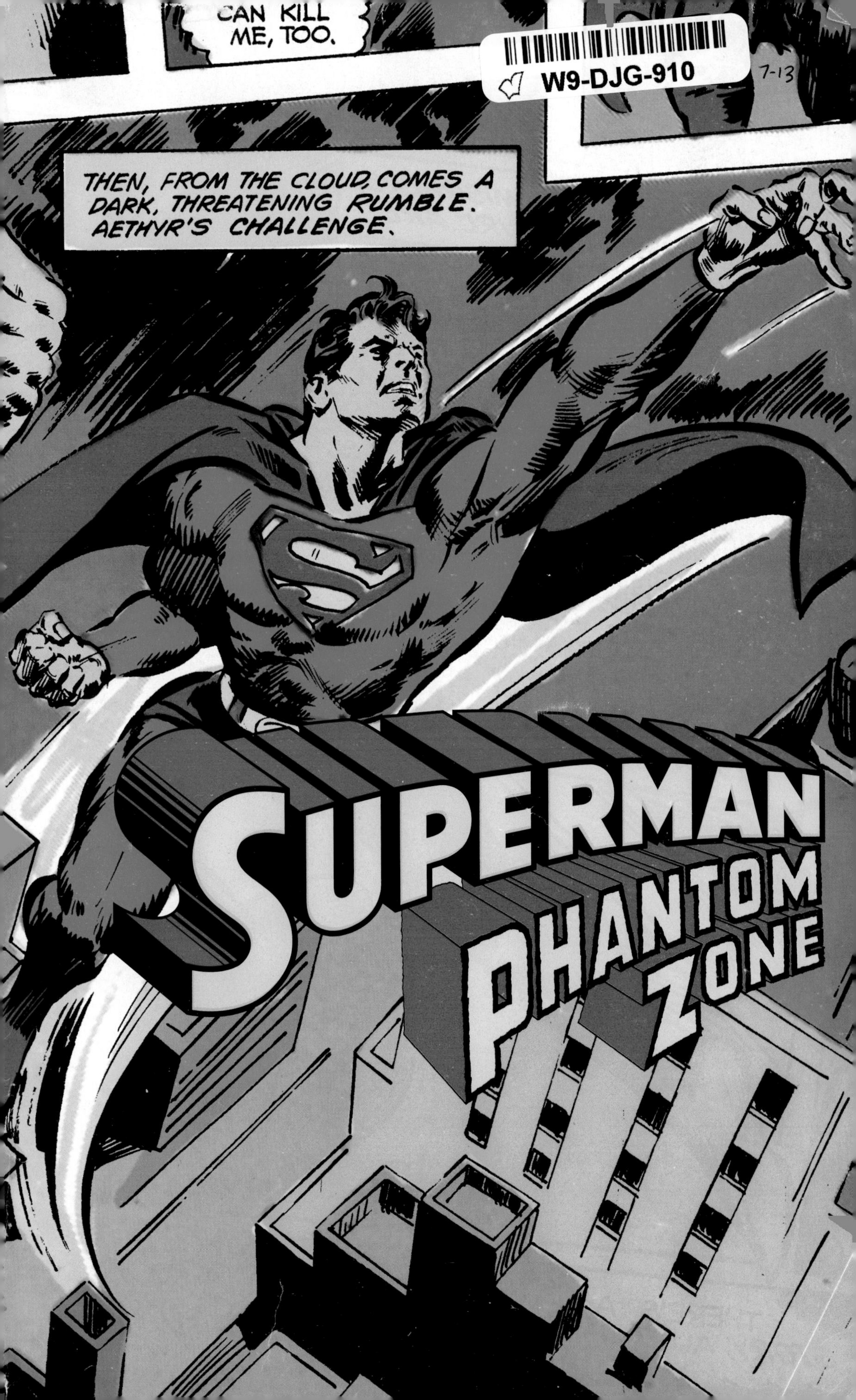
CAN KILL ME, TOO.
THEN, FROM THE CLOUD, COMES A DARK, THREATENING RUMBLE. AETHYR'S CHALLENGE.
SUPERMAN
PHANTOM ZONE

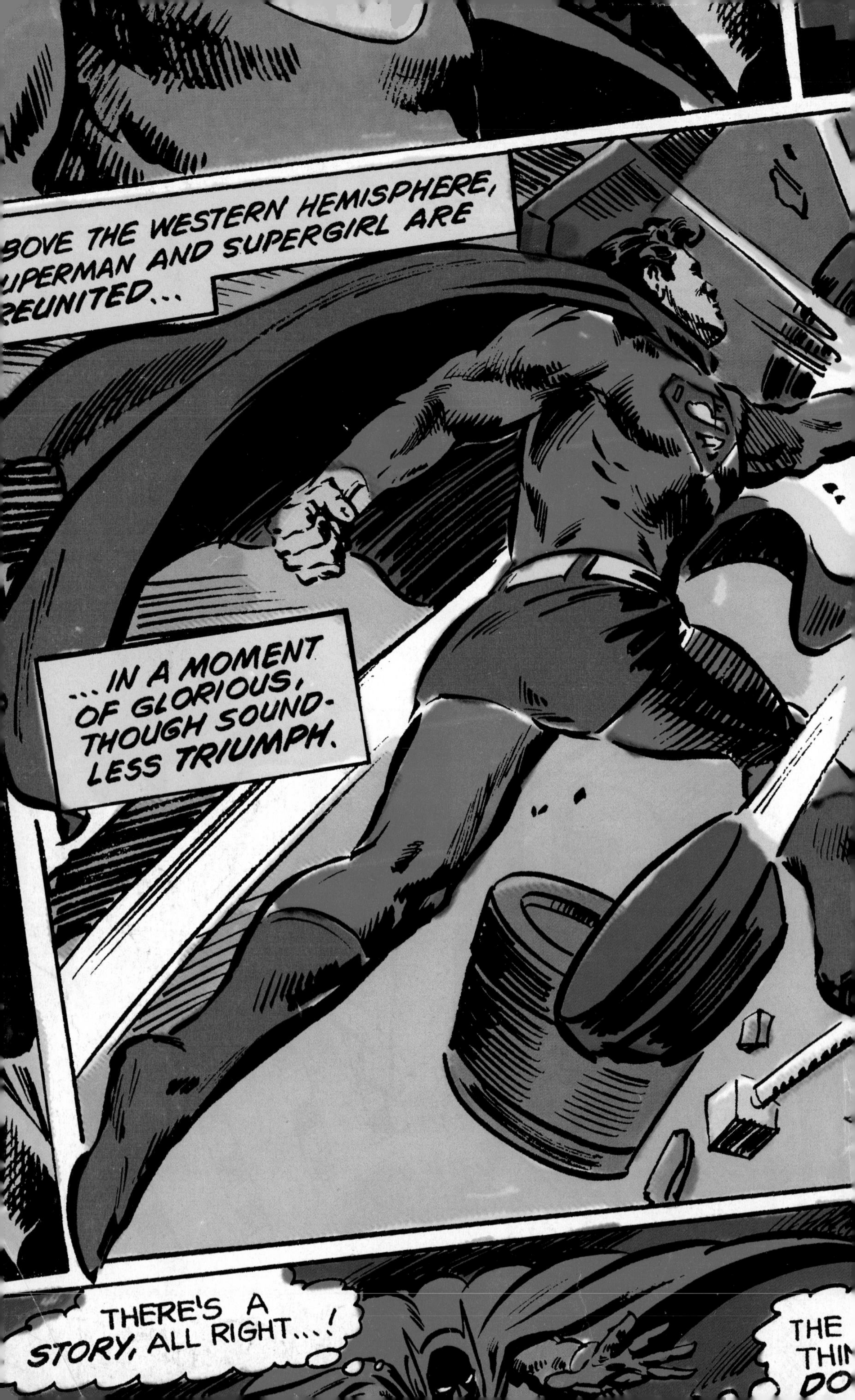
BOVE THE WESTERN HEMISPHERE, UPERMAN AND SUPERGIRL ARE REUNITED...
...IN A MOMENT OF GLORIOUS, THOUGH SOUND- LESS TRIUMPH.
THERE'S A STORY, ALL RIGHT...!

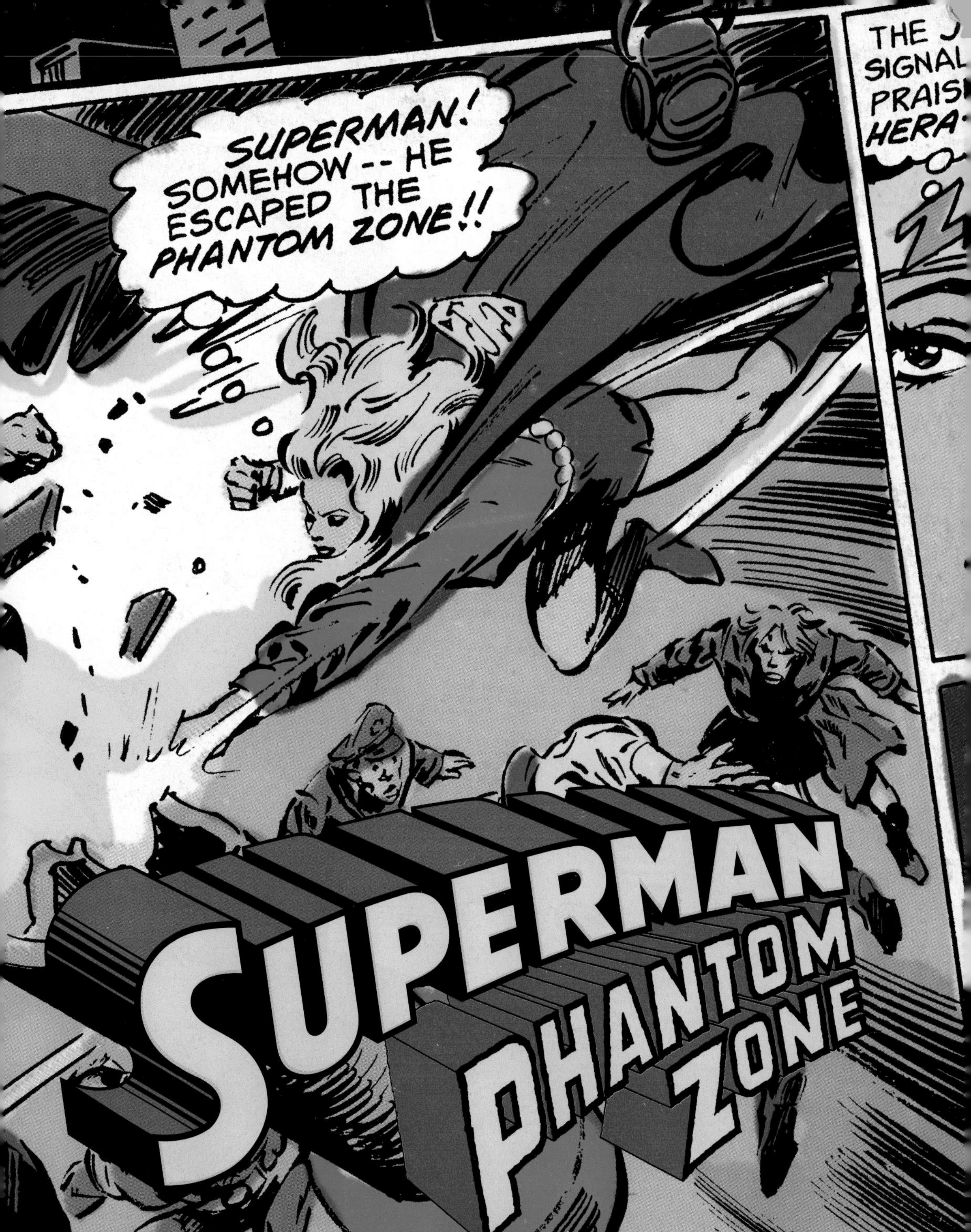
SUPERMAN! SOMEHOW -- HE ESCAPED THE PHANTOM ZONE!!

SUPERMAN PHANTOM ZONE

Steve Gerber Writer Gene Colan Tony DeZuniga Rick Veitch Bob Smith Artists
Milt Snapinn Ben Oda John Costanza Letterers
Carl Gafford Gene D'Angelo Colorists
Gene Colan Dick Giordano Cover Art
Gene Colan Dick Giordano Rick Veitch Bob Smith Original Series Covers

SUPERMAN created by Jerry Siegel and Joe Shuster
SUPERGIRL based on the characters created by Jerry Siegel and Joe Shuster
By Special Arrangement with the Jerry Siegel Family

Dick Giordano Julius Schwartz Editors – Original Series
Scott Nybakken Editor
Robbin Brosterman Design Director – Books
Louis Prandi Publication Design

Bob Harras Senior VP – Editor-in-Chief, DC Comics

Diane Nelson President
Dan DiDio and Jim Lee Co-Publishers
Geoff Johns Chief Creative Officer
John Rood Executive VP – Sales, Marketing & Business Development
Amy Genkins Senior VP – Business & Legal Affairs
Nairi Gardiner Senior VP – Finance
Jeff Boison VP – Publishing Planning
Mark Chiarello VP – Art Direction & Design
John Cunningham VP – Marketing
Terri Cunningham VP – Editorial Administration
Alison Gill Senior VP – Manufacturing & Operations
Jay Kogan VP – Business & Legal Affairs, Publishing
Jack Mahan VP – Business Affairs, Talent
Nick Napolitano VP – Manufacturing Administration
Sue Pohja VP – Book Sales
Courtney Simmons Senior VP – Publicity
Bob Wayne Senior VP – Sales

Color reconstruction on
covers and interior pages
by Tom Valente.

SUPERMAN: PHANTOM ZONE
Published by DC Comics. Cover and
compilation Copyright © 2013 DC
Comics. All Rights Reserved.
Originally published in single magazine
form in THE PHANTOM ZONE 1-4
and DC COMICS PRESENTS 97.
Copyright © 1982, 1986 DC Comics.
All Rights Reserved. All characters,
their distinctive likenesses and related
elements featured in this publication are
trademarks of DC Comics. The stories,
characters and incidents featured in
this publication are entirely fictional.
DC Comics does not read or accept
unsolicited submissions of
ideas, stories or artwork.
DC Comics, 1700 Broadway,
New York, NY 10019
A Warner Bros. Entertainment Company
Printed by RR Donnelley, Salem VA,
USA. 6/14/13 First Printing.
ISBN:978-1-4012-4051-6

Library of Congress Cataloging-in-
Publication Data

Gerber, Steve, 1947-2008.
Superman : phantom zone / Steve
Gerber, Gene Colan.
pages cm
"Originally published in single
magazine form in Phantom Zone 1-4,
DC Comics Presents 97."
ISBN 978-1-4012-4051-6
1. Graphic novels. I. Colan, Gene,
illustrator. II. Title. III. Title: Phantom
zone.
PN6728.S9G476 2013
741.5'973—dc23

2013009137

HIGH OVER THE SNOW-SWEPT BERING STRAIT, A DESPERATE AMAZON PRINCESS ADDRESSES JUST THAT QUESTION...

Table of Contents

The Haunting of Charlie Kweskill! 7
From THE PHANTOM ZONE #1
Cover art by **Gene Colan** and **Dick Giordano**

Earth Under Siege! 35
From THE PHANTOM ZONE #2
Cover art by **Gene Colan** and **Dick Giordano**

The Terror Beyond Twilight! 63
From THE PHANTOM ZONE #3
Cover art by **Gene Colan** and **Dick Giordano**

The Phantom Planet! 91
From THE PHANTOM ZONE #4
Cover art by **Gene Colan** and **Dick Giordano**

The Final Chapter 119
From DC COMICS PRESENTS #97
Cover art by **Rick Veitch** and **Bob Smith**

IN MOMENTS, THE COMBINED MIGHT OF THE TWO MOST POWERFUL WOMEN ON EARTH REDUCES THE MISSILES TO A HAIL OF FLAMING METAL...

ARTEMIS GUIDE MY HAND! MY FIRST TOSS MUST FIND ITS MARK.!

THERE WON'T BE TIME FOR A SECOND!

...THAT SIZZLES AND SINKS INTO THE ICY STRAIT

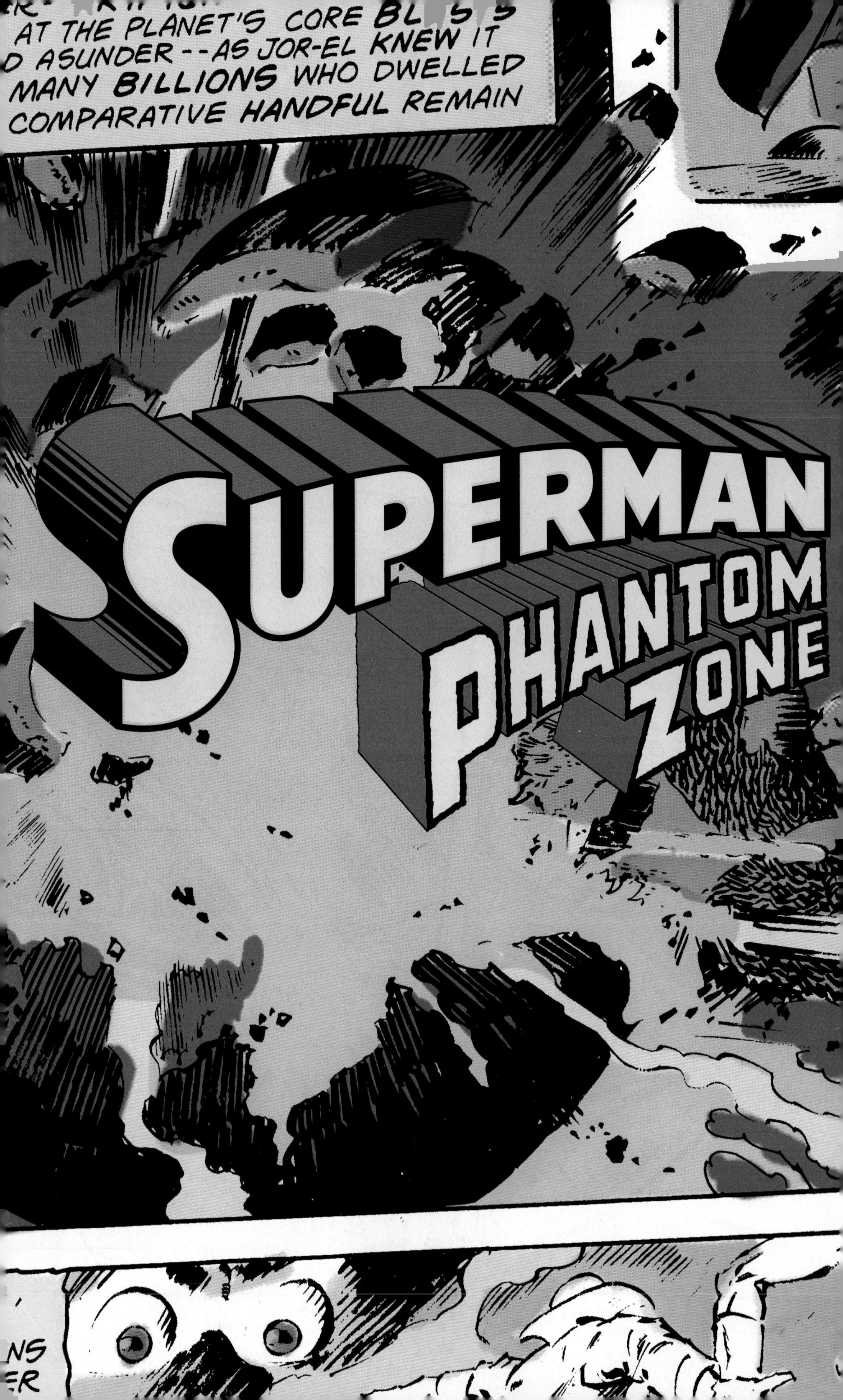
AT THE PLANET'S CORE
ASUNDER -- AS JOR-EL KNEW IT
MANY BILLIONS WHO DWELLED
COMPARATIVE HANDFUL REMAIN
SUPERMAN
PHANTOM ZONE

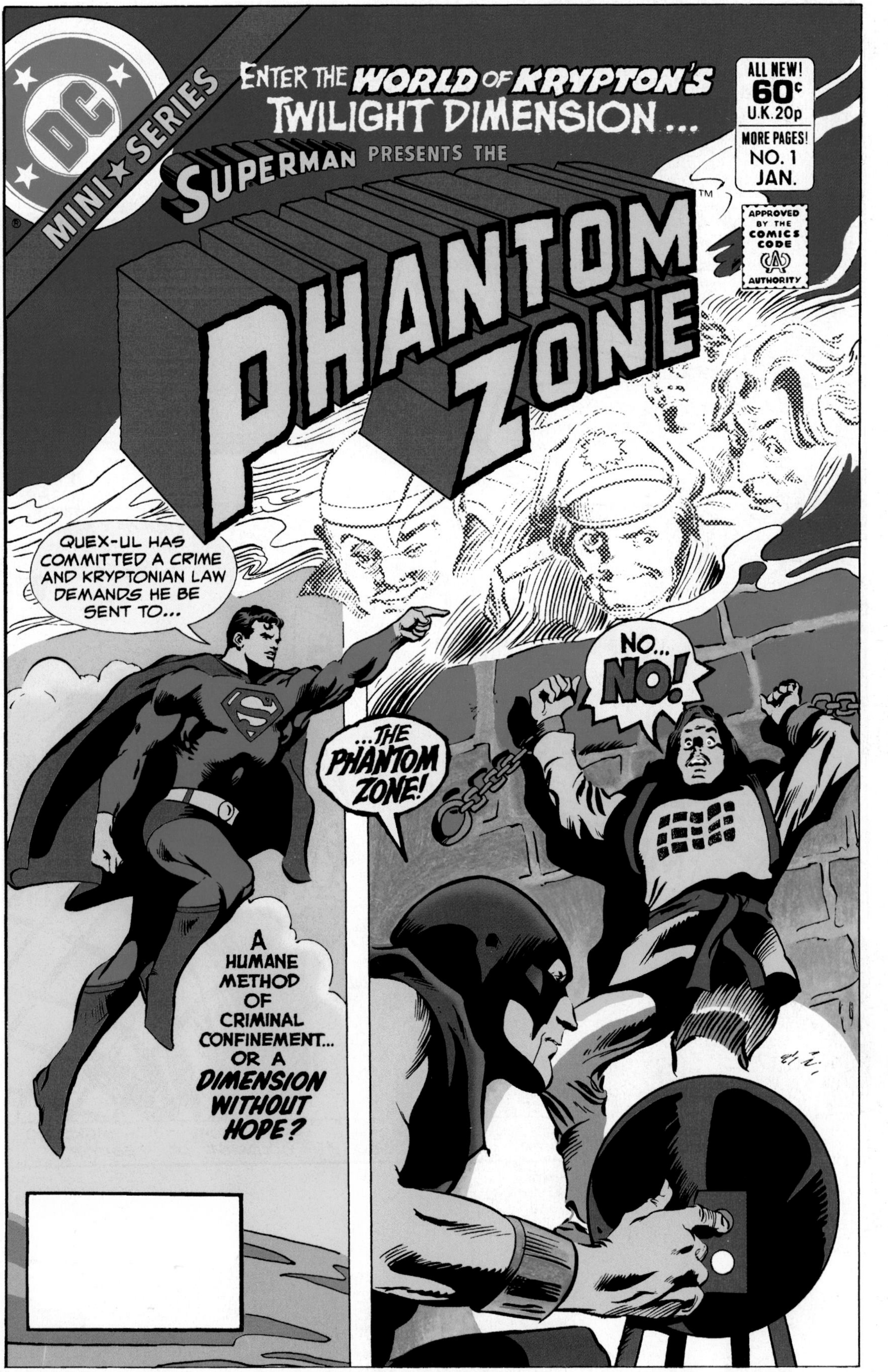
DC
MINI ★ SERIES
ENTER THE WORLD OF KRYPTON'S
TWILIGHT DIMENSION...
ALL NEW!
60¢
U.K. 20p
MORE PAGES!
NO. 1
JAN.
SUPERMAN PRESENTS THE
PHANTOM ZONE
APPROVED BY THE COMICS CODE AUTHORITY
QUEX-UL HAS COMMITTED A CRIME AND KRYPTONIAN LAW DEMANDS HE BE SENT TO...
NO... NO!
...THE PHANTOM ZONE!
A HUMANE METHOD OF CRIMINAL CONFINEMENT... OR A DIMENSION WITHOUT HOPE?

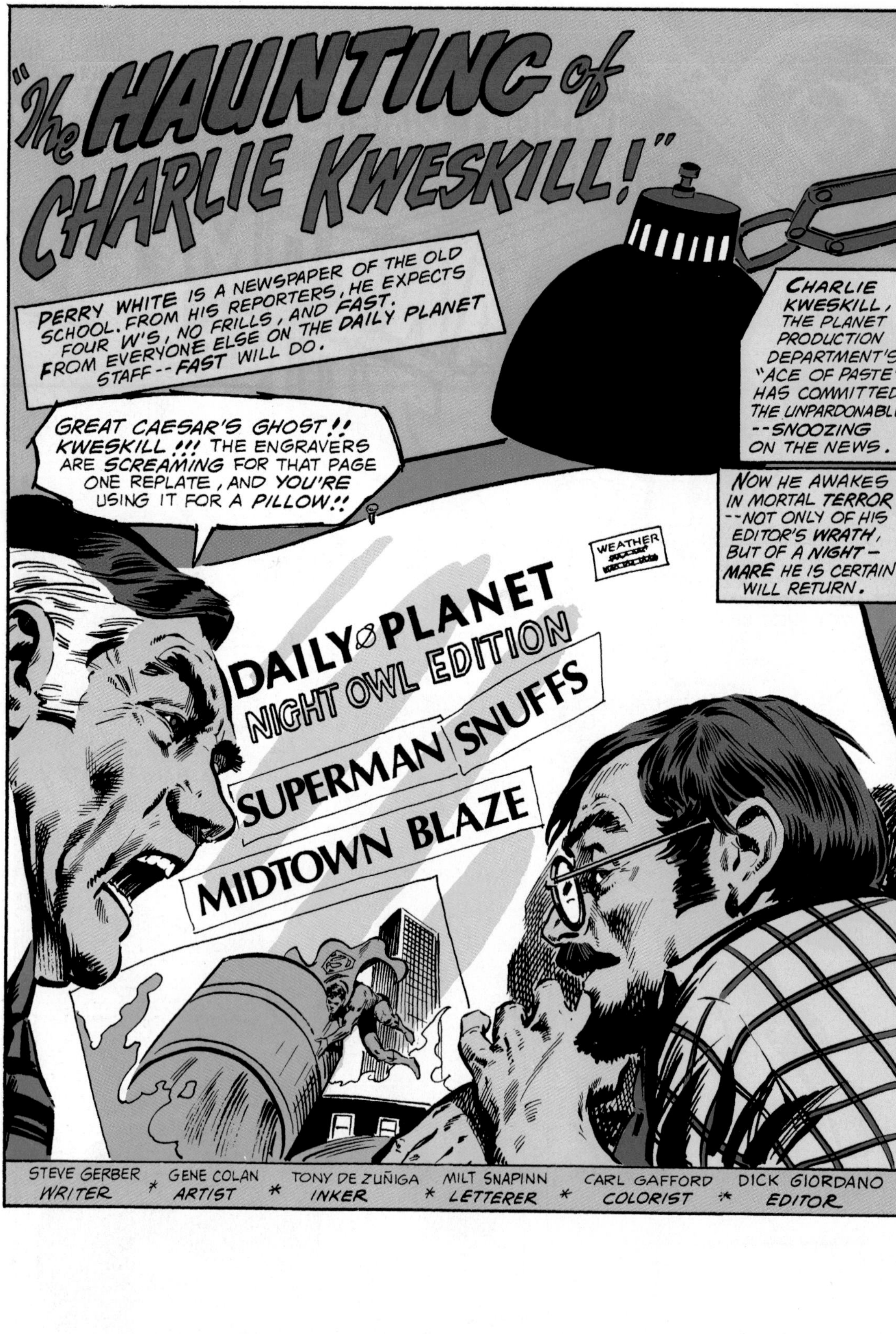
"The HAUNTING of CHARLIE KWESKILL!"
PERRY WHITE IS A NEWSPAPER OF THE OLD SCHOOL. FROM HIS REPORTERS, HE EXPECTS FOUR W'S, NO FRILLS, AND FAST. FROM EVERYONE ELSE ON THE DAILY PLANET STAFF--FAST WILL DO.
CHARLIE KWESKILL, THE PLANET PRODUCTION DEPARTMENT'S "ACE OF PASTE", HAS COMMITTED THE UNPARDONABLE --SNOOZING ON THE NEWS.
GREAT CAESAR'S GHOST!! KWESKILL!!! THE ENGRAVERS ARE SCREAMING FOR THAT PAGE ONE REPLATE, AND YOU'RE USING IT FOR A PILLOW!!
NOW HE AWAKES IN MORTAL TERROR --NOT ONLY OF HIS EDITOR'S WRATH, BUT OF A NIGHT-MARE HE IS CERTAIN WILL RETURN.
WEATHER
DAILY PLANET
NIGHT OWL EDITION
SUPERMAN SNUFFS
MIDTOWN BLAZE
STEVE GERBER WRITER * GENE COLAN ARTIST * TONY DE ZUÑIGA INKER * MILT SNAPINN LETTERER * CARL GAFFORD COLORIST * DICK GIORDANO EDITOR

BLAST IT, KWESKILL, STOP *SHAKING!* I'M NOT GOING TO *BITE* YOU! I *MAY* HAVE YOUR *HEAD* HANDED TO ME, THOUGH, IF THAT PASTE-UP ISN'T FINISHED BY--

I--I'M SORRY-- MR. WHITE-- I'LL *TRY*--!

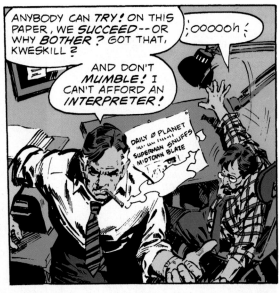

ANYBODY CAN *TRY!* ON THIS PAPER, WE *SUCCEED*--OR WHY *BOTHER?* GOT THAT, KWESKILL?

;OOOOOH;

AND DON'T *MUMBLE!* I CAN'T AFFORD AN *INTERPRETER!*

DAILY Ø PLANET
SUPERMAN SNUFFS MIDTOWN BLATE

YOU'LL HAVE TO *SPEAK UP* IF--

K-THUNK

WHAT IN THE NAME OF--?!

CHARLIE'S BEEN OUT OF *SORTS* LATELY, MR. WHITE--HE HASN'T BEEN *HIMSELF.*

WELL, WHO *HAS* HE BEEN? HAS HE SEEN A *DOCTOR?* HE HASN'T BEEN *DRINKING,* HAS HE?

CHARLIE? I DOUBT IT, MR. WHITE!

IT'S HARD TO GET HIM TO SAMPLE ANYTHING STRONGER THAN *HERBAL TEA!*

IS IT YOUR *HEART,* CHARLIE? WANNA GO TO A HOSPITAL?

NO... TIRED... SO, SO TIRED... NEED *SLEEP*...!

DON'T...FIRE ME... MR. WHITE...PLEASE, I'VE BEEN...VERY DEPENDABLE...!

I KNOW, KWESKILL, I KNOW. BANDAGE THAT CUT--AND GET HIM A *CAB,* GARRITY. AND SEE THAT HE GETS HOME *SAFELY.* THE *PLANET* NEVER LOSES A VALUED EMPLOYEE--UNLESS I FIRE HIM *PERSONALLY!*

2

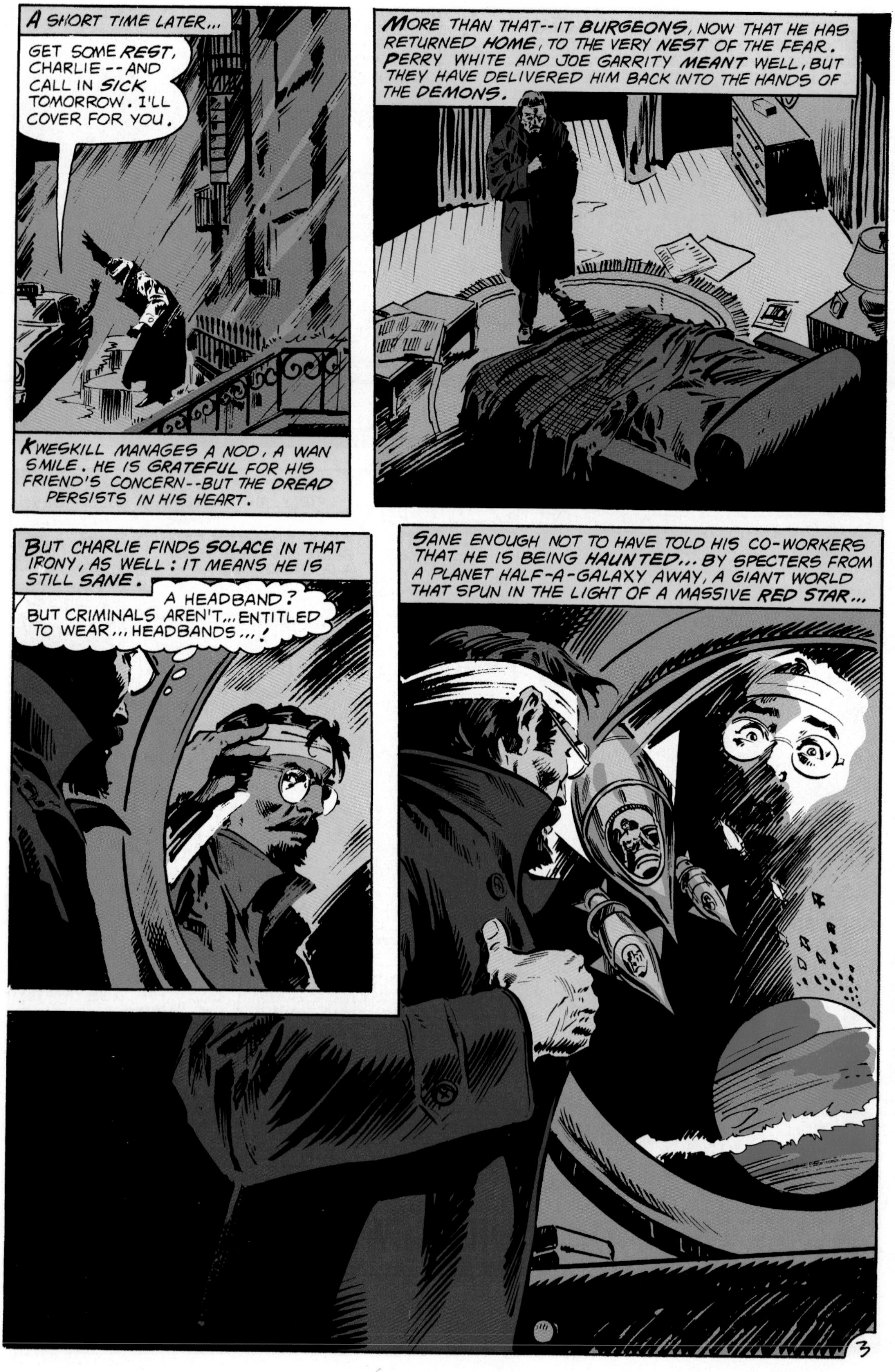
A SHORT TIME LATER...
GET SOME REST, CHARLIE--AND CALL IN SICK TOMORROW. I'LL COVER FOR YOU.
KWESKILL MANAGES A NOD, A WAN SMILE. HE IS GRATEFUL FOR HIS FRIEND'S CONCERN--BUT THE DREAD PERSISTS IN HIS HEART.
MORE THAN THAT--IT BURGEONS, NOW THAT HE HAS RETURNED HOME, TO THE VERY NEST OF THE FEAR. PERRY WHITE AND JOE GARRITY MEANT WELL, BUT THEY HAVE DELIVERED HIM BACK INTO THE HANDS OF THE DEMONS.
BUT CHARLIE FINDS SOLACE IN THAT IRONY, AS WELL: IT MEANS HE IS STILL SANE.
A HEADBAND? BUT CRIMINALS AREN'T... ENTITLED TO WEAR... HEADBANDS...!
SANE ENOUGH NOT TO HAVE TOLD HIS CO-WORKERS THAT HE IS BEING HAUNTED... BY SPECTERS FROM A PLANET HALF-A-GALAXY AWAY, A GIANT WORLD THAT SPUN IN THE LIGHT OF A MASSIVE RED STAR...
3

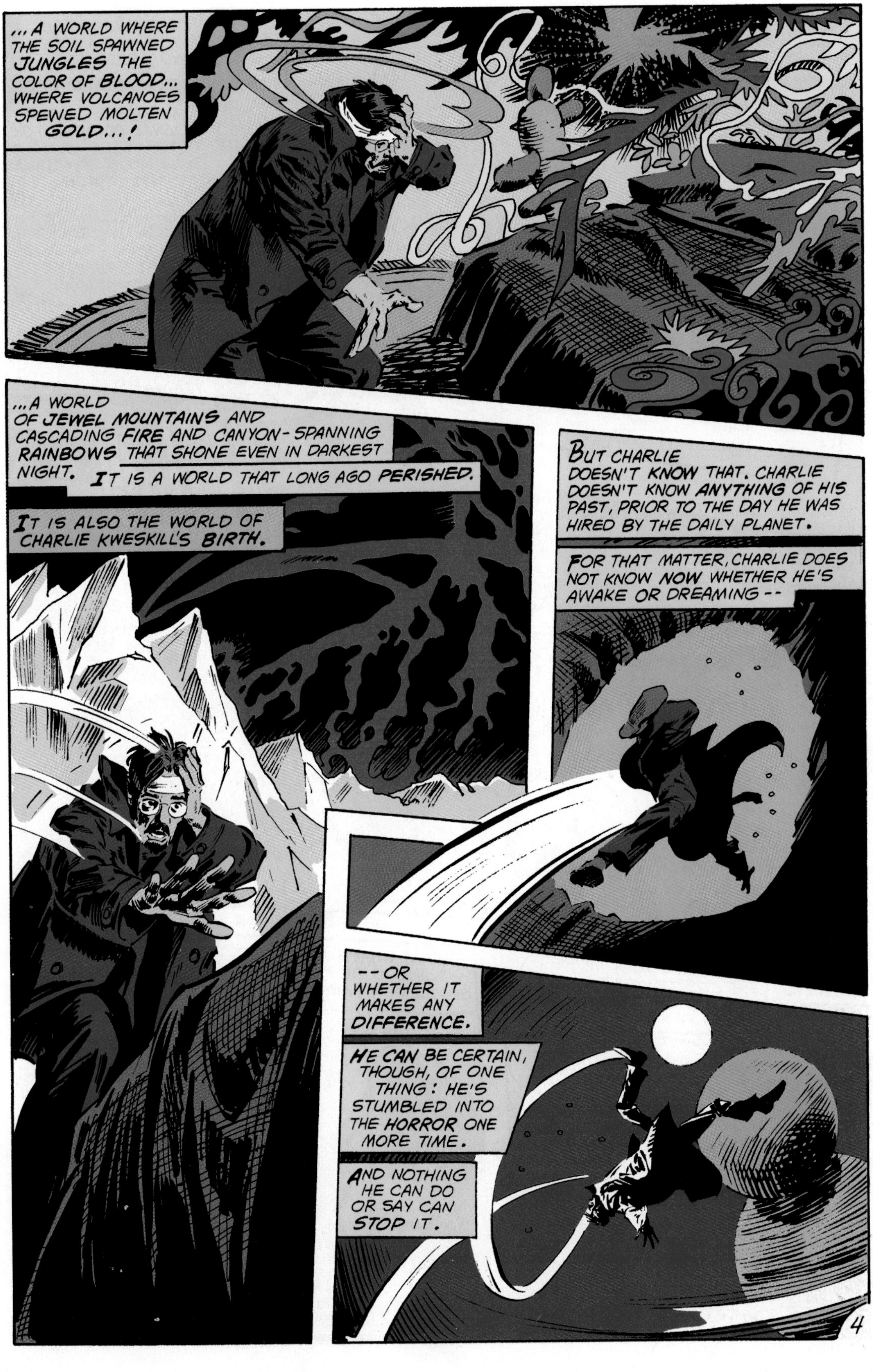
...A WORLD WHERE THE SOIL SPAWNED JUNGLES THE COLOR OF BLOOD... WHERE VOLCANOES SPEWED MOLTEN GOLD...!
...A WORLD OF JEWEL MOUNTAINS AND CASCADING FIRE AND CANYON-SPANNING RAINBOWS THAT SHONE EVEN IN DARKEST NIGHT.
IT IS A WORLD THAT LONG AGO PERISHED.
IT IS ALSO THE WORLD OF CHARLIE KWESKILL'S BIRTH.
BUT CHARLIE DOESN'T KNOW THAT. CHARLIE DOESN'T KNOW ANYTHING OF HIS PAST, PRIOR TO THE DAY HE WAS HIRED BY THE DAILY PLANET.
FOR THAT MATTER, CHARLIE DOES NOT KNOW NOW WHETHER HE'S AWAKE OR DREAMING --
--OR WHETHER IT MAKES ANY DIFFERENCE.
HE CAN BE CERTAIN, THOUGH, OF ONE THING: HE'S STUMBLED INTO THE HORROR ONE MORE TIME.
AND NOTHING HE CAN DO OR SAY CAN STOP IT.
4

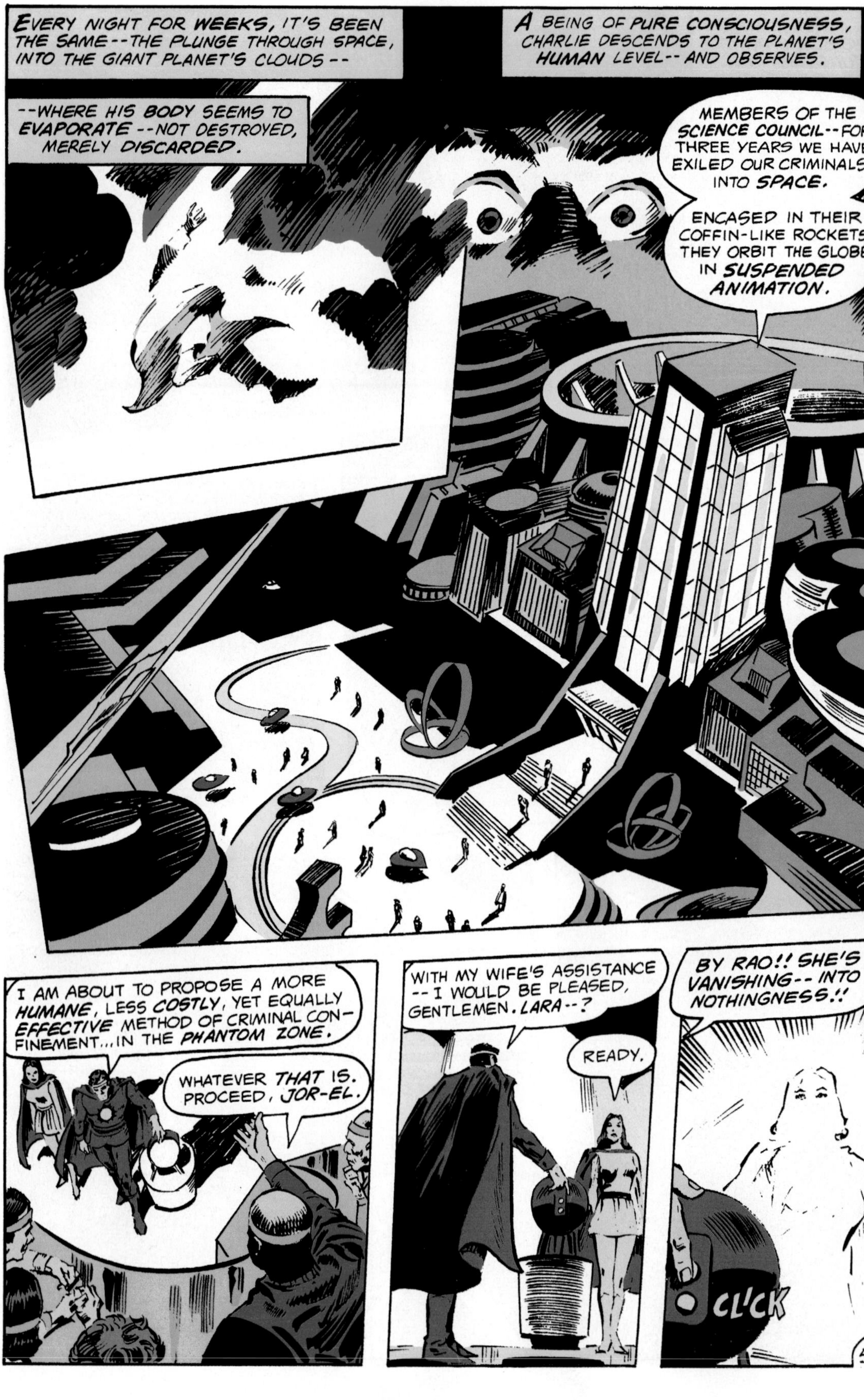
EVERY NIGHT FOR WEEKS, IT'S BEEN THE SAME--THE PLUNGE THROUGH SPACE, INTO THE GIANT PLANET'S CLOUDS--
A BEING OF PURE CONSCIOUSNESS, CHARLIE DESCENDS TO THE PLANET'S HUMAN LEVEL--AND OBSERVES.
--WHERE HIS BODY SEEMS TO EVAPORATE--NOT DESTROYED, MERELY DISCARDED.
MEMBERS OF THE SCIENCE COUNCIL--FOR THREE YEARS WE HAVE EXILED OUR CRIMINALS INTO SPACE.
ENCASED IN THEIR COFFIN-LIKE ROCKETS, THEY ORBIT THE GLOBE IN SUSPENDED ANIMATION.
I AM ABOUT TO PROPOSE A MORE HUMANE, LESS COSTLY, YET EQUALLY EFFECTIVE METHOD OF CRIMINAL CONFINEMENT...IN THE PHANTOM ZONE.
WHATEVER THAT IS. PROCEED, JOR-EL.
WITH MY WIFE'S ASSISTANCE--I WOULD BE PLEASED, GENTLEMEN. LARA--?
READY.
BY RAO!! SHE'S VANISHING--INTO NOTHINGNESS!!
CLICK
5

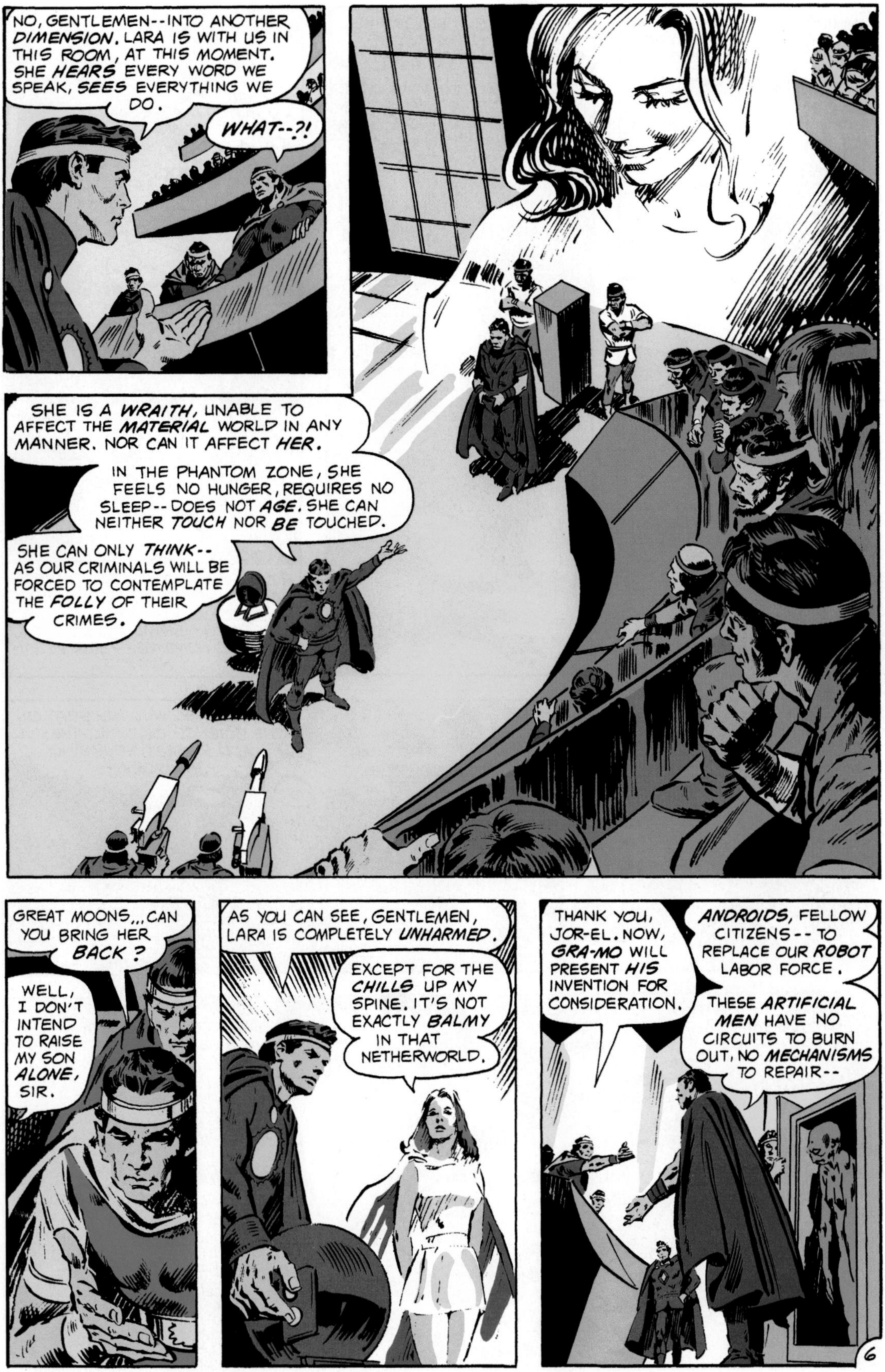
NO, GENTLEMEN--INTO ANOTHER DIMENSION. LARA IS WITH US IN THIS ROOM, AT THIS MOMENT. SHE HEARS EVERY WORD WE SPEAK, SEES EVERYTHING WE DO.
WHAT--?!
SHE IS A WRAITH, UNABLE TO AFFECT THE MATERIAL WORLD IN ANY MANNER. NOR CAN IT AFFECT HER.
IN THE PHANTOM ZONE, SHE FEELS NO HUNGER, REQUIRES NO SLEEP--DOES NOT AGE. SHE CAN NEITHER TOUCH NOR BE TOUCHED.
SHE CAN ONLY THINK--AS OUR CRIMINALS WILL BE FORCED TO CONTEMPLATE THE FOLLY OF THEIR CRIMES.
GREAT MOONS... CAN YOU BRING HER BACK?
WELL, I DON'T INTEND TO RAISE MY SON ALONE, SIR.
AS YOU CAN SEE, GENTLEMEN, LARA IS COMPLETELY UNHARMED.
EXCEPT FOR THE CHILLS UP MY SPINE. IT'S NOT EXACTLY BALMY IN THAT NETHERWORLD.
THANK YOU, JOR-EL. NOW, GRA-MO WILL PRESENT HIS INVENTION FOR CONSIDERATION.
ANDROIDS, FELLOW CITIZENS--TO REPLACE OUR ROBOT LABOR FORCE.
THESE ARTIFICIAL MEN HAVE NO CIRCUITS TO BURN OUT, NO MECHANISMS TO REPAIR--
6

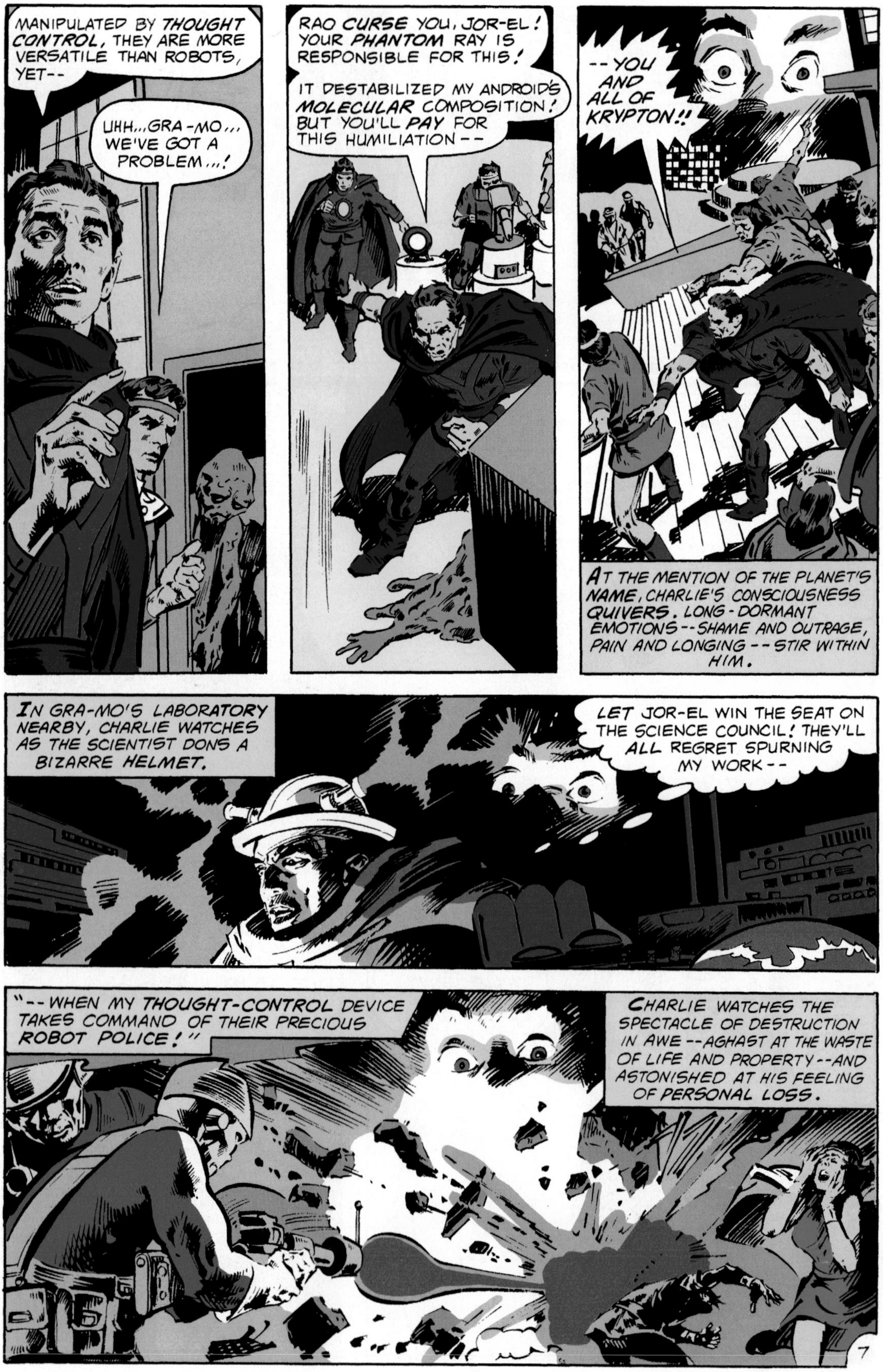
MANIPULATED BY THOUGHT CONTROL, THEY ARE MORE VERSATILE THAN ROBOTS, YET--
UHH...GRA-MO... WE'VE GOT A PROBLEM...!
RAO CURSE YOU, JOR-EL! YOUR PHANTOM RAY IS RESPONSIBLE FOR THIS!
IT DESTABILIZED MY ANDROID'S MOLECULAR COMPOSITION! BUT YOU'LL PAY FOR THIS HUMILIATION--
--YOU AND ALL OF KRYPTON!!
AT THE MENTION OF THE PLANET'S NAME, CHARLIE'S CONSCIOUSNESS QUIVERS. LONG-DORMANT EMOTIONS--SHAME AND OUTRAGE, PAIN AND LONGING--STIR WITHIN HIM.
IN GRA-MO'S LABORATORY NEARBY, CHARLIE WATCHES AS THE SCIENTIST DONS A BIZARRE HELMET.
LET JOR-EL WIN THE SEAT ON THE SCIENCE COUNCIL! THEY'LL ALL REGRET SPURNING MY WORK--
"--WHEN MY THOUGHT-CONTROL DEVICE TAKES COMMAND OF THEIR PRECIOUS ROBOT POLICE!"
CHARLIE WATCHES THE SPECTACLE OF DESTRUCTION IN AWE--AGHAST AT THE WASTE OF LIFE AND PROPERTY--AND ASTONISHED AT HIS FEELING OF PERSONAL LOSS.
7

BEFORE THE NEXT DAWN, GRA-MO IS APPREHENDED BY THE *SCIENCE POLICE*, AND THE "ROBOT REBELLION" IS QUELLED.

TRIAL AND SENTENCING FOLLOW QUICKLY...

...AND GRA-MO AND HIS ASSISTANTS ARE ROCKETED INTO *EXILE.*

THEY'LL BE THE *LAST* TO SUFFER THAT PUNISHMENT, JOR-EL.

THE COUNCIL HAS APPROVED THE *PHANTOM ZONE* AS KRYPTON'S OFFICIAL METHOD OF CRIMINAL CONFINEMENT.

AND CHARLIE DREAMS ON, WEEKS PASSING IN *INSTANTS* -- THE GIANT PLANET TURNING ON ITS MIGHTY AXIS, SWINGING IN ITS INEXORABLE ORBIT --

-- ON A COLLISION COURSE WITH DESTINY.

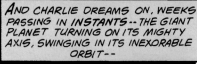

IT IS THE 62ND DAY OF THE MONTH OF EORX IN THE YEAR 9999. RENEGADE SCIENTIST JAX-UR LAUNCHES A MISSILE WITH AN *EXPLOSIVE PAY-LOAD* INTO SPACE.

HIS INTENT IS TO INTERCEPT A *METEOR* AND BLAST IT INTO *VAPOR*, AS A TEST OF HIS NEW GUIDANCE SYSTEM AND NUCLEAR DEVICE.

THE GUIDANCE SYSTEM *FAILS.* THE MISSILE HURTLES ON PAST ITS TARGET...

8

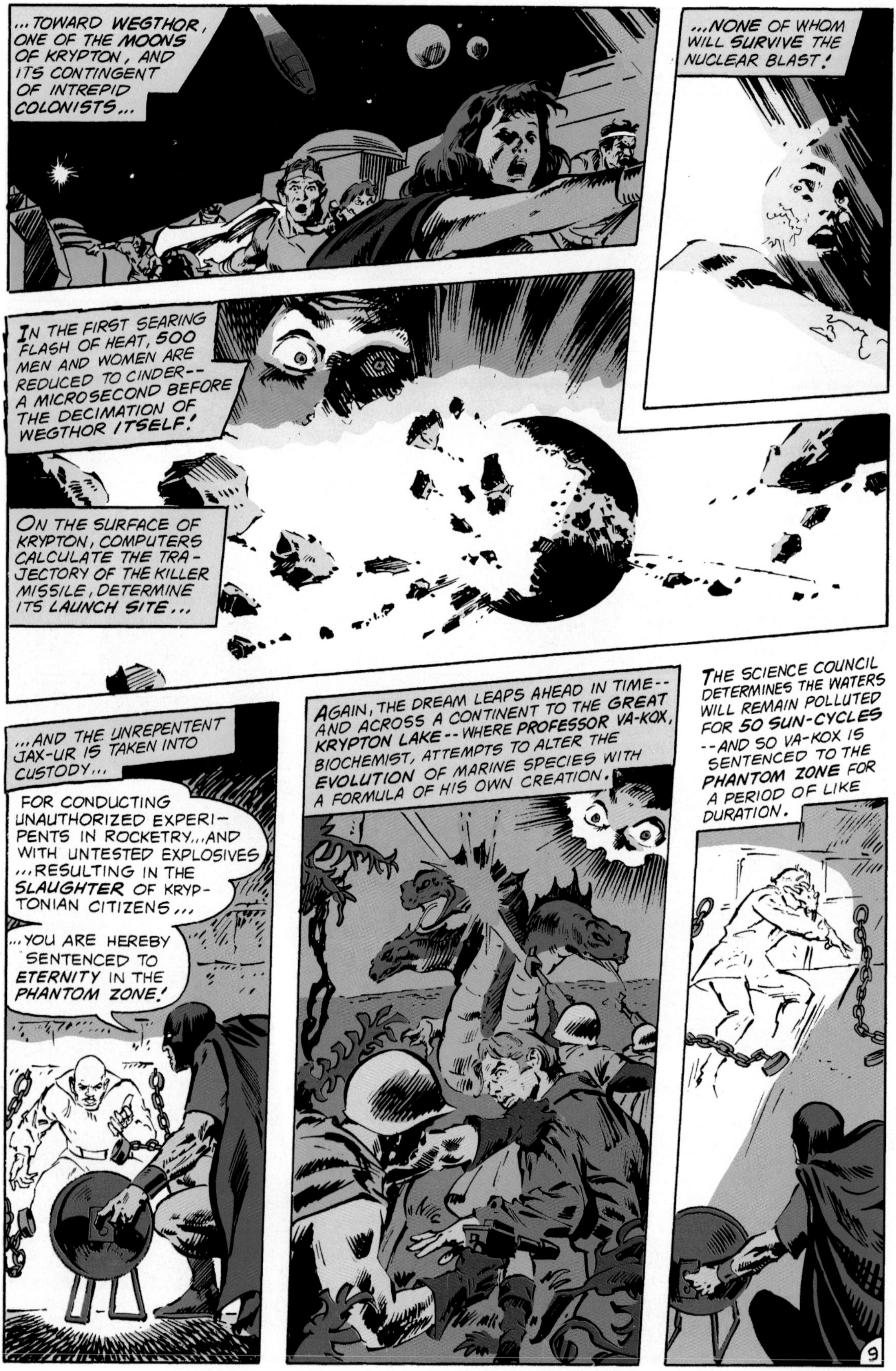
...TOWARD WEGTHOR, ONE OF THE MOONS OF KRYPTON, AND ITS CONTINGENT OF INTREPID COLONISTS...
...NONE OF WHOM WILL SURVIVE THE NUCLEAR BLAST!
IN THE FIRST SEARING FLASH OF HEAT, 500 MEN AND WOMEN ARE REDUCED TO CINDER-- A MICROSECOND BEFORE THE DECIMATION OF WEGTHOR ITSELF!
ON THE SURFACE OF KRYPTON, COMPUTERS CALCULATE THE TRAJECTORY OF THE KILLER MISSILE, DETERMINE ITS LAUNCH SITE...
...AND THE UNREPENTENT JAX-UR IS TAKEN INTO CUSTODY...
FOR CONDUCTING UNAUTHORIZED EXPERIPENTS IN ROCKETRY,..AND WITH UNTESTED EXPLOSIVES ...RESULTING IN THE SLAUGHTER OF KRYPTONIAN CITIZENS...
...YOU ARE HEREBY SENTENCED TO ETERNITY IN THE PHANTOM ZONE!
AGAIN, THE DREAM LEAPS AHEAD IN TIME-- AND ACROSS A CONTINENT TO THE GREAT KRYPTON LAKE--WHERE PROFESSOR VA-KOX, BIOCHEMIST, ATTEMPTS TO ALTER THE EVOLUTION OF MARINE SPECIES WITH A FORMULA OF HIS OWN CREATION.
THE SCIENCE COUNCIL DETERMINES THE WATERS WILL REMAIN POLLUTED FOR 50 SUN-CYCLES --AND SO VA-KOX IS SENTENCED TO THE PHANTOM ZONE FOR A PERIOD OF LIKE DURATION.
9

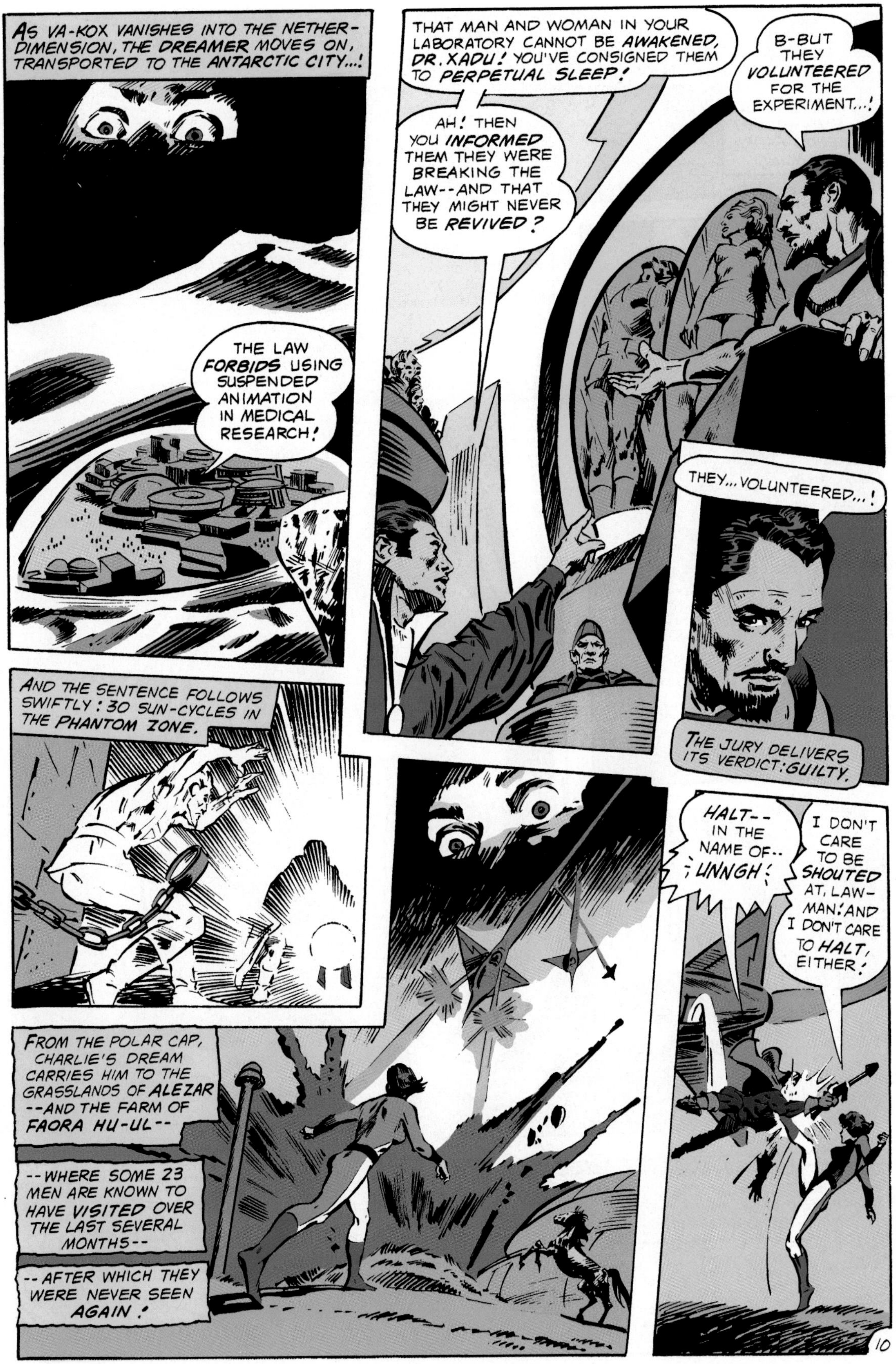

AS VA-KOX VANISHES INTO THE NETHER-DIMENSION, THE DREAMER MOVES ON, TRANSPORTED TO THE ANTARCTIC CITY...!
THE LAW FORBIDS USING SUSPENDED ANIMATION IN MEDICAL RESEARCH!
THAT MAN AND WOMAN IN YOUR LABORATORY CANNOT BE AWAKENED, DR. XADU! YOU'VE CONSIGNED THEM TO PERPETUAL SLEEP!
B-BUT THEY VOLUNTEERED FOR THE EXPERIMENT...!
AH! THEN YOU INFORMED THEM THEY WERE BREAKING THE LAW--AND THAT THEY MIGHT NEVER BE REVIVED?
THEY... VOLUNTEERED...!
THE JURY DELIVERS ITS VERDICT: GUILTY.
AND THE SENTENCE FOLLOWS SWIFTLY: 30 SUN-CYCLES IN THE PHANTOM ZONE.
HALT-- IN THE NAME OF-- UNNGH!
I DON'T CARE TO BE SHOUTED AT, LAW-MAN! AND I DON'T CARE TO HALT, EITHER!
FROM THE POLAR CAP, CHARLIE'S DREAM CARRIES HIM TO THE GRASSLANDS OF ALEZAR --AND THE FARM OF FAORA HU-UL--
--WHERE SOME 23 MEN ARE KNOWN TO HAVE VISITED OVER THE LAST SEVERAL MONTHS--
--AFTER WHICH THEY WERE NEVER SEEN AGAIN!
10

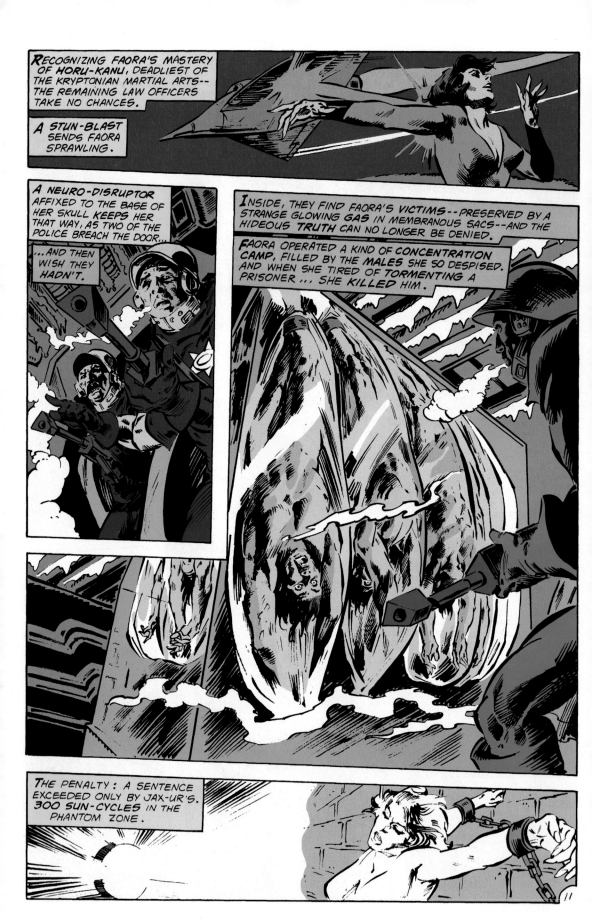

RECOGNIZING FAORA'S MASTERY OF *HORU-KANU*, DEADLIEST OF THE KRYPTONIAN MARTIAL ARTS-- THE REMAINING LAW OFFICERS TAKE NO CHANCES.

A *STUN-BLAST* SENDS FAORA SPRAWLING.

A *NEURO-DISRUPTOR* AFFIXED TO THE BASE OF HER SKULL *KEEPS* HER THAT WAY, AS TWO OF THE POLICE BREACH THE DOOR...

...AND THEN WISH THEY *HADN'T*.

*I*NSIDE, THEY FIND FAORA'S *VICTIMS*--PRESERVED BY A STRANGE GLOWING *GAS* IN MEMBRANOUS SACS--AND THE HIDEOUS *TRUTH* CAN NO LONGER BE DENIED.

*F*AORA OPERATED A KIND OF *CONCENTRATION CAMP*, FILLED BY THE *MALES* SHE SO DESPISED. AND WHEN SHE TIRED OF *TORMENTING* A PRISONER ... SHE *KILLED* HIM.

*T*HE *PENALTY*: A SENTENCE EXCEEDED ONLY BY JAX-UR'S. *300 SUN-CYCLES* IN THE PHANTOM ZONE.

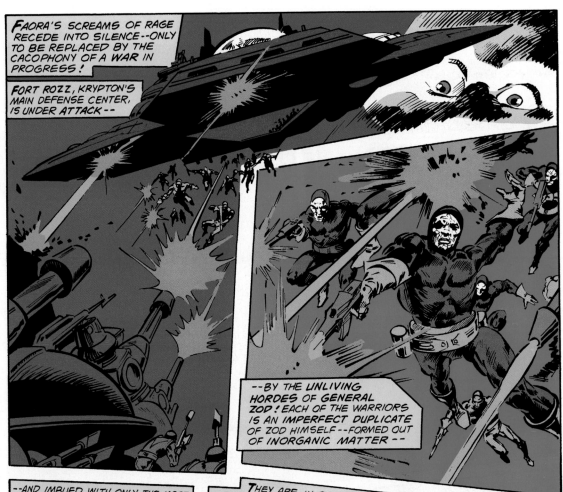

FAORA'S SCREAMS OF RAGE RECEDE INTO SILENCE--ONLY TO BE REPLACED BY THE CACOPHONY OF A *WAR* IN PROGRESS!

FORT ROZZ, KRYPTON'S MAIN DEFENSE CENTER, IS UNDER ATTACK--

--BY THE *UNLIVING HORDES OF GENERAL ZOD!* EACH OF THE WARRIORS IS AN *IMPERFECT DUPLICATE* OF ZOD HIMSELF--FORMED OUT OF *INORGANIC MATTER* --

--AND IMBUED WITH ONLY THE MOST *RUDIMENTARY* INTELLIGENCE. THEY LEAP FROM THE SKY, INTO THE *BLASTER* CANNONADES, TO THEIR "*DEATHS*", WITHOUT *HESITATION*, WITHOUT *QUESTION*.

THEY ARE, IN SHORT, THE *IDEAL TROOPS* FOR A *MEGALO-MANIACAL MILITARY DICTATOR*"--WHICH, IN TURN, IS THE *IDEAL* DESCRIPTION OF *GENERAL ZOD.*

HE HAD PLANNED TO USHER IN THE *ELEVENTH MILLENIUM* OF KRYPTON'S CIVILIZATION AS ITS PLANET-ARY *RULER*...
...TO *DISCIPLINE* ITS POPULATION FOR THEIR *INESCAPABLE MISSION*, CONQUEST OF THE *STARS!*

12

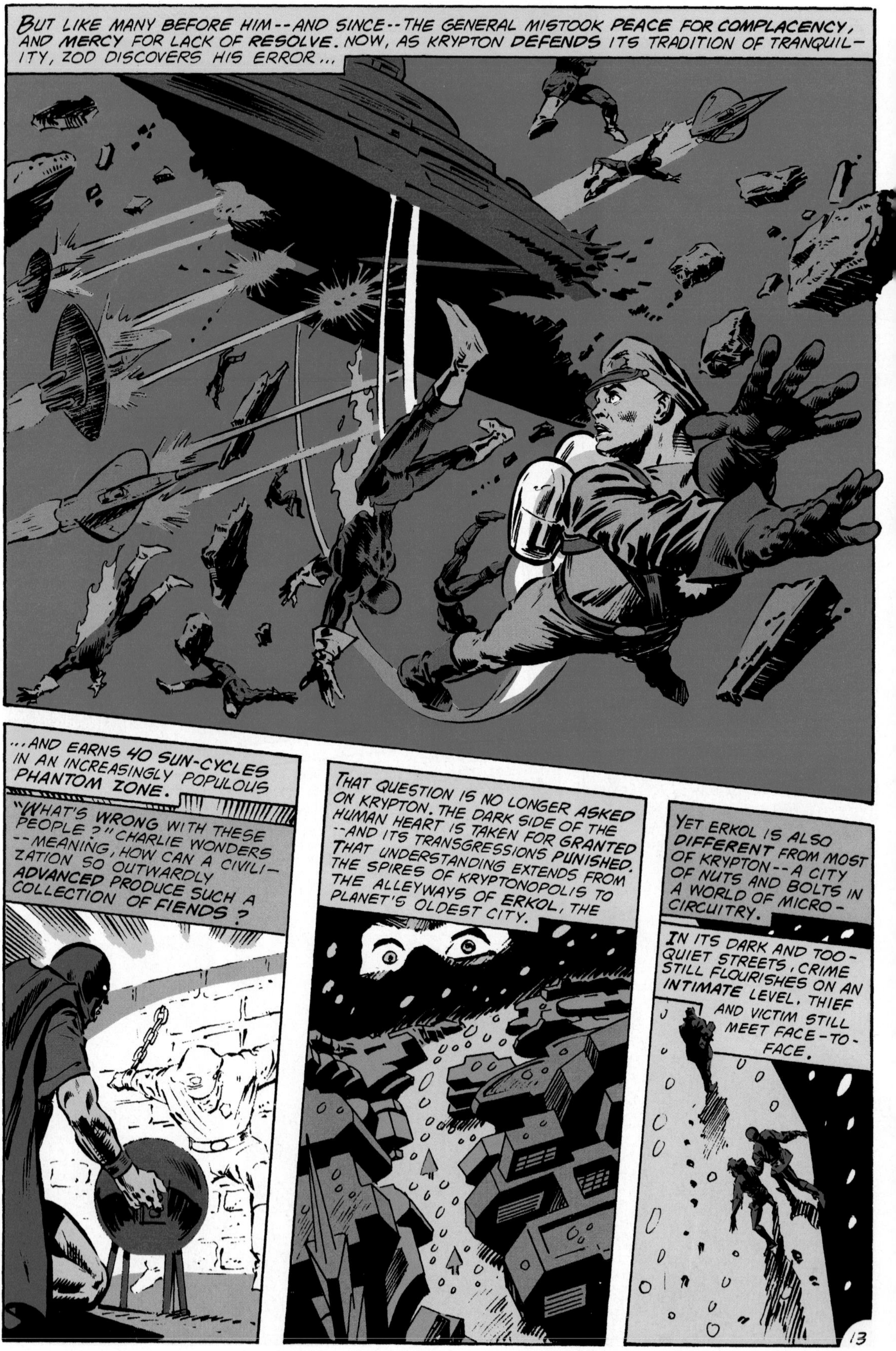

BUT LIKE MANY BEFORE HIM--AND SINCE--THE GENERAL MISTOOK PEACE FOR COMPLACENCY, AND MERCY FOR LACK OF RESOLVE. NOW, AS KRYPTON DEFENDS ITS TRADITION OF TRANQUILITY, ZOD DISCOVERS HIS ERROR...
...AND EARNS 40 SUN-CYCLES IN AN INCREASINGLY POPULOUS PHANTOM ZONE.
"WHAT'S WRONG WITH THESE PEOPLE?" CHARLIE WONDERS --MEANING, HOW CAN A CIVILIZATION SO OUTWARDLY ADVANCED PRODUCE SUCH A COLLECTION OF FIENDS?
THAT QUESTION IS NO LONGER ASKED ON KRYPTON. THE DARK SIDE OF THE HUMAN HEART IS TAKEN FOR GRANTED --AND ITS TRANSGRESSIONS PUNISHED. THAT UNDERSTANDING EXTENDS FROM THE SPIRES OF KRYPTONOPOLIS TO THE ALLEYWAYS OF ERKOL, THE PLANET'S OLDEST CITY.
YET ERKOL IS ALSO DIFFERENT FROM MOST OF KRYPTON--A CITY OF NUTS AND BOLTS IN A WORLD OF MICRO-CIRCUITRY.
IN ITS DARK AND TOO-QUIET STREETS, CRIME STILL FLOURISHES ON AN INTIMATE LEVEL. THIEF AND VICTIM STILL MEET FACE-TO-FACE.
13

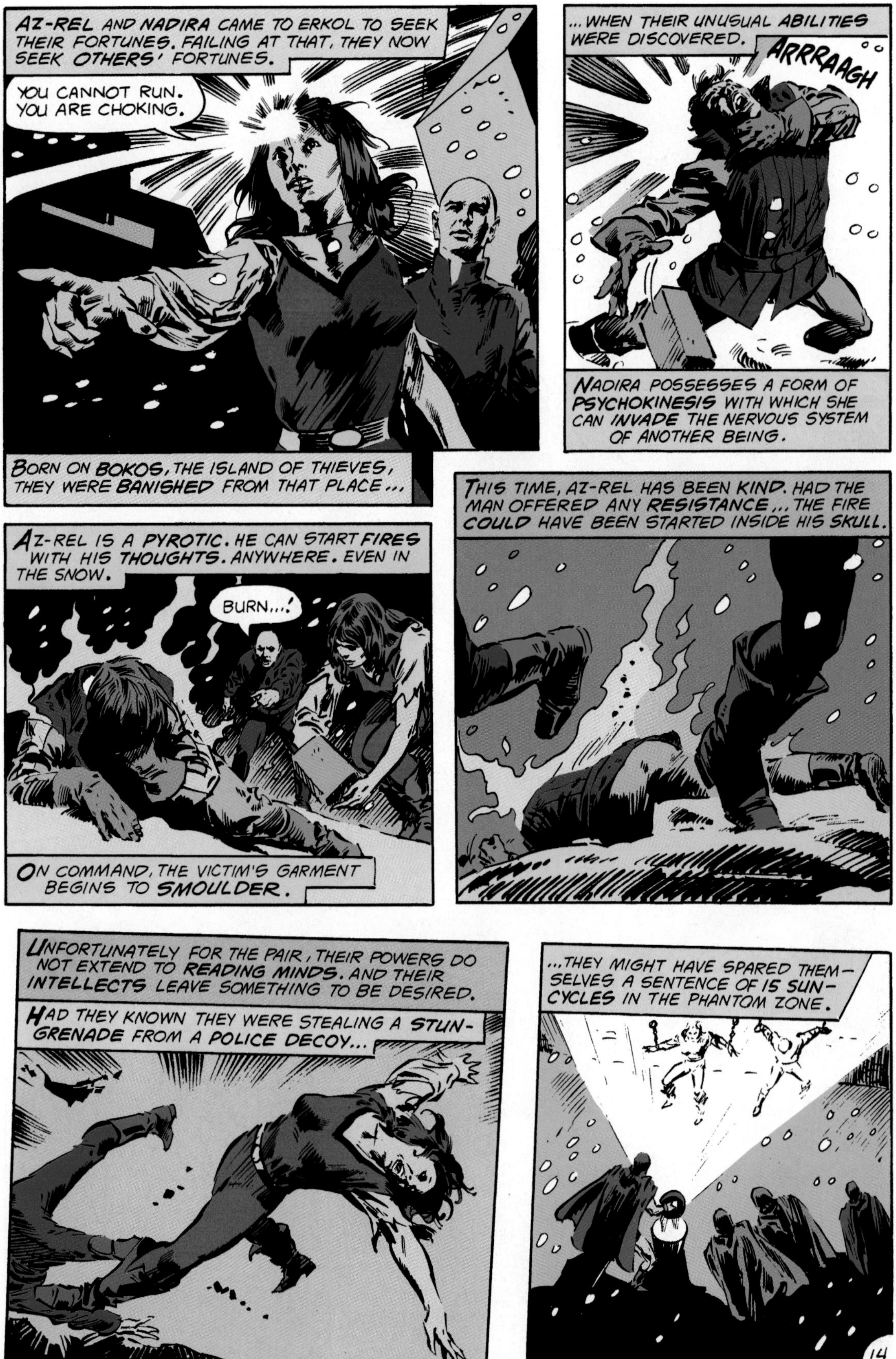
AZ-REL AND NADIRA CAME TO ERKOL TO SEEK THEIR FORTUNES. FAILING AT THAT, THEY NOW SEEK OTHERS' FORTUNES.
YOU CANNOT RUN. YOU ARE CHOKING.
BORN ON BOKOS, THE ISLAND OF THIEVES, THEY WERE BANISHED FROM THAT PLACE...
...WHEN THEIR UNUSUAL ABILITIES WERE DISCOVERED.
ARRRAAGH
NADIRA POSSESSES A FORM OF PSYCHOKINESIS WITH WHICH SHE CAN INVADE THE NERVOUS SYSTEM OF ANOTHER BEING.
AZ-REL IS A PYROTIC. HE CAN START FIRES WITH HIS THOUGHTS. ANYWHERE. EVEN IN THE SNOW.
BURN...!
ON COMMAND, THE VICTIM'S GARMENT BEGINS TO SMOULDER.
THIS TIME, AZ-REL HAS BEEN KIND. HAD THE MAN OFFERED ANY RESISTANCE... THE FIRE COULD HAVE BEEN STARTED INSIDE HIS SKULL.
UNFORTUNATELY FOR THE PAIR, THEIR POWERS DO NOT EXTEND TO READING MINDS. AND THEIR INTELLECTS LEAVE SOMETHING TO BE DESIRED.
HAD THEY KNOWN THEY WERE STEALING A STUN-GRENADE FROM A POLICE DECOY...
...THEY MIGHT HAVE SPARED THEMSELVES A SENTENCE OF 15 SUN-CYCLES IN THE PHANTOM ZONE.
14

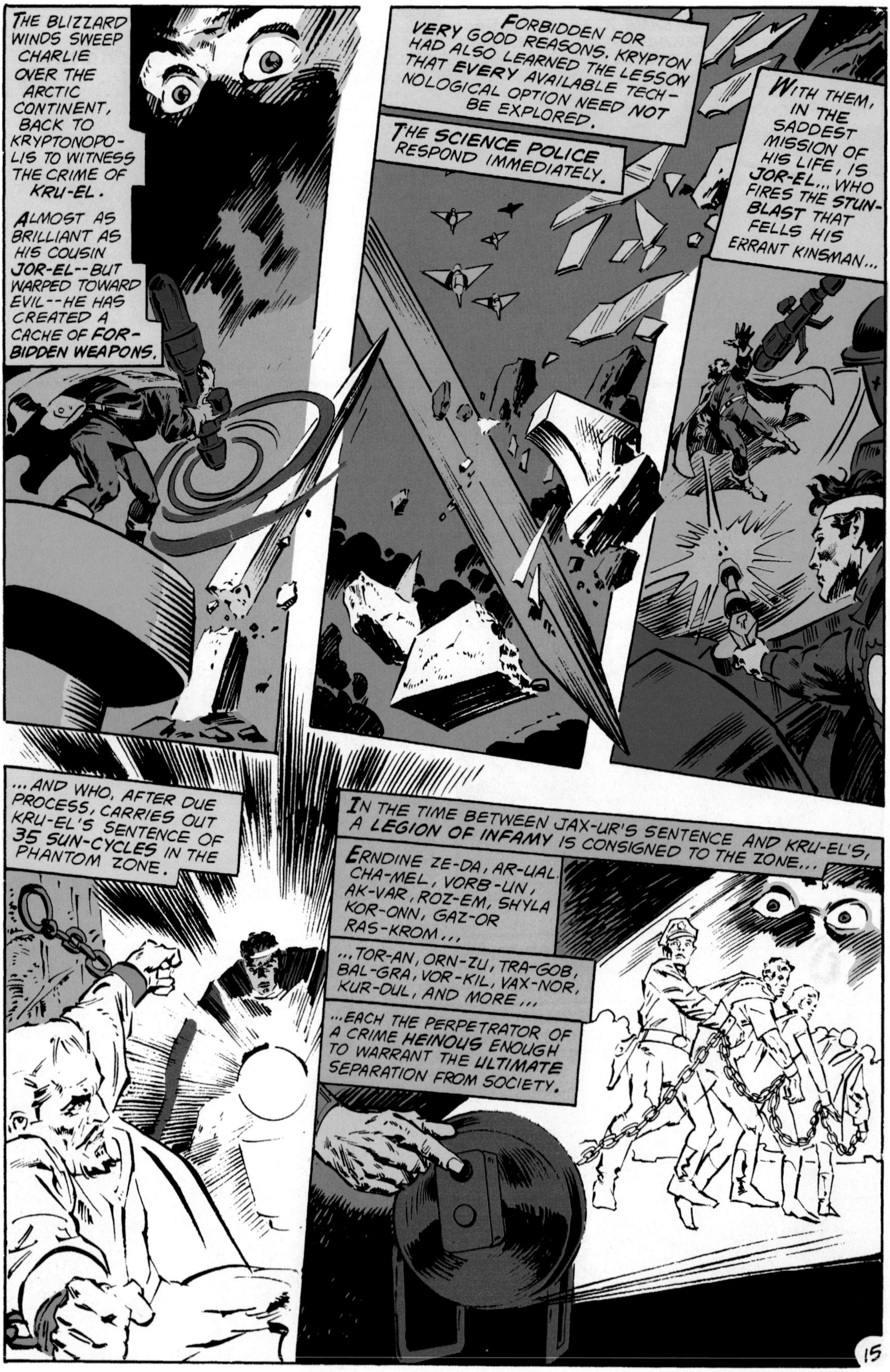
THE BLIZZARD WINDS SWEEP CHARLIE OVER THE ARCTIC CONTINENT, BACK TO KRYPTONOPOLIS TO WITNESS THE CRIME OF KRU-EL.
ALMOST AS BRILLIANT AS HIS COUSIN JOR-EL--BUT WARPED TOWARD EVIL--HE HAS CREATED A CACHE OF FORBIDDEN WEAPONS.
FORBIDDEN FOR VERY GOOD REASONS. KRYPTON HAD ALSO LEARNED THE LESSON THAT EVERY AVAILABLE TECHNOLOGICAL OPTION NEED NOT BE EXPLORED.
THE SCIENCE POLICE RESPOND IMMEDIATELY.
WITH THEM, IN THE SADDEST MISSION OF HIS LIFE, IS JOR-EL... WHO FIRES THE STUN-BLAST THAT FELLS HIS ERRANT KINSMAN...
...AND WHO, AFTER DUE PROCESS, CARRIES OUT KRU-EL'S SENTENCE OF 35 SUN-CYCLES IN THE PHANTOM ZONE.
IN THE TIME BETWEEN JAX-UR'S SENTENCE AND KRU-EL'S, A LEGION OF INFAMY IS CONSIGNED TO THE ZONE...
ERNDINE ZE-DA, AR-UAL CHA-MEL, VORB-UN, AK-VAR, ROZ-EM, SHYLA KOR-ONN, GAZ-OR RAS-KROM...
...TOR-AN, ORN-ZU, TRA-GOB, BAL-GRA, VOR-KIL, VAX-NOR, KUR-DUL, AND MORE...
...EACH THE PERPETRATOR OF A CRIME HEINOUS ENOUGH TO WARRANT THE ULTIMATE SEPARATION FROM SOCIETY.
15

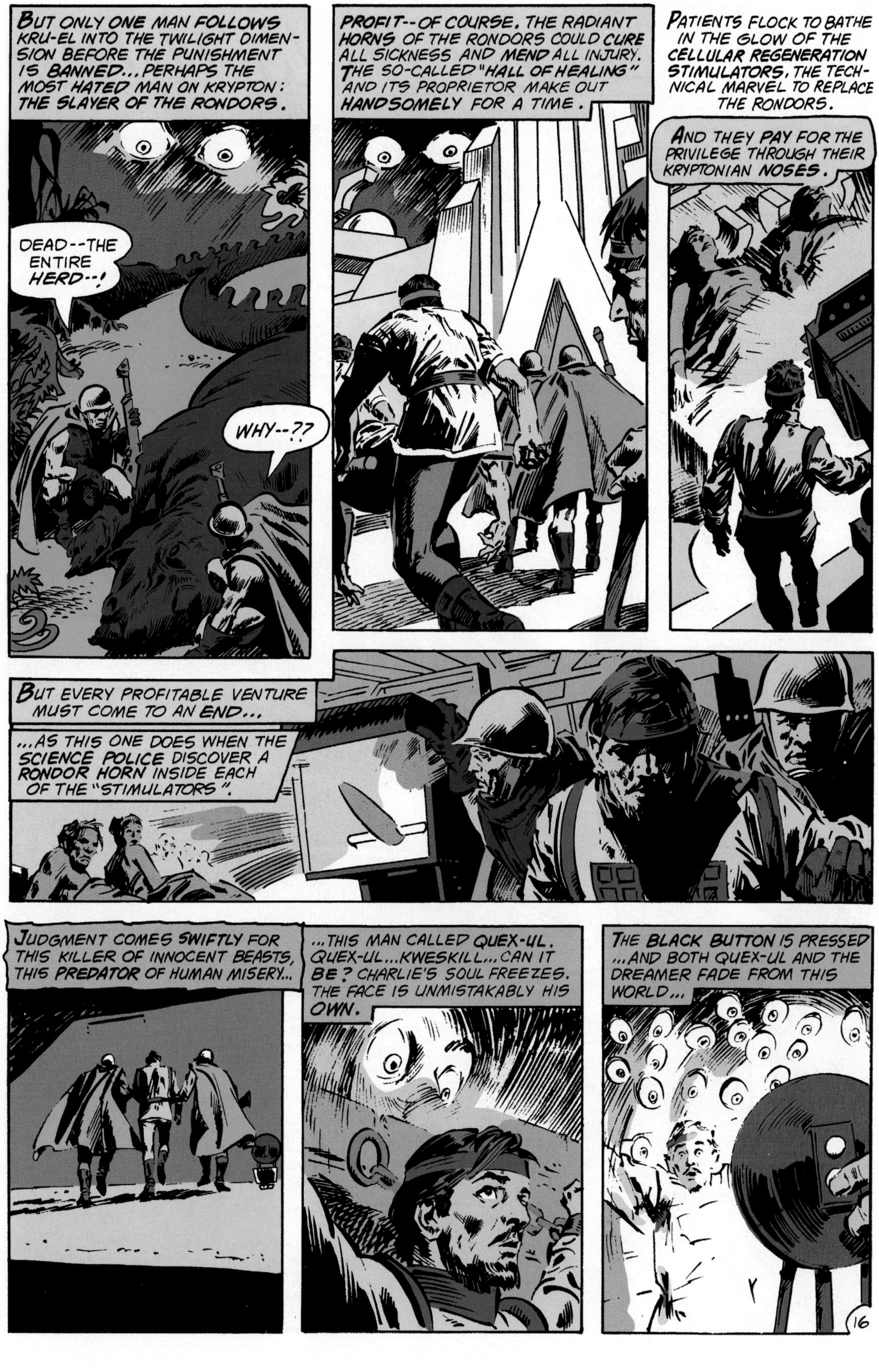

BUT ONLY ONE MAN FOLLOWS KRU-EL INTO THE TWILIGHT DIMENSION BEFORE THE PUNISHMENT IS BANNED... PERHAPS THE MOST HATED MAN ON KRYPTON: THE SLAYER OF THE RONDORS.
DEAD--THE ENTIRE HERD--!
WHY--??
PROFIT--OF COURSE. THE RADIANT HORNS OF THE RONDORS COULD CURE ALL SICKNESS AND MEND ALL INJURY. THE SO-CALLED "HALL OF HEALING" AND ITS PROPRIETOR MAKE OUT HANDSOMELY FOR A TIME.
PATIENTS FLOCK TO BATHE IN THE GLOW OF THE CELLULAR REGENERATION STIMULATORS, THE TECHNICAL MARVEL TO REPLACE THE RONDORS.
AND THEY PAY FOR THE PRIVILEGE THROUGH THEIR KRYPTONIAN NOSES.
BUT EVERY PROFITABLE VENTURE MUST COME TO AN END...
...AS THIS ONE DOES WHEN THE SCIENCE POLICE DISCOVER A RONDOR HORN INSIDE EACH OF THE "STIMULATORS".
JUDGMENT COMES SWIFTLY FOR THIS KILLER OF INNOCENT BEASTS, THIS PREDATOR OF HUMAN MISERY...
...THIS MAN CALLED QUEX-UL. QUEX-UL...KWESKILL...CAN IT BE? CHARLIE'S SOUL FREEZES. THE FACE IS UNMISTAKABLY HIS OWN.
THE BLACK BUTTON IS PRESSED ...AND BOTH QUEX-UL AND THE DREAMER FADE FROM THIS WORLD...
16

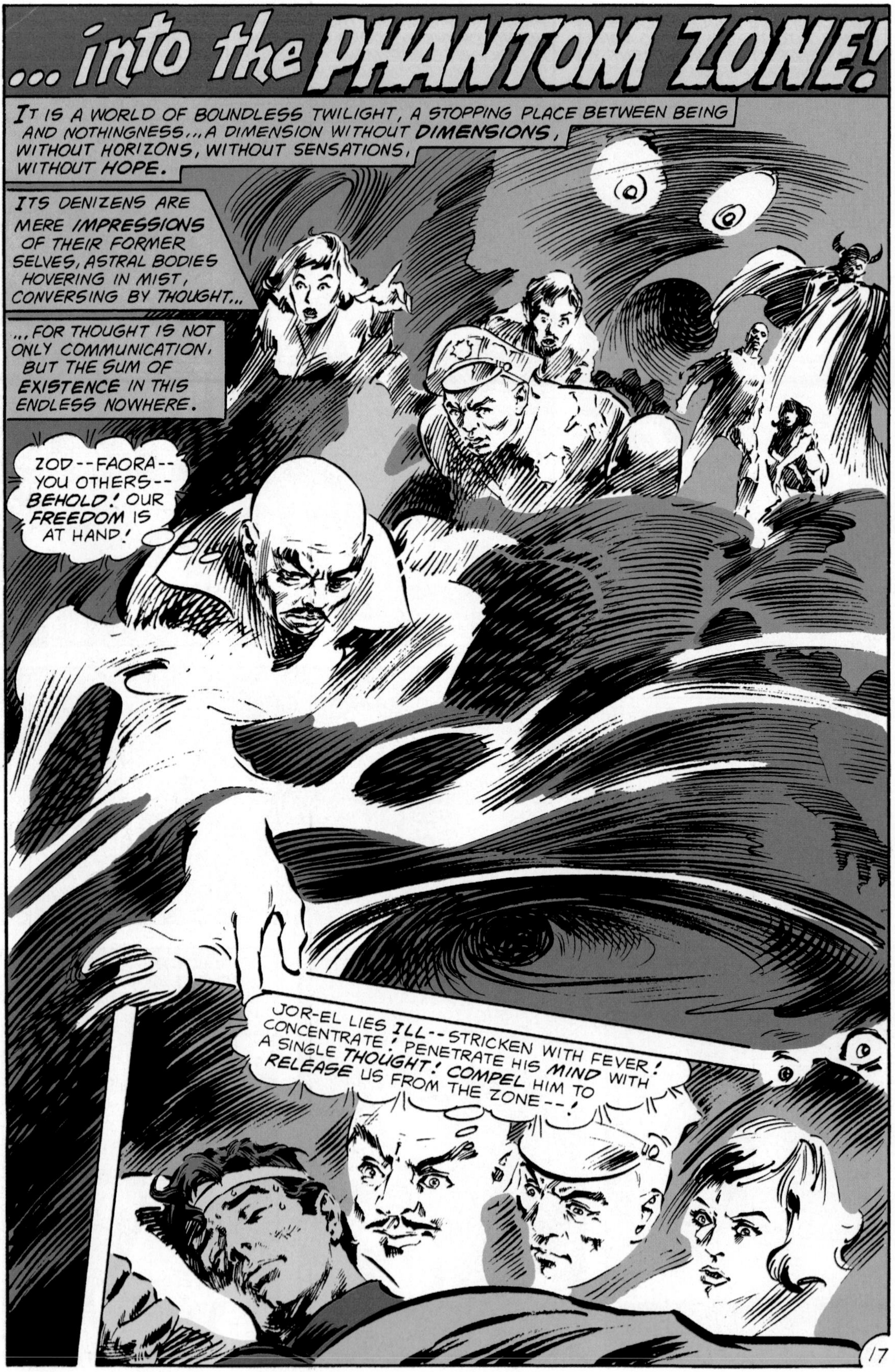
...into the PHANTOM ZONE!
IT IS A WORLD OF BOUNDLESS TWILIGHT, A STOPPING PLACE BETWEEN BEING AND NOTHINGNESS... A DIMENSION WITHOUT DIMENSIONS, WITHOUT HORIZONS, WITHOUT SENSATIONS, WITHOUT HOPE.
ITS DENIZENS ARE MERE IMPRESSIONS OF THEIR FORMER SELVES, ASTRAL BODIES HOVERING IN MIST, CONVERSING BY THOUGHT...
...FOR THOUGHT IS NOT ONLY COMMUNICATION, BUT THE SUM OF EXISTENCE IN THIS ENDLESS NOWHERE.
ZOD--FAORA--YOU OTHERS--BEHOLD! OUR FREEDOM IS AT HAND!
JOR-EL LIES ILL--STRICKEN WITH FEVER! CONCENTRATE! PENETRATE HIS MIND WITH A SINGLE THOUGHT! COMPEL HIM TO RELEASE US FROM THE ZONE--!
17

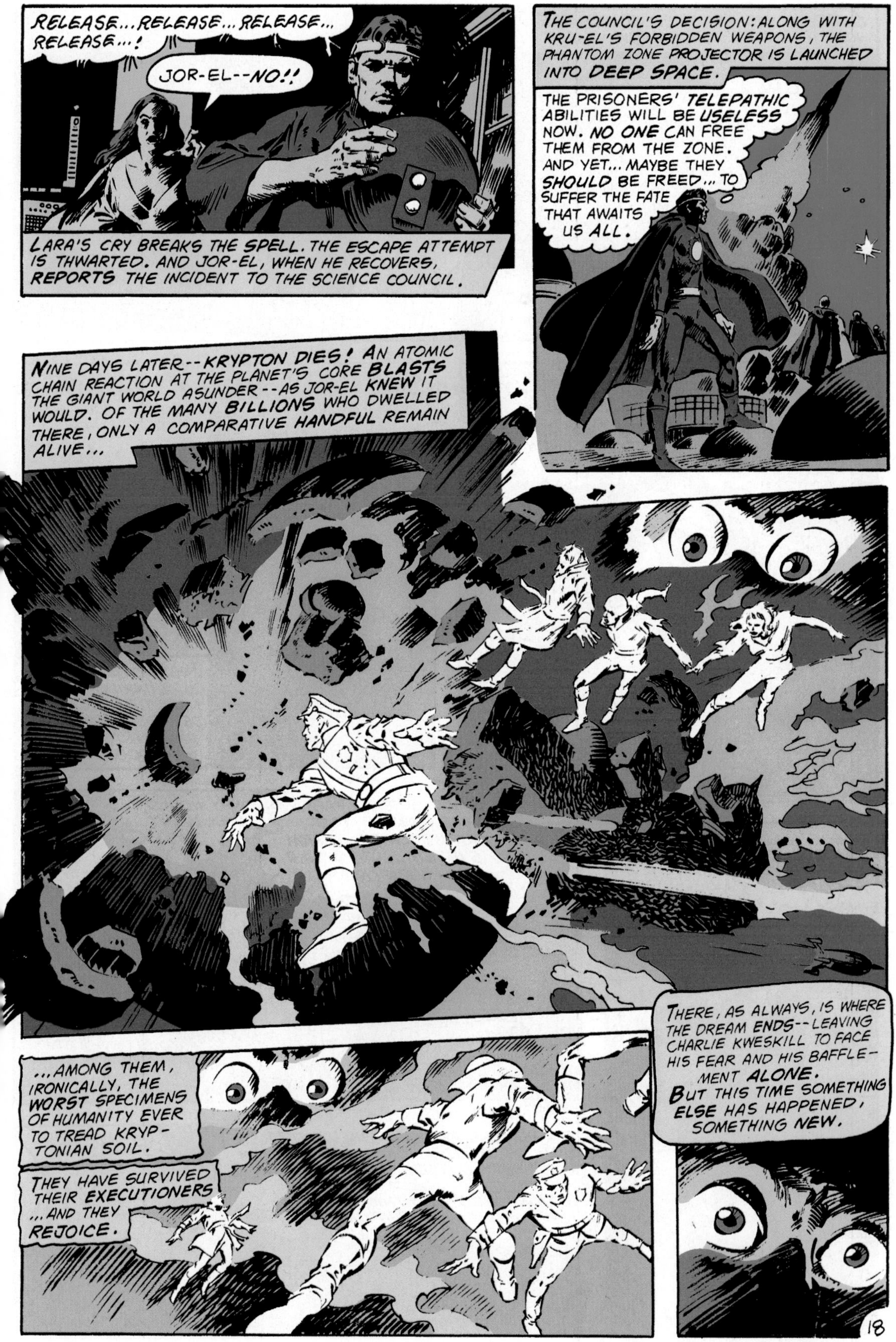
RELEASE... RELEASE... RELEASE... RELEASE...!
JOR-EL--NO!!
LARA'S CRY BREAKS THE SPELL. THE ESCAPE ATTEMPT IS THWARTED. AND JOR-EL, WHEN HE RECOVERS, REPORTS THE INCIDENT TO THE SCIENCE COUNCIL.
THE COUNCIL'S DECISION: ALONG WITH KRU-EL'S FORBIDDEN WEAPONS, THE PHANTOM ZONE PROJECTOR IS LAUNCHED INTO DEEP SPACE.
THE PRISONERS' TELEPATHIC ABILITIES WILL BE USELESS NOW. NO ONE CAN FREE THEM FROM THE ZONE. AND YET... MAYBE THEY SHOULD BE FREED... TO SUFFER THE FATE THAT AWAITS US ALL.
NINE DAYS LATER--KRYPTON DIES! AN ATOMIC CHAIN REACTION AT THE PLANET'S CORE BLASTS THE GIANT WORLD ASUNDER--AS JOR-EL KNEW IT WOULD. OF THE MANY BILLIONS WHO DWELLED THERE, ONLY A COMPARATIVE HANDFUL REMAIN ALIVE...
...AMONG THEM, IRONICALLY, THE WORST SPECIMENS OF HUMANITY EVER TO TREAD KRYPTONIAN SOIL.
THEY HAVE SURVIVED THEIR EXECUTIONERS ...AND THEY REJOICE.
THERE, AS ALWAYS, IS WHERE THE DREAM ENDS--LEAVING CHARLIE KWESKILL TO FACE HIS FEAR AND HIS BAFFLEMENT ALONE.
BUT THIS TIME SOMETHING ELSE HAS HAPPENED, SOMETHING NEW.
18

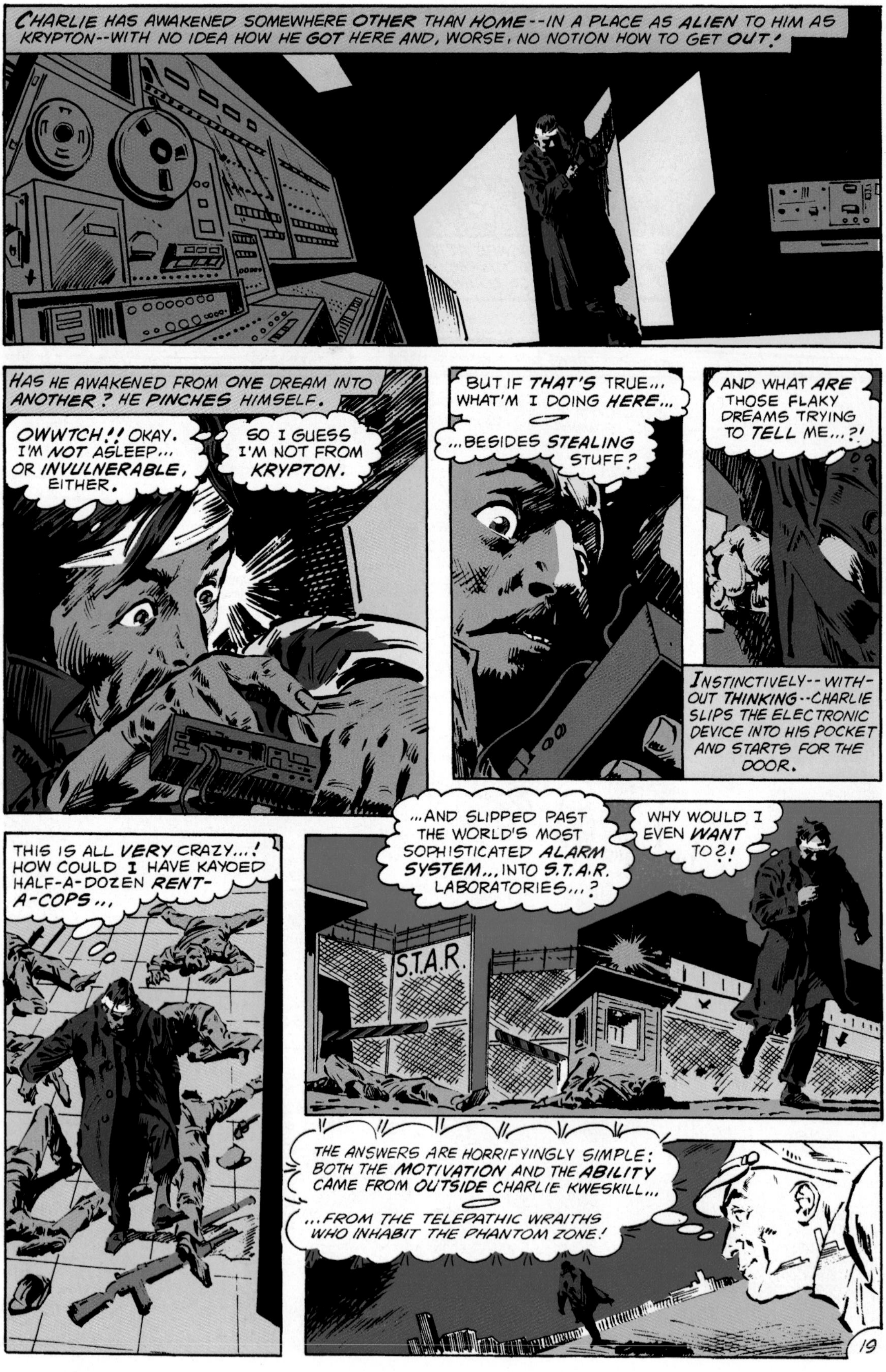

CHARLIE HAS AWAKENED SOMEWHERE OTHER THAN HOME--IN A PLACE AS ALIEN TO HIM AS KRYPTON--WITH NO IDEA HOW HE GOT HERE AND, WORSE, NO NOTION HOW TO GET OUT!
HAS HE AWAKENED FROM ONE DREAM INTO ANOTHER? HE PINCHES HIMSELF.
OWWTCH!! OKAY. I'M NOT ASLEEP... OR INVULNERABLE, EITHER.
SO I GUESS I'M NOT FROM KRYPTON.
BUT IF THAT'S TRUE... WHAT'M I DOING HERE...
...BESIDES STEALING STUFF?
AND WHAT ARE THOSE FLAKY DREAMS TRYING TO TELL ME...?!
INSTINCTIVELY--WITHOUT THINKING--CHARLIE SLIPS THE ELECTRONIC DEVICE INTO HIS POCKET AND STARTS FOR THE DOOR.
THIS IS ALL VERY CRAZY...! HOW COULD I HAVE KAYOED HALF-A-DOZEN RENT-A-COPS...
...AND SLIPPED PAST THE WORLD'S MOST SOPHISTICATED ALARM SYSTEM... INTO S.T.A.R. LABORATORIES...?
WHY WOULD I EVEN WANT TO?!
S.T.A.R.
THE ANSWERS ARE HORRIFYINGLY SIMPLE: BOTH THE MOTIVATION AND THE ABILITY CAME FROM OUTSIDE CHARLIE KWESKILL...
...FROM THE TELEPATHIC WRAITHS WHO INHABIT THE PHANTOM ZONE!
19

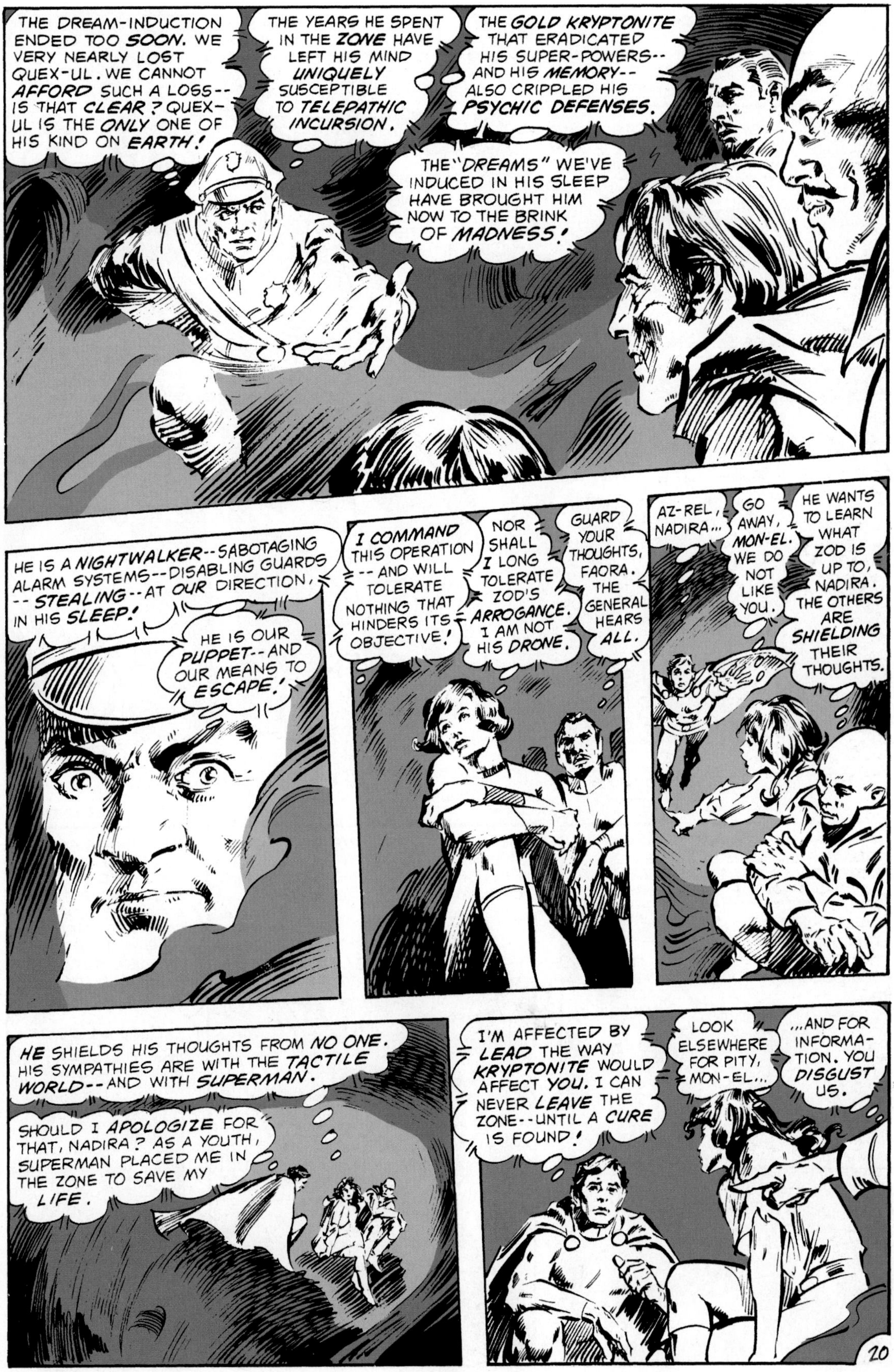
THE DREAM-INDUCTION ENDED TOO SOON. WE VERY NEARLY LOST QUEX-UL. WE CANNOT AFFORD SUCH A LOSS-- IS THAT CLEAR? QUEX-UL IS THE ONLY ONE OF HIS KIND ON EARTH!
THE YEARS HE SPENT IN THE ZONE HAVE LEFT HIS MIND UNIQUELY SUSCEPTIBLE TO TELEPATHIC INCURSION.
THE GOLD KRYPTONITE THAT ERADICATED HIS SUPER-POWERS-- AND HIS MEMORY-- ALSO CRIPPLED HIS PSYCHIC DEFENSES.
THE "DREAMS" WE'VE INDUCED IN HIS SLEEP HAVE BROUGHT HIM NOW TO THE BRINK OF MADNESS!
HE IS A NIGHTWALKER--SABOTAGING ALARM SYSTEMS--DISABLING GUARDS --STEALING--AT OUR DIRECTION, IN HIS SLEEP!
HE IS OUR PUPPET--AND OUR MEANS TO ESCAPE!
I COMMAND THIS OPERATION --AND WILL TOLERATE NOTHING THAT HINDERS ITS OBJECTIVE!
NOR SHALL I LONG TOLERATE ZOD'S ARROGANCE. I AM NOT HIS DRONE.
GUARD YOUR THOUGHTS, FAORA. THE GENERAL HEARS ALL.
AZ-REL, NADIRA...
GO AWAY, MON-EL. WE DO NOT LIKE YOU.
HE WANTS TO LEARN WHAT ZOD IS UP TO, NADIRA. THE OTHERS ARE SHIELDING THEIR THOUGHTS.
HE SHIELDS HIS THOUGHTS FROM NO ONE. HIS SYMPATHIES ARE WITH THE TACTILE WORLD--AND WITH SUPERMAN.
SHOULD I APOLOGIZE FOR THAT, NADIRA? AS A YOUTH, SUPERMAN PLACED ME IN THE ZONE TO SAVE MY LIFE.
I'M AFFECTED BY LEAD THE WAY KRYPTONITE WOULD AFFECT YOU. I CAN NEVER LEAVE THE ZONE--UNTIL A CURE IS FOUND!
LOOK ELSEWHERE FOR PITY, MON-EL...
...AND FOR INFORMATION. YOU DISGUST US.
20

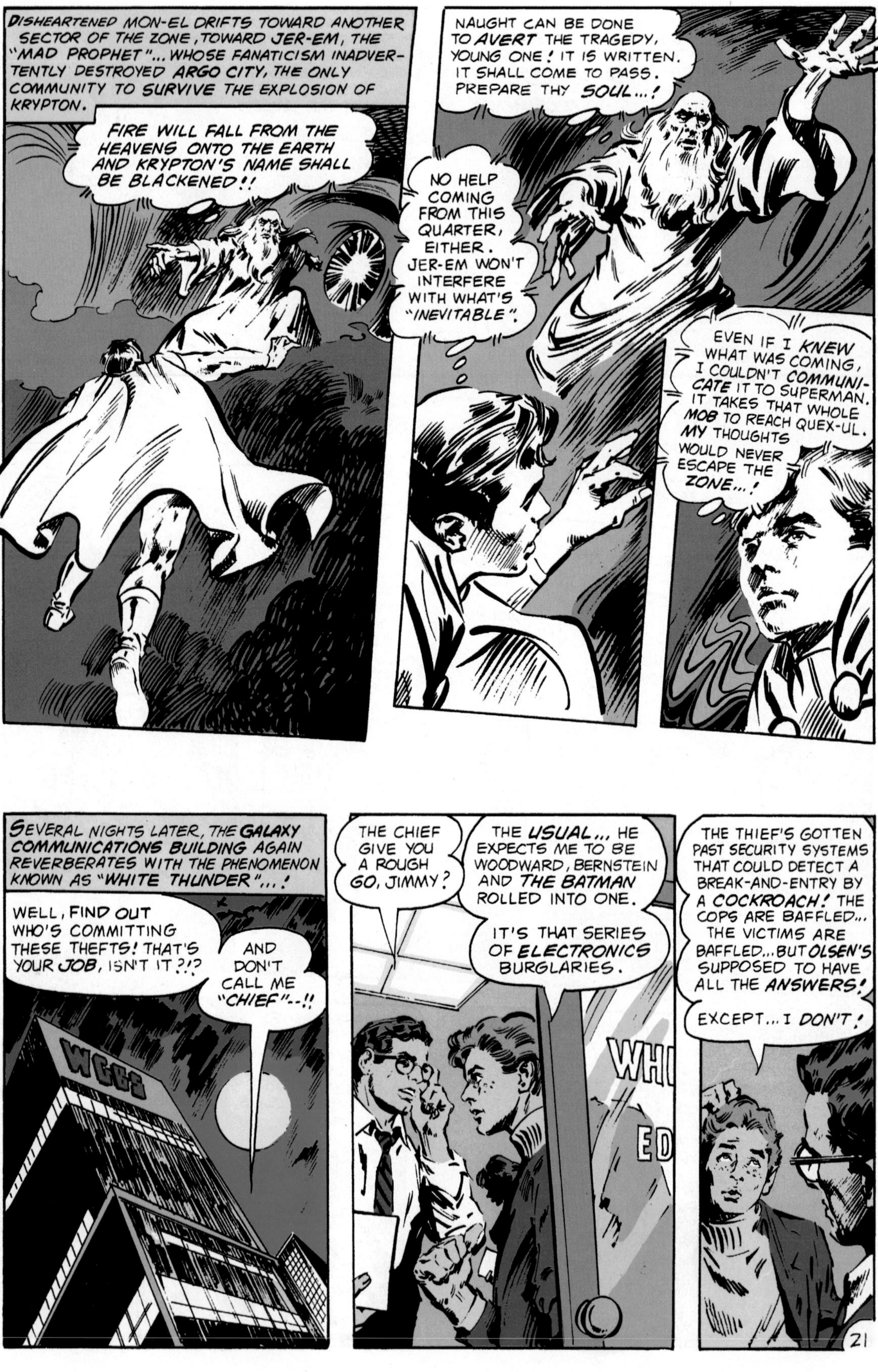
DISHEARTENED MON-EL DRIFTS TOWARD ANOTHER SECTOR OF THE ZONE, TOWARD JER-EM, THE "MAD PROPHET"... WHOSE FANATICISM INADVERTENTLY DESTROYED ARGO CITY, THE ONLY COMMUNITY TO SURVIVE THE EXPLOSION OF KRYPTON.
FIRE WILL FALL FROM THE HEAVENS ONTO THE EARTH AND KRYPTON'S NAME SHALL BE BLACKENED!!
NAUGHT CAN BE DONE TO AVERT THE TRAGEDY, YOUNG ONE! IT IS WRITTEN. IT SHALL COME TO PASS. PREPARE THY SOUL...!
NO HELP COMING FROM THIS QUARTER, EITHER. JER-EM WON'T INTERFERE WITH WHAT'S "INEVITABLE".
EVEN IF I KNEW WHAT WAS COMING, I COULDN'T COMMUNICATE IT TO SUPERMAN. IT TAKES THAT WHOLE MOB TO REACH QUEX-UL. MY THOUGHTS WOULD NEVER ESCAPE THE ZONE...!
SEVERAL NIGHTS LATER, THE GALAXY COMMUNICATIONS BUILDING AGAIN REVERBERATES WITH THE PHENOMENON KNOWN AS "WHITE THUNDER"...!
WELL, FIND OUT WHO'S COMMITTING THESE THEFTS! THAT'S YOUR JOB, ISN'T IT?!?
AND DON'T CALL ME "CHIEF"--!!
WGBS
THE CHIEF GIVE YOU A ROUGH GO, JIMMY?
THE USUAL... HE EXPECTS ME TO BE WOODWARD, BERNSTEIN AND THE BATMAN ROLLED INTO ONE.
IT'S THAT SERIES OF ELECTRONICS BURGLARIES.
THE THIEF'S GOTTEN PAST SECURITY SYSTEMS THAT COULD DETECT A BREAK-AND-ENTRY BY A COCKROACH! THE COPS ARE BAFFLED... THE VICTIMS ARE BAFFLED... BUT OLSEN'S SUPPOSED TO HAVE ALL THE ANSWERS!
EXCEPT... I DON'T!
21

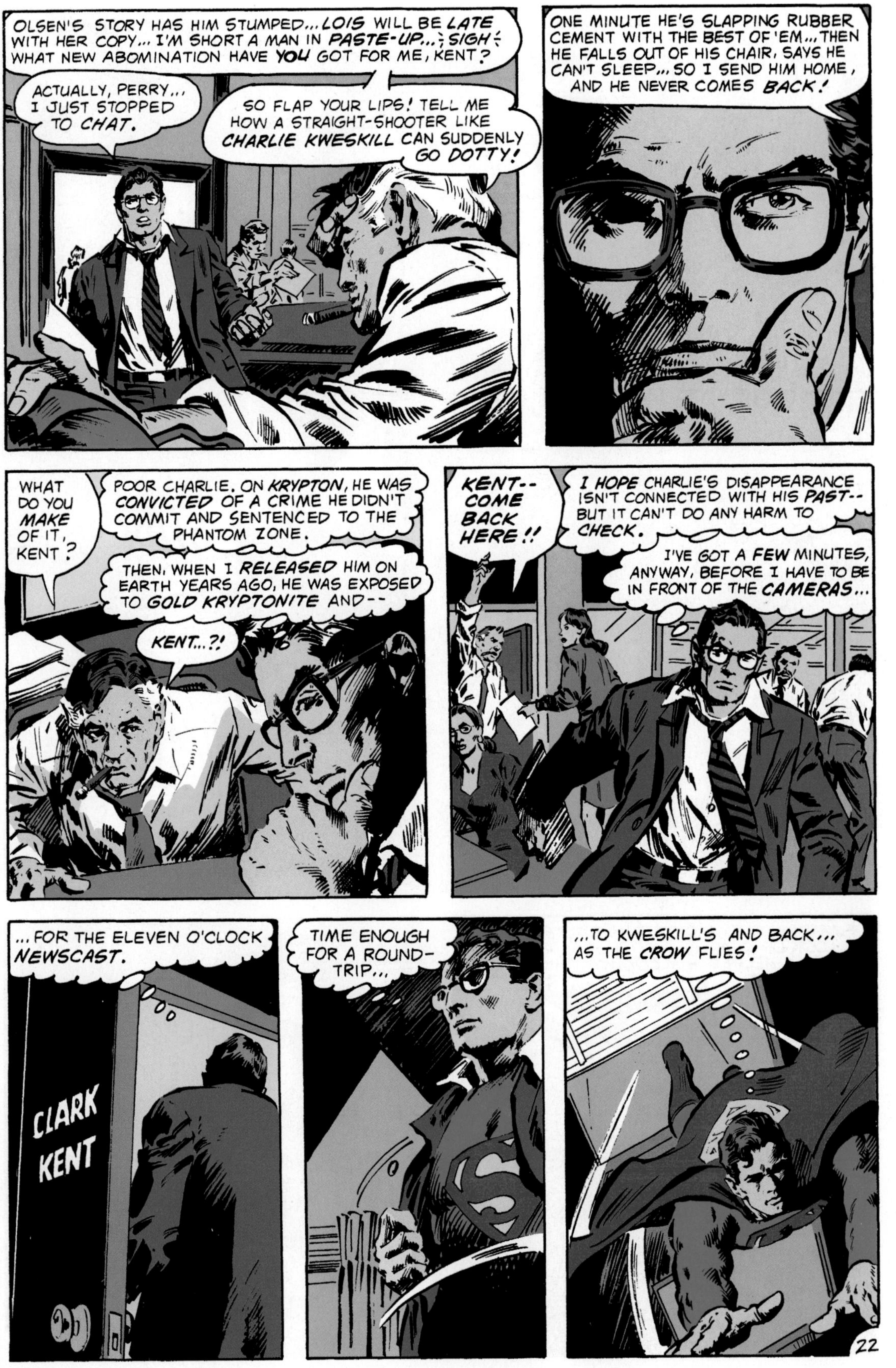

OLSEN'S STORY HAS HIM STUMPED... LOIS WILL BE LATE WITH HER COPY... I'M SHORT A MAN IN PASTE-UP... -SIGH- WHAT NEW ABOMINATION HAVE YOU GOT FOR ME, KENT?
ACTUALLY, PERRY... I JUST STOPPED TO CHAT.
SO FLAP YOUR LIPS! TELL ME HOW A STRAIGHT-SHOOTER LIKE CHARLIE KWESKILL CAN SUDDENLY GO DOTTY!
ONE MINUTE HE'S SLAPPING RUBBER CEMENT WITH THE BEST OF 'EM... THEN HE FALLS OUT OF HIS CHAIR, SAYS HE CAN'T SLEEP... SO I SEND HIM HOME, AND HE NEVER COMES BACK!
WHAT DO YOU MAKE OF IT, KENT?
POOR CHARLIE. ON KRYPTON, HE WAS CONVICTED OF A CRIME HE DIDN'T COMMIT AND SENTENCED TO THE PHANTOM ZONE.
THEN, WHEN I RELEASED HIM ON EARTH YEARS AGO, HE WAS EXPOSED TO GOLD KRYPTONITE AND--
KENT...?!
KENT-- COME BACK HERE!!
I HOPE CHARLIE'S DISAPPEARANCE ISN'T CONNECTED WITH HIS PAST-- BUT IT CAN'T DO ANY HARM TO CHECK.
I'VE GOT A FEW MINUTES, ANYWAY, BEFORE I HAVE TO BE IN FRONT OF THE CAMERAS...
...FOR THE ELEVEN O'CLOCK NEWSCAST.
CLARK KENT
TIME ENOUGH FOR A ROUND-TRIP...
...TO KWESKILL'S AND BACK... AS THE CROW FLIES!
22

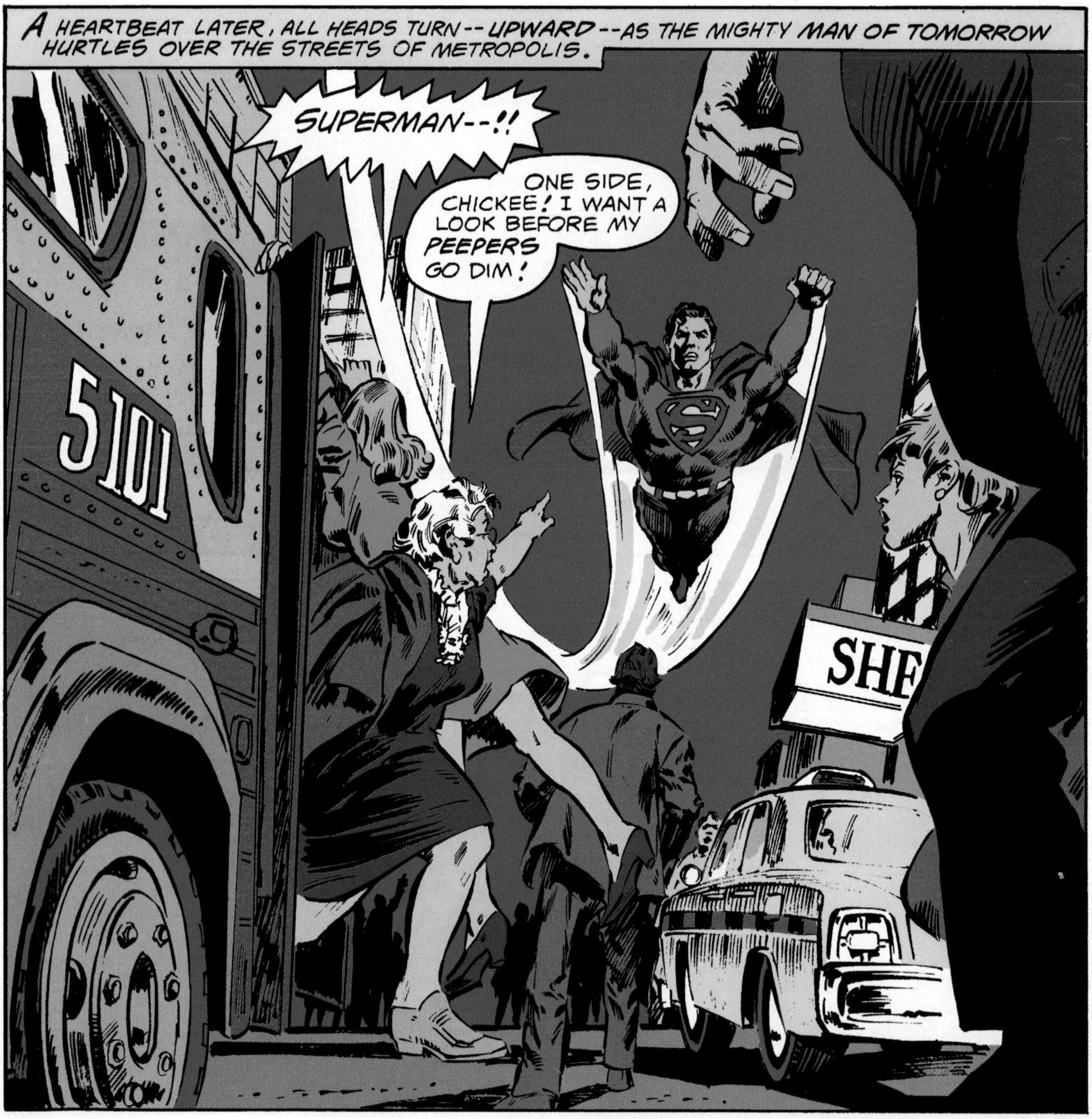
A HEARTBEAT LATER, ALL HEADS TURN--UPWARD--AS THE MIGHTY MAN OF TOMORROW HURTLES OVER THE STREETS OF METROPOLIS.
SUPERMAN--!!
ONE SIDE, CHICKEE! I WANT A LOOK BEFORE MY PEEPERS GO DIM!
5101
SHE

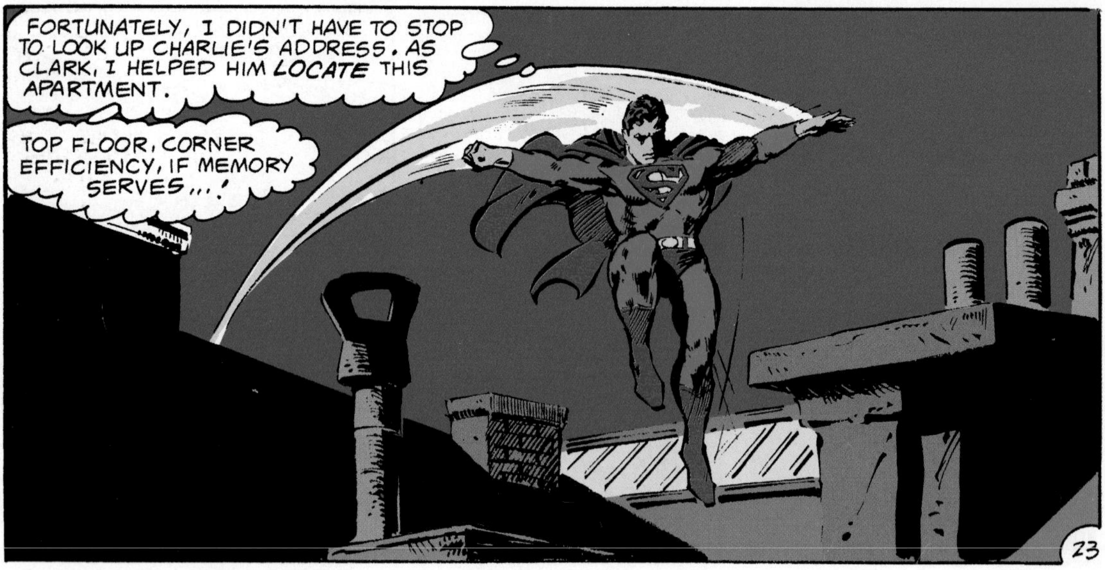
FORTUNATELY, I DIDN'T HAVE TO STOP TO LOOK UP CHARLIE'S ADDRESS. AS CLARK, I HELPED HIM LOCATE THIS APARTMENT.
TOP FLOOR, CORNER EFFICIENCY, IF MEMORY SERVES...!
23

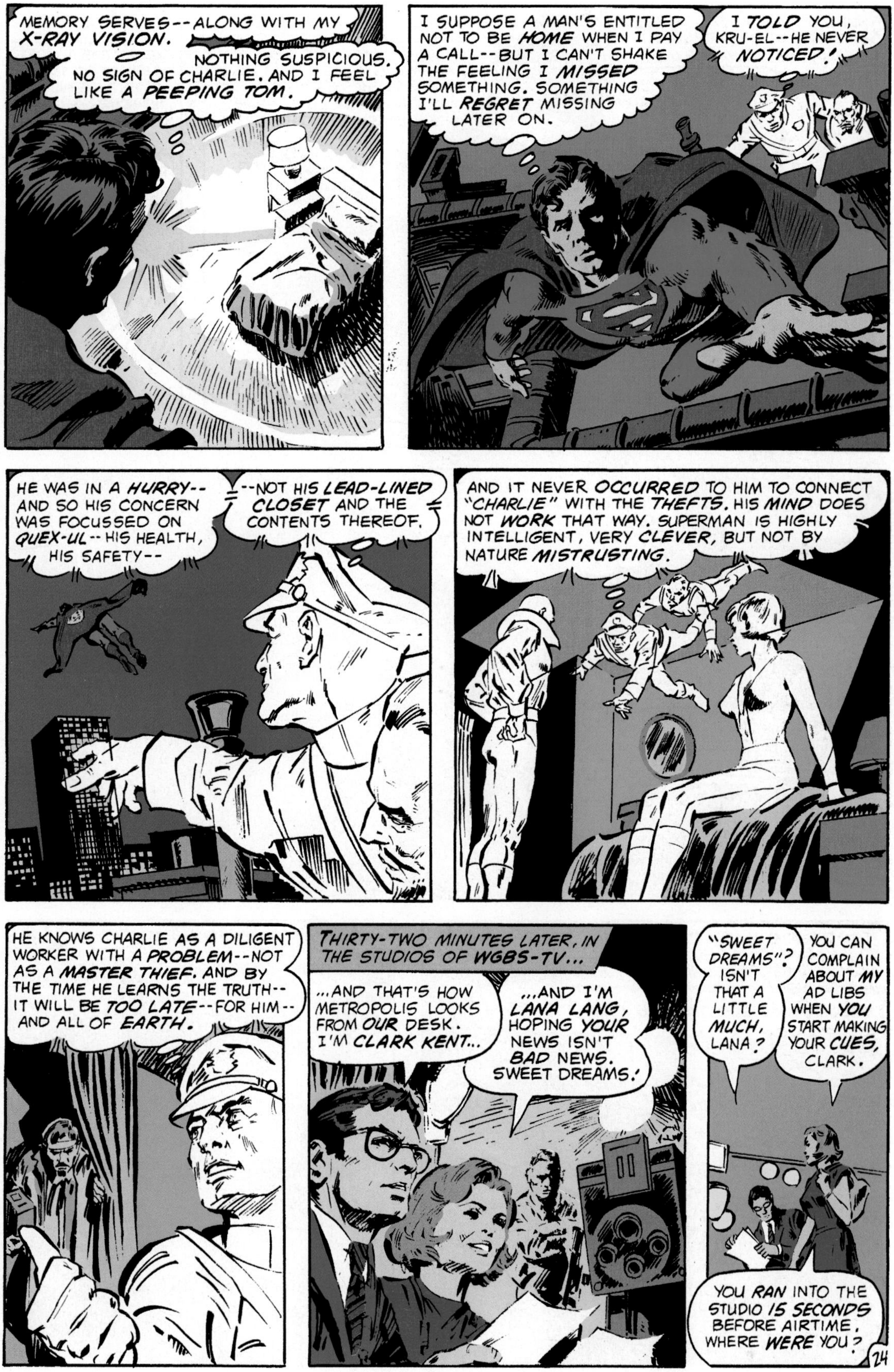
MEMORY SERVES--ALONG WITH MY X-RAY VISION.
NOTHING SUSPICIOUS. NO SIGN OF CHARLIE. AND I FEEL LIKE A PEEPING TOM.
I SUPPOSE A MAN'S ENTITLED NOT TO BE HOME WHEN I PAY A CALL--BUT I CAN'T SHAKE THE FEELING I MISSED SOMETHING. SOMETHING I'LL REGRET MISSING LATER ON.
I TOLD YOU, KRU-EL--HE NEVER NOTICED!
HE WAS IN A HURRY--AND SO HIS CONCERN WAS FOCUSSED ON QUEX-UL--HIS HEALTH, HIS SAFETY--
--NOT HIS LEAD-LINED CLOSET AND THE CONTENTS THEREOF.
AND IT NEVER OCCURRED TO HIM TO CONNECT "CHARLIE" WITH THE THEFTS. HIS MIND DOES NOT WORK THAT WAY. SUPERMAN IS HIGHLY INTELLIGENT, VERY CLEVER, BUT NOT BY NATURE MISTRUSTING.
HE KNOWS CHARLIE AS A DILIGENT WORKER WITH A PROBLEM--NOT AS A MASTER THIEF. AND BY THE TIME HE LEARNS THE TRUTH--IT WILL BE TOO LATE--FOR HIM--AND ALL OF EARTH.
THIRTY-TWO MINUTES LATER, IN THE STUDIOS OF WGBS-TV...
...AND THAT'S HOW METROPOLIS LOOKS FROM OUR DESK. I'M CLARK KENT...
...AND I'M LANA LANG, HOPING YOUR NEWS ISN'T BAD NEWS. SWEET DREAMS!
"SWEET DREAMS"? ISN'T THAT A LITTLE MUCH, LANA?
YOU CAN COMPLAIN ABOUT MY AD LIBS WHEN YOU START MAKING YOUR CUES, CLARK.
YOU RAN INTO THE STUDIO 15 SECONDS BEFORE AIRTIME. WHERE WERE YOU?
24

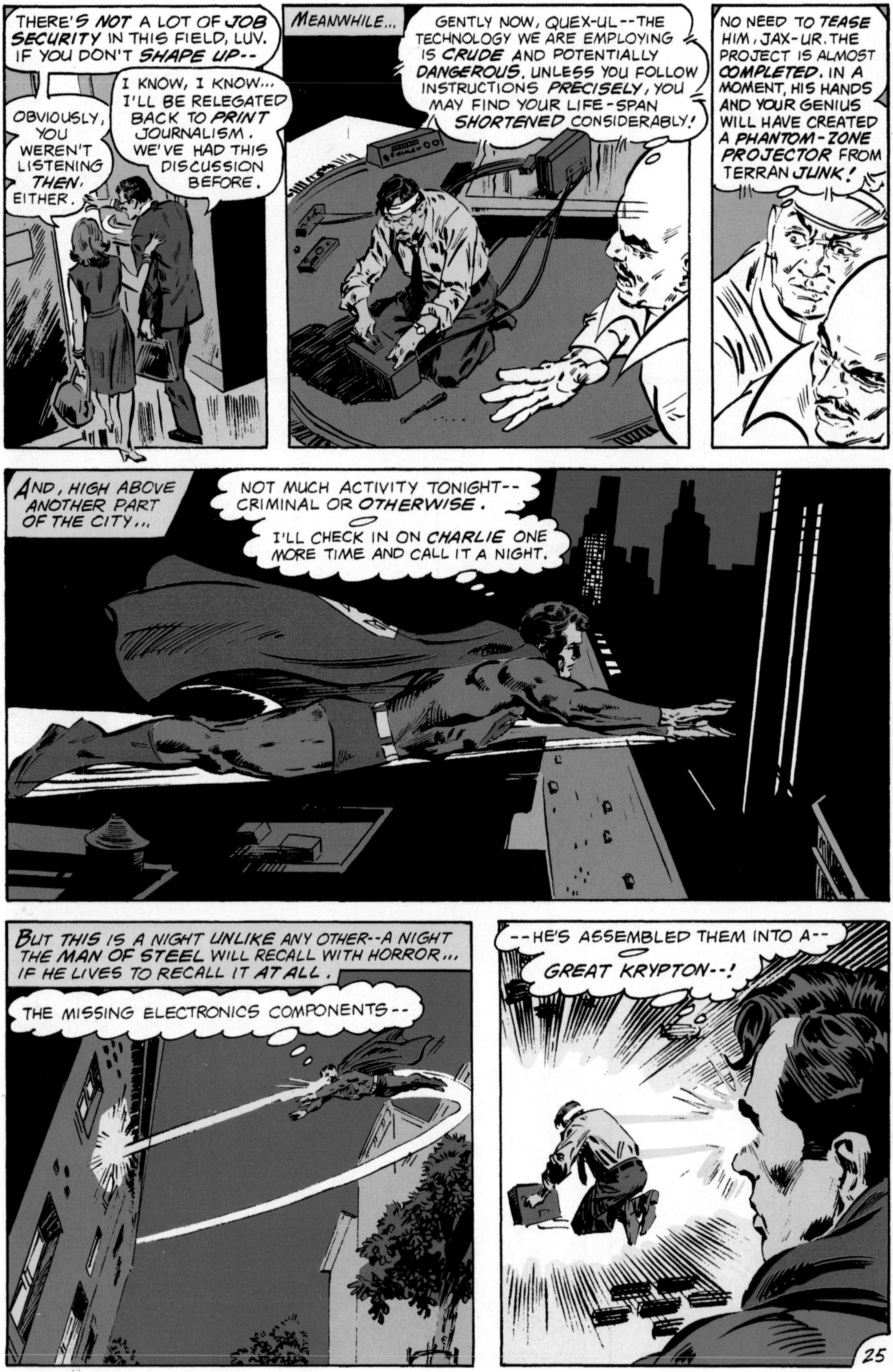
THERE'S NOT A LOT OF JOB SECURITY IN THIS FIELD, LUV. IF YOU DON'T SHAPE UP--
I KNOW, I KNOW... I'LL BE RELEGATED BACK TO PRINT JOURNALISM. WE'VE HAD THIS DISCUSSION BEFORE.
OBVIOUSLY, YOU WEREN'T LISTENING THEN, EITHER.
MEANWHILE...
GENTLY NOW, QUEX-UL--THE TECHNOLOGY WE ARE EMPLOYING IS CRUDE AND POTENTIALLY DANGEROUS. UNLESS YOU FOLLOW INSTRUCTIONS PRECISELY, YOU MAY FIND YOUR LIFE-SPAN SHORTENED CONSIDERABLY!
NO NEED TO TEASE HIM, JAX-UR. THE PROJECT IS ALMOST COMPLETED. IN A MOMENT, HIS HANDS AND YOUR GENIUS WILL HAVE CREATED A PHANTOM-ZONE PROJECTOR FROM TERRAN JUNK!
AND, HIGH ABOVE ANOTHER PART OF THE CITY...
NOT MUCH ACTIVITY TONIGHT--CRIMINAL OR OTHERWISE.
I'LL CHECK IN ON CHARLIE ONE MORE TIME AND CALL IT A NIGHT.
BUT THIS IS A NIGHT UNLIKE ANY OTHER--A NIGHT THE MAN OF STEEL WILL RECALL WITH HORROR... IF HE LIVES TO RECALL IT AT ALL.
THE MISSING ELECTRONICS COMPONENTS--
--HE'S ASSEMBLED THEM INTO A--
GREAT KRYPTON--!
25

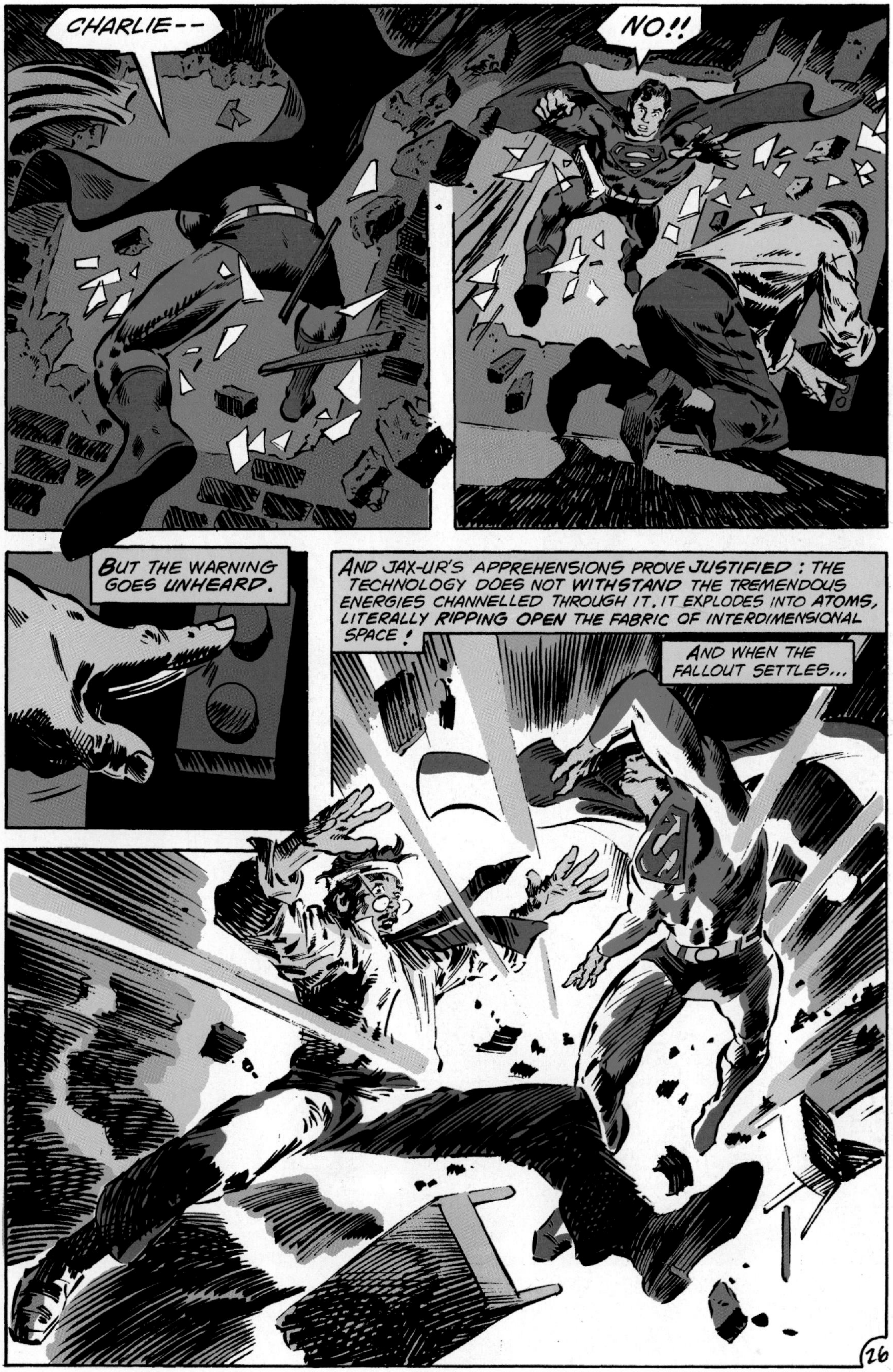

CHARLIE--
NO!!
BUT THE WARNING GOES UNHEARD.
AND JAX-UR'S APPREHENSIONS PROVE JUSTIFIED: THE TECHNOLOGY DOES NOT WITHSTAND THE TREMENDOUS ENERGIES CHANNELLED THROUGH IT. IT EXPLODES INTO ATOMS, LITERALLY RIPPING OPEN THE FABRIC OF INTERDIMENSIONAL SPACE!
AND WHEN THE FALLOUT SETTLES...
26

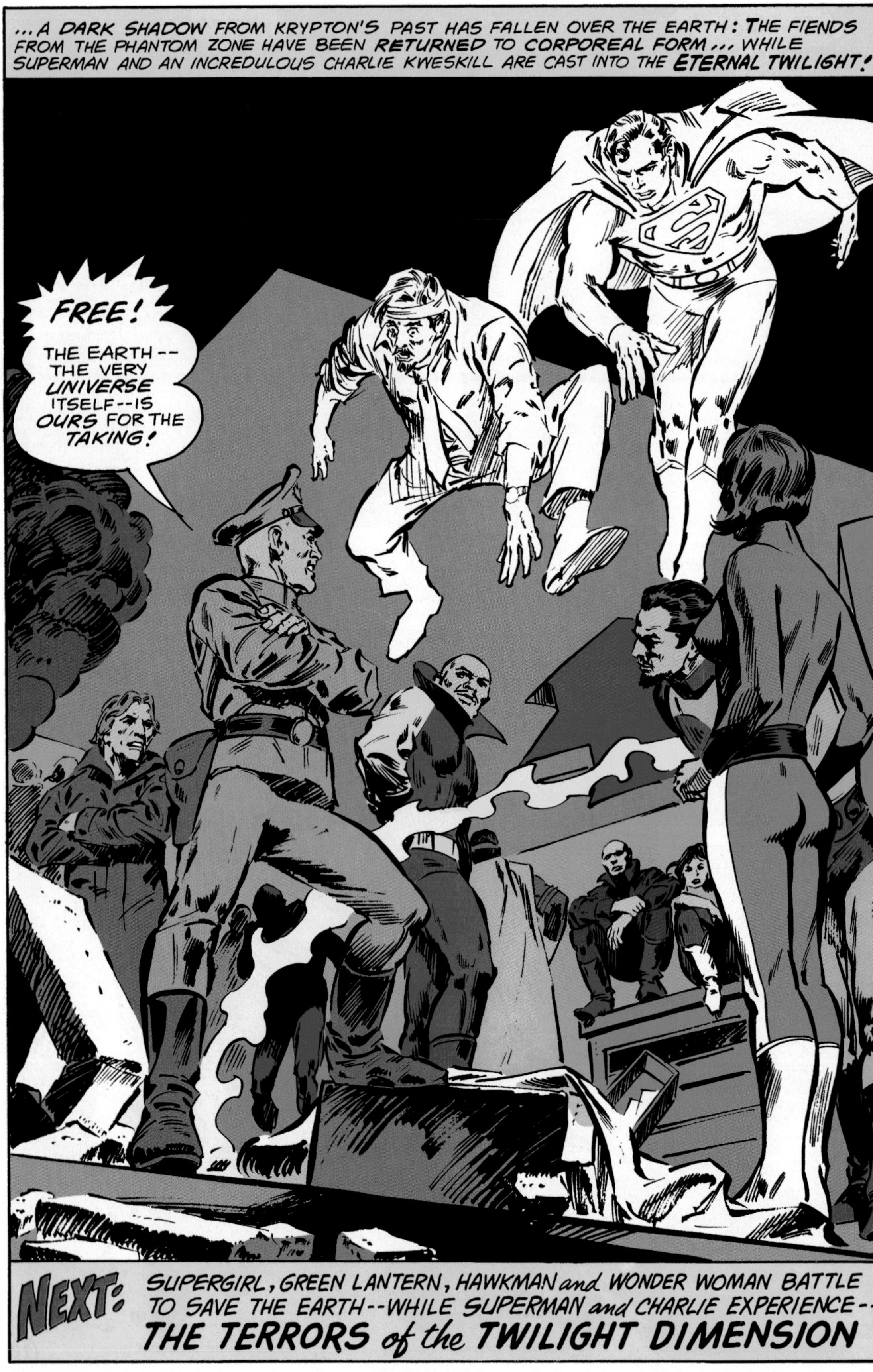
...A DARK SHADOW FROM KRYPTON'S PAST HAS FALLEN OVER THE EARTH: THE FIENDS FROM THE PHANTOM ZONE HAVE BEEN RETURNED TO CORPOREAL FORM... WHILE SUPERMAN AND AN INCREDULOUS CHARLIE KWESKILL ARE CAST INTO THE ETERNAL TWILIGHT!
FREE!
THE EARTH -- THE VERY UNIVERSE ITSELF--IS OURS FOR THE TAKING!
NEXT: SUPERGIRL, GREEN LANTERN, HAWKMAN and WONDER WOMAN BATTLE TO SAVE THE EARTH--WHILE SUPERMAN and CHARLIE EXPERIENCE--
THE TERRORS of the TWILIGHT DIMENSION

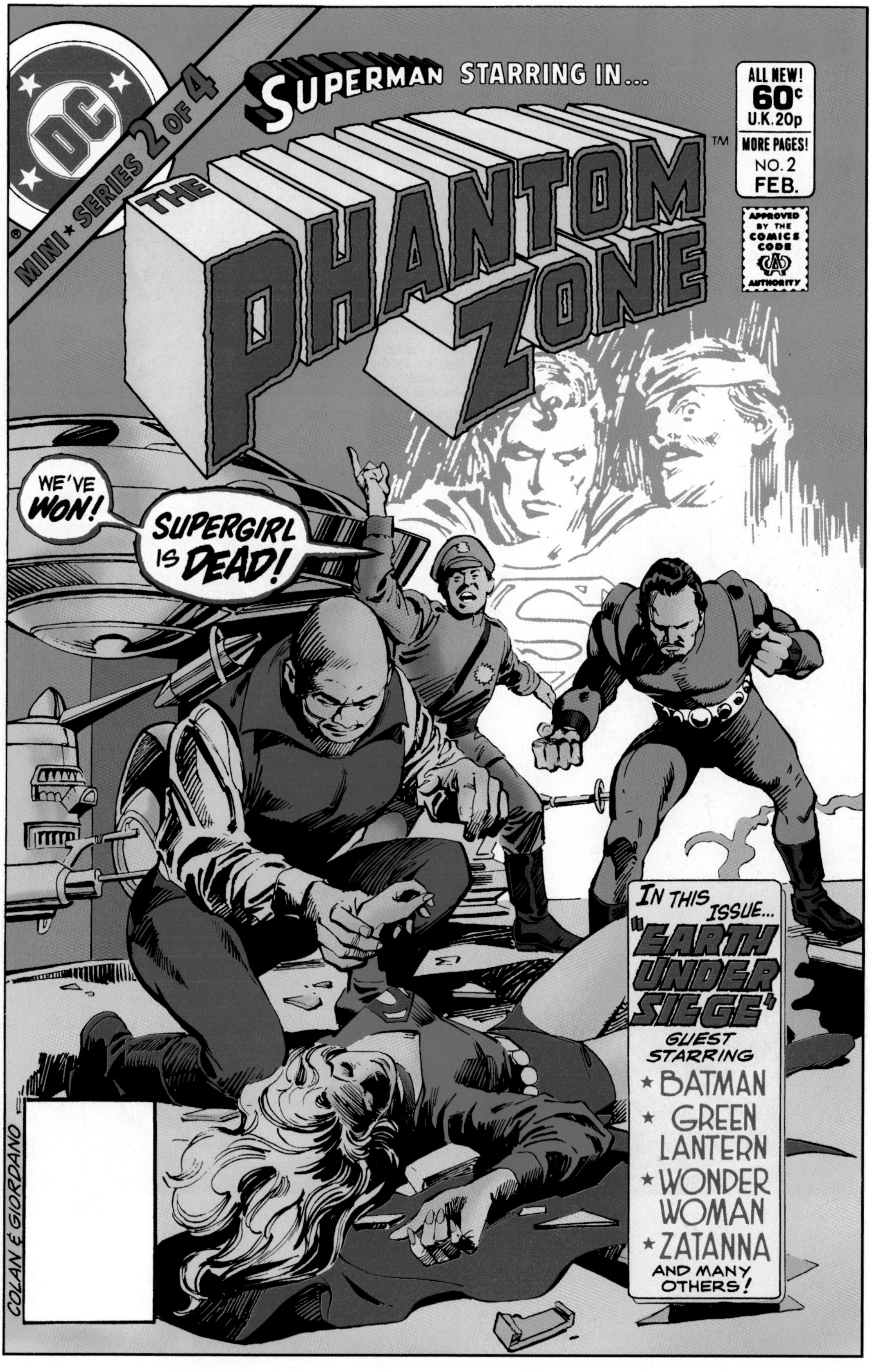

MINI★SERIES 2 OF 4
DC
SUPERMAN STARRING IN...
THE PHANTOM ZONE
ALL NEW! 60¢ U.K.20p
MORE PAGES!
NO. 2 FEB.
APPROVED BY THE COMICS CODE AUTHORITY
WE'VE WON!
SUPERGIRL IS DEAD!
IN THIS ISSUE... "EARTH UNDER SIEGE"
GUEST STARRING
★BATMAN
★GREEN LANTERN
★WONDER WOMAN
★ZATANNA
AND MANY OTHERS!
COLAN & GIORDANO

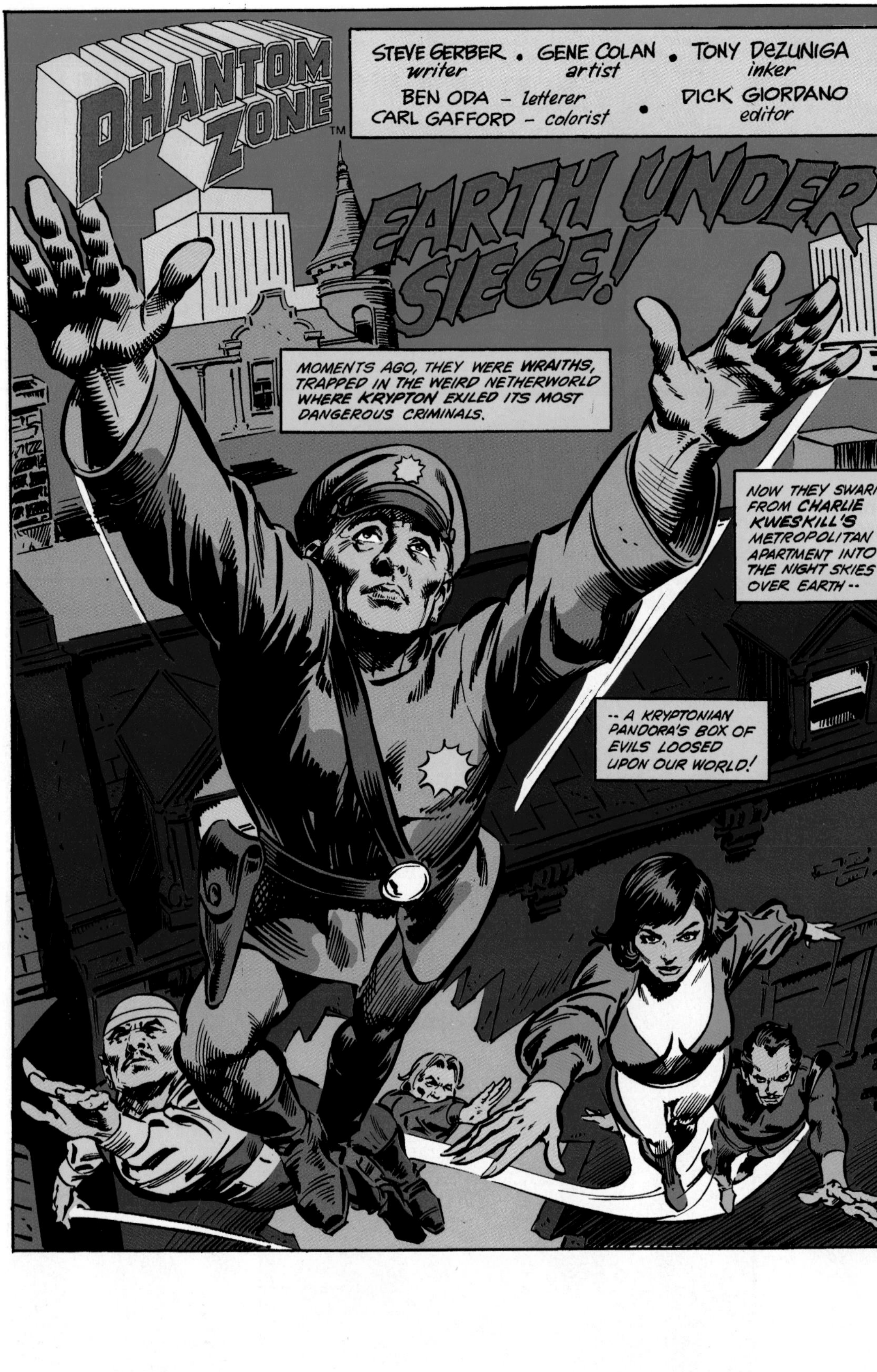

PHANTOM ZONE™
STEVE GERBER writer • GENE COLAN artist • TONY DeZUNIGA inker
BEN ODA - letterer
CARL GAFFORD - colorist • DICK GIORDANO editor
EARTH UNDER SIEGE!
MOMENTS AGO, THEY WERE WRAITHS, TRAPPED IN THE WEIRD NETHERWORLD WHERE KRYPTON EXILED ITS MOST DANGEROUS CRIMINALS.
NOW THEY SWARM FROM CHARLIE KWESKILL'S METROPOLITAN APARTMENT INTO THE NIGHT SKIES OVER EARTH --
-- A KRYPTONIAN PANDORA'S BOX OF EVILS LOOSED UPON OUR WORLD!

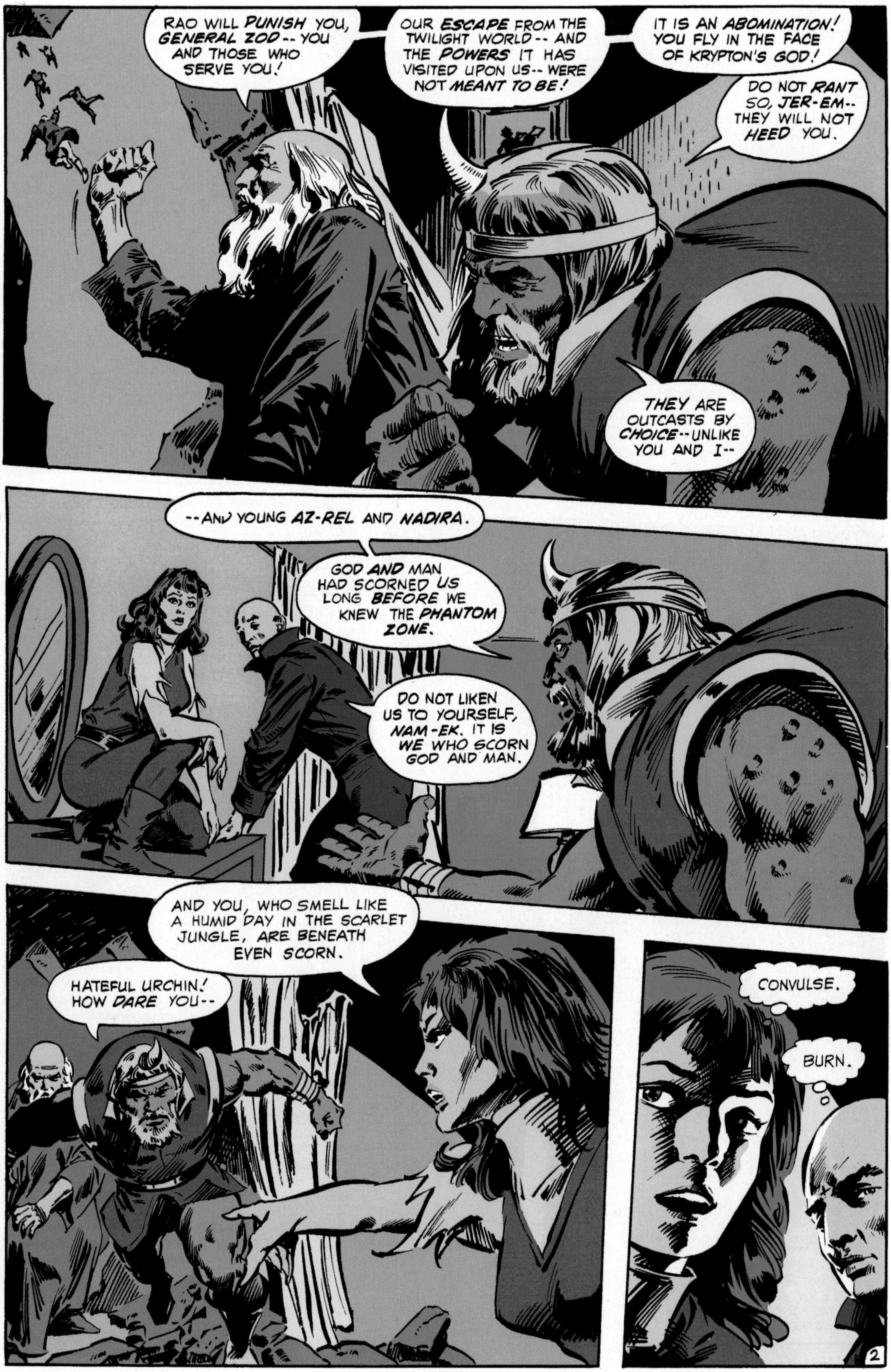
RAO WILL PUNISH YOU, GENERAL ZOD -- YOU AND THOSE WHO SERVE YOU!
OUR ESCAPE FROM THE TWILIGHT WORLD -- AND THE POWERS IT HAS VISITED UPON US -- WERE NOT MEANT TO BE!
IT IS AN ABOMINATION! YOU FLY IN THE FACE OF KRYPTON'S GOD!
DO NOT RANT SO, JER-EM -- THEY WILL NOT HEED YOU.
THEY ARE OUTCASTS BY CHOICE -- UNLIKE YOU AND I --
-- AND YOUNG AZ-REL AND NADIRA.
GOD AND MAN HAD SCORNED US LONG BEFORE WE KNEW THE PHANTOM ZONE.
DO NOT LIKEN US TO YOURSELF, NAM-EK. IT IS WE WHO SCORN GOD AND MAN.
AND YOU, WHO SMELL LIKE A HUMID DAY IN THE SCARLET JUNGLE, ARE BENEATH EVEN SCORN.
HATEFUL URCHIN! HOW DARE YOU --
CONVULSE.
BURN.
2

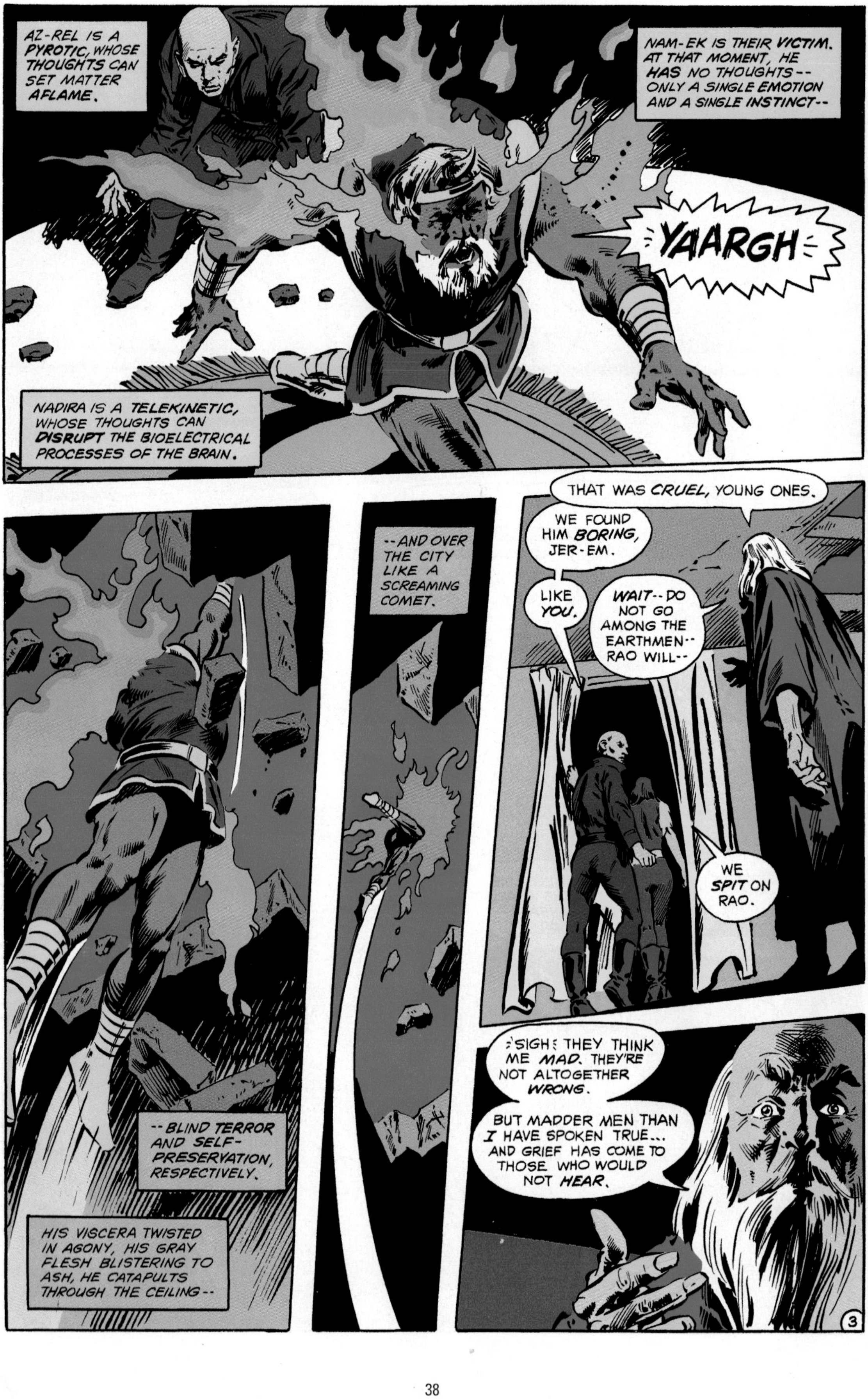

AZ-REL IS A PYROTIC, WHOSE THOUGHTS CAN SET MATTER AFLAME.
NAM-EK IS THEIR VICTIM. AT THAT MOMENT, HE HAS NO THOUGHTS-- ONLY A SINGLE EMOTION AND A SINGLE INSTINCT--
YAARGH
NADIRA IS A TELEKINETIC, WHOSE THOUGHTS CAN DISRUPT THE BIOELECTRICAL PROCESSES OF THE BRAIN.
--BLIND TERROR AND SELF-PRESERVATION, RESPECTIVELY.
HIS VISCERA TWISTED IN AGONY, HIS GRAY FLESH BLISTERING TO ASH, HE CATAPULTS THROUGH THE CEILING--
--AND OVER THE CITY LIKE A SCREAMING COMET.
THAT WAS CRUEL, YOUNG ONES.
WE FOUND HIM BORING, JER-EM.
LIKE YOU.
WAIT--DO NOT GO AMONG THE EARTHMEN-- RAO WILL--
WE SPIT ON RAO.
:SIGH: THEY THINK ME MAD. THEY'RE NOT ALTOGETHER WRONG.
BUT MADDER MEN THAN I HAVE SPOKEN TRUE... AND GRIEF HAS COME TO THOSE WHO WOULD NOT HEAR.
3

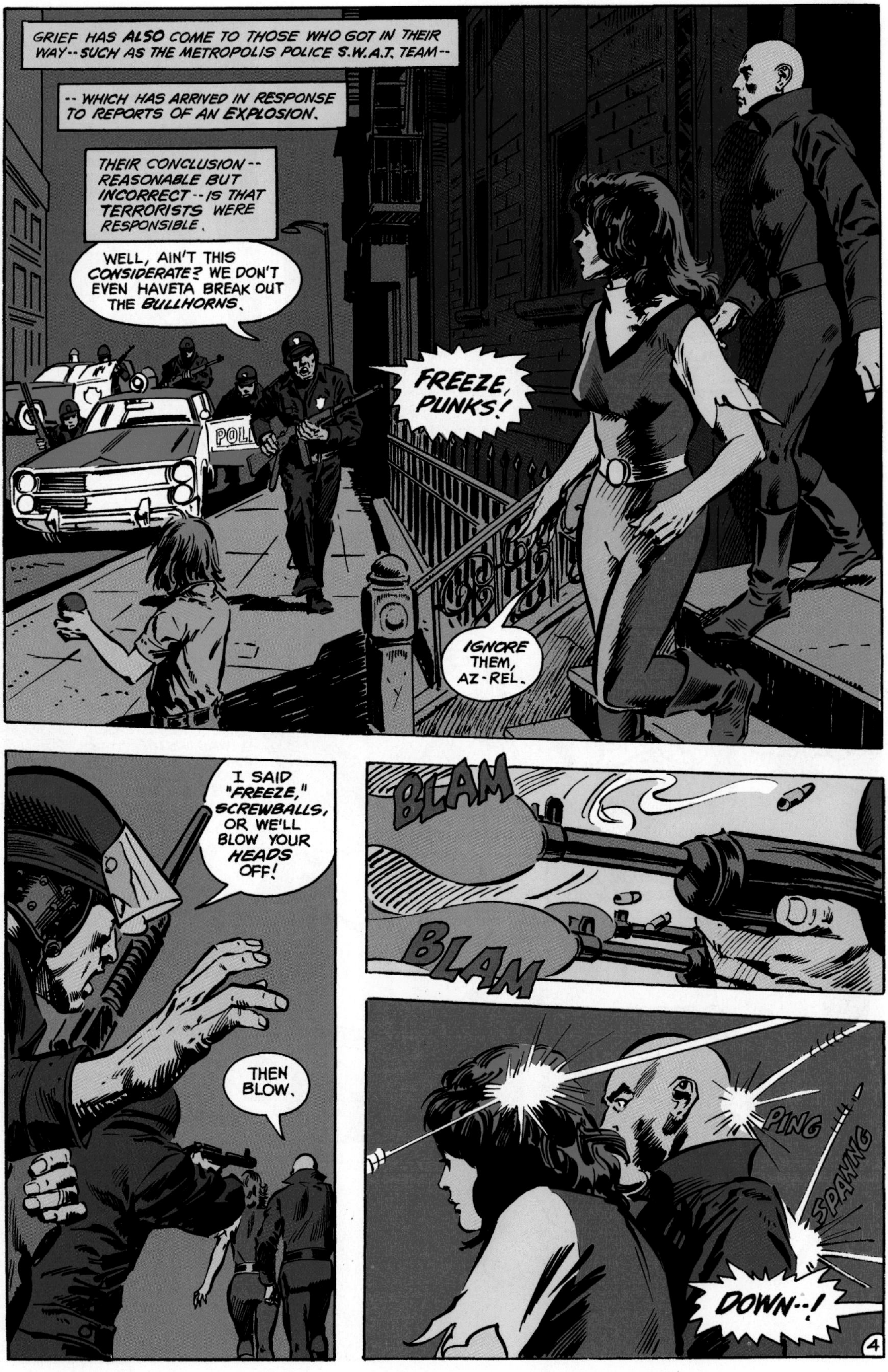
GRIEF HAS ALSO COME TO THOSE WHO GOT IN THEIR WAY--SUCH AS THE METROPOLIS POLICE S.W.A.T. TEAM--
--WHICH HAS ARRIVED IN RESPONSE TO REPORTS OF AN EXPLOSION.
THEIR CONCLUSION--REASONABLE BUT INCORRECT--IS THAT TERRORISTS WERE RESPONSIBLE.
WELL, AIN'T THIS CONSIDERATE? WE DON'T EVEN HAVETA BREAK OUT THE BULLHORNS.
FREEZE, PUNKS!
IGNORE THEM, AZ-REL.
I SAID "FREEZE," SCREWBALLS, OR WE'LL BLOW YOUR HEADS OFF!
THEN BLOW.
BLAM
BLAM
PING
SPAWNG
DOWN--!
4

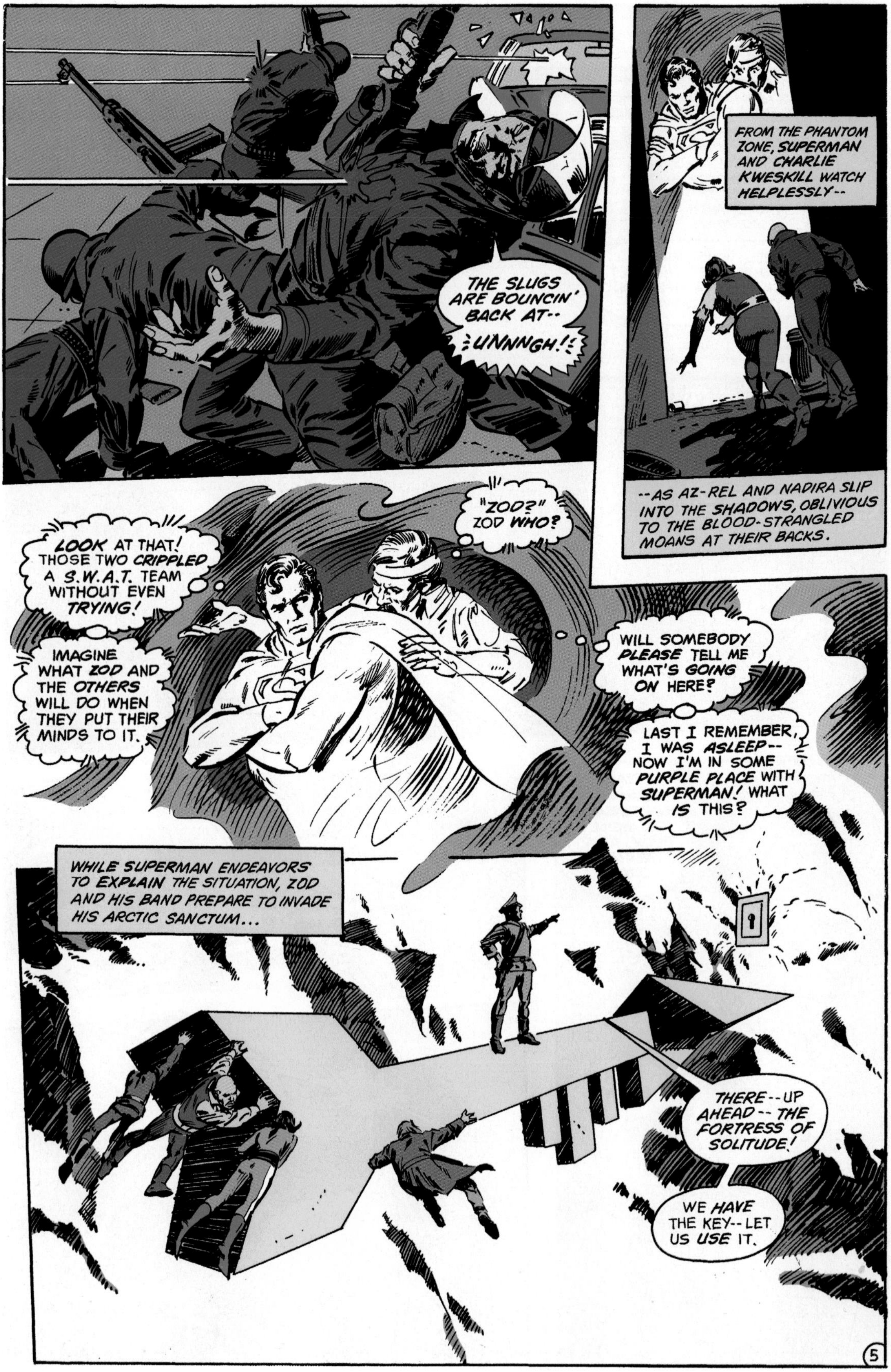
THE SLUGS ARE BOUNCIN' BACK AT--
UNNNGH!
FROM THE PHANTOM ZONE, SUPERMAN AND CHARLIE KWESKILL WATCH HELPLESSLY--
--AS AZ-REL AND NADIRA SLIP INTO THE SHADOWS, OBLIVIOUS TO THE BLOOD-STRANGLED MOANS AT THEIR BACKS.
LOOK AT THAT! THOSE TWO CRIPPLED A S.W.A.T. TEAM WITHOUT EVEN TRYING!
IMAGINE WHAT ZOD AND THE OTHERS WILL DO WHEN THEY PUT THEIR MINDS TO IT.
"ZOD?" ZOD WHO?
WILL SOMEBODY PLEASE TELL ME WHAT'S GOING ON HERE?
LAST I REMEMBER, I WAS ASLEEP-- NOW I'M IN SOME PURPLE PLACE WITH SUPERMAN! WHAT IS THIS?
WHILE SUPERMAN ENDEAVORS TO EXPLAIN THE SITUATION, ZOD AND HIS BAND PREPARE TO INVADE HIS ARCTIC SANCTUM...
THERE--UP AHEAD--THE FORTRESS OF SOLITUDE!
WE HAVE THE KEY--LET US USE IT.
5

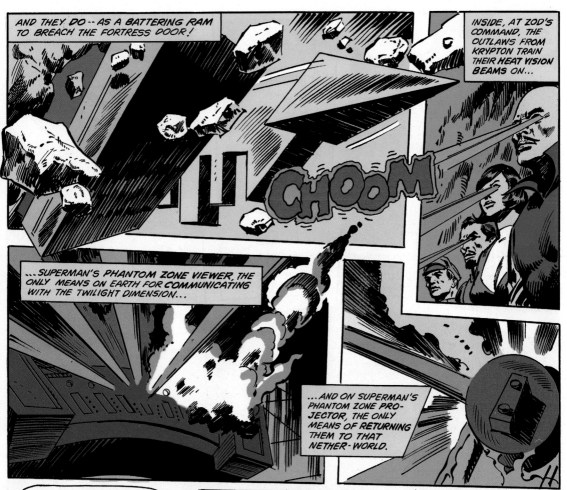

AND THEY *DO* -- AS A BATTERING RAM TO BREACH THE FORTRESS DOOR!

INSIDE, AT ZOD'S COMMAND, THE OUTLAWS FROM KRYPTON TRAIN THEIR *HEAT VISION* BEAMS ON...

CHOOM

...SUPERMAN'S *PHANTOM ZONE VIEWER*, THE ONLY MEANS ON EARTH FOR *COMMUNICATING* WITH THE TWILIGHT DIMENSION...

...AND ON SUPERMAN'S *PHANTOM ZONE PRO-JECTOR*, THE ONLY MEANS OF *RETURNING* THEM TO THAT *NETHER-WORLD*.

WELL DONE. SUPERMAN IS TRAPPED--*INCOMMUNICADO*-- IN THE ZONE.

AND WE ARE FREE TO PURSUE OUR PROGRAM FOR THE *ELIMINATION OF EARTH*.

YOU KNOW YOUR ORDERS.

"CARRY THEM OUT-- WITHOUT *DELAY!*"

WITHOUT COMMENT, PROF. VA-KOX, JAX-UR, AND KRU-EL BURST THROUGH THE FORTRESS WALL AND SOAR SKYWARD.

I DO NOT THINK THEY LIKED YOUR *TONE*, ZOD...

I AM A *GENERAL*, FAORA. I GIVE COMMANDS, NOT *SUGGESTIONS*.

... AND *I* DO NOT LIKE THE *PRESUMPTION* IN YOUR *TOUCH*.

6

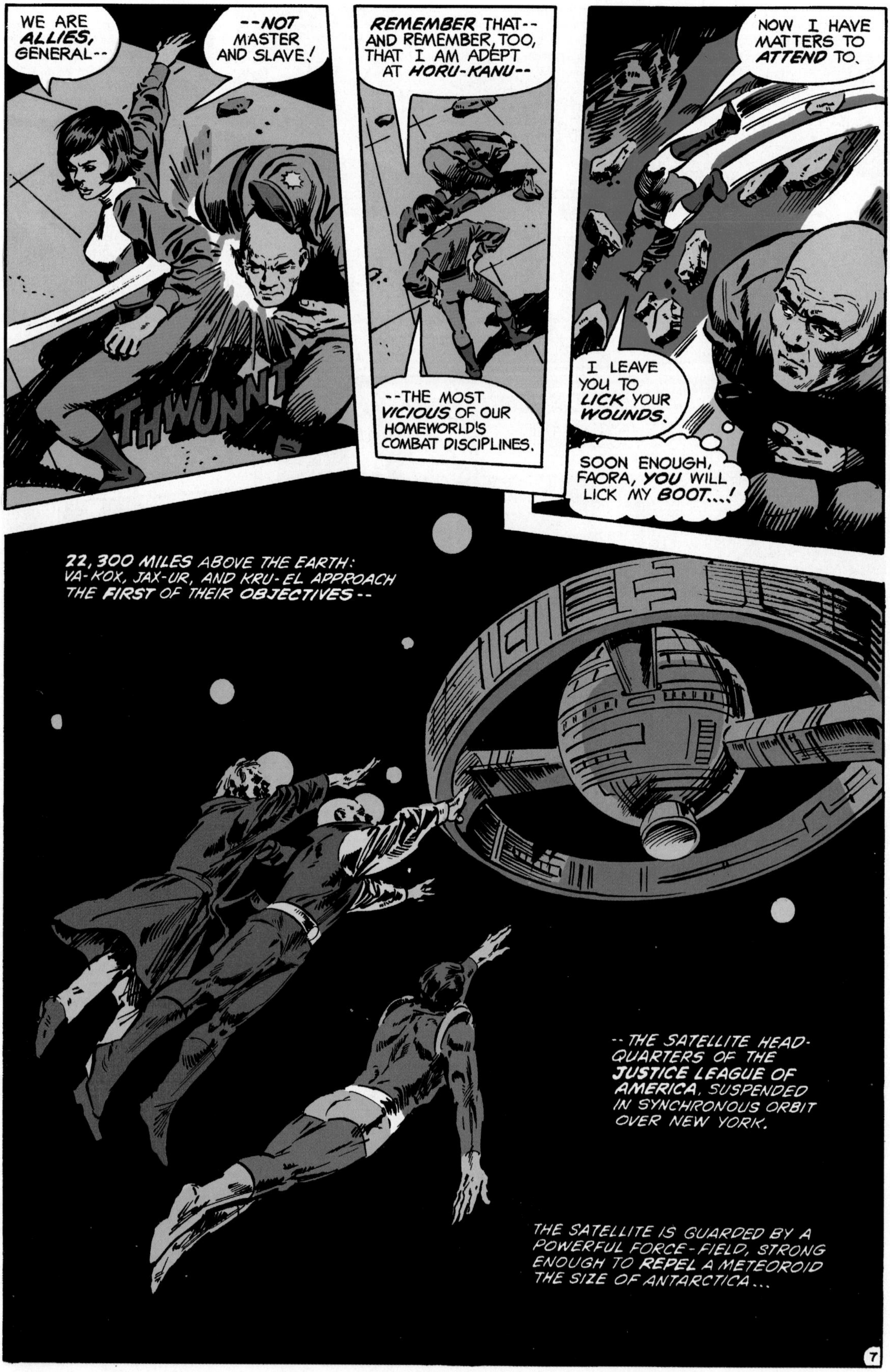
WE ARE ALLIES, GENERAL--
--NOT MASTER AND SLAVE!
THWUNN!
REMEMBER THAT-- AND REMEMBER, TOO, THAT I AM ADEPT AT HORU-KANU--
--THE MOST VICIOUS OF OUR HOMEWORLD'S COMBAT DISCIPLINES.
NOW I HAVE MATTERS TO ATTEND TO.
I LEAVE YOU TO LICK YOUR WOUNDS.
SOON ENOUGH, FAORA, YOU WILL LICK MY BOOT...!
22,300 MILES ABOVE THE EARTH: VA-KOX, JAX-UR, AND KRU-EL APPROACH THE FIRST OF THEIR OBJECTIVES--
--THE SATELLITE HEAD-QUARTERS OF THE JUSTICE LEAGUE OF AMERICA, SUSPENDED IN SYNCHRONOUS ORBIT OVER NEW YORK.
THE SATELLITE IS GUARDED BY A POWERFUL FORCE-FIELD, STRONG ENOUGH TO REPEL A METEOROID THE SIZE OF ANTARCTICA...
7

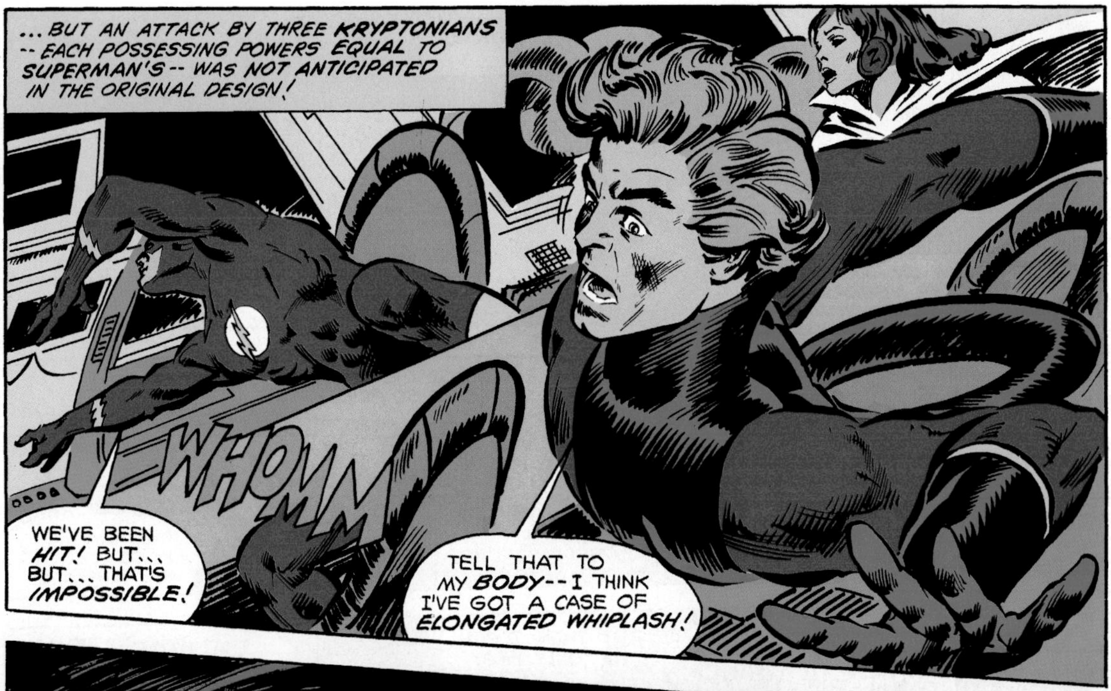
... BUT AN ATTACK BY THREE KRYPTONIANS -- EACH POSSESSING POWERS EQUAL TO SUPERMAN'S -- WAS NOT ANTICIPATED IN THE ORIGINAL DESIGN!
WHOMM
WE'VE BEEN HIT! BUT... BUT... THAT'S IMPOSSIBLE!
TELL THAT TO MY BODY -- I THINK I'VE GOT A CASE OF ELONGATED WHIPLASH!

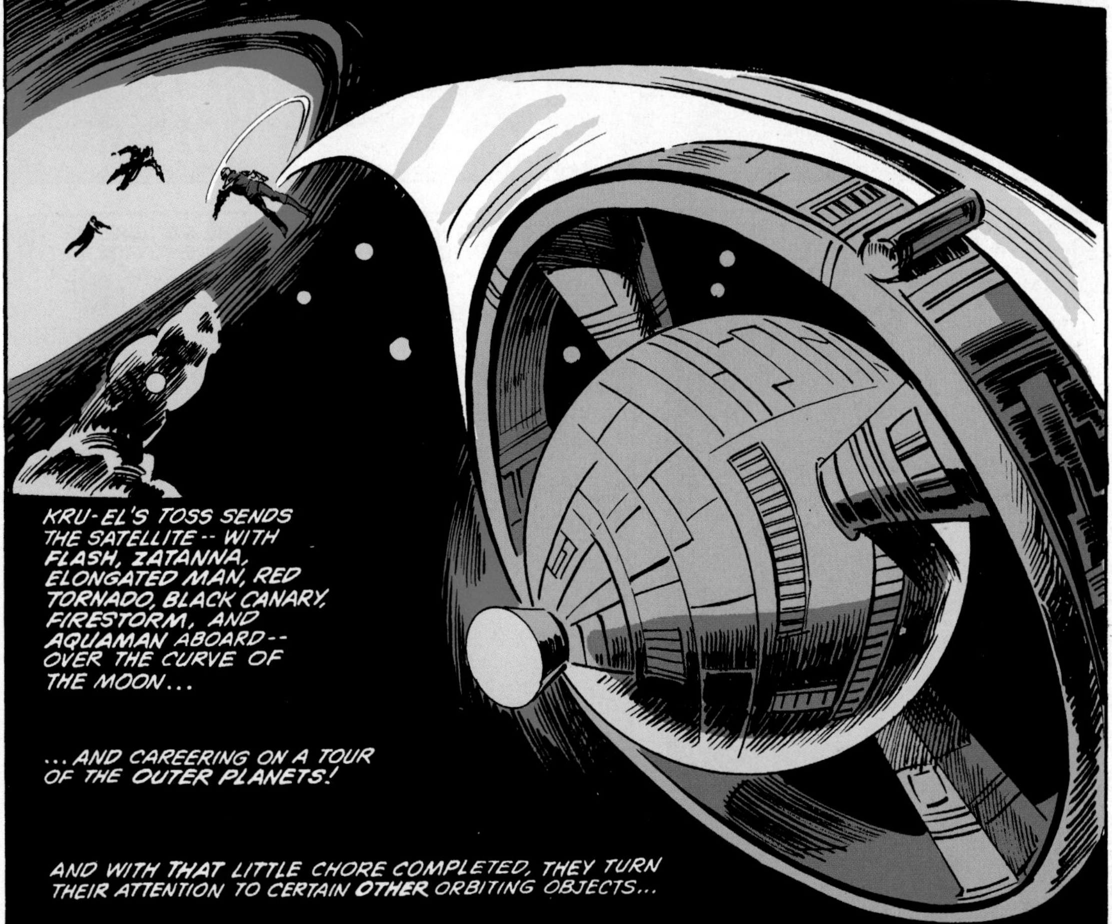
KRU-EL'S TOSS SENDS THE SATELLITE -- WITH FLASH, ZATANNA, ELONGATED MAN, RED TORNADO, BLACK CANARY, FIRESTORM, AND AQUAMAN ABOARD -- OVER THE CURVE OF THE MOON...
... AND CAREERING ON A TOUR OF THE OUTER PLANETS!
AND WITH THAT LITTLE CHORE COMPLETED, THEY TURN THEIR ATTENTION TO CERTAIN OTHER ORBITING OBJECTS...
8

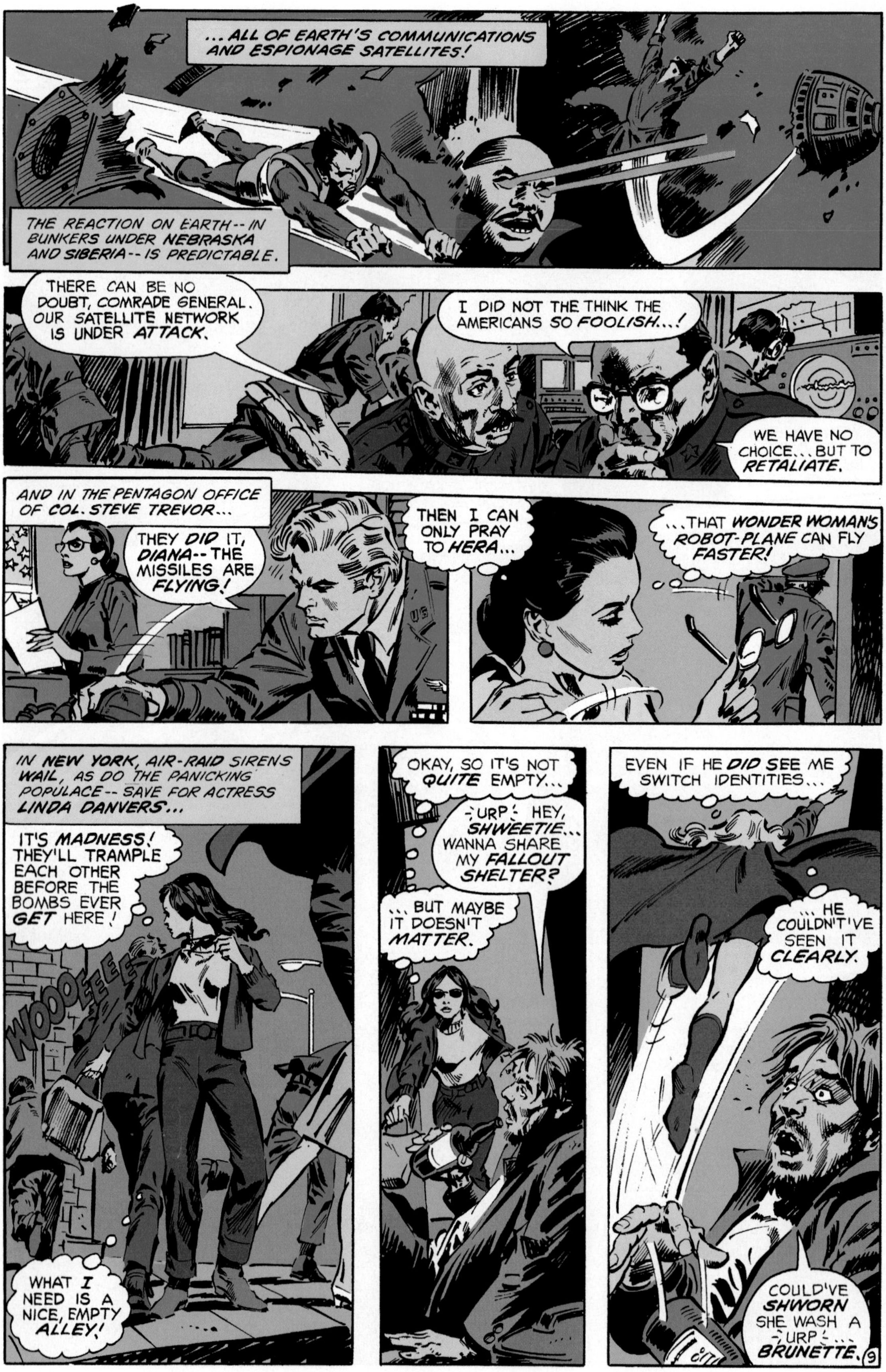

...ALL OF EARTH'S COMMUNICATIONS AND ESPIONAGE SATELLITES!
THE REACTION ON EARTH -- IN BUNKERS UNDER NEBRASKA AND SIBERIA -- IS PREDICTABLE.
THERE CAN BE NO DOUBT, COMRADE GENERAL. OUR SATELLITE NETWORK IS UNDER ATTACK.
I DID NOT THE THINK THE AMERICANS SO FOOLISH...!
WE HAVE NO CHOICE... BUT TO RETALIATE.
AND IN THE PENTAGON OFFICE OF COL. STEVE TREVOR...
THEY DID IT, DIANA-- THE MISSILES ARE FLYING!
THEN I CAN ONLY PRAY TO HERA...
...THAT WONDER WOMAN'S ROBOT-PLANE CAN FLY FASTER!
IN NEW YORK, AIR-RAID SIRENS WAIL, AS DO THE PANICKING POPULACE -- SAVE FOR ACTRESS LINDA DANVERS...
IT'S MADNESS! THEY'LL TRAMPLE EACH OTHER BEFORE THE BOMBS EVER GET HERE!
WOOOEEEE
WHAT I NEED IS A NICE, EMPTY ALLEY!
OKAY, SO IT'S NOT QUITE EMPTY...
-URP- HEY, SHWEETIE... WANNA SHARE MY FALLOUT SHELTER?
...BUT MAYBE IT DOESN'T MATTER.
EVEN IF HE DID SEE ME SWITCH IDENTITIES...
...HE COULDN'T'VE SEEN IT CLEARLY.
COULD'VE SHWORN SHE WASH A -URP-... BRUNETTE.
9

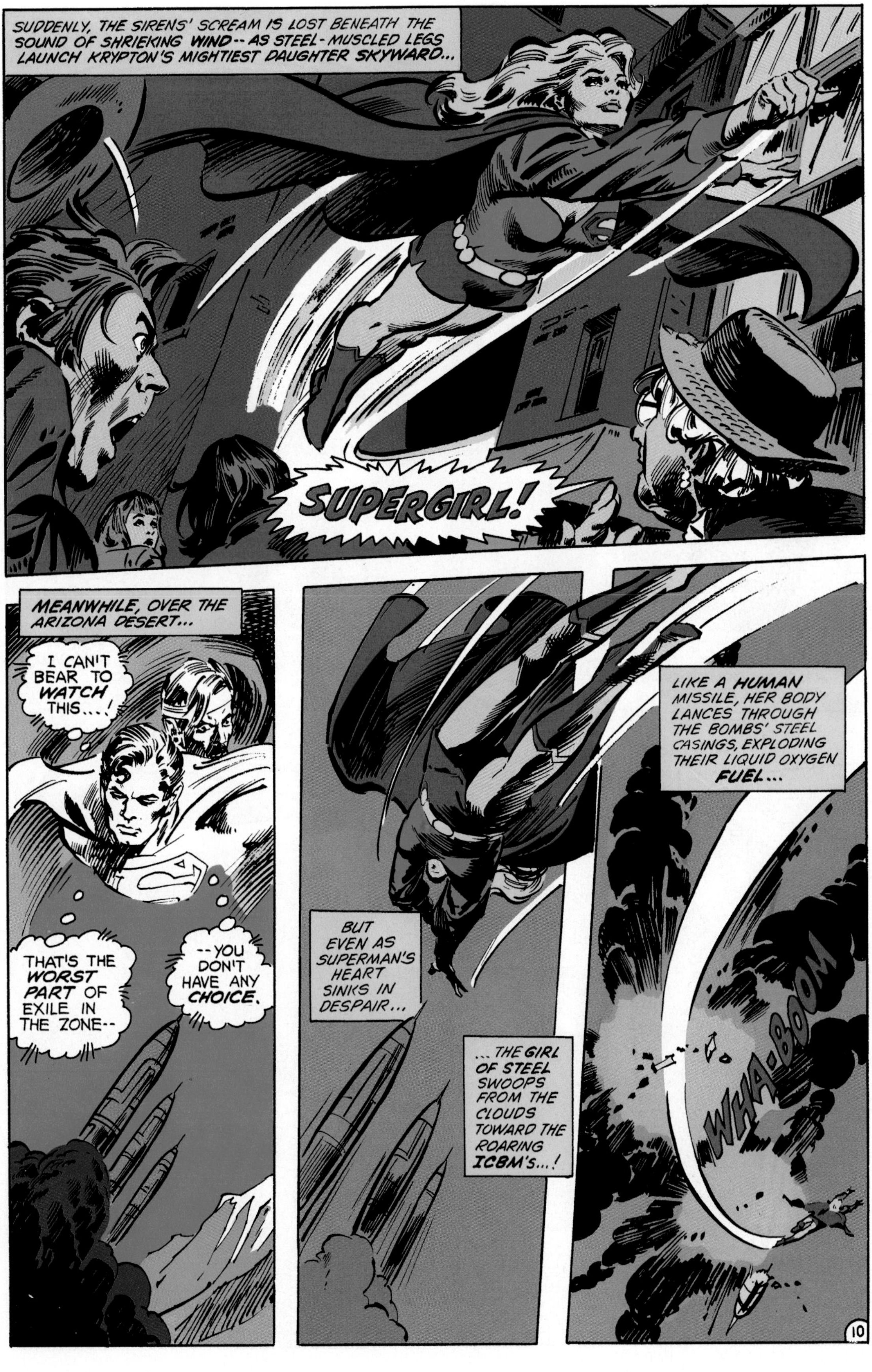
SUDDENLY, THE SIRENS' SCREAM IS LOST BENEATH THE SOUND OF SHRIEKING WIND-- AS STEEL-MUSCLED LEGS LAUNCH KRYPTON'S MIGHTIEST DAUGHTER SKYWARD...
SUPERGIRL!
MEANWHILE, OVER THE ARIZONA DESERT...
I CAN'T BEAR TO WATCH THIS...!
THAT'S THE WORST PART OF EXILE IN THE ZONE--
--YOU DON'T HAVE ANY CHOICE.
BUT EVEN AS SUPERMAN'S HEART SINKS IN DESPAIR...
...THE GIRL OF STEEL SWOOPS FROM THE CLOUDS TOWARD THE ROARING ICBM's...!
LIKE A HUMAN MISSILE, HER BODY LANCES THROUGH THE BOMBS' STEEL CASINGS, EXPLODING THEIR LIQUID OXYGEN FUEL...
WHA-BOOM
10

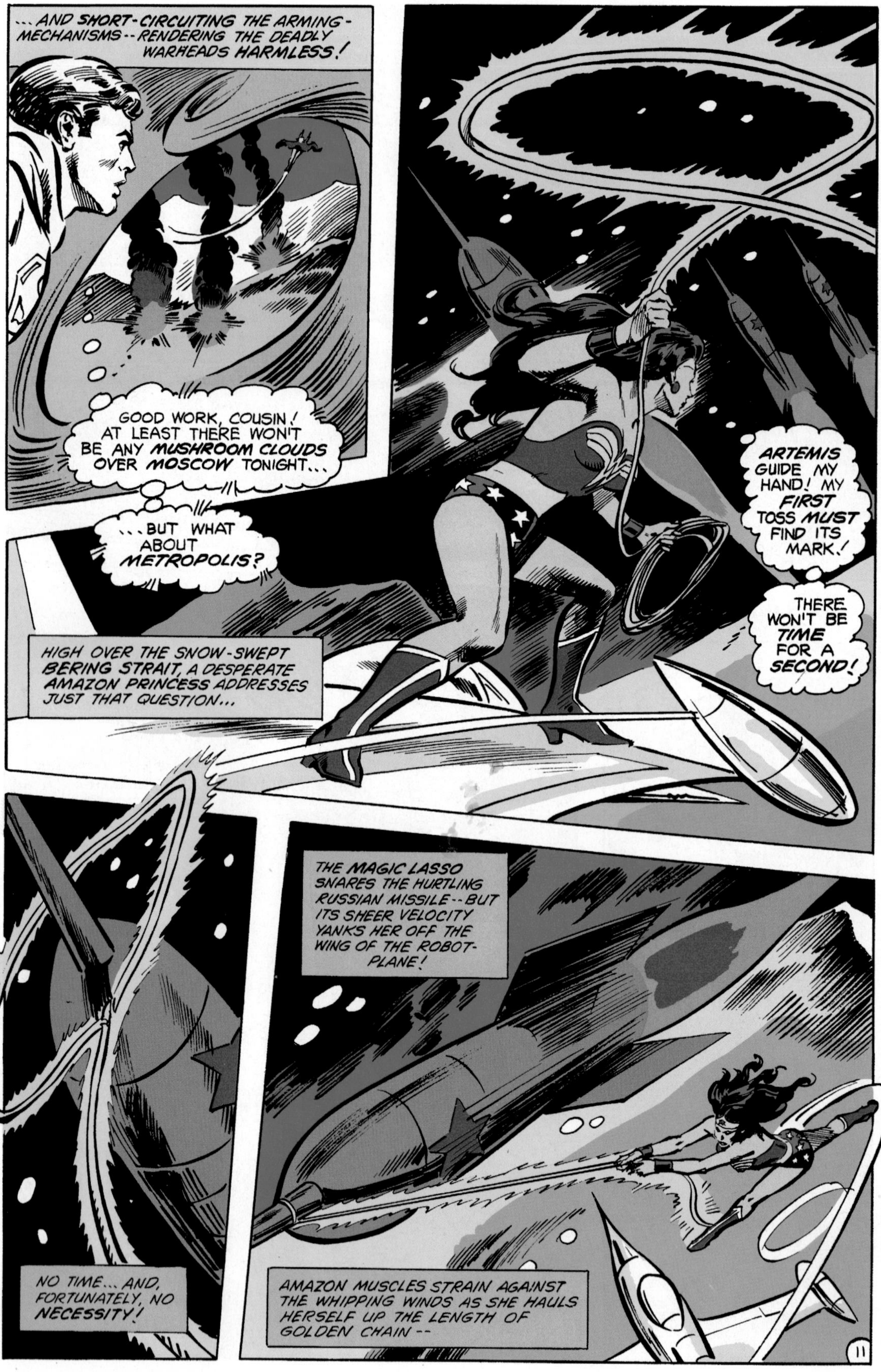
...AND SHORT-CIRCUITING THE ARMING-MECHANISMS--RENDERING THE DEADLY WARHEADS HARMLESS!
GOOD WORK, COUSIN! AT LEAST THERE WON'T BE ANY MUSHROOM CLOUDS OVER MOSCOW TONIGHT...
...BUT WHAT ABOUT METROPOLIS?
HIGH OVER THE SNOW-SWEPT BERING STRAIT, A DESPERATE AMAZON PRINCESS ADDRESSES JUST THAT QUESTION...
ARTEMIS GUIDE MY HAND! MY FIRST TOSS MUST FIND ITS MARK!
THERE WON'T BE TIME FOR A SECOND!
NO TIME... AND, FORTUNATELY, NO NECESSITY!
THE MAGIC LASSO SNARES THE HURTLING RUSSIAN MISSILE--BUT ITS SHEER VELOCITY YANKS HER OFF THE WING OF THE ROBOT-PLANE!
AMAZON MUSCLES STRAIN AGAINST THE WHIPPING WINDS AS SHE HAULS HERSELF UP THE LENGTH OF GOLDEN CHAIN--
11

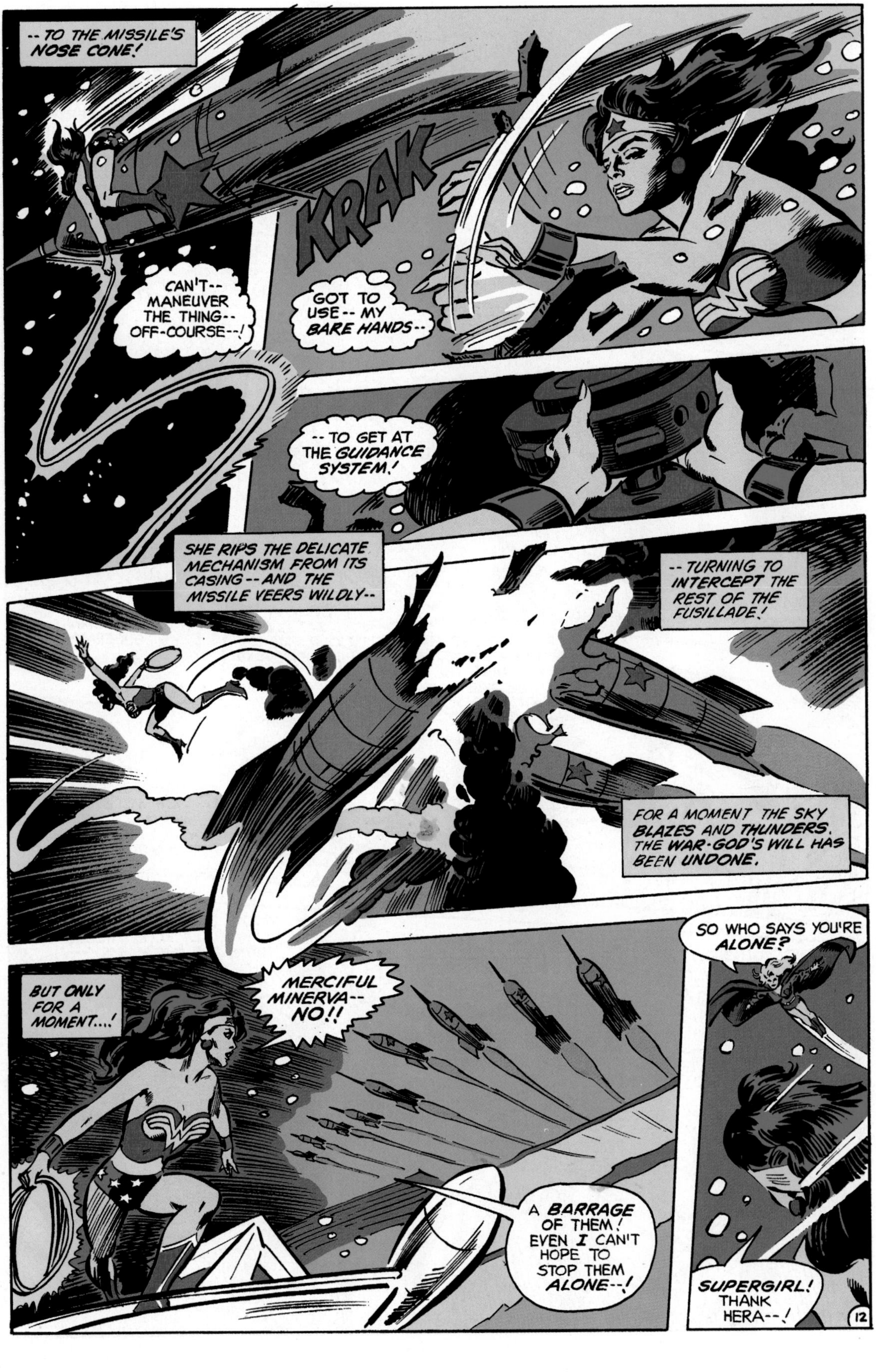
--TO THE MISSILE'S NOSE CONE!
KRAK
CAN'T--MANEUVER THE THING--OFF-COURSE--!
GOT TO USE--MY BARE HANDS--
--TO GET AT THE GUIDANCE SYSTEM!
SHE RIPS THE DELICATE MECHANISM FROM ITS CASING--AND THE MISSILE VEERS WILDLY--
--TURNING TO INTERCEPT THE REST OF THE FUSILLADE!
FOR A MOMENT THE SKY BLAZES AND THUNDERS. THE WAR-GOD'S WILL HAS BEEN UNDONE.
BUT ONLY FOR A MOMENT...!
MERCIFUL MINERVA--NO!!
A BARRAGE OF THEM! EVEN I CAN'T HOPE TO STOP THEM ALONE--!
SO WHO SAYS YOU'RE ALONE?
SUPERGIRL! THANK HERA--!
12

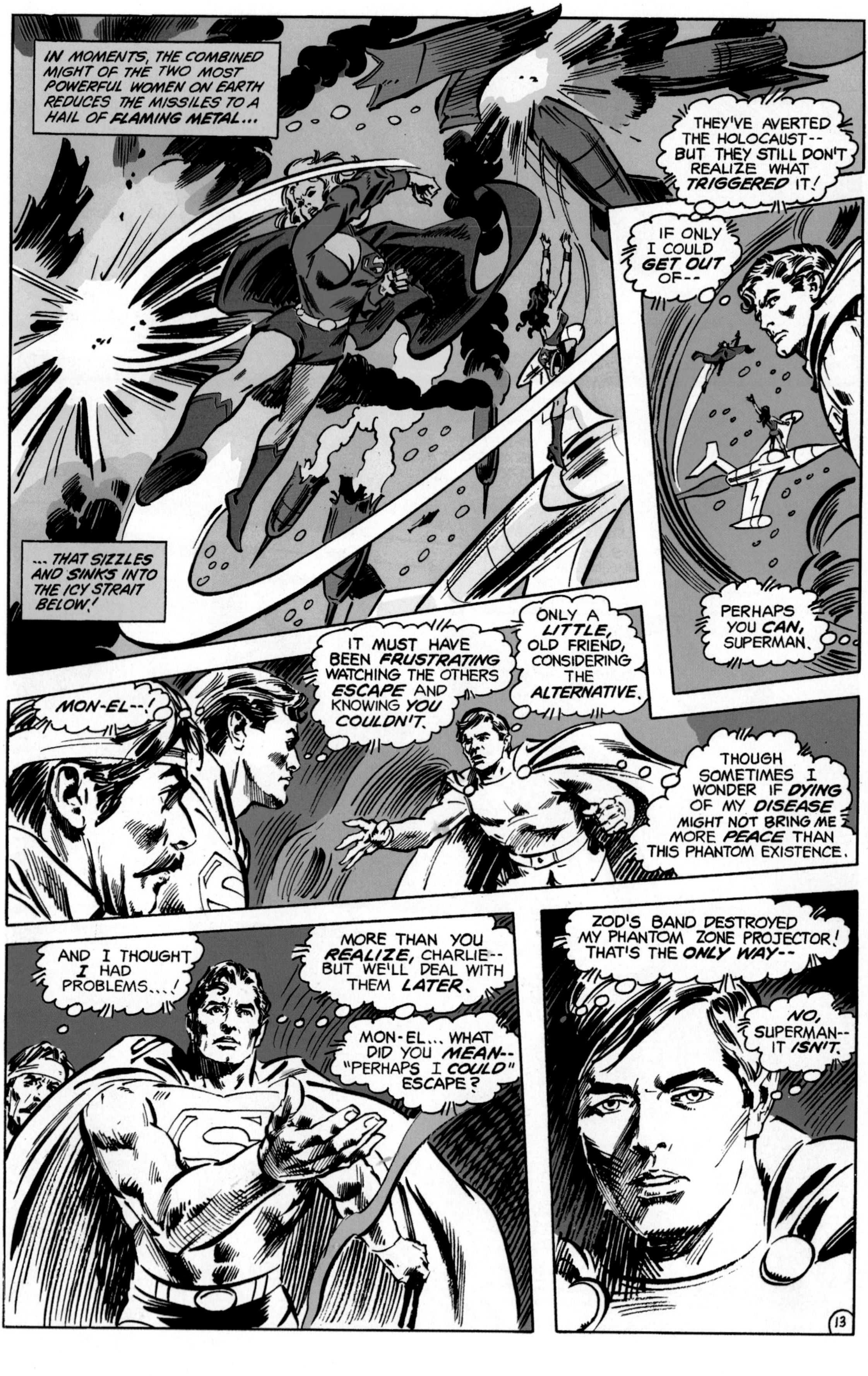
IN MOMENTS, THE COMBINED MIGHT OF THE TWO MOST POWERFUL WOMEN ON EARTH REDUCES THE MISSILES TO A HAIL OF FLAMING METAL...
THEY'VE AVERTED THE HOLOCAUST-- BUT THEY STILL DON'T REALIZE WHAT TRIGGERED IT!
IF ONLY I COULD GET OUT OF--
...THAT SIZZLES AND SINKS INTO THE ICY STRAIT BELOW!
PERHAPS YOU CAN, SUPERMAN.
MON-EL--!
IT MUST HAVE BEEN FRUSTRATING WATCHING THE OTHERS ESCAPE AND KNOWING YOU COULDN'T.
ONLY A LITTLE, OLD FRIEND, CONSIDERING THE ALTERNATIVE.
THOUGH SOMETIMES I WONDER IF DYING OF MY DISEASE MIGHT NOT BRING ME MORE PEACE THAN THIS PHANTOM EXISTENCE.
AND I THOUGHT I HAD PROBLEMS...!
MORE THAN YOU REALIZE, CHARLIE-- BUT WE'LL DEAL WITH THEM LATER.
MON-EL... WHAT DID YOU MEAN-- "PERHAPS I COULD" ESCAPE?
ZOD'S BAND DESTROYED MY PHANTOM ZONE PROJECTOR! THAT'S THE ONLY WAY--
NO, SUPERMAN-- IT ISN'T.
13

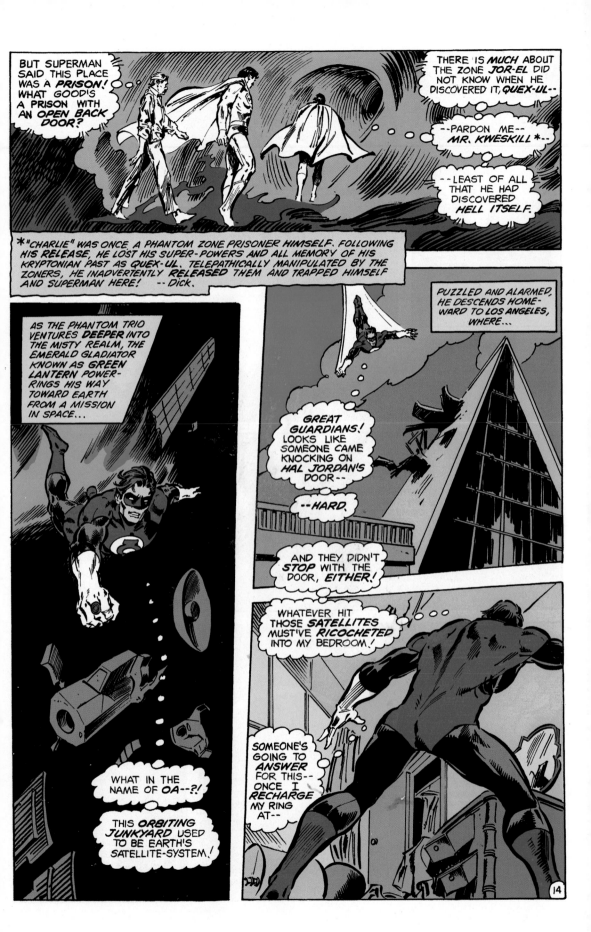

BUT SUPERMAN SAID THIS PLACE WAS A *PRISON!* WHAT GOOD'S A PRISON WITH AN *OPEN BACK DOOR?*

THERE IS *MUCH* ABOUT THE ZONE *JOR-EL* DID NOT KNOW WHEN HE DISCOVERED IT, *QUEX-UL--*

--PARDON ME-- MR. *KWESKILL* *--

--LEAST OF ALL THAT HE HAD DISCOVERED *HELL ITSELF.*

*"CHARLIE" WAS ONCE A PHANTOM ZONE PRISONER HIMSELF. FOLLOWING HIS *RELEASE,* HE LOST HIS SUPER-POWERS AND ALL MEMORY OF HIS KRYPTONIAN PAST AS *QUEX-UL.* TELEPATHICALLY MANIPULATED BY THE ZONERS, HE INADVERTENTLY *RELEASED* THEM AND TRAPPED HIMSELF AND SUPERMAN HERE! -- Dick.

AS THE PHANTOM TRIO VENTURES *DEEPER* INTO THE MISTY REALM, THE EMERALD GLADIATOR KNOWN AS *GREEN LANTERN* POWER-RINGS HIS WAY TOWARD EARTH FROM A MISSION IN SPACE...

PUZZLED AND ALARMED, HE DESCENDS HOME-WARD TO LOS ANGELES, WHERE...

GREAT GUARDIANS! LOOKS LIKE SOMEONE CAME KNOCKING ON *HAL JORDAN'S* DOOR--

--*HARD.*

AND THEY DIDN'T *STOP* WITH THE DOOR, *EITHER!*

WHATEVER HIT THOSE *SATELLITES* MUST'VE *RICOCHETED* INTO MY BEDROOM!

WHAT IN THE NAME OF *OA--?!*

THIS *ORBITING JUNKYARD* USED TO BE EARTH'S SATELLITE-SYSTEM!

SOMEONE'S GOING TO *ANSWER* FOR THIS-- ONCE I *RECHARGE* MY RING AT--

14

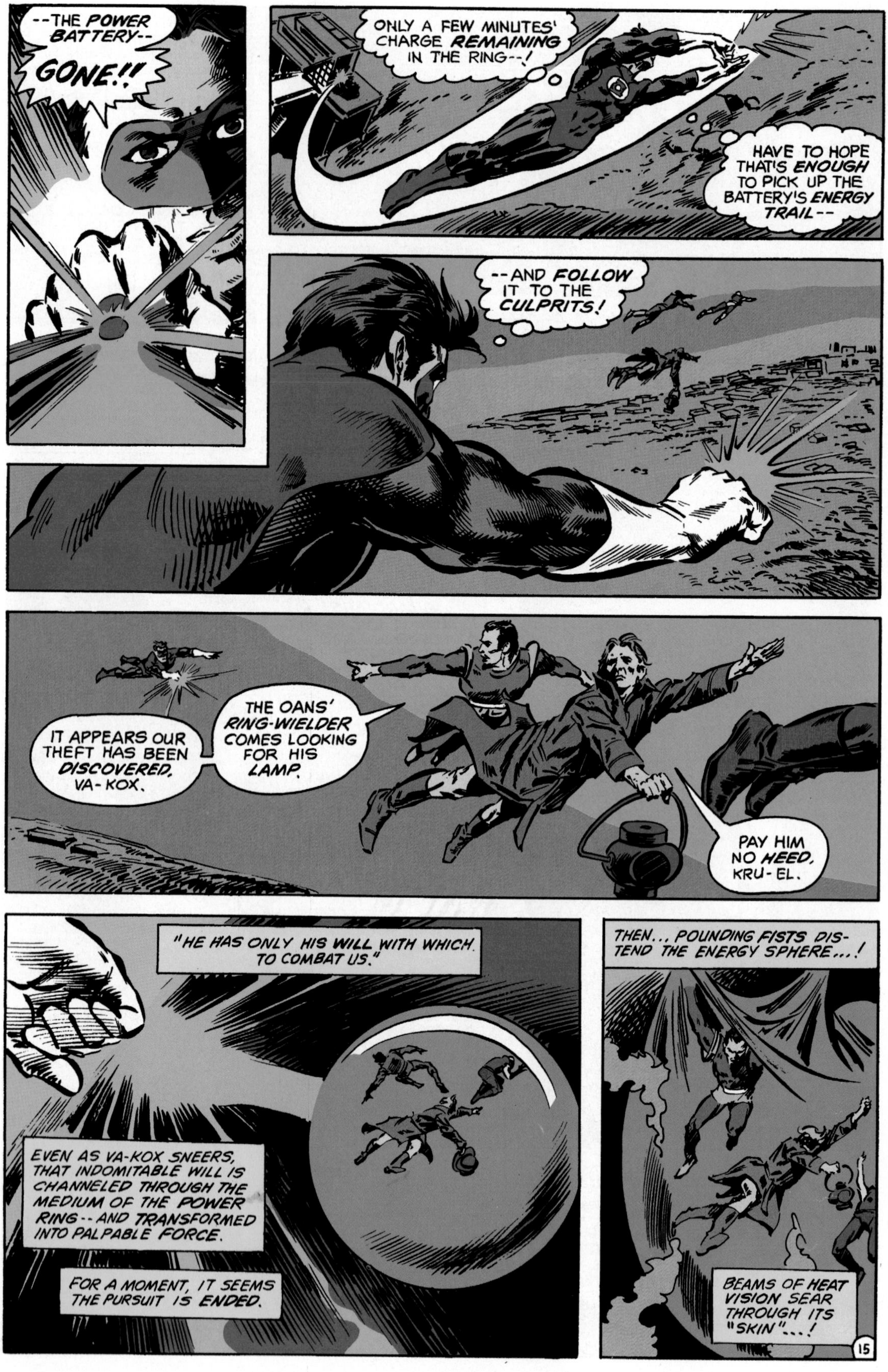
--THE POWER BATTERY--
GONE!!
ONLY A FEW MINUTES' CHARGE REMAINING IN THE RING--!
HAVE TO HOPE THAT'S ENOUGH TO PICK UP THE BATTERY'S ENERGY TRAIL--
--AND FOLLOW IT TO THE CULPRITS!
IT APPEARS OUR THEFT HAS BEEN DISCOVERED, VA-KOX.
THE OANS' RING-WIELDER COMES LOOKING FOR HIS LAMP.
PAY HIM NO HEED, KRU-EL.
"HE HAS ONLY HIS WILL WITH WHICH TO COMBAT US."
EVEN AS VA-KOX SNEERS, THAT INDOMITABLE WILL IS CHANNELED THROUGH THE MEDIUM OF THE POWER RING--AND TRANSFORMED INTO PALPABLE FORCE.
FOR A MOMENT, IT SEEMS THE PURSUIT IS ENDED.
THEN..., POUNDING FISTS DISTEND THE ENERGY SPHERE...!
BEAMS OF HEAT VISION SEAR THROUGH ITS "SKIN"...!
15

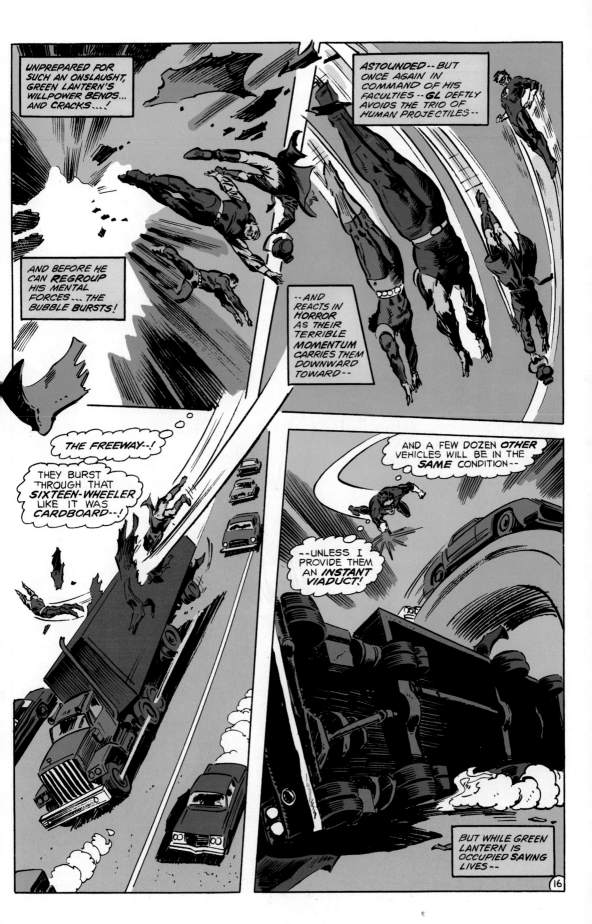

UNPREPARED FOR SUCH AN ONSLAUGHT, GREEN LANTERN'S WILLPOWER BENDS... AND CRACKS....!

ASTOUNDED -- BUT ONCE AGAIN IN COMMAND OF HIS FACULTIES -- *GL* DEFTLY AVOIDS THE TRIO OF HUMAN PROJECTILES --

AND BEFORE HE CAN *REGROUP* HIS MENTAL FORCES... THE BUBBLE BURSTS!

--AND REACTS IN HORROR AS THEIR TERRIBLE MOMENTUM CARRIES THEM DOWNWARD TOWARD --

THE FREEWAY--!

THEY BURST THROUGH THAT *SIXTEEN-WHEELER* LIKE IT WAS *CARDBOARD*--!

AND A FEW DOZEN *OTHER* VEHICLES WILL BE IN THE *SAME* CONDITION --

--UNLESS I PROVIDE THEM AN *INSTANT* VIADUCT!

BUT WHILE GREEN LANTERN IS OCCUPIED *SAVING* LIVES --

16

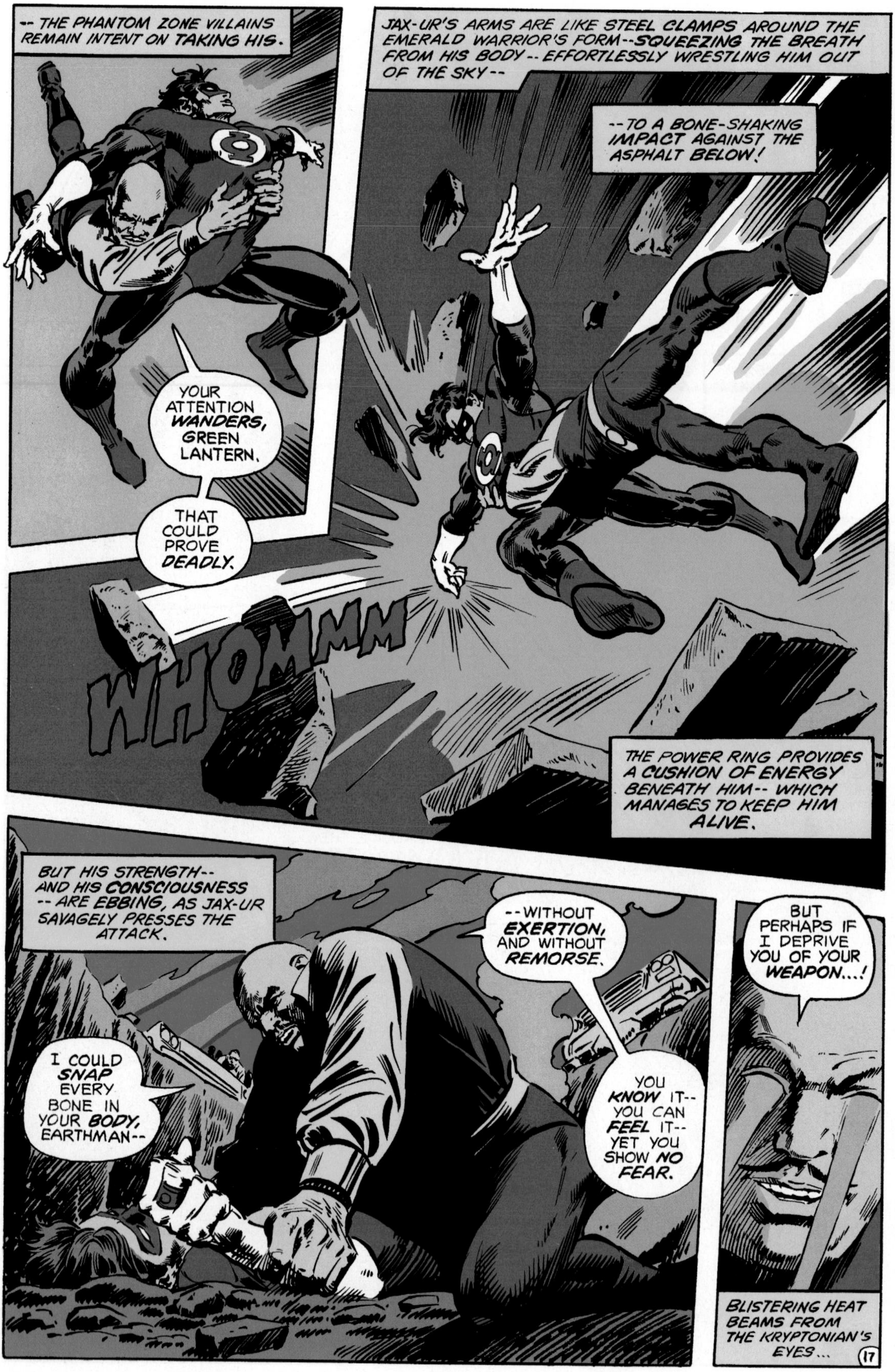
-- THE PHANTOM ZONE VILLAINS REMAIN INTENT ON TAKING HIS.
YOUR ATTENTION WANDERS, GREEN LANTERN.
THAT COULD PROVE DEADLY.
JAX-UR'S ARMS ARE LIKE STEEL CLAMPS AROUND THE EMERALD WARRIOR'S FORM--SQUEEZING THE BREATH FROM HIS BODY -- EFFORTLESSLY WRESTLING HIM OUT OF THE SKY --
--TO A BONE-SHAKING IMPACT AGAINST THE ASPHALT BELOW!
WHOMMM
THE POWER RING PROVIDES A CUSHION OF ENERGY BENEATH HIM -- WHICH MANAGES TO KEEP HIM ALIVE.
BUT HIS STRENGTH-- AND HIS CONSCIOUSNESS -- ARE EBBING, AS JAX-UR SAVAGELY PRESSES THE ATTACK.
I COULD SNAP EVERY BONE IN YOUR BODY, EARTHMAN--
--WITHOUT EXERTION, AND WITHOUT REMORSE.
YOU KNOW IT-- YOU CAN FEEL IT-- YET YOU SHOW NO FEAR.
BUT PERHAPS IF I DEPRIVE YOU OF YOUR WEAPON...!
BLISTERING HEAT BEAMS FROM THE KRYPTONIAN'S EYES...
17

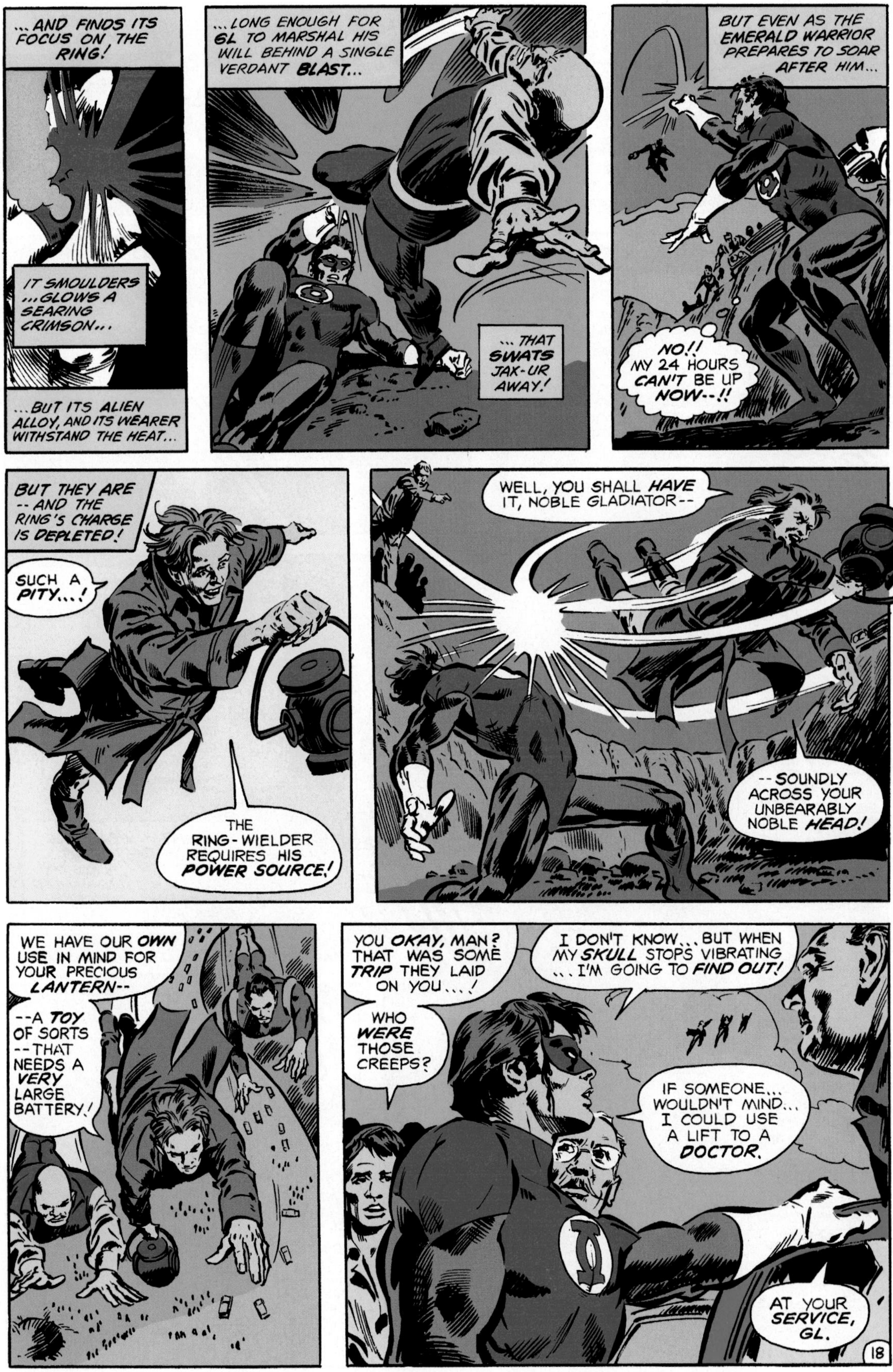

...AND FINDS ITS FOCUS ON THE RING!
IT SMOULDERS ...GLOWS A SEARING CRIMSON...
...BUT ITS ALIEN ALLOY, AND ITS WEARER WITHSTAND THE HEAT...
...LONG ENOUGH FOR GL TO MARSHAL HIS WILL BEHIND A SINGLE VERDANT BLAST...
...THAT SWATS JAX-UR AWAY!
BUT EVEN AS THE EMERALD WARRIOR PREPARES TO SOAR AFTER HIM...
NO!! MY 24 HOURS CAN'T BE UP NOW--!!
BUT THEY ARE -- AND THE RING'S CHARGE IS DEPLETED!
SUCH A PITY...!
THE RING-WIELDER REQUIRES HIS POWER SOURCE!
WELL, YOU SHALL HAVE IT, NOBLE GLADIATOR--
--SOUNDLY ACROSS YOUR UNBEARABLY NOBLE HEAD!
WE HAVE OUR OWN USE IN MIND FOR YOUR PRECIOUS LANTERN--
--A TOY OF SORTS --THAT NEEDS A VERY LARGE BATTERY!
YOU OKAY, MAN? THAT WAS SOME TRIP THEY LAID ON YOU...!
I DON'T KNOW... BUT WHEN MY SKULL STOPS VIBRATING ...I'M GOING TO FIND OUT!
WHO WERE THOSE CREEPS?
IF SOMEONE... WOULDN'T MIND... I COULD USE A LIFT TO A DOCTOR.
AT YOUR SERVICE, GL.
18

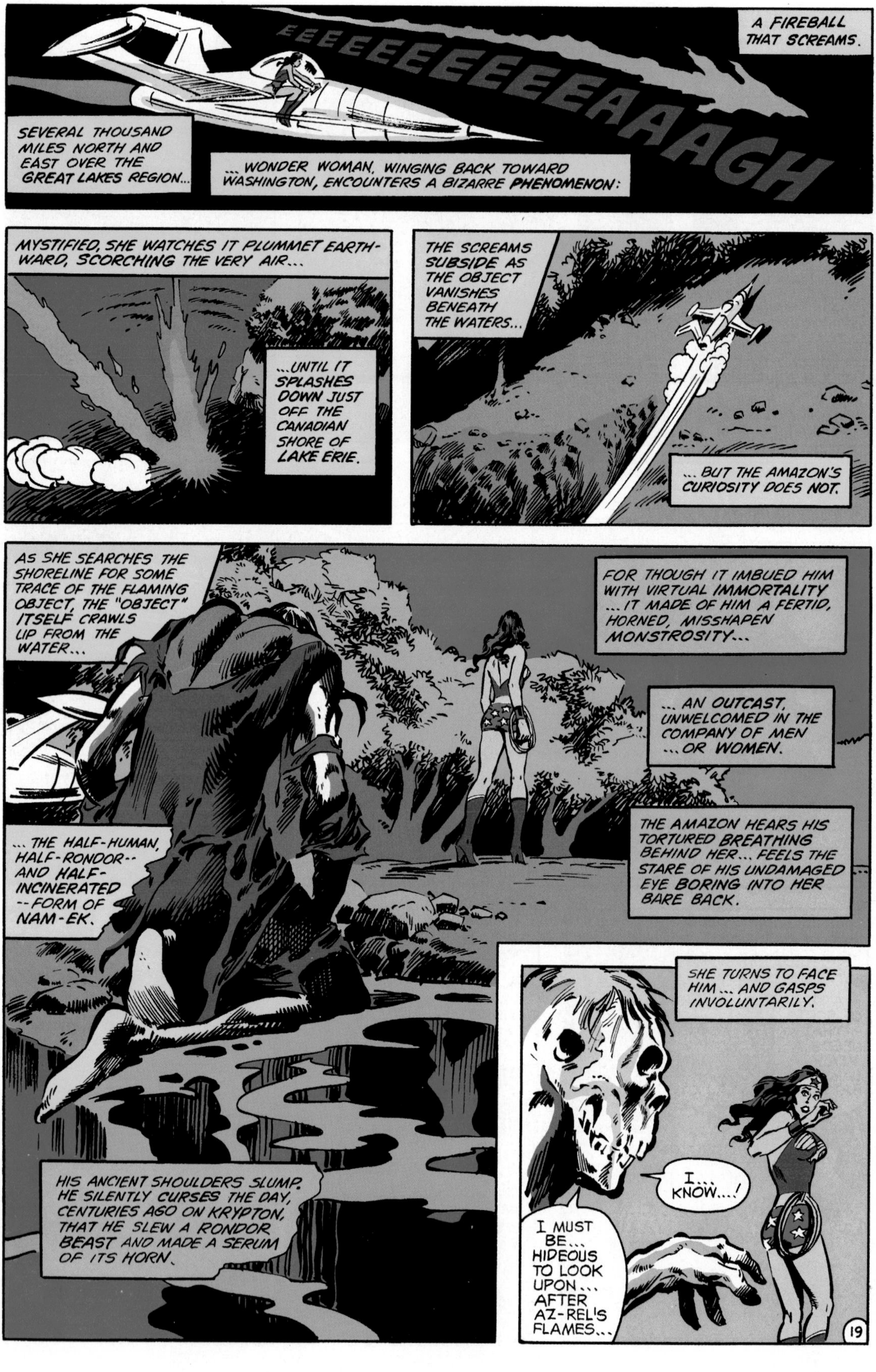
SEVERAL THOUSAND MILES NORTH AND EAST OVER THE GREAT LAKES REGION...
...WONDER WOMAN, WINGING BACK TOWARD WASHINGTON, ENCOUNTERS A BIZARRE PHENOMENON:
EEEEEEEEEEEEAAAAGH
A FIREBALL THAT SCREAMS.
MYSTIFIED, SHE WATCHES IT PLUMMET EARTH-WARD, SCORCHING THE VERY AIR...
...UNTIL IT SPLASHES DOWN JUST OFF THE CANADIAN SHORE OF LAKE ERIE.
THE SCREAMS SUBSIDE AS THE OBJECT VANISHES BENEATH THE WATERS...
...BUT THE AMAZON'S CURIOSITY DOES NOT.
AS SHE SEARCHES THE SHORELINE FOR SOME TRACE OF THE FLAMING OBJECT, THE "OBJECT" ITSELF CRAWLS UP FROM THE WATER...
...THE HALF-HUMAN, HALF-RONDOR-- AND HALF-INCINERATED --FORM OF NAM-EK.
HIS ANCIENT SHOULDERS SLUMP. HE SILENTLY CURSES THE DAY, CENTURIES AGO ON KRYPTON, THAT HE SLEW A RONDOR BEAST AND MADE A SERUM OF ITS HORN.
FOR THOUGH IT IMBUED HIM WITH VIRTUAL IMMORTALITY ...IT MADE OF HIM A FERTID, HORNED, MISSHAPEN MONSTROSITY...
...AN OUTCAST, UNWELCOMED IN THE COMPANY OF MEN ...OR WOMEN.
THE AMAZON HEARS HIS TORTURED BREATHING BEHIND HER... FEELS THE STARE OF HIS UNDAMAGED EYE BORING INTO HER BARE BACK.
SHE TURNS TO FACE HIM... AND GASPS INVOLUNTARILY.
I MUST BE... HIDEOUS TO LOOK UPON... AFTER AZ-REL'S FLAMES...
I... KNOW...!
19

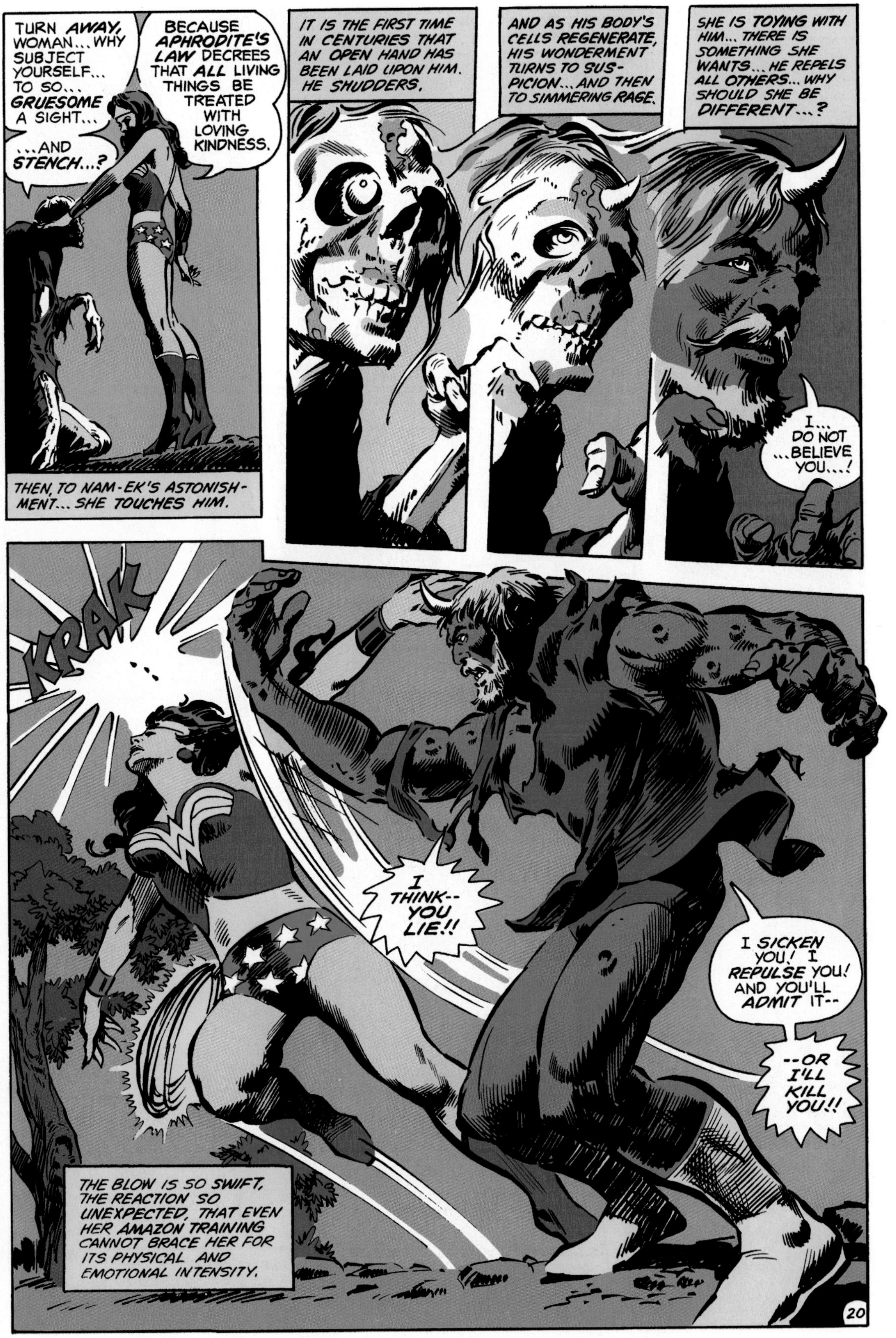

TURN AWAY, WOMAN... WHY SUBJECT YOURSELF... TO SO... GRUESOME A SIGHT...
...AND STENCH...?
BECAUSE APHRODITE'S LAW DECREES THAT ALL LIVING THINGS BE TREATED WITH LOVING KINDNESS.
THEN, TO NAM-EK'S ASTONISHMENT... SHE TOUCHES HIM.
IT IS THE FIRST TIME IN CENTURIES THAT AN OPEN HAND HAS BEEN LAID UPON HIM. HE SHUDDERS.
AND AS HIS BODY'S CELLS REGENERATE, HIS WONDERMENT TURNS TO SUSPICION... AND THEN TO SIMMERING RAGE.
SHE IS TOYING WITH HIM... THERE IS SOMETHING SHE WANTS... HE REPELS ALL OTHERS... WHY SHOULD SHE BE DIFFERENT...?
I... DO NOT ...BELIEVE YOU...!
KRAK
I THINK-- YOU LIE!!
I SICKEN YOU! I REPULSE YOU! AND YOU'LL ADMIT IT--
--OR I'LL KILL YOU!!
THE BLOW IS SO SWIFT, THE REACTION SO UNEXPECTED, THAT EVEN HER AMAZON TRAINING CANNOT BRACE HER FOR ITS PHYSICAL AND EMOTIONAL INTENSITY.
20

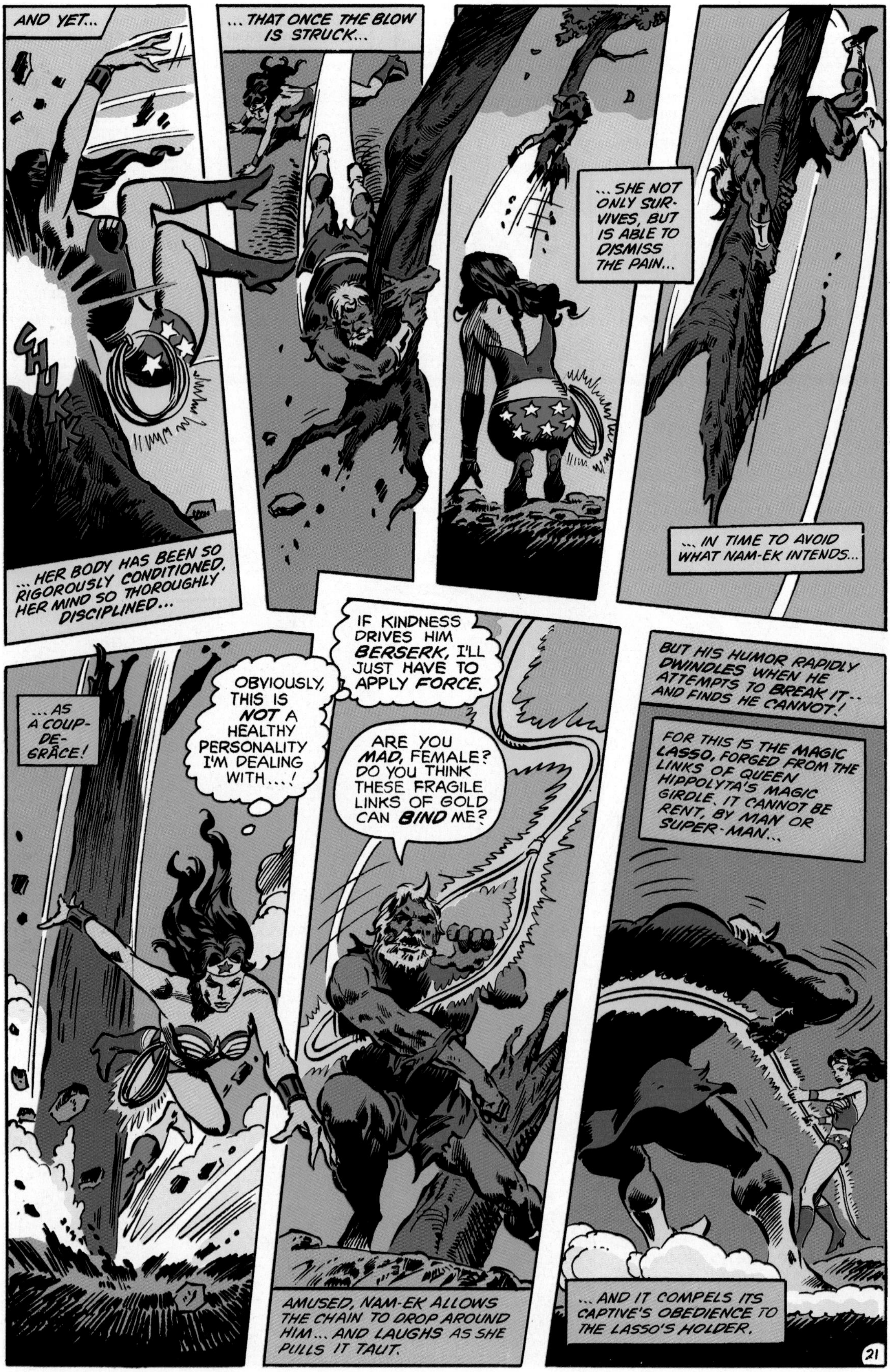
AND YET...
...HER BODY HAS BEEN SO RIGOROUSLY CONDITIONED, HER MIND SO THOROUGHLY DISCIPLINED...
CHUKK
...THAT ONCE THE BLOW IS STRUCK...
...SHE NOT ONLY SURVIVES, BUT IS ABLE TO DISMISS THE PAIN...
...IN TIME TO AVOID WHAT NAM-EK INTENDS...
...AS A COUP-DE-GRÂCE!
OBVIOUSLY, THIS IS NOT A HEALTHY PERSONALITY I'M DEALING WITH...!
IF KINDNESS DRIVES HIM BERSERK, I'LL JUST HAVE TO APPLY FORCE.
ARE YOU MAD, FEMALE? DO YOU THINK THESE FRAGILE LINKS OF GOLD CAN BIND ME?
AMUSED, NAM-EK ALLOWS THE CHAIN TO DROP AROUND HIM... AND LAUGHS AS SHE PULLS IT TAUT.
BUT HIS HUMOR RAPIDLY DWINDLES WHEN HE ATTEMPTS TO BREAK IT... AND FINDS HE CANNOT!
FOR THIS IS THE MAGIC LASSO, FORGED FROM THE LINKS OF QUEEN HIPPOLYTA'S MAGIC GIRDLE. IT CANNOT BE RENT, BY MAN OR SUPER-MAN...
...AND IT COMPELS ITS CAPTIVE'S OBEDIENCE TO THE LASSO'S HOLDER.
21

NOW--YOU AND I ARE GOING TO HAVE A PEACEFUL LITTLE *CHAT*.

WE CAN *START* WITH YOUR *AUTOBIOGRAPHY*...!

GOTHAM CITY: THE AIR-RAID PANIC-- WITH ITS TERRIFIED MOBS BATTLING FOR SPACE IN CLOSET-SIZED FALLOUT SHELTERS --*IS OVER*--

SOME *DIED* IN THE RIOTING. MOST HAVE JUST GONE *HOME*, THOUGH, LEAVING THE *RUBBLE-STREWN* STREETS TO THE INEVITABLE *LOOTERS* AND THEIR ETERNAL *NEMESIS*.

BATMAN--!!

L-LEMME GO-- I MEAN IT-- OR I'LL *CUT YA*--!

YOUR *HAND* IS SHAKING, SCUM.

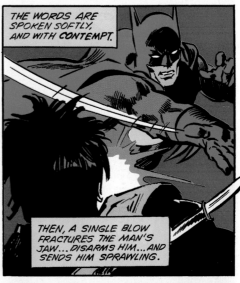

THE WORDS ARE SPOKEN SOFTLY, AND WITH *CONTEMPT*.

THEN, A SINGLE BLOW FRACTURES THE MAN'S JAW...DISARMS HIM...AND SENDS HIM SPRAWLING.

≈ WHEW ≈ *HE'LL* THINK TWICE BEFORE *HE* STEALS HIS NEXT TOASTER...!

POSSIBLY-- BUT THEN HE'LL STEAL IT, *ANYWAY*!

THE WORLD MIGHT'VE *ENDED* TONIGHT...

...AND LOOK HOW HE CHOSE TO CELEBRATE ITS *SURVIVAL*.

THEY DON'T *LEARN*, SOME OF THEM...!

22

WHAT BRINGS YOU TO *GOTHAM*, SUPERGIRL?

YOU.

I'VE GOT A *MISSING PERSONS* PROBLEM--THE KIND OF THING YOU'RE GOOD AT.

WHO'S *MISSING?*

MY COUSIN... YOUR BEST FRIEND.

SUPERMAN NEVER SHOWED UP WHILE THE MISSILES WERE FLYING...

...AND HE HASN'T BEEN SPOTTED *SINCE* EITHER.

IT ALL HAPPENED VERY *QUICKLY.* HE MIGHT BE *OFF-PLANET...*

...OR TRAVELING THROUGH *TIME* ...OR ON EARTH-2.

EVEN HE CAN'T ANTICIPATE *EVERY* CRISIS.

I TRIED ON ALL THOSE EXPLANATIONS, TOO.

OBVIOUSLY, YOU WEREN'T CONVINCED.

ABOUT AS MUCH AS *YOU* ARE.

THEN I THINK WE OUGHT TO LOOK INTO THE MATTER.

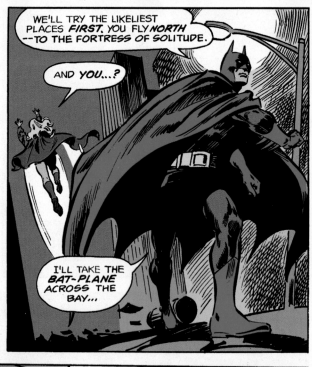

WE'LL TRY THE LIKELIEST PLACES *FIRST.* YOU FLY *NORTH* --TO THE FORTRESS OF SOLITUDE.

AND *YOU...?*

I'LL TAKE THE *BAT-PLANE* ACROSS THE BAY...

"...TO METROPOLIS."

OLSEN, YOU HAVE THE REPORTORIAL INSTINCTS OF A *DWARF MAPLE!*

ONLY *YOU* COULD FAIL TO SEE THE JOURNALISTIC POSSIBILITIES...

...IN *WORLD WAR III*...

...AND BRING ME COPY OF AN *APARTMENT BOMBING* INSTEAD!

23

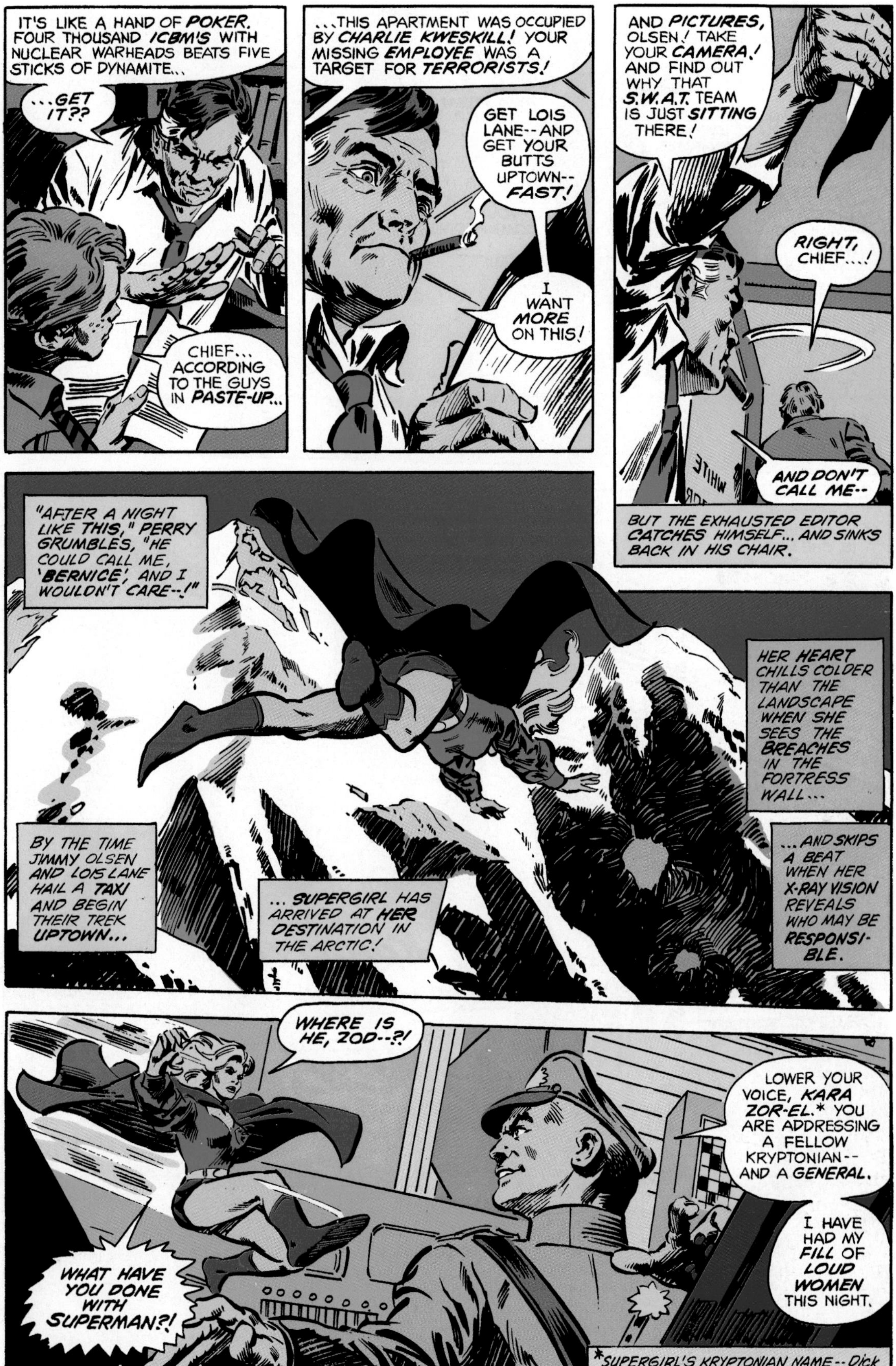

IT'S LIKE A HAND OF POKER. FOUR THOUSAND ICBM'S WITH NUCLEAR WARHEADS BEATS FIVE STICKS OF DYNAMITE...
...GET IT??
CHIEF... ACCORDING TO THE GUYS IN PASTE-UP...
...THIS APARTMENT WAS OCCUPIED BY CHARLIE KWESKILL! YOUR MISSING EMPLOYEE WAS A TARGET FOR TERRORISTS!
GET LOIS LANE--AND GET YOUR BUTTS UPTOWN--FAST!
I WANT MORE ON THIS!
AND PICTURES, OLSEN! TAKE YOUR CAMERA! AND FIND OUT WHY THAT S.W.A.T. TEAM IS JUST SITTING THERE!
RIGHT, CHIEF...!
AND DON'T CALL ME--
BUT THE EXHAUSTED EDITOR CATCHES HIMSELF... AND SINKS BACK IN HIS CHAIR.
"AFTER A NIGHT LIKE THIS," PERRY GRUMBLES, "HE COULD CALL ME, 'BERNICE', AND I WOULDN'T CARE--!"
HER HEART CHILLS COLDER THAN THE LANDSCAPE WHEN SHE SEES THE BREACHES IN THE FORTRESS WALL...
BY THE TIME JIMMY OLSEN AND LOIS LANE HAIL A TAXI AND BEGIN THEIR TREK UPTOWN...
... SUPERGIRL HAS ARRIVED AT HER DESTINATION IN THE ARCTIC!
...AND SKIPS A BEAT WHEN HER X-RAY VISION REVEALS WHO MAY BE RESPONSI-BLE.
WHERE IS HE, ZOD--?!
WHAT HAVE YOU DONE WITH SUPERMAN?!
LOWER YOUR VOICE, KARA ZOR-EL.* YOU ARE ADDRESSING A FELLOW KRYPTONIAN--AND A GENERAL.
I HAVE HAD MY FILL OF LOUD WOMEN THIS NIGHT.
*SUPERGIRL'S KRYPTONIAN NAME--Dick

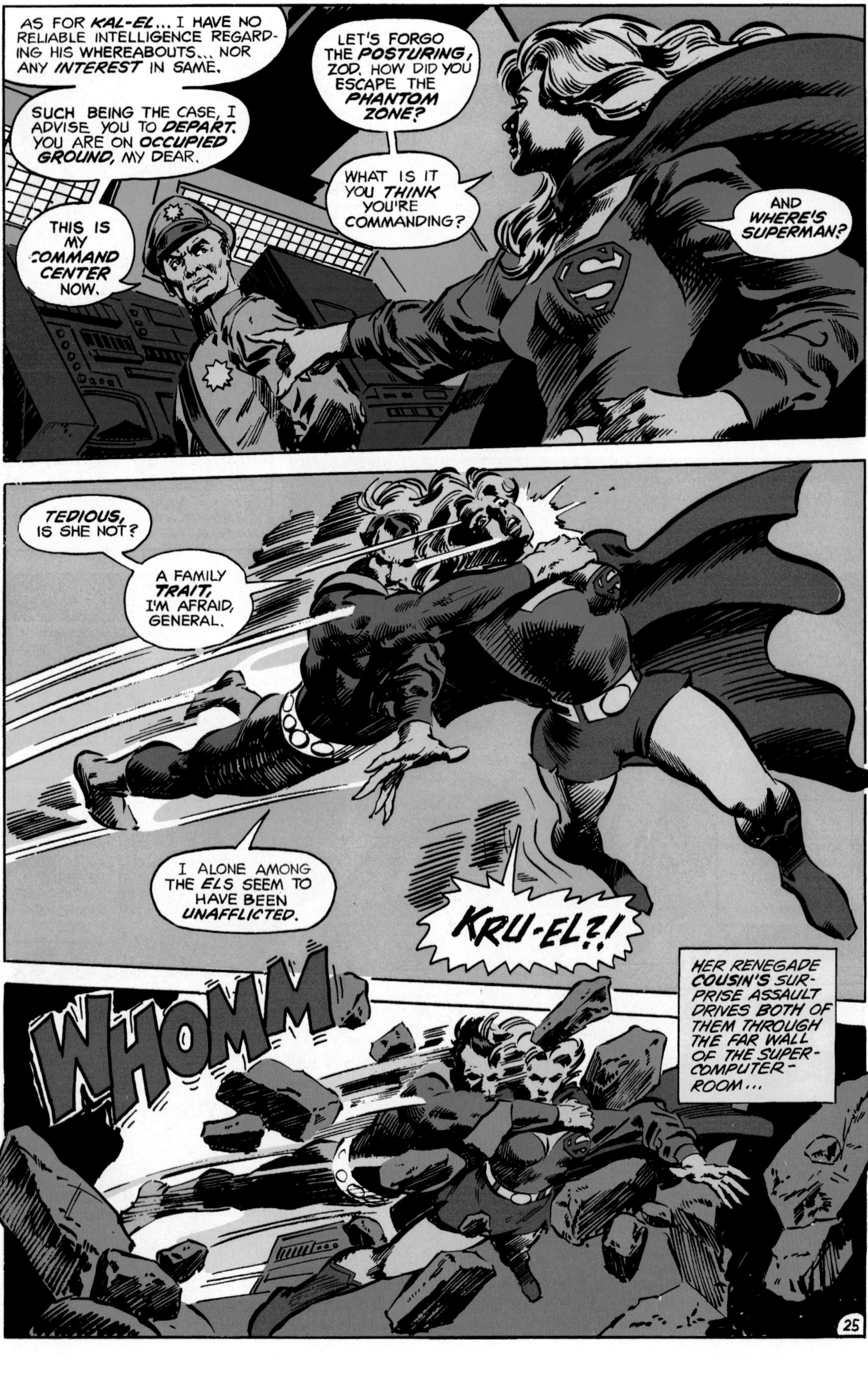
AS FOR KAL-EL... I HAVE NO RELIABLE INTELLIGENCE REGARDING HIS WHEREABOUTS... NOR ANY INTEREST IN SAME.
SUCH BEING THE CASE, I ADVISE YOU TO DEPART. YOU ARE ON OCCUPIED GROUND, MY DEAR.
THIS IS MY COMMAND CENTER NOW.
LET'S FORGO THE POSTURING, ZOD. HOW DID YOU ESCAPE THE PHANTOM ZONE?
WHAT IS IT YOU THINK YOU'RE COMMANDING?
AND WHERE'S SUPERMAN?
TEDIOUS, IS SHE NOT?
A FAMILY TRAIT, I'M AFRAID, GENERAL.
I ALONE AMONG THE ELS SEEM TO HAVE BEEN UNAFFLICTED.
KRU-EL?!
WHOMM
HER RENEGADE COUSIN'S SURPRISE ASSAULT DRIVES BOTH OF THEM THROUGH THE FAR WALL OF THE SUPER-COMPUTER-ROOM...
25

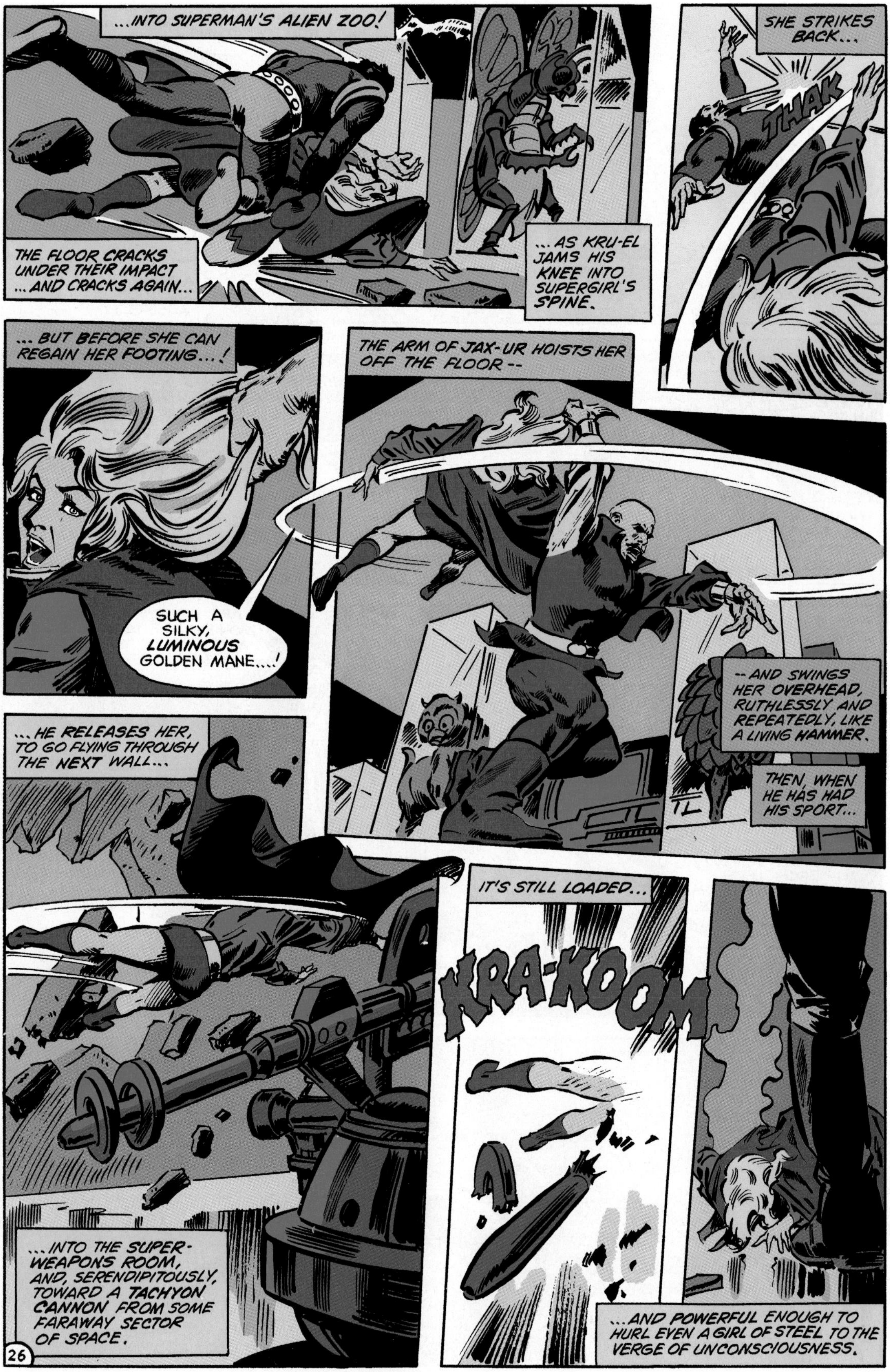
...INTO SUPERMAN'S ALIEN ZOO!
THE FLOOR CRACKS UNDER THEIR IMPACT ...AND CRACKS AGAIN...
...AS KRU-EL JAMS HIS KNEE INTO SUPERGIRL'S SPINE.
SHE STRIKES BACK...
THAK
... BUT BEFORE SHE CAN REGAIN HER FOOTING...!
SUCH A SILKY, LUMINOUS GOLDEN MANE...!
THE ARM OF JAX-UR HOISTS HER OFF THE FLOOR --
--AND SWINGS HER OVERHEAD, RUTHLESSLY AND REPEATEDLY, LIKE A LIVING HAMMER.
THEN, WHEN HE HAS HAD HIS SPORT...
...HE RELEASES HER, TO GO FLYING THROUGH THE NEXT WALL...
...INTO THE SUPER-WEAPONS ROOM, AND, SERENDIPITOUSLY, TOWARD A TACHYON CANNON FROM SOME FARAWAY SECTOR OF SPACE.
26
IT'S STILL LOADED...
KRA-KOOM
...AND POWERFUL ENOUGH TO HURL EVEN A GIRL OF STEEL TO THE VERGE OF UNCONSCIOUSNESS.

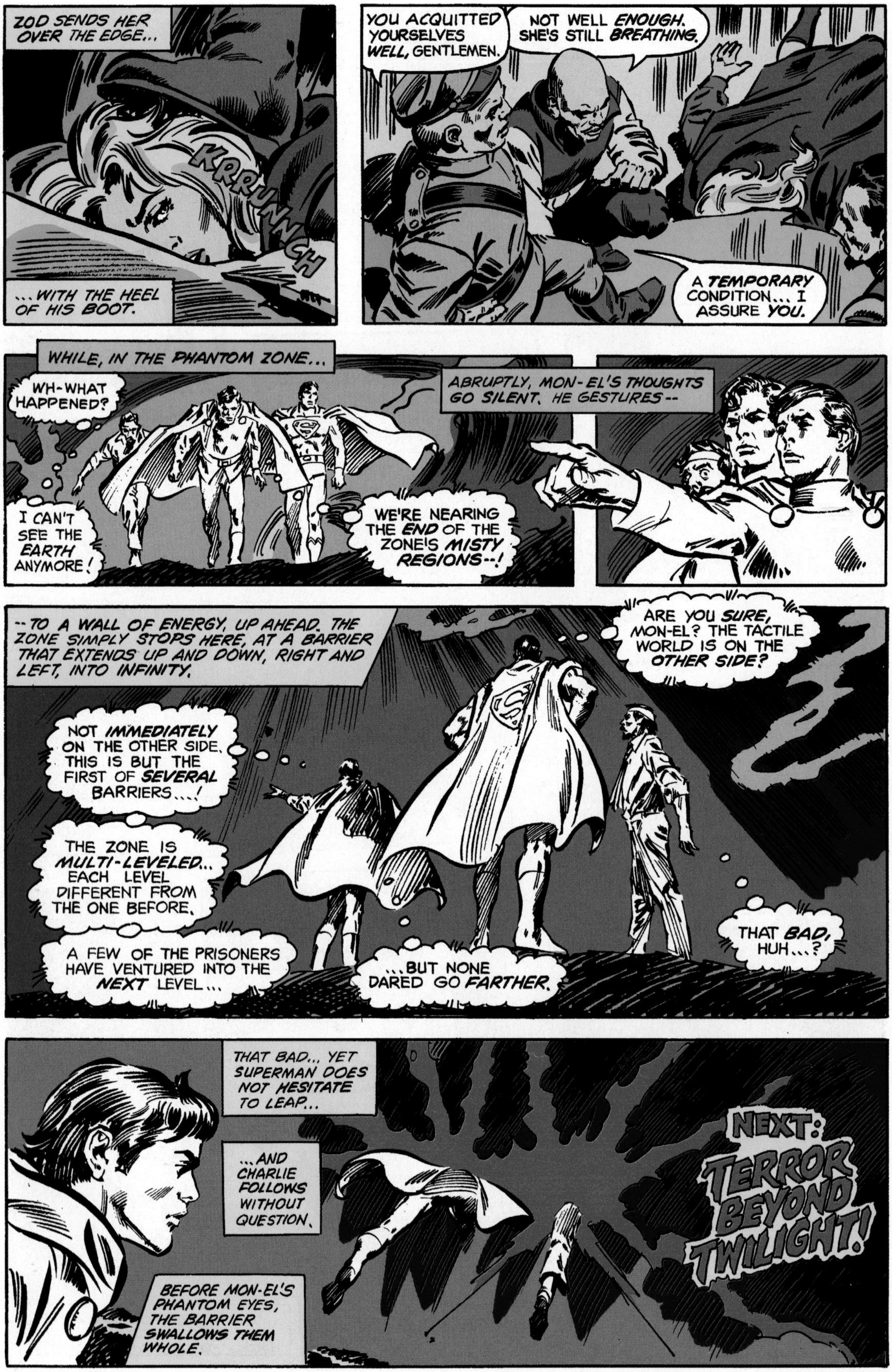

ZOD SENDS HER OVER THE EDGE...
KRRUNNCH
...WITH THE HEEL OF HIS BOOT.
YOU ACQUITTED YOURSELVES WELL, GENTLEMEN.
NOT WELL ENOUGH. SHE'S STILL BREATHING.
A TEMPORARY CONDITION... I ASSURE YOU.
WHILE, IN THE PHANTOM ZONE...
WH-WHAT HAPPENED?
I CAN'T SEE THE EARTH ANYMORE!
WE'RE NEARING THE END OF THE ZONE'S MISTY REGIONS--!
ABRUPTLY, MON-EL'S THOUGHTS GO SILENT. HE GESTURES--
--TO A WALL OF ENERGY, UP AHEAD. THE ZONE SIMPLY STOPS HERE, AT A BARRIER THAT EXTENDS UP AND DOWN, RIGHT AND LEFT, INTO INFINITY.
ARE YOU SURE, MON-EL? THE TACTILE WORLD IS ON THE OTHER SIDE?
NOT IMMEDIATELY ON THE OTHER SIDE. THIS IS BUT THE FIRST OF SEVERAL BARRIERS...!
THE ZONE IS MULTI-LEVELED... EACH LEVEL DIFFERENT FROM THE ONE BEFORE.
A FEW OF THE PRISONERS HAVE VENTURED INTO THE NEXT LEVEL...
...BUT NONE DARED GO FARTHER.
THAT BAD, HUH...?
THAT BAD... YET SUPERMAN DOES NOT HESITATE TO LEAP...
...AND CHARLIE FOLLOWS WITHOUT QUESTION.
BEFORE MON-EL'S PHANTOM EYES, THE BARRIER SWALLOWS THEM WHOLE.
NEXT: TERROR BEYOND TWILIGHT!

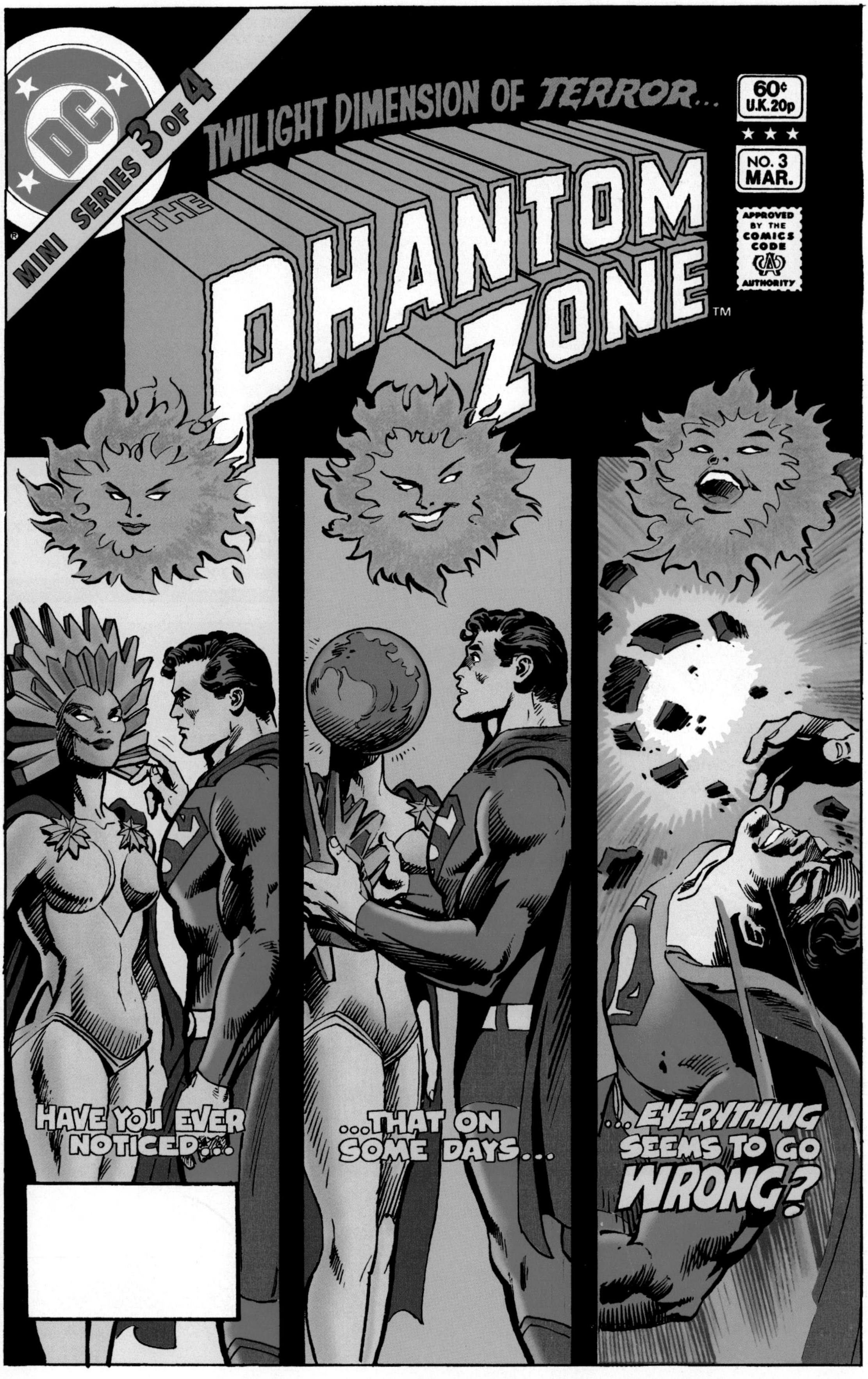
MINI SERIES 3 OF 4
TWILIGHT DIMENSION OF TERROR...
60¢ U.K.20p
NO. 3 MAR.
APPROVED BY THE COMICS CODE AUTHORITY
THE PHANTOM ZONE™
HAVE YOU EVER NOTICED...
...THAT ON SOME DAYS...
...EVERYTHING SEEMS TO GO WRONG?

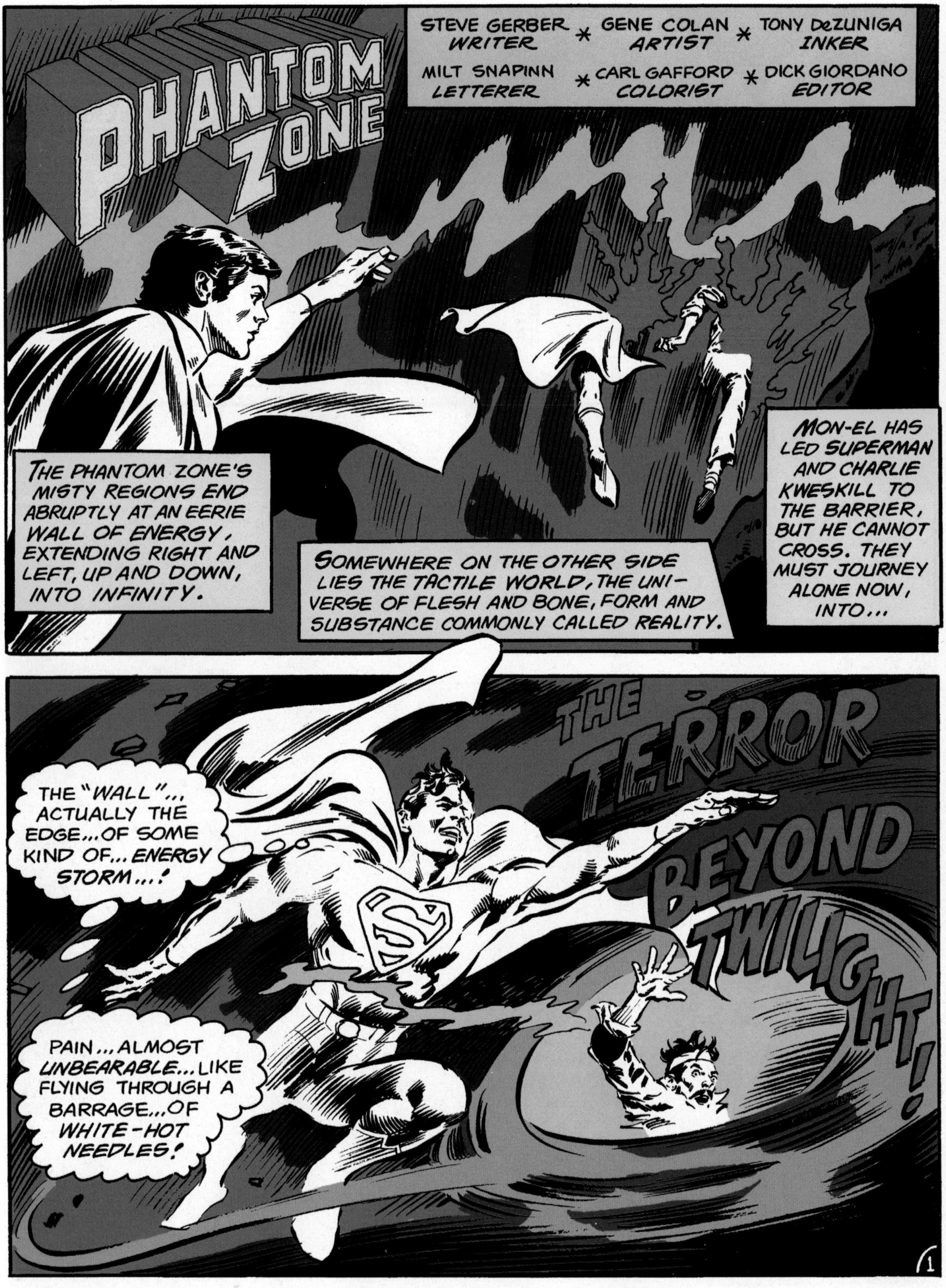

PHANTOM ZONE
STEVE GERBER WRITER * GENE COLAN ARTIST * TONY DeZUNIGA INKER
MILT SNAPINN LETTERER * CARL GAFFORD COLORIST * DICK GIORDANO EDITOR
THE PHANTOM ZONE'S MISTY REGIONS END ABRUPTLY AT AN EERIE WALL OF ENERGY, EXTENDING RIGHT AND LEFT, UP AND DOWN, INTO INFINITY.
SOMEWHERE ON THE OTHER SIDE LIES THE TACTILE WORLD, THE UNI-VERSE OF FLESH AND BONE, FORM AND SUBSTANCE COMMONLY CALLED REALITY.
MON-EL HAS LED SUPERMAN AND CHARLIE KWESKILL TO THE BARRIER, BUT HE CANNOT CROSS. THEY MUST JOURNEY ALONE NOW, INTO...
THE TERROR BEYOND TWILIGHT!
THE "WALL"... ACTUALLY THE EDGE... OF SOME KIND OF... ENERGY STORM...!
PAIN... ALMOST UNBEARABLE... LIKE FLYING THROUGH A BARRAGE... OF WHITE-HOT NEEDLES!
1

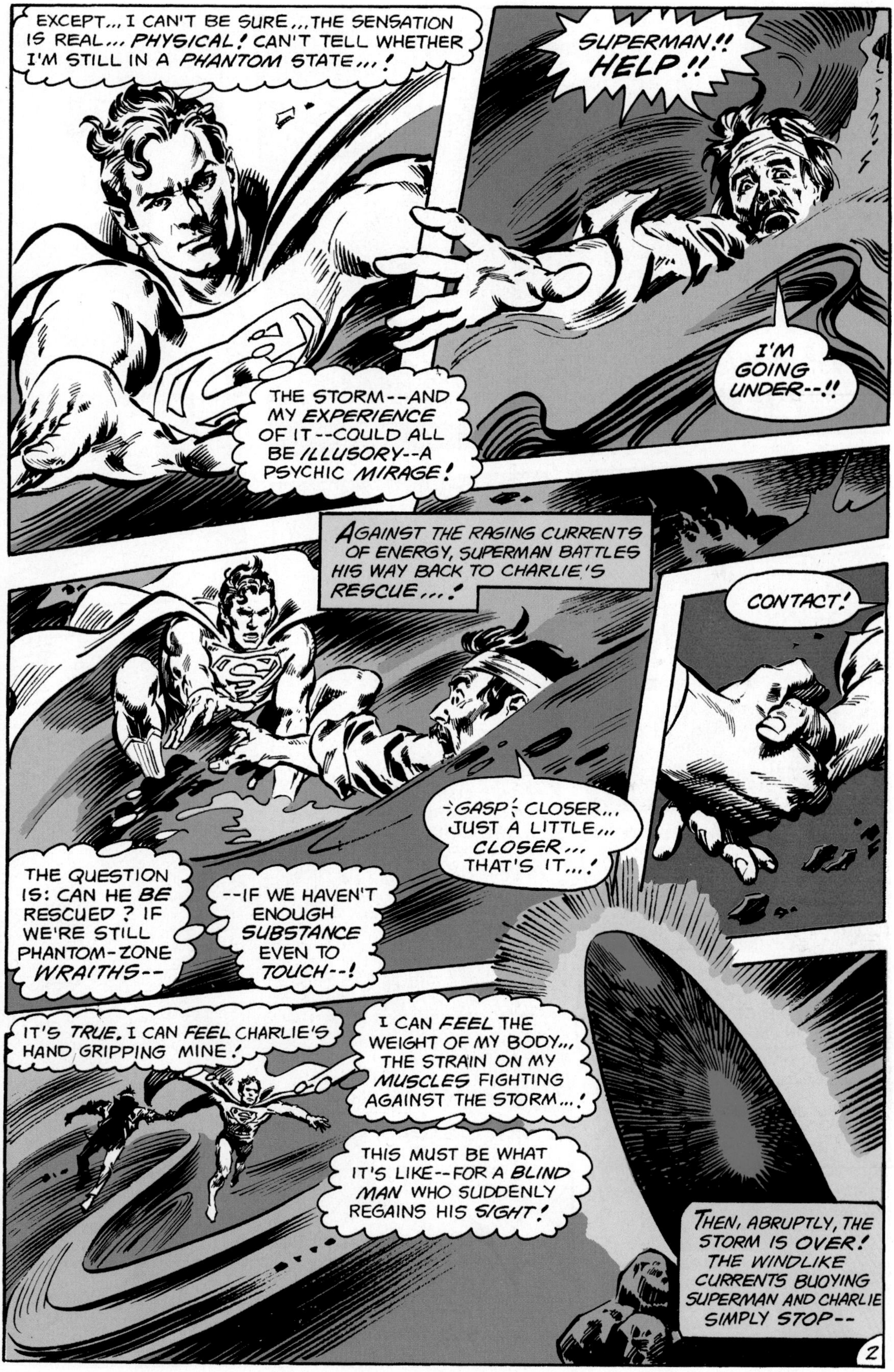

EXCEPT... I CAN'T BE SURE... THE SENSATION IS REAL... PHYSICAL! CAN'T TELL WHETHER I'M STILL IN A PHANTOM STATE...!
THE STORM--AND MY EXPERIENCE OF IT--COULD ALL BE ILLUSORY--A PSYCHIC MIRAGE!
SUPERMAN!! HELP!!
I'M GOING UNDER--!!
AGAINST THE RAGING CURRENTS OF ENERGY, SUPERMAN BATTLES HIS WAY BACK TO CHARLIE'S RESCUE...!
GASP CLOSER... JUST A LITTLE... CLOSER... THAT'S IT...!
THE QUESTION IS: CAN HE BE RESCUED? IF WE'RE STILL PHANTOM-ZONE WRAITHS--
--IF WE HAVEN'T ENOUGH SUBSTANCE EVEN TO TOUCH--!
CONTACT!
IT'S TRUE. I CAN FEEL CHARLIE'S HAND GRIPPING MINE!
I CAN FEEL THE WEIGHT OF MY BODY... THE STRAIN ON MY MUSCLES FIGHTING AGAINST THE STORM...!
THIS MUST BE WHAT IT'S LIKE--FOR A BLIND MAN WHO SUDDENLY REGAINS HIS SIGHT!
THEN, ABRUPTLY, THE STORM IS OVER! THE WINDLIKE CURRENTS BUOYING SUPERMAN AND CHARLIE SIMPLY STOP--
2

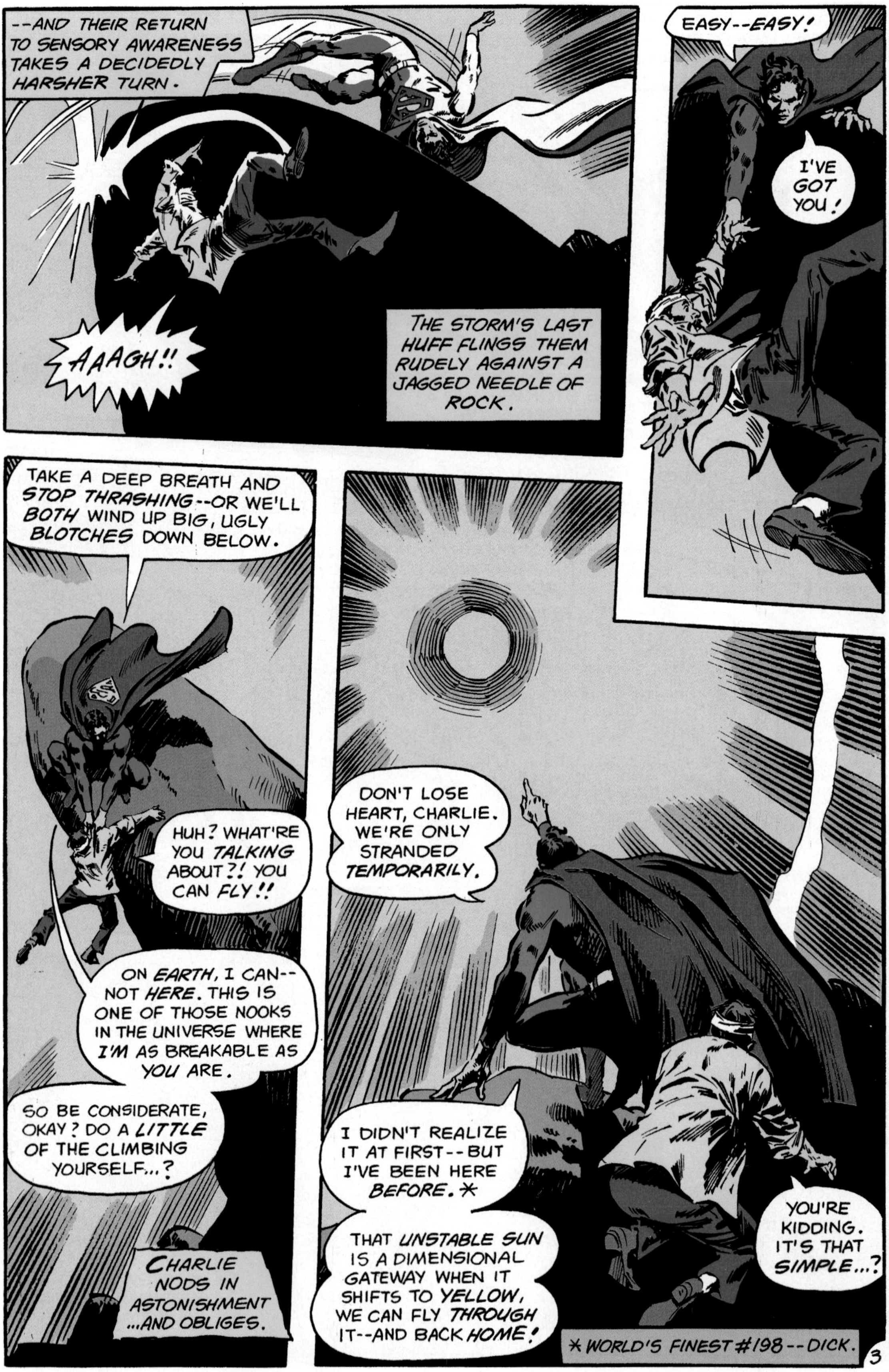
--AND THEIR RETURN TO SENSORY AWARENESS TAKES A DECIDEDLY HARSHER TURN.
AAAGH!!
THE STORM'S LAST HUFF FLINGS THEM RUDELY AGAINST A JAGGED NEEDLE OF ROCK.
EASY--EASY!
I'VE GOT YOU!
TAKE A DEEP BREATH AND STOP THRASHING--OR WE'LL BOTH WIND UP BIG, UGLY BLOTCHES DOWN BELOW.
HUH? WHAT'RE YOU TALKING ABOUT?! YOU CAN FLY!!
ON EARTH, I CAN--NOT HERE. THIS IS ONE OF THOSE NOOKS IN THE UNIVERSE WHERE I'M AS BREAKABLE AS YOU ARE.
SO BE CONSIDERATE, OKAY? DO A LITTLE OF THE CLIMBING YOURSELF...?
CHARLIE NODS IN ASTONISHMENT ...AND OBLIGES.
DON'T LOSE HEART, CHARLIE. WE'RE ONLY STRANDED TEMPORARILY.
I DIDN'T REALIZE IT AT FIRST--BUT I'VE BEEN HERE BEFORE.*
THAT UNSTABLE SUN IS A DIMENSIONAL GATEWAY WHEN IT SHIFTS TO YELLOW, WE CAN FLY THROUGH IT--AND BACK HOME!
YOU'RE KIDDING. IT'S THAT SIMPLE...?
*WORLD'S FINEST #198--DICK.
3

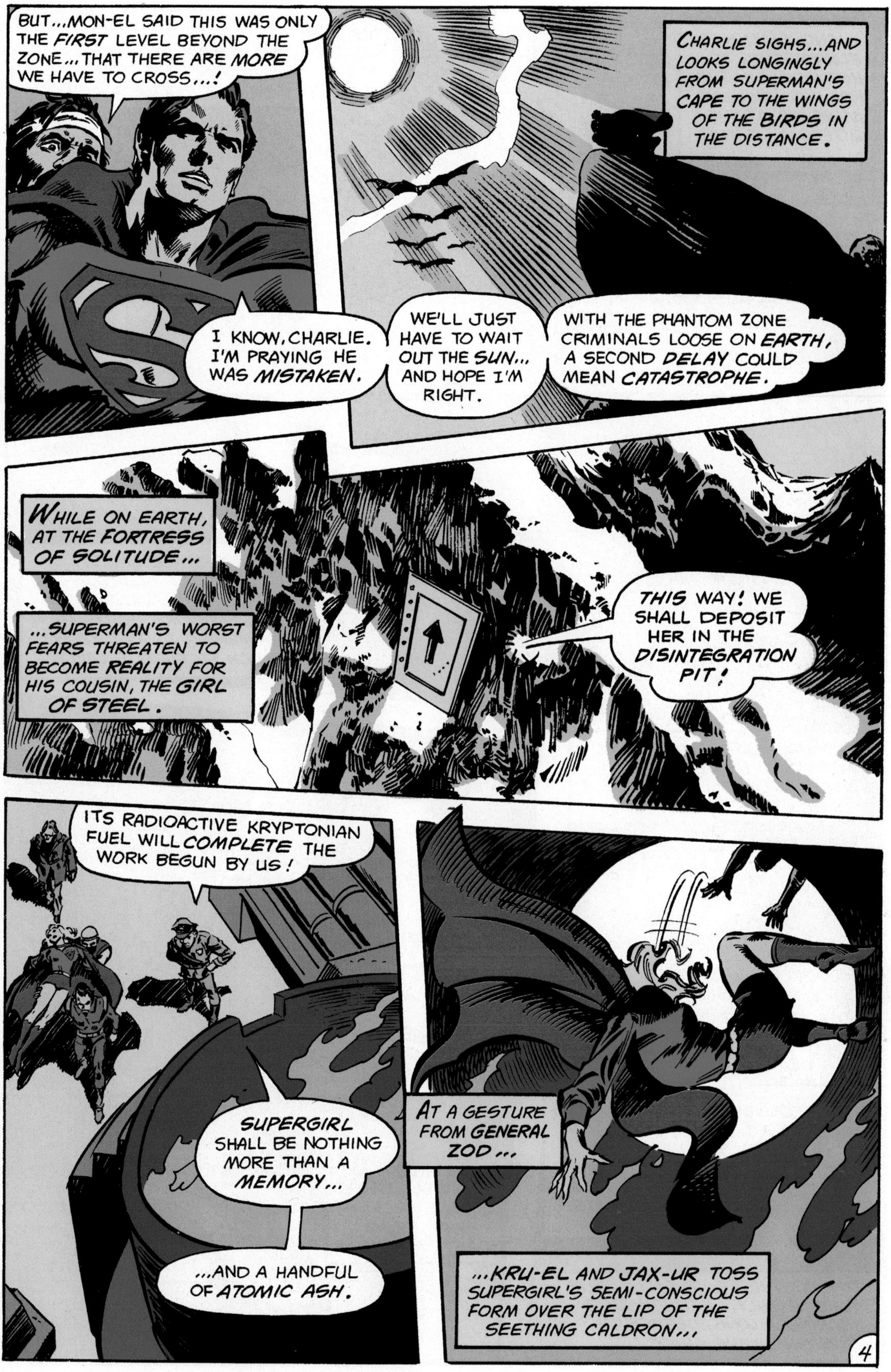

BUT...MON-EL SAID THIS WAS ONLY THE FIRST LEVEL BEYOND THE ZONE...THAT THERE ARE MORE WE HAVE TO CROSS...!
CHARLIE SIGHS...AND LOOKS LONGINGLY FROM SUPERMAN'S CAPE TO THE WINGS OF THE BIRDS IN THE DISTANCE.
I KNOW, CHARLIE. I'M PRAYING HE WAS MISTAKEN.
WE'LL JUST HAVE TO WAIT OUT THE SUN... AND HOPE I'M RIGHT.
WITH THE PHANTOM ZONE CRIMINALS LOOSE ON EARTH, A SECOND DELAY COULD MEAN CATASTROPHE.
WHILE ON EARTH, AT THE FORTRESS OF SOLITUDE...
...SUPERMAN'S WORST FEARS THREATEN TO BECOME REALITY FOR HIS COUSIN, THE GIRL OF STEEL.
THIS WAY! WE SHALL DEPOSIT HER IN THE DISINTEGRATION PIT!
ITS RADIOACTIVE KRYPTONIAN FUEL WILL COMPLETE THE WORK BEGUN BY US!
SUPERGIRL SHALL BE NOTHING MORE THAN A MEMORY...
...AND A HANDFUL OF ATOMIC ASH.
AT A GESTURE FROM GENERAL ZOD...
...KRU-EL AND JAX-UR TOSS SUPERGIRL'S SEMI-CONSCIOUS FORM OVER THE LIP OF THE SEETHING CALDRON...
4

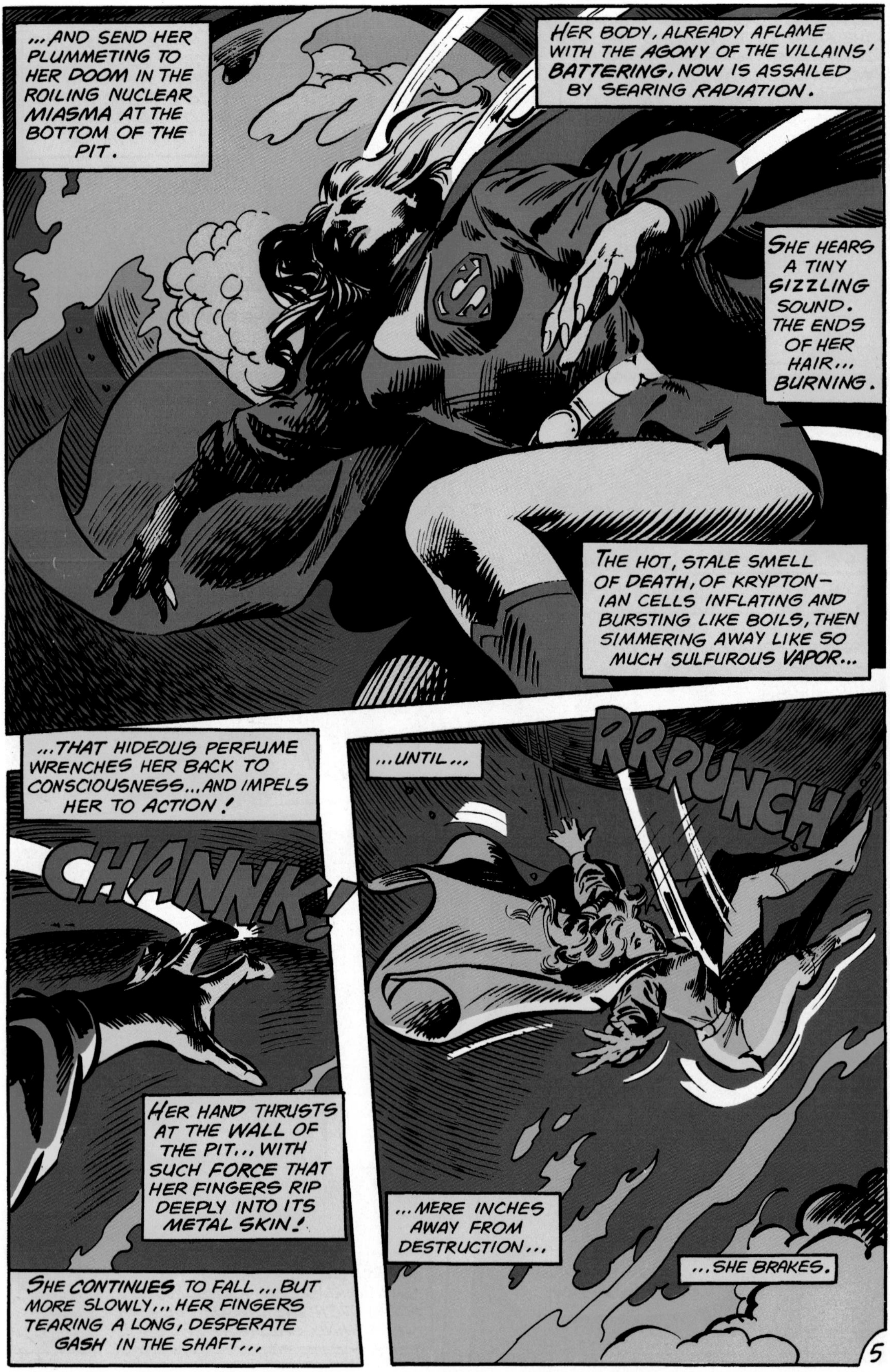
...AND SEND HER PLUMMETING TO HER DOOM IN THE ROILING NUCLEAR MIASMA AT THE BOTTOM OF THE PIT.
HER BODY, ALREADY AFLAME WITH THE AGONY OF THE VILLAINS' BATTERING, NOW IS ASSAILED BY SEARING RADIATION.
SHE HEARS A TINY SIZZLING SOUND. THE ENDS OF HER HAIR... BURNING.
THE HOT, STALE SMELL OF DEATH, OF KRYPTON-IAN CELLS INFLATING AND BURSTING LIKE BOILS, THEN SIMMERING AWAY LIKE SO MUCH SULFUROUS VAPOR...
...THAT HIDEOUS PERFUME WRENCHES HER BACK TO CONSCIOUSNESS...AND IMPELS HER TO ACTION!
CHANNK!
HER HAND THRUSTS AT THE WALL OF THE PIT... WITH SUCH FORCE THAT HER FINGERS RIP DEEPLY INTO ITS METAL SKIN!
SHE CONTINUES TO FALL... BUT MORE SLOWLY... HER FINGERS TEARING A LONG, DESPERATE GASH IN THE SHAFT...
...UNTIL...
RRRUNCH
...MERE INCHES AWAY FROM DESTRUCTION...
...SHE BRAKES.
5

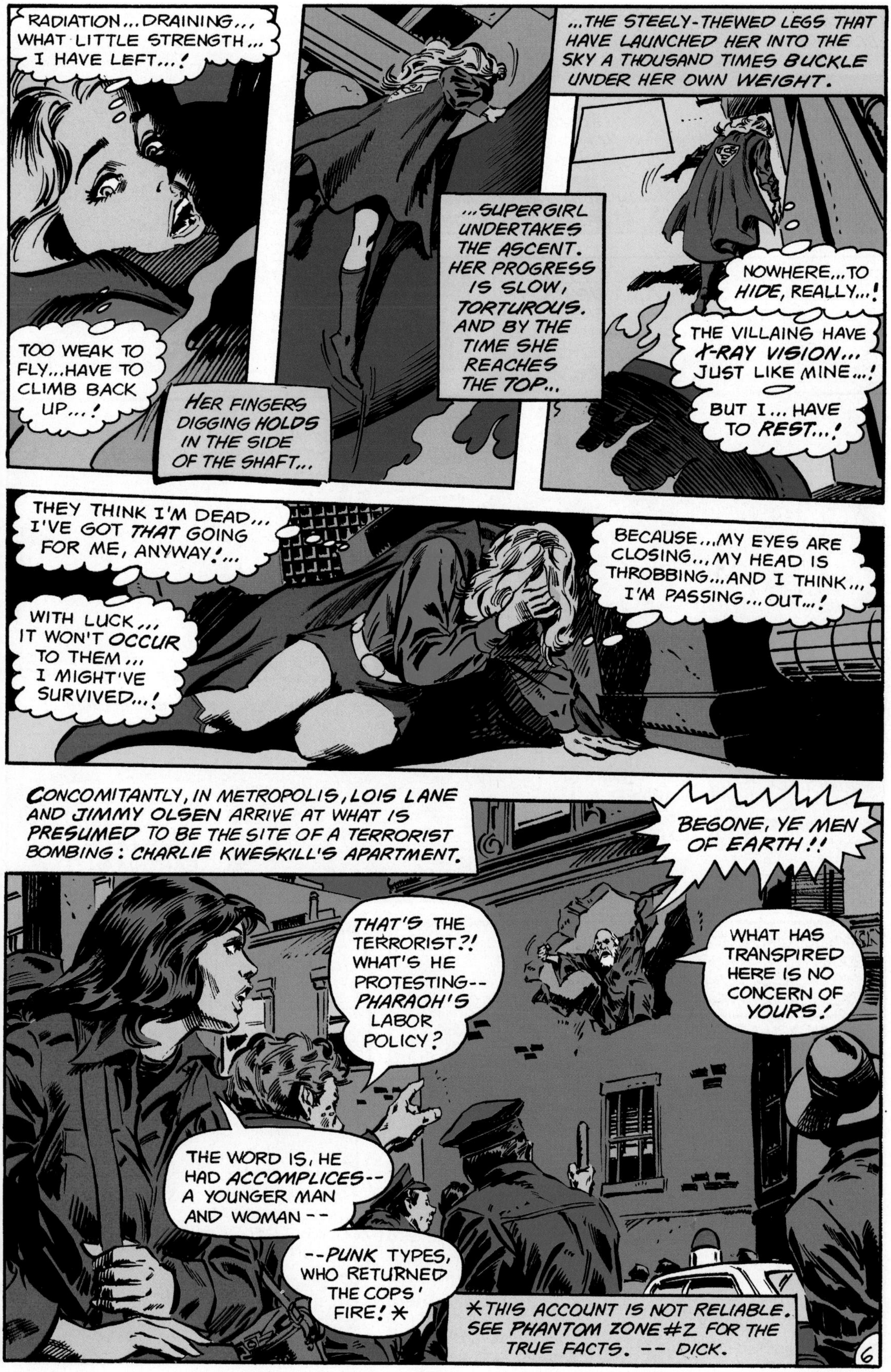

RADIATION... DRAINING... WHAT LITTLE STRENGTH... I HAVE LEFT...!
TOO WEAK TO FLY... HAVE TO CLIMB BACK UP...!
HER FINGERS DIGGING HOLDS IN THE SIDE OF THE SHAFT...
...SUPERGIRL UNDERTAKES THE ASCENT. HER PROGRESS IS SLOW, TORTUROUS. AND BY THE TIME SHE REACHES THE TOP...
...THE STEELY-THEWED LEGS THAT HAVE LAUNCHED HER INTO THE SKY A THOUSAND TIMES BUCKLE UNDER HER OWN WEIGHT.
NOWHERE... TO HIDE, REALLY...!
THE VILLAINS HAVE X-RAY VISION... JUST LIKE MINE...!
BUT I... HAVE TO REST...!
THEY THINK I'M DEAD... I'VE GOT THAT GOING FOR ME, ANYWAY!...
WITH LUCK... IT WON'T OCCUR TO THEM... I MIGHT'VE SURVIVED...!
BECAUSE... MY EYES ARE CLOSING... MY HEAD IS THROBBING... AND I THINK... I'M PASSING... OUT...!
CONCOMITANTLY, IN METROPOLIS, LOIS LANE AND JIMMY OLSEN ARRIVE AT WHAT IS PRESUMED TO BE THE SITE OF A TERRORIST BOMBING: CHARLIE KWESKILL'S APARTMENT.
BEGONE, YE MEN OF EARTH!!
THAT'S THE TERRORIST?! WHAT'S HE PROTESTING-- PHARAOH'S LABOR POLICY?
WHAT HAS TRANSPIRED HERE IS NO CONCERN OF YOURS!
THE WORD IS, HE HAD ACCOMPLICES-- A YOUNGER MAN AND WOMAN--
--PUNK TYPES, WHO RETURNED THE COPS' FIRE! *
* THIS ACCOUNT IS NOT RELIABLE. SEE PHANTOM ZONE #2 FOR THE TRUE FACTS. -- DICK.
6

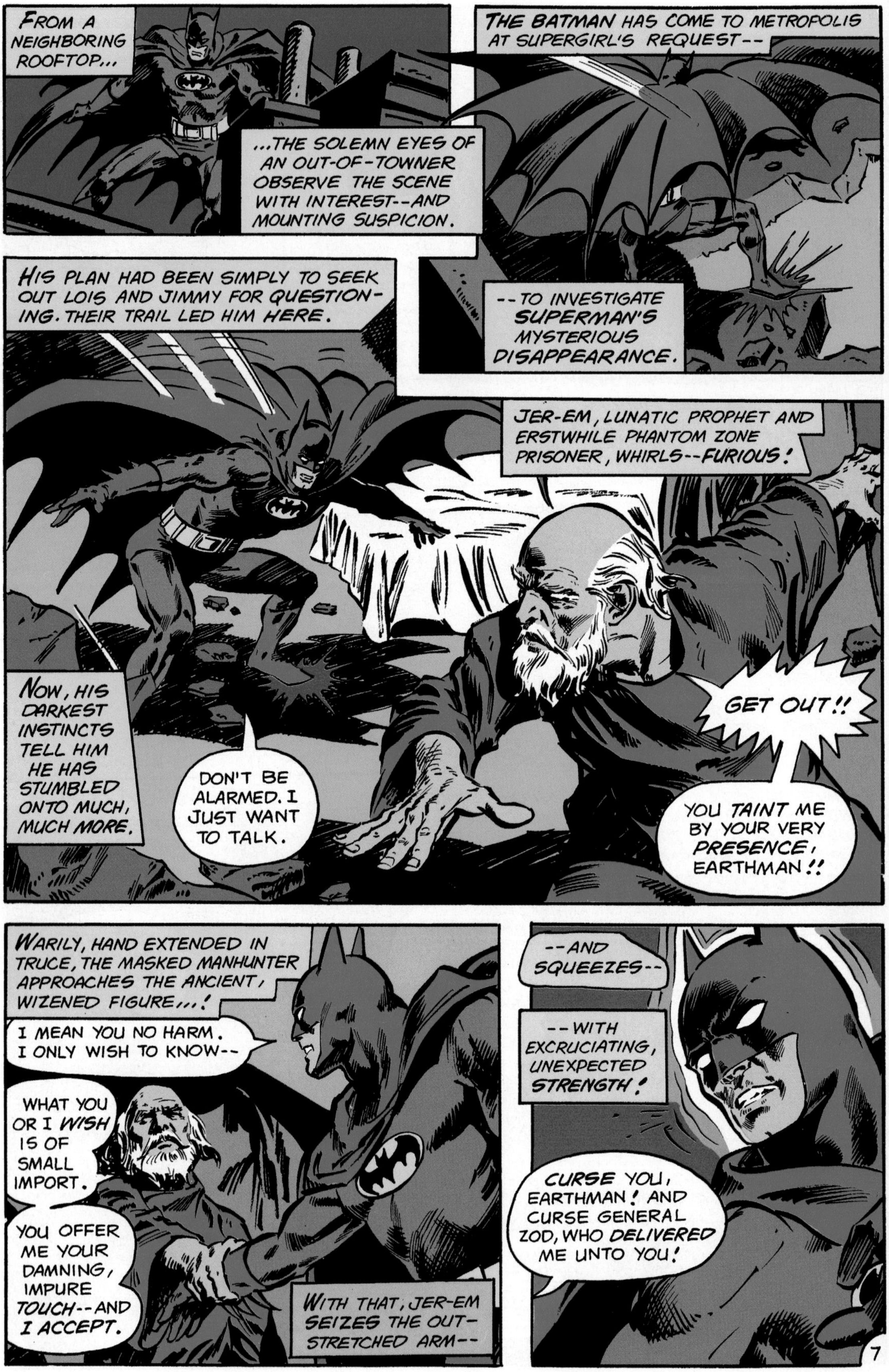
FROM A NEIGHBORING ROOFTOP...
...THE SOLEMN EYES OF AN OUT-OF-TOWNER OBSERVE THE SCENE WITH INTEREST--AND MOUNTING SUSPICION.
THE BATMAN HAS COME TO METROPOLIS AT SUPERGIRL'S REQUEST--
--TO INVESTIGATE SUPERMAN'S MYSTERIOUS DISAPPEARANCE.
HIS PLAN HAD BEEN SIMPLY TO SEEK OUT LOIS AND JIMMY FOR QUESTIONING. THEIR TRAIL LED HIM HERE.
JER-EM, LUNATIC PROPHET AND ERSTWHILE PHANTOM ZONE PRISONER, WHIRLS--FURIOUS!
NOW, HIS DARKEST INSTINCTS TELL HIM HE HAS STUMBLED ONTO MUCH, MUCH MORE.
DON'T BE ALARMED. I JUST WANT TO TALK.
GET OUT!!
YOU TAINT ME BY YOUR VERY PRESENCE, EARTHMAN!!
WARILY, HAND EXTENDED IN TRUCE, THE MASKED MANHUNTER APPROACHES THE ANCIENT, WIZENED FIGURE...!
I MEAN YOU NO HARM. I ONLY WISH TO KNOW--
WHAT YOU OR I WISH IS OF SMALL IMPORT.
YOU OFFER ME YOUR DAMNING, IMPURE TOUCH--AND I ACCEPT.
WITH THAT, JER-EM SEIZES THE OUT-STRETCHED ARM--
--AND SQUEEZES--
--WITH EXCRUCIATING, UNEXPECTED STRENGTH!
CURSE YOU, EARTHMAN! AND CURSE GENERAL ZOD, WHO DELIVERED ME UNTO YOU!
7

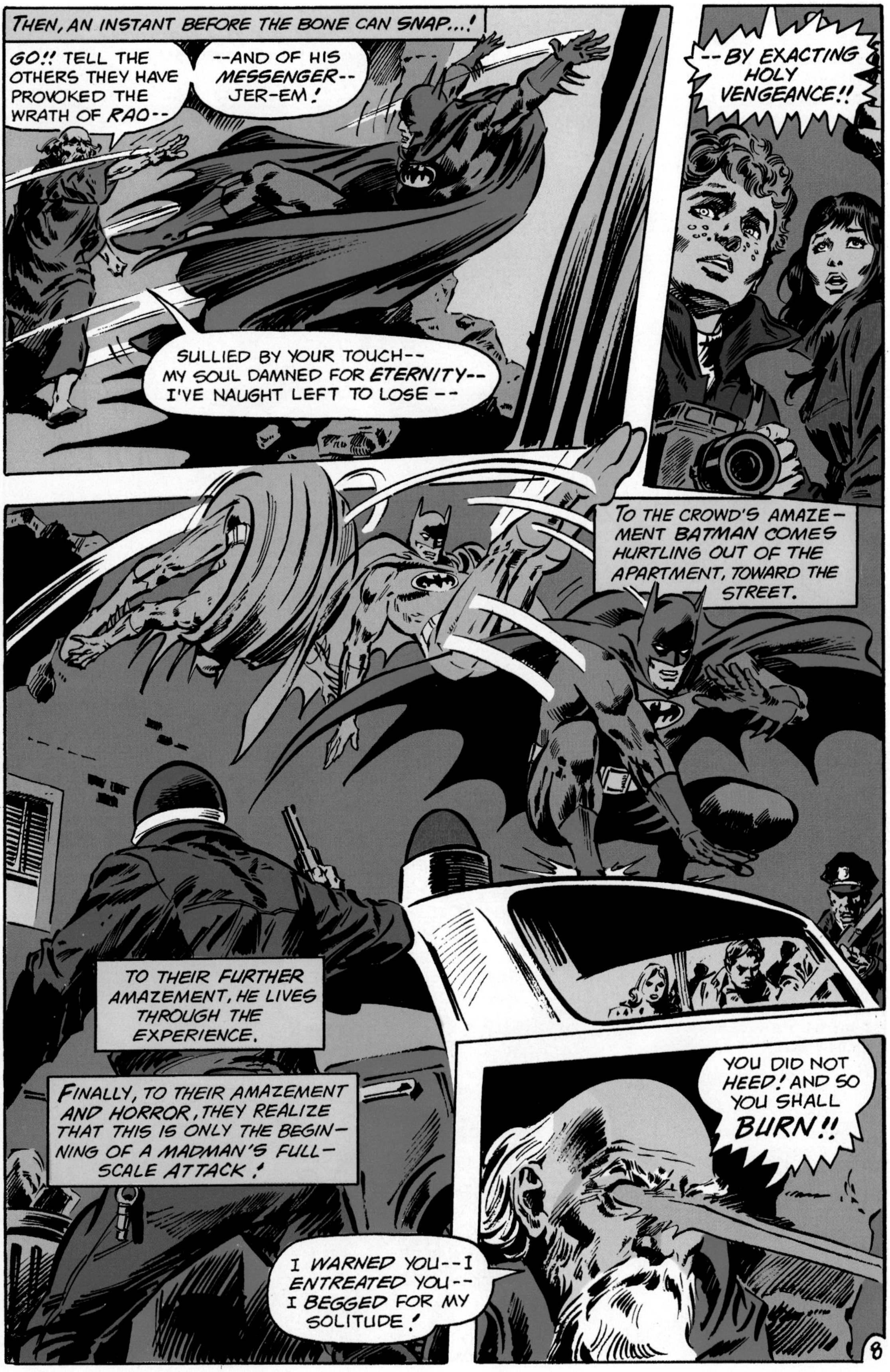

THEN, AN INSTANT BEFORE THE BONE CAN SNAP...!
GO!! TELL THE OTHERS THEY HAVE PROVOKED THE WRATH OF RAO--
--AND OF HIS MESSENGER-- JER-EM!
SULLIED BY YOUR TOUCH-- MY SOUL DAMNED FOR ETERNITY-- I'VE NAUGHT LEFT TO LOSE --
--BY EXACTING HOLY VENGEANCE!!
TO THE CROWD'S AMAZE-MENT BATMAN COMES HURTLING OUT OF THE APARTMENT, TOWARD THE STREET.
TO THEIR FURTHER AMAZEMENT, HE LIVES THROUGH THE EXPERIENCE.
FINALLY, TO THEIR AMAZEMENT AND HORROR, THEY REALIZE THAT THIS IS ONLY THE BEGIN-NING OF A MADMAN'S FULL-SCALE ATTACK!
YOU DID NOT HEED! AND SO YOU SHALL BURN!!
I WARNED YOU--I ENTREATED YOU-- I BEGGED FOR MY SOLITUDE!
8

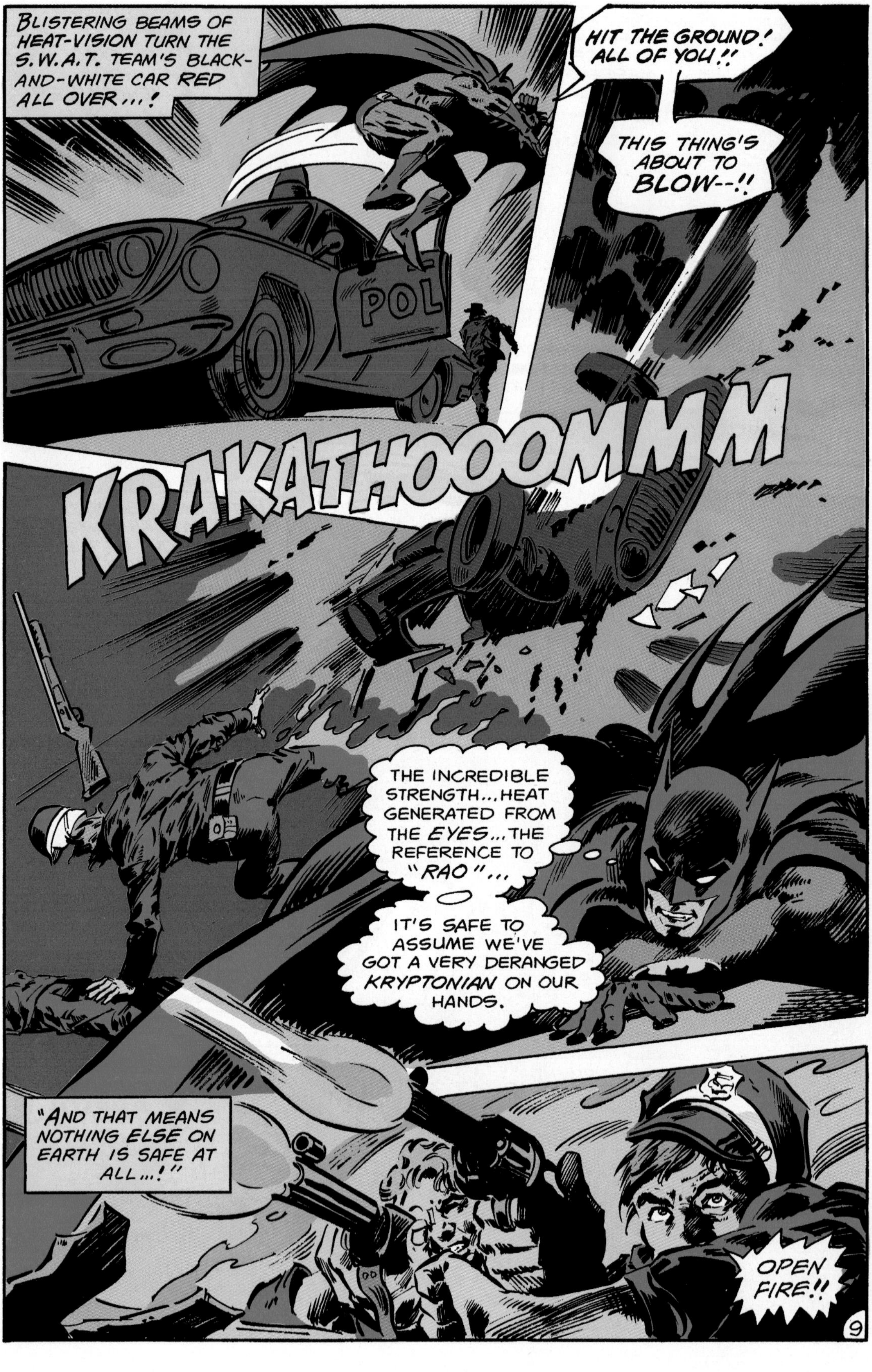
BLISTERING BEAMS OF HEAT-VISION TURN THE S.W.A.T. TEAM'S BLACK-AND-WHITE CAR RED ALL OVER...!
HIT THE GROUND! ALL OF YOU!!
THIS THING'S ABOUT TO BLOW--!!
POL
KRAKATHOOOMMM
THE INCREDIBLE STRENGTH...HEAT GENERATED FROM THE EYES...THE REFERENCE TO "RAO"...
IT'S SAFE TO ASSUME WE'VE GOT A VERY DERANGED KRYPTONIAN ON OUR HANDS.
"AND THAT MEANS NOTHING ELSE ON EARTH IS SAFE AT ALL...!"
OPEN FIRE!!
9

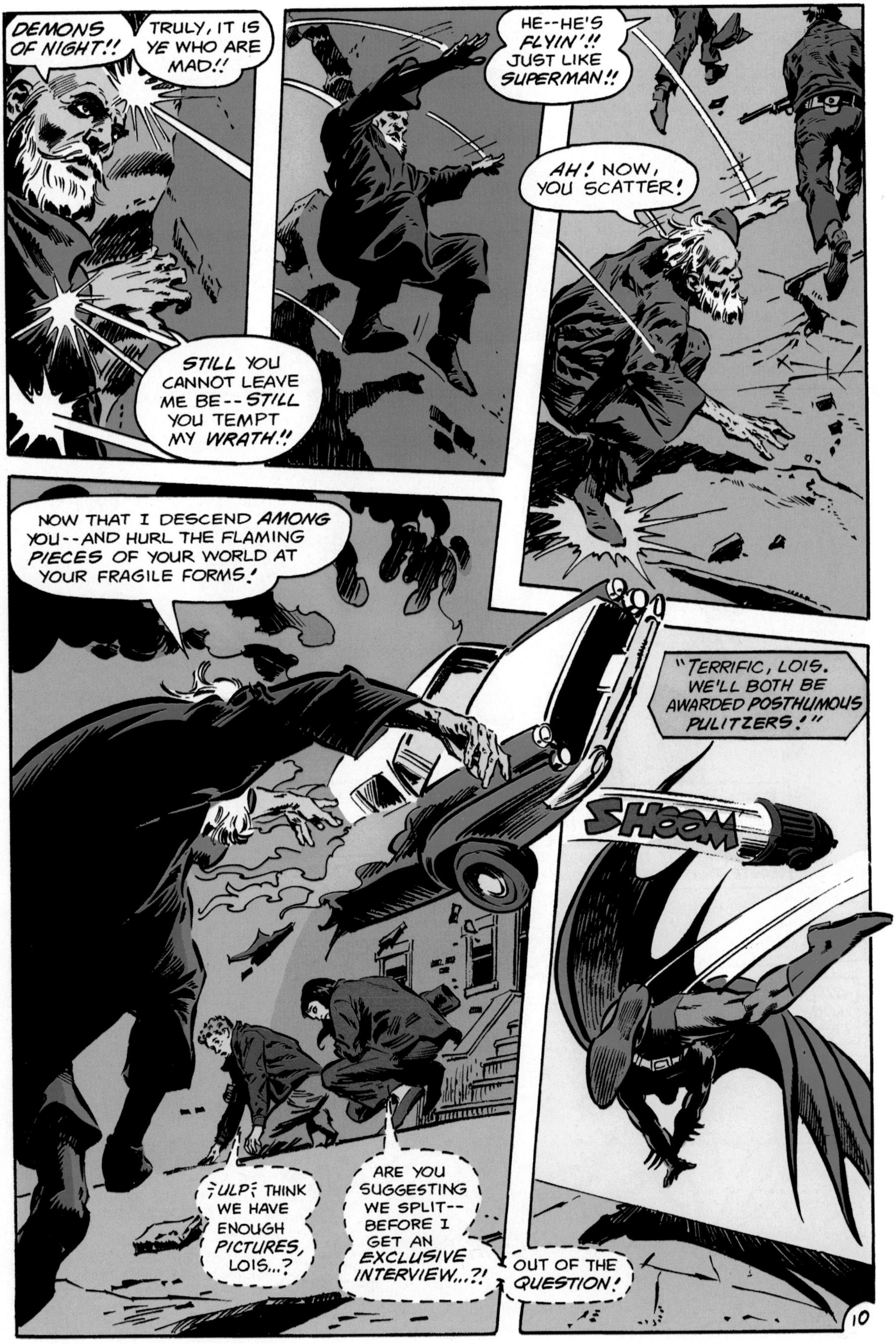
DEMONS OF NIGHT!!
TRULY, IT IS YE WHO ARE MAD!!
STILL YOU CANNOT LEAVE ME BE--STILL YOU TEMPT MY WRATH!!
HE--HE'S FLYIN'!! JUST LIKE SUPERMAN!!
AH! NOW, YOU SCATTER!
NOW THAT I DESCEND AMONG YOU--AND HURL THE FLAMING PIECES OF YOUR WORLD AT YOUR FRAGILE FORMS!
¡ULP¡ THINK WE HAVE ENOUGH PICTURES, LOIS...?
ARE YOU SUGGESTING WE SPLIT--BEFORE I GET AN EXCLUSIVE INTERVIEW...?!
"TERRIFIC, LOIS. WE'LL BOTH BE AWARDED POSTHUMOUS PULITZERS!"
SHOOM
OUT OF THE QUESTION!
10

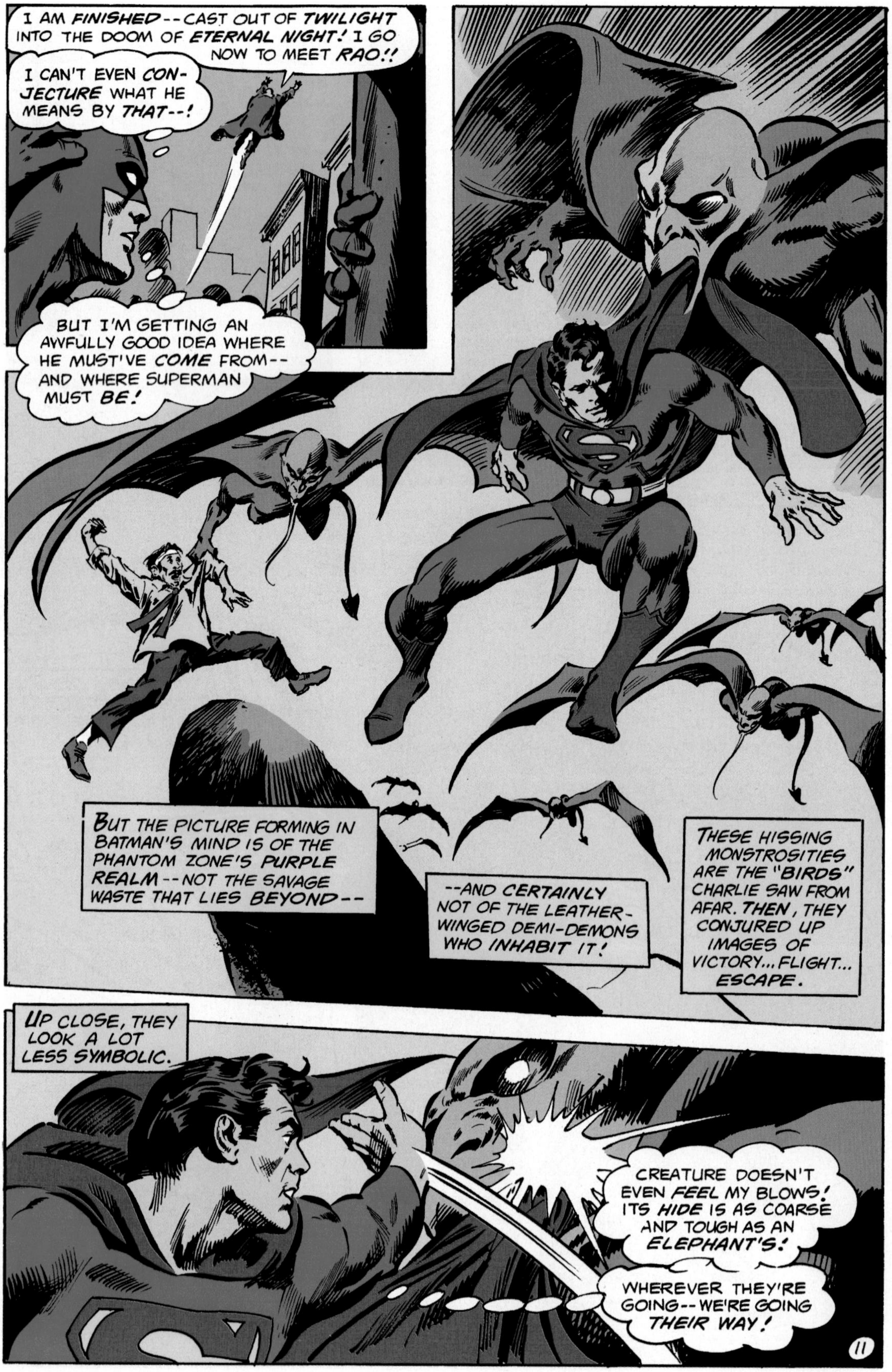

I AM FINISHED--CAST OUT OF TWILIGHT INTO THE DOOM OF ETERNAL NIGHT! I GO NOW TO MEET RAO!!
I CAN'T EVEN CONJECTURE WHAT HE MEANS BY THAT--!
BUT I'M GETTING AN AWFULLY GOOD IDEA WHERE HE MUST'VE COME FROM--AND WHERE SUPERMAN MUST BE!
BUT THE PICTURE FORMING IN BATMAN'S MIND IS OF THE PHANTOM ZONE'S PURPLE REALM--NOT THE SAVAGE WASTE THAT LIES BEYOND--
--AND CERTAINLY NOT OF THE LEATHER-WINGED DEMI-DEMONS WHO INHABIT IT!
THESE HISSING MONSTROSITIES ARE THE "BIRDS" CHARLIE SAW FROM AFAR. THEN, THEY CONJURED UP IMAGES OF VICTORY... FLIGHT... ESCAPE.
UP CLOSE, THEY LOOK A LOT LESS SYMBOLIC.
CREATURE DOESN'T EVEN FEEL MY BLOWS! ITS HIDE IS AS COARSE AND TOUGH AS AN ELEPHANT'S!
WHEREVER THEY'RE GOING--WE'RE GOING THEIR WAY!
11

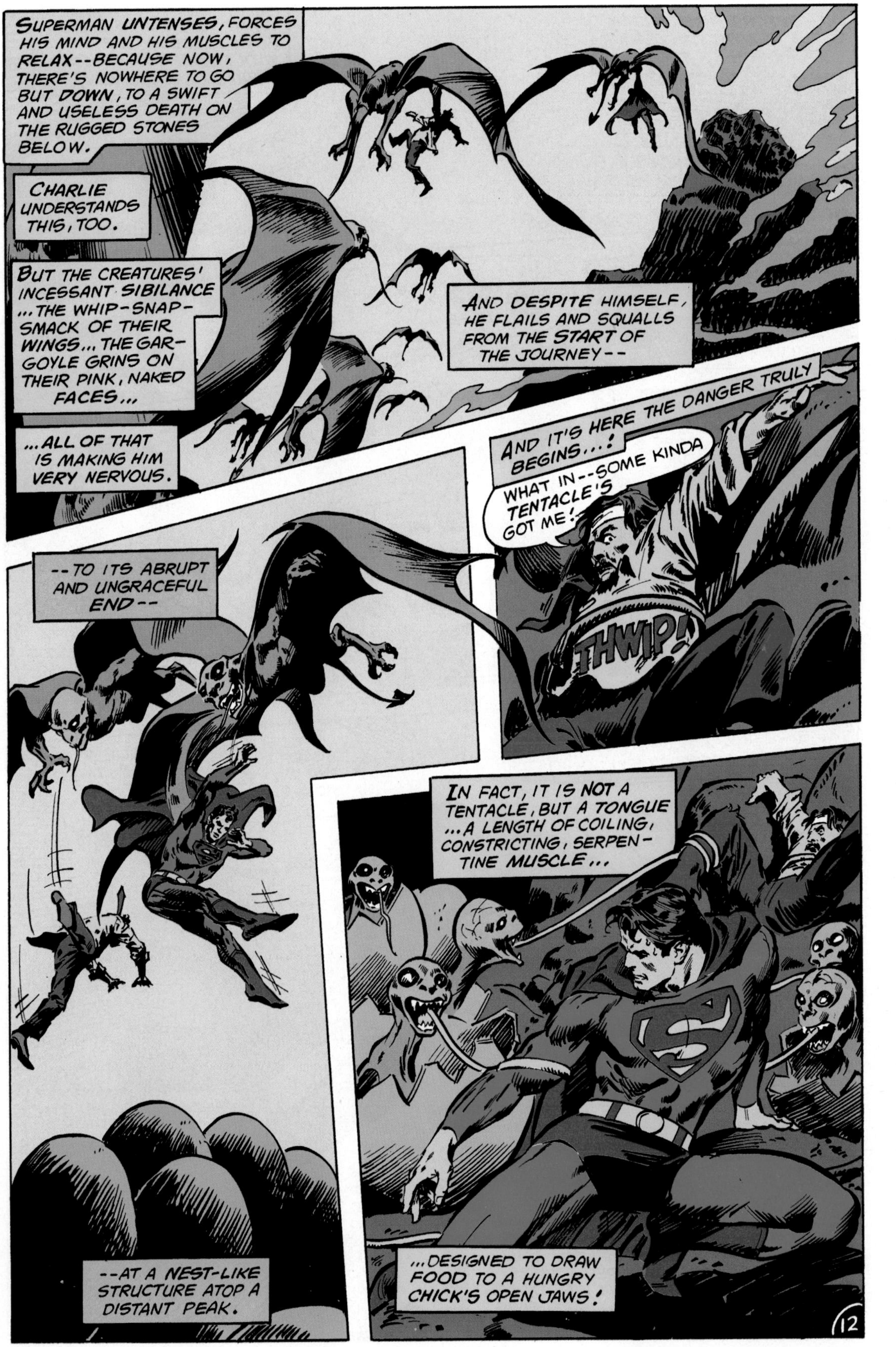
SUPERMAN UNTENSES, FORCES HIS MIND AND HIS MUSCLES TO RELAX--BECAUSE NOW, THERE'S NOWHERE TO GO BUT DOWN, TO A SWIFT AND USELESS DEATH ON THE RUGGED STONES BELOW.
CHARLIE UNDERSTANDS THIS, TOO.
BUT THE CREATURES' INCESSANT SIBILANCE ...THE WHIP-SNAP-SMACK OF THEIR WINGS... THE GARGOYLE GRINS ON THEIR PINK, NAKED FACES...
...ALL OF THAT IS MAKING HIM VERY NERVOUS.
AND DESPITE HIMSELF, HE FLAILS AND SQUALLS FROM THE START OF THE JOURNEY--
--TO ITS ABRUPT AND UNGRACEFUL END--
--AT A NEST-LIKE STRUCTURE ATOP A DISTANT PEAK.
AND IT'S HERE THE DANGER TRULY BEGINS...!
WHAT IN--SOME KINDA TENTACLE'S GOT ME!
THWIP!
IN FACT, IT IS NOT A TENTACLE, BUT A TONGUE ...A LENGTH OF COILING, CONSTRICTING, SERPENTINE MUSCLE...
...DESIGNED TO DRAW FOOD TO A HUNGRY CHICK'S OPEN JAWS!
12

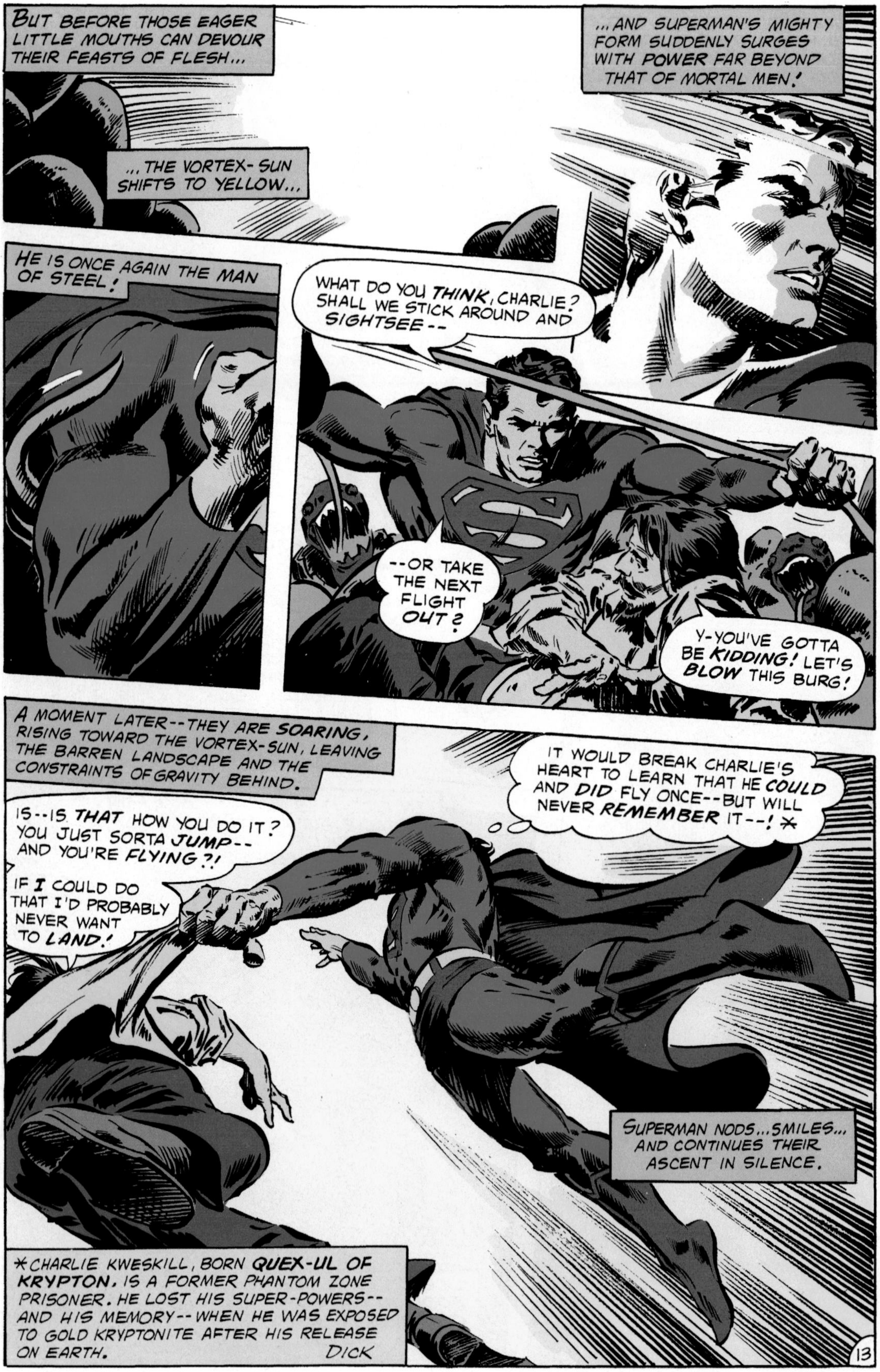

BUT BEFORE THOSE EAGER LITTLE MOUTHS CAN DEVOUR THEIR FEASTS OF FLESH...
...THE VORTEX-SUN SHIFTS TO YELLOW...
...AND SUPERMAN'S MIGHTY FORM SUDDENLY SURGES WITH POWER FAR BEYOND THAT OF MORTAL MEN!
HE IS ONCE AGAIN THE MAN OF STEEL!
WHAT DO YOU THINK, CHARLIE? SHALL WE STICK AROUND AND SIGHTSEE--
--OR TAKE THE NEXT FLIGHT OUT?
Y-YOU'VE GOTTA BE KIDDING! LET'S BLOW THIS BURG!
A MOMENT LATER--THEY ARE SOARING, RISING TOWARD THE VORTEX-SUN, LEAVING THE BARREN LANDSCAPE AND THE CONSTRAINTS OF GRAVITY BEHIND.
IS--IS THAT HOW YOU DO IT? YOU JUST SORTA JUMP-- AND YOU'RE FLYING?!
IF I COULD DO THAT I'D PROBABLY NEVER WANT TO LAND!
IT WOULD BREAK CHARLIE'S HEART TO LEARN THAT HE COULD AND DID FLY ONCE--BUT WILL NEVER REMEMBER IT--! *
SUPERMAN NODS...SMILES... AND CONTINUES THEIR ASCENT IN SILENCE.
*CHARLIE KWESKILL, BORN QUEX-UL OF KRYPTON, IS A FORMER PHANTOM ZONE PRISONER. HE LOST HIS SUPER-POWERS-- AND HIS MEMORY--WHEN HE WAS EXPOSED TO GOLD KRYPTONITE AFTER HIS RELEASE ON EARTH. DICK
13

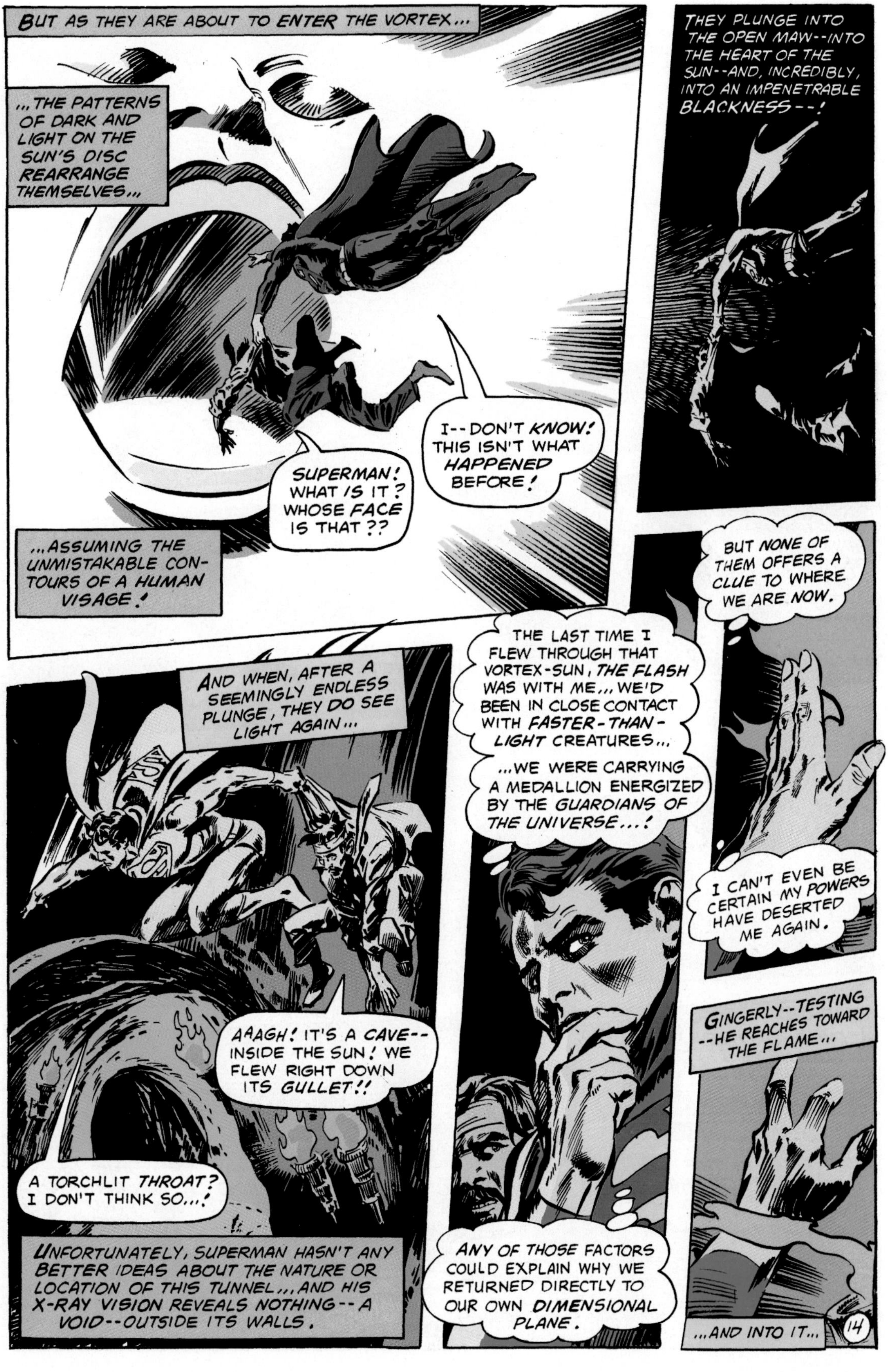

BUT AS THEY ARE ABOUT TO ENTER THE VORTEX...
...THE PATTERNS OF DARK AND LIGHT ON THE SUN'S DISC REARRANGE THEMSELVES...
...ASSUMING THE UNMISTAKABLE CONTOURS OF A HUMAN VISAGE!
SUPERMAN! WHAT IS IT? WHOSE FACE IS THAT??
I--DON'T KNOW! THIS ISN'T WHAT HAPPENED BEFORE!
THEY PLUNGE INTO THE OPEN MAW--INTO THE HEART OF THE SUN--AND, INCREDIBLY, INTO AN IMPENETRABLE BLACKNESS--!
AND WHEN, AFTER A SEEMINGLY ENDLESS PLUNGE, THEY DO SEE LIGHT AGAIN...
AAAGH! IT'S A CAVE--INSIDE THE SUN! WE FLEW RIGHT DOWN ITS GULLET!!
A TORCHLIT THROAT? I DON'T THINK SO...!
UNFORTUNATELY, SUPERMAN HASN'T ANY BETTER IDEAS ABOUT THE NATURE OR LOCATION OF THIS TUNNEL... AND HIS X-RAY VISION REVEALS NOTHING--A VOID--OUTSIDE ITS WALLS.
THE LAST TIME I FLEW THROUGH THAT VORTEX-SUN, THE FLASH WAS WITH ME... WE'D BEEN IN CLOSE CONTACT WITH FASTER-THAN-LIGHT CREATURES...
...WE WERE CARRYING A MEDALLION ENERGIZED BY THE GUARDIANS OF THE UNIVERSE...!
ANY OF THOSE FACTORS COULD EXPLAIN WHY WE RETURNED DIRECTLY TO OUR OWN DIMENSIONAL PLANE.
BUT NONE OF THEM OFFERS A CLUE TO WHERE WE ARE NOW.
I CAN'T EVEN BE CERTAIN MY POWERS HAVE DESERTED ME AGAIN.
GINGERLY--TESTING--HE REACHES TOWARD THE FLAME...
...AND INTO IT...
14

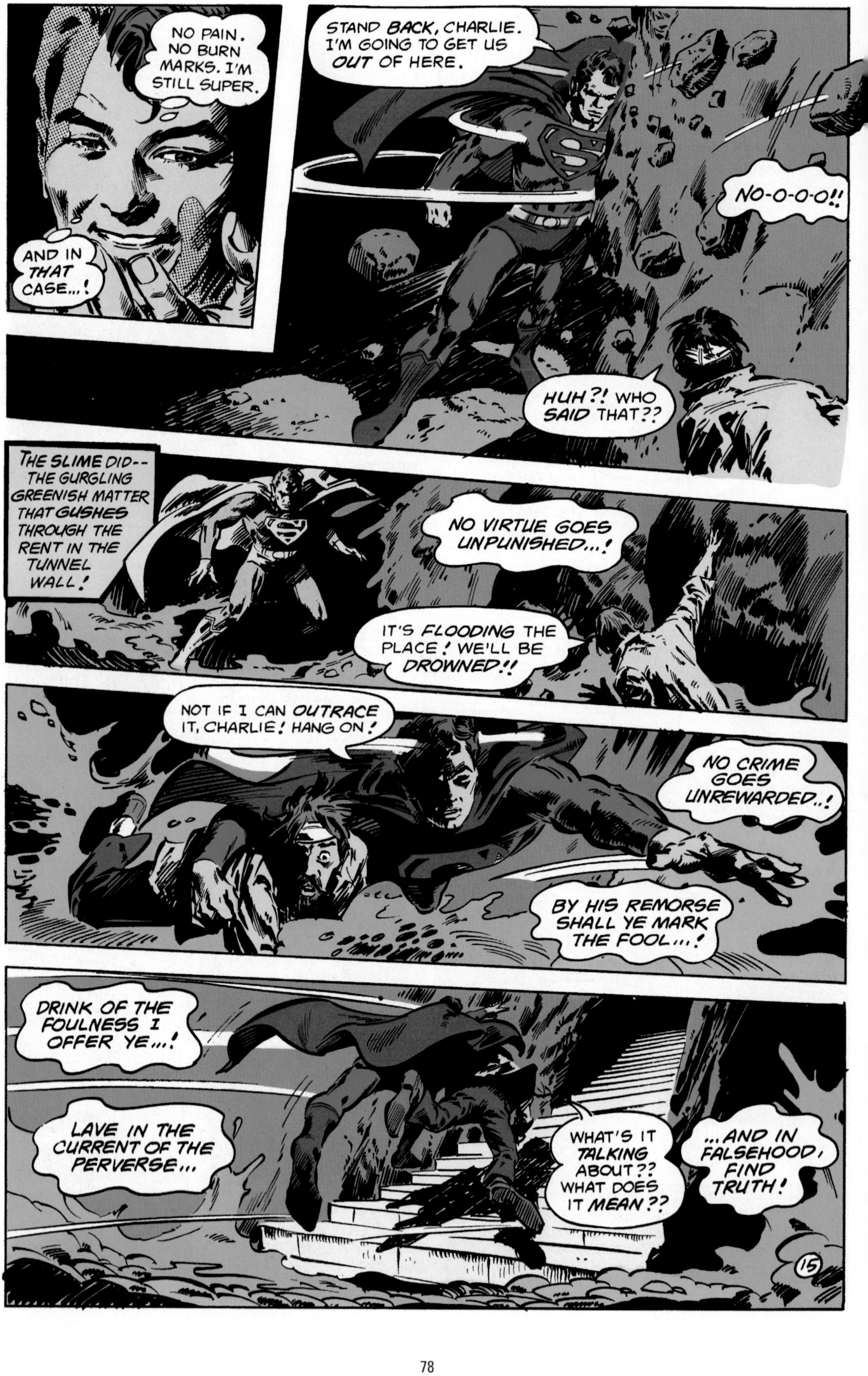
NO PAIN. NO BURN MARKS. I'M STILL SUPER.
AND IN THAT CASE...!
STAND BACK, CHARLIE. I'M GOING TO GET US OUT OF HERE.
NO-O-O-O!!
HUH?! WHO SAID THAT??
THE SLIME DID-- THE GURGLING GREENISH MATTER THAT GUSHES THROUGH THE RENT IN THE TUNNEL WALL!
NO VIRTUE GOES UNPUNISHED...!
IT'S FLOODING THE PLACE! WE'LL BE DROWNED!!
NOT IF I CAN OUTRACE IT, CHARLIE! HANG ON!
NO CRIME GOES UNREWARDED..!
BY HIS REMORSE SHALL YE MARK THE FOOL...!
DRINK OF THE FOULNESS I OFFER YE...!
LAVE IN THE CURRENT OF THE PERVERSE...
WHAT'S IT TALKING ABOUT?? WHAT DOES IT MEAN??
...AND IN FALSEHOOD, FIND TRUTH!
15

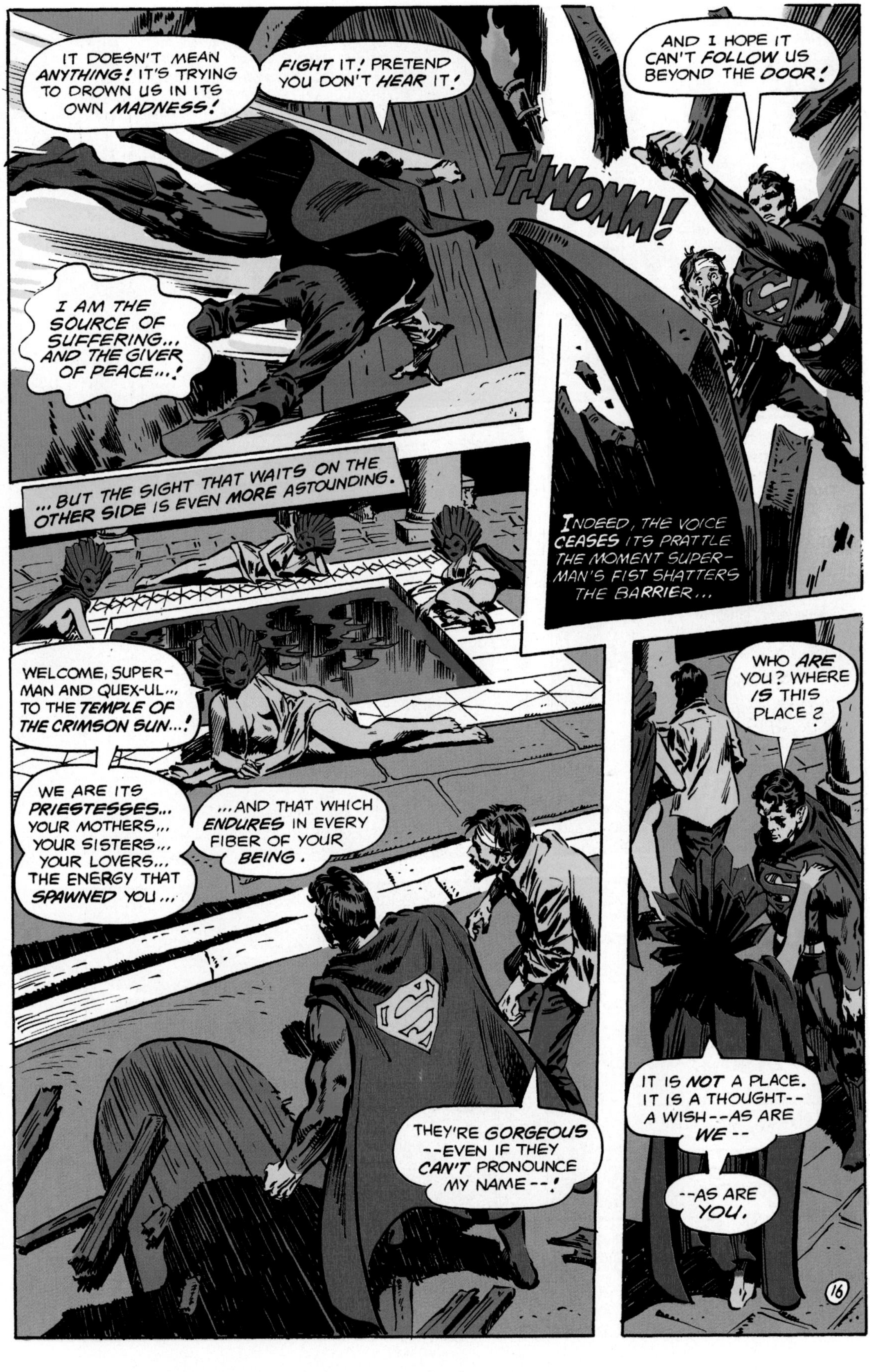
IT DOESN'T MEAN ANYTHING! IT'S TRYING TO DROWN US IN ITS OWN MADNESS!
FIGHT IT! PRETEND YOU DON'T HEAR IT!
AND I HOPE IT CAN'T FOLLOW US BEYOND THE DOOR!
THWOMM!
I AM THE SOURCE OF SUFFERING... AND THE GIVER OF PEACE...!
INDEED, THE VOICE CEASES ITS PRATTLE THE MOMENT SUPER-MAN'S FIST SHATTERS THE BARRIER...
...BUT THE SIGHT THAT WAITS ON THE OTHER SIDE IS EVEN MORE ASTOUNDING.
WELCOME, SUPER-MAN AND QUEX-UL... TO THE TEMPLE OF THE CRIMSON SUN...!
WE ARE ITS PRIESTESSES... YOUR MOTHERS... YOUR SISTERS... YOUR LOVERS... THE ENERGY THAT SPAWNED YOU...
...AND THAT WHICH ENDURES IN EVERY FIBER OF YOUR BEING.
THEY'RE GORGEOUS --EVEN IF THEY CAN'T PRONOUNCE MY NAME--!
WHO ARE YOU? WHERE IS THIS PLACE?
IT IS NOT A PLACE. IT IS A THOUGHT-- A WISH--AS ARE WE--
--AS ARE YOU.
16

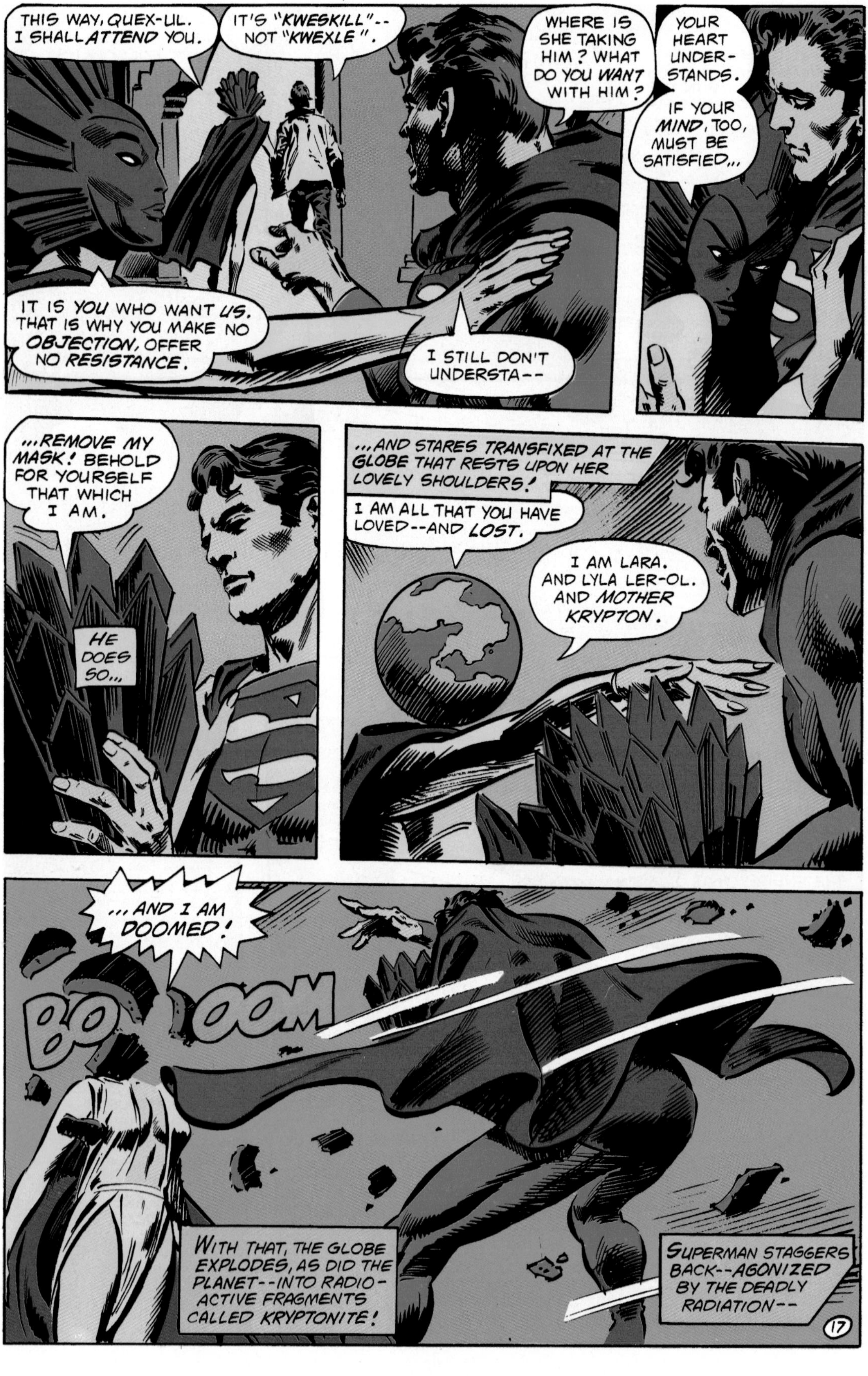
THIS WAY, QUEX-UL. I SHALL ATTEND YOU.
IT'S "KWESKILL"-- NOT "KWEXLE".
IT IS YOU WHO WANT US. THAT IS WHY YOU MAKE NO OBJECTION, OFFER NO RESISTANCE.
I STILL DON'T UNDERSTA--
WHERE IS SHE TAKING HIM? WHAT DO YOU WANT WITH HIM?
YOUR HEART UNDER-STANDS.
IF YOUR MIND, TOO, MUST BE SATISFIED,..
...REMOVE MY MASK! BEHOLD FOR YOURSELF THAT WHICH I AM.
HE DOES SO...
...AND STARES TRANSFIXED AT THE GLOBE THAT RESTS UPON HER LOVELY SHOULDERS!
I AM ALL THAT YOU HAVE LOVED--AND LOST.
I AM LARA. AND LYLA LER-OL. AND MOTHER KRYPTON.
...AND I AM DOOMED!
BOOOOM
WITH THAT, THE GLOBE EXPLODES, AS DID THE PLANET--INTO RADIO-ACTIVE FRAGMENTS CALLED KRYPTONITE!
SUPERMAN STAGGERS BACK--AGONIZED BY THE DEADLY RADIATION--
17

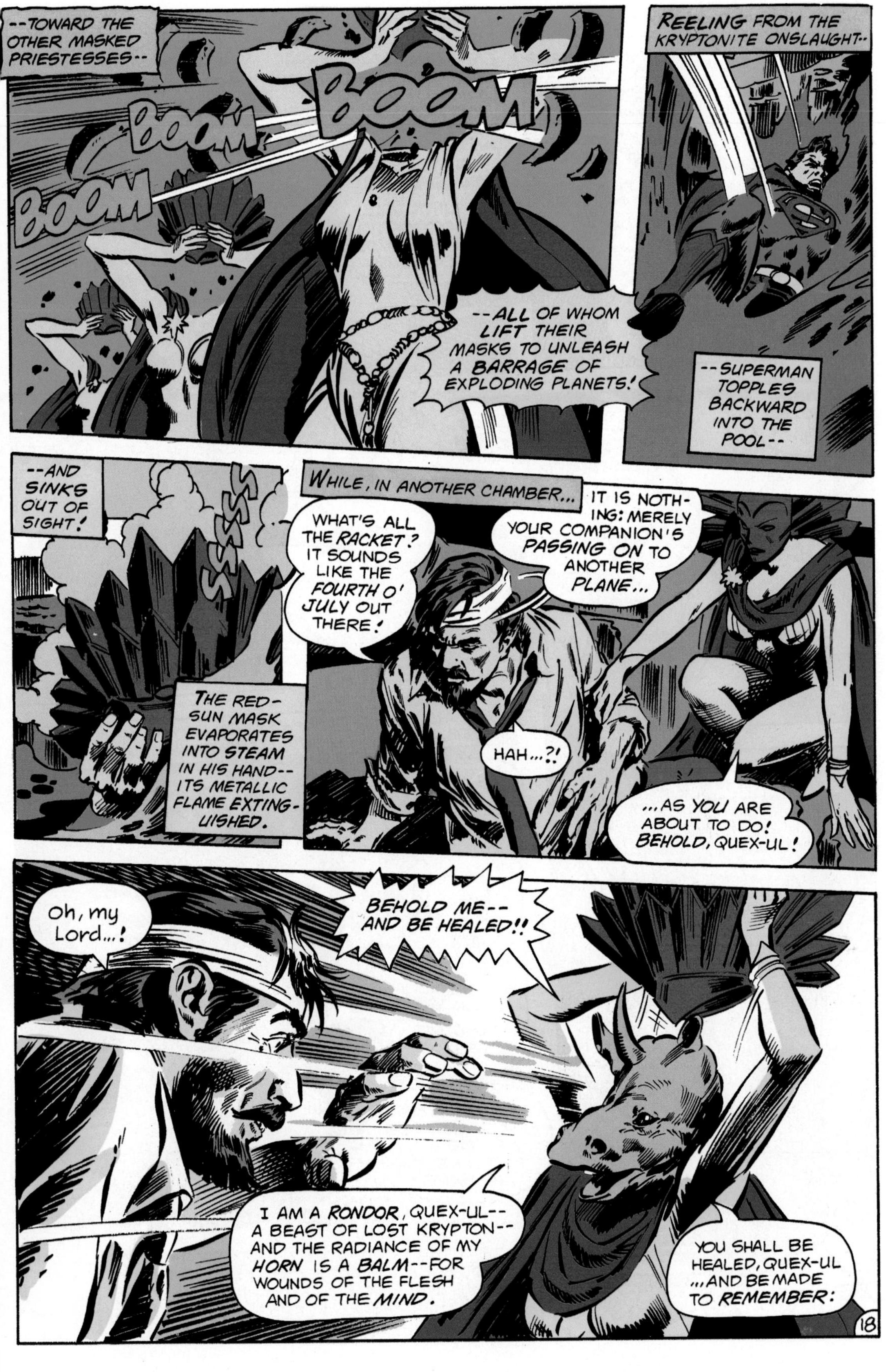
--TOWARD THE OTHER MASKED PRIESTESSES--
BOOM
BOOM
BOOM
--ALL OF WHOM LIFT THEIR MASKS TO UNLEASH A BARRAGE OF EXPLODING PLANETS!
REELING FROM THE KRYPTONITE ONSLAUGHT--
--SUPERMAN TOPPLES BACKWARD INTO THE POOL--
--AND SINKS OUT OF SIGHT!
SSSSSS
THE RED-SUN MASK EVAPORATES INTO STEAM IN HIS HAND--ITS METALLIC FLAME EXTINGUISHED.
WHILE, IN ANOTHER CHAMBER...
WHAT'S ALL THE RACKET? IT SOUNDS LIKE THE FOURTH O' JULY OUT THERE!
IT IS NOTHING; MERELY YOUR COMPANION'S PASSING ON TO ANOTHER PLANE...
HAH...?!
...AS YOU ARE ABOUT TO DO! BEHOLD, QUEX-UL!
Oh, my Lord...!
BEHOLD ME--AND BE HEALED!!
I AM A RONDOR, QUEX-UL--A BEAST OF LOST KRYPTON--AND THE RADIANCE OF MY HORN IS A BALM--FOR WOUNDS OF THE FLESH AND OF THE MIND.
YOU SHALL BE HEALED, QUEX-UL ...AND BE MADE TO REMEMBER:
18

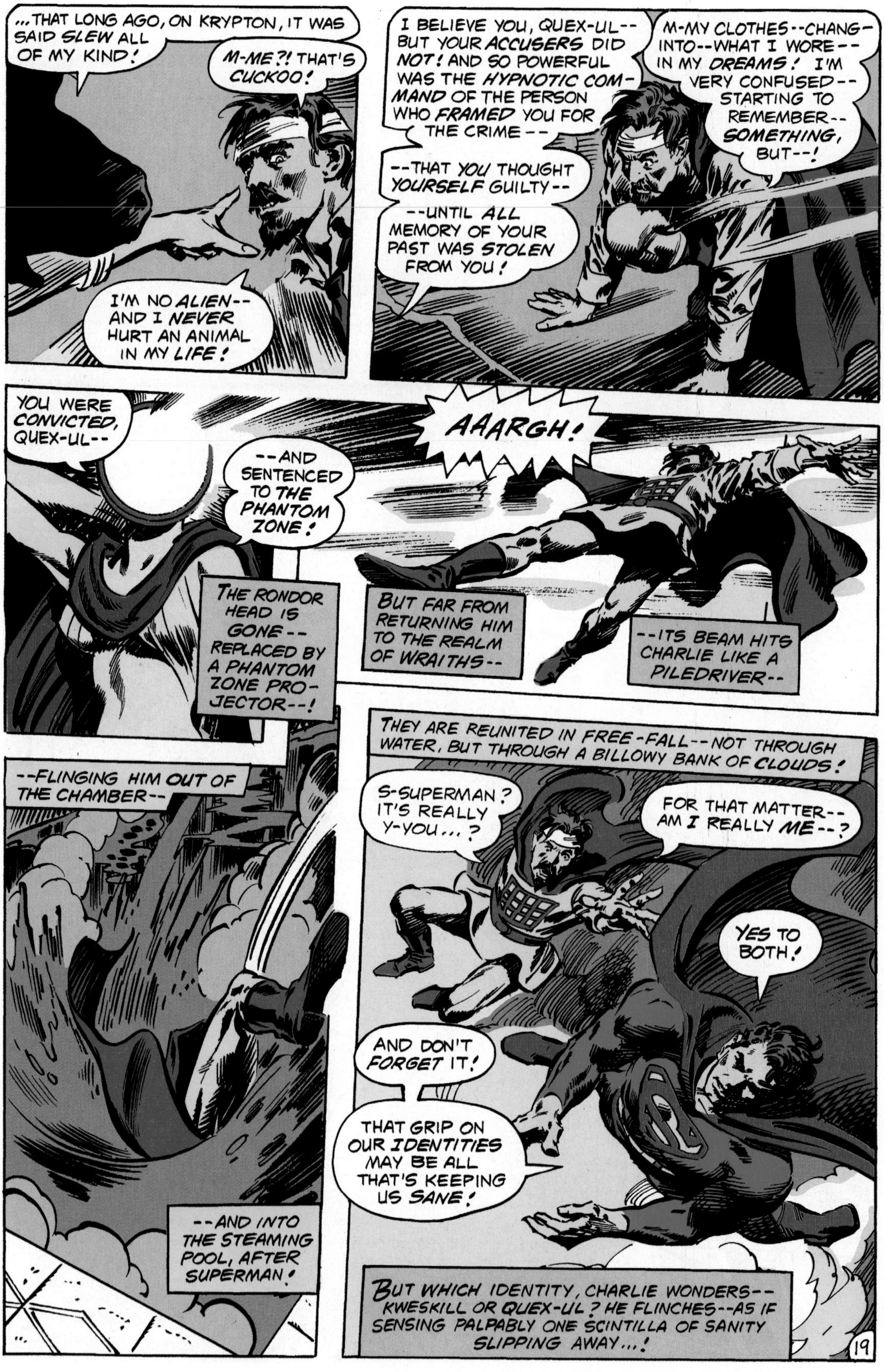
...THAT LONG AGO, ON KRYPTON, IT WAS SAID SLEW ALL OF MY KIND!
M-ME?! THAT'S CUCKOO!
I'M NO ALIEN-- AND I NEVER HURT AN ANIMAL IN MY LIFE!
I BELIEVE YOU, QUEX-UL-- BUT YOUR ACCUSERS DID NOT! AND SO POWERFUL WAS THE HYPNOTIC COMMAND OF THE PERSON WHO FRAMED YOU FOR THE CRIME--
--THAT YOU THOUGHT YOURSELF GUILTY--
--UNTIL ALL MEMORY OF YOUR PAST WAS STOLEN FROM YOU!
M-MY CLOTHES--CHANGINTO--WHAT I WORE-- IN MY DREAMS! I'M VERY CONFUSED-- STARTING TO REMEMBER-- SOMETHING, BUT--!
YOU WERE CONVICTED, QUEX-UL--
--AND SENTENCED TO THE PHANTOM ZONE!
AAARGH!
THE RONDOR HEAD IS GONE-- REPLACED BY A PHANTOM ZONE PROJECTOR--!
BUT FAR FROM RETURNING HIM TO THE REALM OF WRAITHS--
--ITS BEAM HITS CHARLIE LIKE A PILEDRIVER--
--FLINGING HIM OUT OF THE CHAMBER--
--AND INTO THE STEAMING POOL, AFTER SUPERMAN!
THEY ARE REUNITED IN FREE-FALL--NOT THROUGH WATER, BUT THROUGH A BILLOWY BANK OF CLOUDS!
S-SUPERMAN? IT'S REALLY Y-YOU...?
FOR THAT MATTER-- AM I REALLY ME--?
YES TO BOTH!
AND DON'T FORGET IT!
THAT GRIP ON OUR IDENTITIES MAY BE ALL THAT'S KEEPING US SANE!
BUT WHICH IDENTITY, CHARLIE WONDERS-- KWESKILL OR QUEX-UL? HE FLINCHES--AS IF SENSING PALPABLY ONE SCINTILLA OF SANITY SLIPPING AWAY...!
19

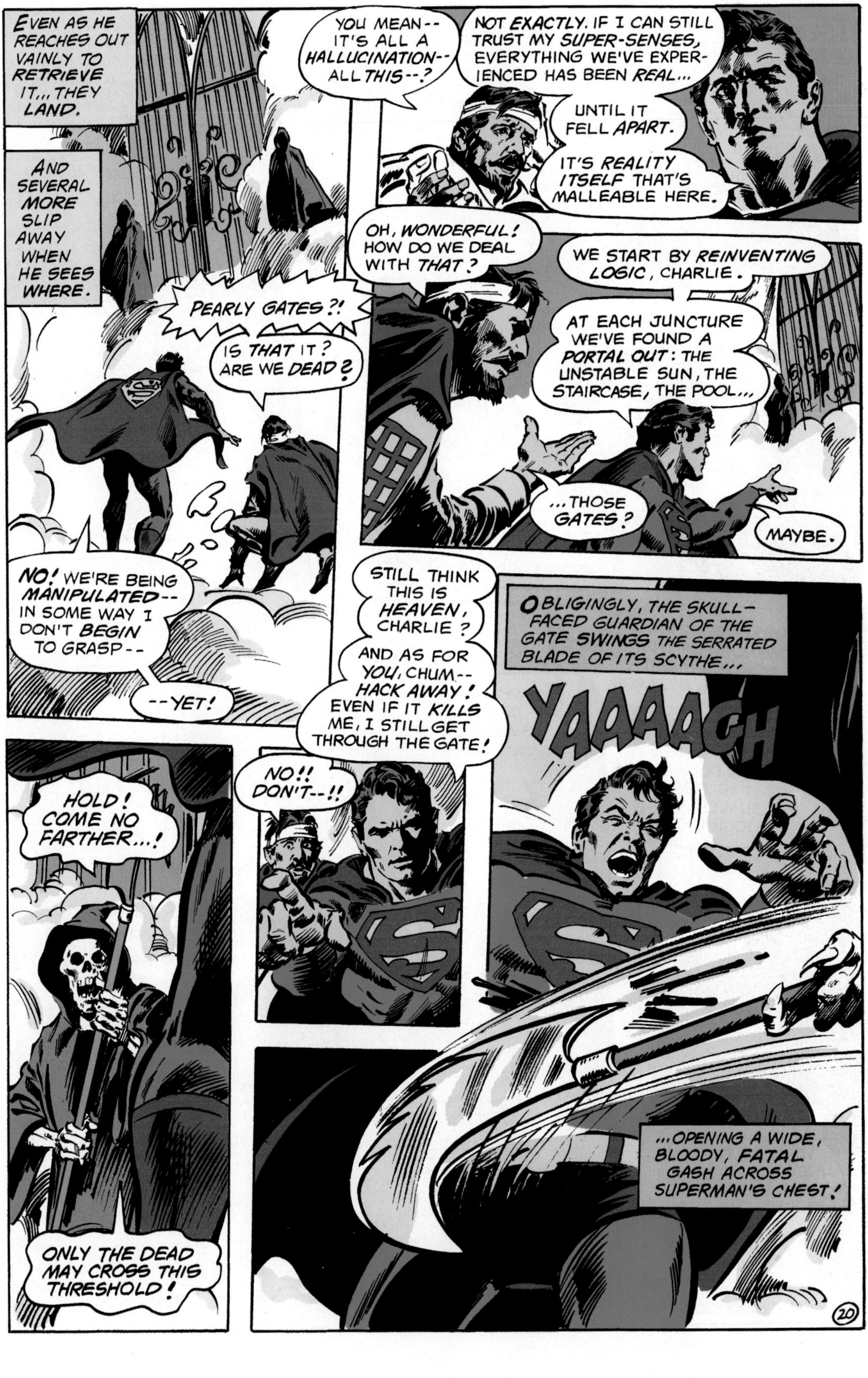
EVEN AS HE REACHES OUT VAINLY TO RETRIEVE IT... THEY LAND.
AND SEVERAL MORE SLIP AWAY WHEN HE SEES WHERE.
YOU MEAN-- IT'S ALL A HALLUCINATION-- ALL THIS--?
NOT EXACTLY. IF I CAN STILL TRUST MY SUPER-SENSES, EVERYTHING WE'VE EXPERIENCED HAS BEEN REAL...
UNTIL IT FELL APART.
IT'S REALITY ITSELF THAT'S MALLEABLE HERE.
PEARLY GATES?!
IS THAT IT? ARE WE DEAD?
NO! WE'RE BEING MANIPULATED-- IN SOME WAY I DON'T BEGIN TO GRASP--
--YET!
OH, WONDERFUL! HOW DO WE DEAL WITH THAT?
WE START BY REINVENTING LOGIC, CHARLIE.
AT EACH JUNCTURE WE'VE FOUND A PORTAL OUT: THE UNSTABLE SUN, THE STAIRCASE, THE POOL...
...THOSE GATES?
MAYBE.
HOLD! COME NO FARTHER...!
ONLY THE DEAD MAY CROSS THIS THRESHOLD!
STILL THINK THIS IS HEAVEN, CHARLIE?
AND AS FOR YOU, CHUM-- HACK AWAY! EVEN IF IT KILLS ME, I STILL GET THROUGH THE GATE!
NO!! DON'T--!!
OBLIGINGLY, THE SKULL-FACED GUARDIAN OF THE GATE SWINGS THE SERRATED BLADE OF ITS SCYTHE...
YAAAAGH
...OPENING A WIDE, BLOODY, FATAL GASH ACROSS SUPERMAN'S CHEST!
20

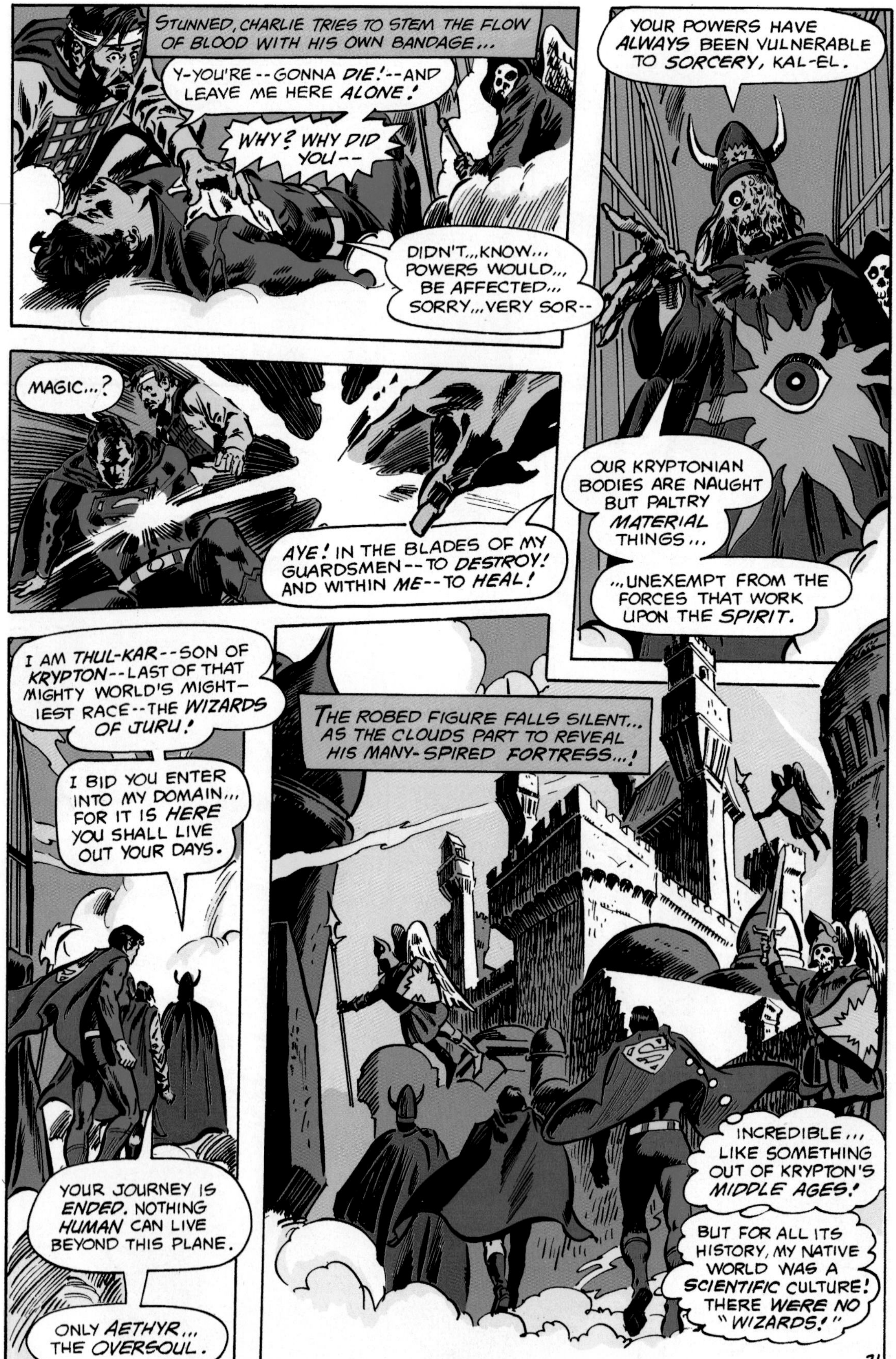
STUNNED, CHARLIE TRIES TO STEM THE FLOW OF BLOOD WITH HIS OWN BANDAGE...
Y-YOU'RE--GONNA DIE!--AND LEAVE ME HERE ALONE!
WHY? WHY DID YOU--
DIDN'T...KNOW... POWERS WOULD... BE AFFECTED... SORRY...VERY SOR--
YOUR POWERS HAVE ALWAYS BEEN VULNERABLE TO SORCERY, KAL-EL.
MAGIC...?
AYE! IN THE BLADES OF MY GUARDSMEN--TO DESTROY! AND WITHIN ME--TO HEAL!
OUR KRYPTONIAN BODIES ARE NAUGHT BUT PALTRY MATERIAL THINGS...
...UNEXEMPT FROM THE FORCES THAT WORK UPON THE SPIRIT.
I AM THUL-KAR--SON OF KRYPTON--LAST OF THAT MIGHTY WORLD'S MIGHTIEST RACE--THE WIZARDS OF JURU!
I BID YOU ENTER INTO MY DOMAIN... FOR IT IS HERE YOU SHALL LIVE OUT YOUR DAYS.
YOUR JOURNEY IS ENDED. NOTHING HUMAN CAN LIVE BEYOND THIS PLANE.
ONLY AETHYR... THE OVERSOUL.
THE ROBED FIGURE FALLS SILENT... AS THE CLOUDS PART TO REVEAL HIS MANY-SPIRED FORTRESS...!
INCREDIBLE... LIKE SOMETHING OUT OF KRYPTON'S MIDDLE AGES!
BUT FOR ALL ITS HISTORY, MY NATIVE WORLD WAS A SCIENTIFIC CULTURE! THERE WERE NO "WIZARDS!"
21

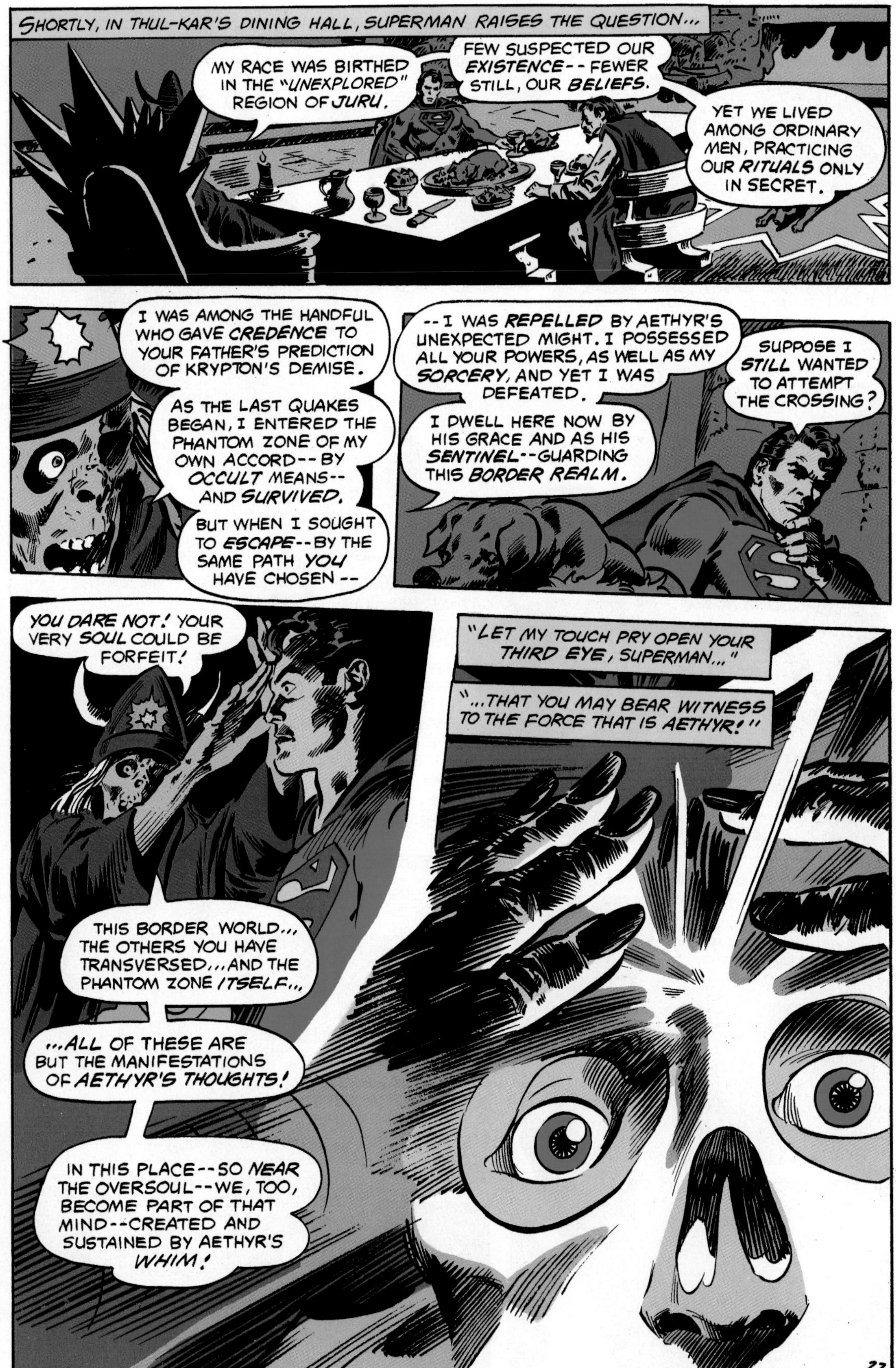
SHORTLY, IN THUL-KAR'S DINING HALL, SUPERMAN RAISES THE QUESTION...
MY RACE WAS BIRTHED IN THE "UNEXPLORED" REGION OF JURU.
FEW SUSPECTED OUR EXISTENCE-- FEWER STILL, OUR BELIEFS.
YET WE LIVED AMONG ORDINARY MEN, PRACTICING OUR RITUALS ONLY IN SECRET.
I WAS AMONG THE HANDFUL WHO GAVE CREDENCE TO YOUR FATHER'S PREDICTION OF KRYPTON'S DEMISE.
AS THE LAST QUAKES BEGAN, I ENTERED THE PHANTOM ZONE OF MY OWN ACCORD-- BY OCCULT MEANS-- AND SURVIVED.
BUT WHEN I SOUGHT TO ESCAPE-- BY THE SAME PATH YOU HAVE CHOSEN --
-- I WAS REPELLED BY AETHYR'S UNEXPECTED MIGHT. I POSSESSED ALL YOUR POWERS, AS WELL AS MY SORCERY, AND YET I WAS DEFEATED.
I DWELL HERE NOW BY HIS GRACE AND AS HIS SENTINEL--GUARDING THIS BORDER REALM.
SUPPOSE I STILL WANTED TO ATTEMPT THE CROSSING?
YOU DARE NOT! YOUR VERY SOUL COULD BE FORFEIT!
THIS BORDER WORLD... THE OTHERS YOU HAVE TRANSVERSED... AND THE PHANTOM ZONE ITSELF...
...ALL OF THESE ARE BUT THE MANIFESTATIONS OF AETHYR'S THOUGHTS!
IN THIS PLACE--SO NEAR THE OVERSOUL--WE, TOO, BECOME PART OF THAT MIND--CREATED AND SUSTAINED BY AETHYR'S WHIM!
"LET MY TOUCH PRY OPEN YOUR THIRD EYE, SUPERMAN..."
"...THAT YOU MAY BEAR WITNESS TO THE FORCE THAT IS AETHYR!"
22

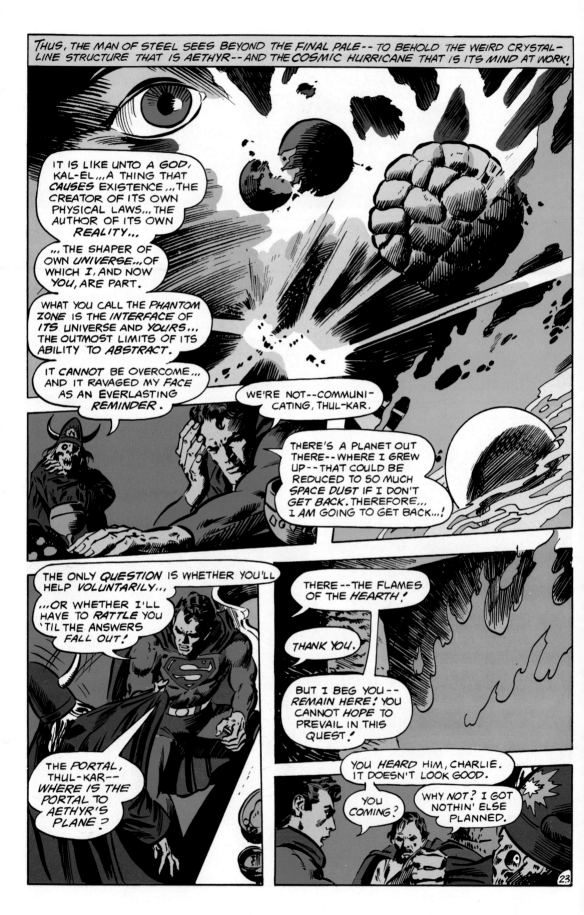

THUS, THE MAN OF STEEL SEES BEYOND THE FINAL PALE-- TO BEHOLD THE WEIRD CRYSTALLINE STRUCTURE THAT IS AETHYR-- AND THE COSMIC HURRICANE THAT IS ITS MIND AT WORK!

IT IS LIKE UNTO A GOD, KAL-EL... A THING THAT *CAUSES* EXISTENCE... THE CREATOR OF ITS OWN PHYSICAL LAWS... THE AUTHOR OF ITS OWN *REALITY*...

... THE SHAPER OF OWN *UNIVERSE*... OF WHICH *I*, AND NOW *YOU*, ARE PART.

WHAT YOU CALL THE *PHANTOM ZONE* IS THE *INTERFACE* OF *ITS* UNIVERSE AND *YOURS*... THE OUTMOST LIMITS OF ITS ABILITY TO *ABSTRACT.*

IT *CANNOT* BE OVERCOME... AND IT RAVAGED MY *FACE* AS AN EVERLASTING *REMINDER.*

WE'RE NOT--COMMUNICATING, THUL-KAR.

THERE'S A PLANET OUT THERE-- WHERE I GREW UP-- THAT COULD BE REDUCED TO SO MUCH *SPACE DUST* IF I DON'T *GET BACK.* THEREFORE... I AM GOING TO GET BACK...!

THE ONLY *QUESTION* IS WHETHER YOU'LL HELP *VOLUNTARILY*...

...OR WHETHER I'LL HAVE TO *RATTLE* YOU 'TIL THE ANSWERS *FALL OUT!*

THE *PORTAL*, THUL-KAR-- *WHERE IS* THE PORTAL TO AETHYR'S PLANE ?

THERE --THE FLAMES OF THE *HEARTH !*

THANK YOU.

BUT I BEG YOU-- *REMAIN HERE !* YOU CANNOT *HOPE* TO PREVAIL IN THIS *QUEST !*

YOU *HEARD* HIM, CHARLIE. IT DOESN'T LOOK GOOD.

YOU COMING ?

WHY *NOT* ? I GOT NOTHIN' ELSE PLANNED.

23

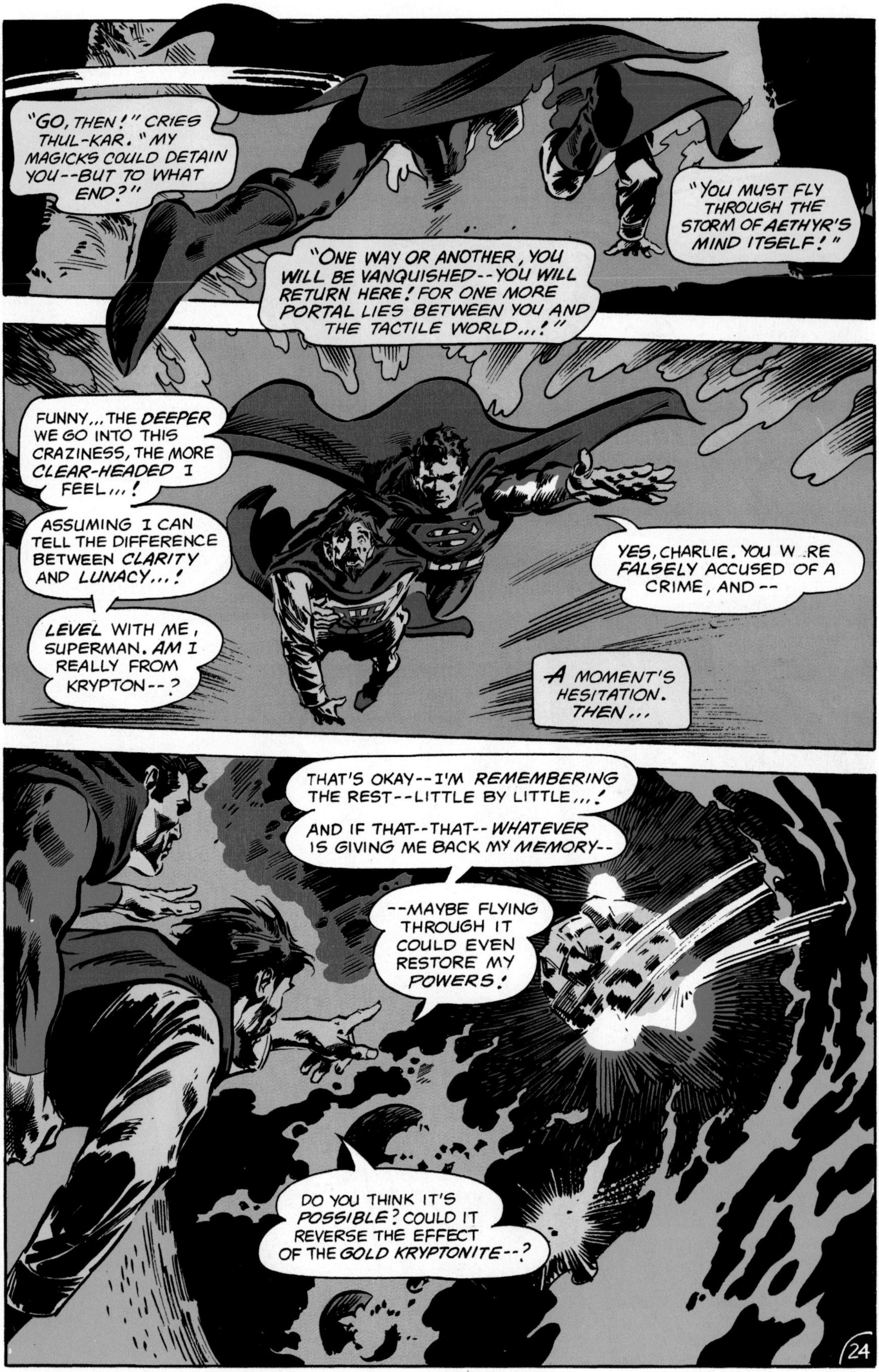
"GO, THEN!" CRIES THUL-KAR. "MY MAGICKS COULD DETAIN YOU--BUT TO WHAT END?"
"ONE WAY OR ANOTHER, YOU WILL BE VANQUISHED--YOU WILL RETURN HERE! FOR ONE MORE PORTAL LIES BETWEEN YOU AND THE TACTILE WORLD...!"
"YOU MUST FLY THROUGH THE STORM OF AETHYR'S MIND ITSELF!"
FUNNY... THE DEEPER WE GO INTO THIS CRAZINESS, THE MORE CLEAR-HEADED I FEEL...!
ASSUMING I CAN TELL THE DIFFERENCE BETWEEN CLARITY AND LUNACY...!
LEVEL WITH ME, SUPERMAN. AM I REALLY FROM KRYPTON--?
YES, CHARLIE. YOU W RE FALSELY ACCUSED OF A CRIME, AND--
A MOMENT'S HESITATION. THEN...
THAT'S OKAY--I'M REMEMBERING THE REST--LITTLE BY LITTLE...!
AND IF THAT--THAT--WHATEVER IS GIVING ME BACK MY MEMORY--
--MAYBE FLYING THROUGH IT COULD EVEN RESTORE MY POWERS!
DO YOU THINK IT'S POSSIBLE? COULD IT REVERSE THE EFFECT OF THE GOLD KRYPTONITE--?
24

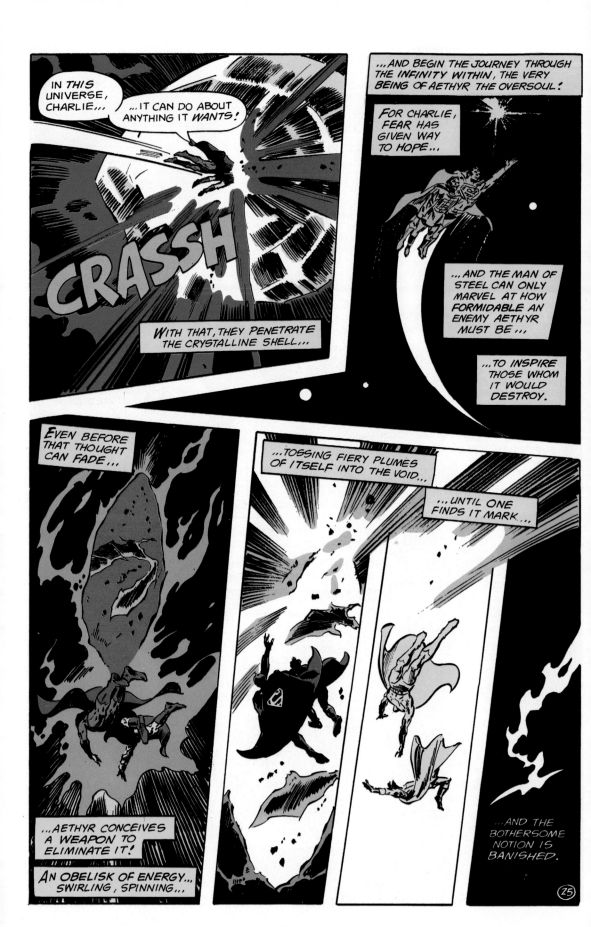

IN *THIS* UNIVERSE, CHARLIE...

...IT CAN DO ABOUT ANYTHING IT *WANTS!*

CRASSH

WITH THAT, THEY PENETRATE THE CRYSTALLINE SHELL...

...AND BEGIN THE JOURNEY THROUGH THE *INFINITY WITHIN*, THE VERY BEING OF AETHYR THE OVERSOUL!

FOR CHARLIE, FEAR HAS GIVEN WAY TO HOPE...

...AND THE MAN OF STEEL CAN ONLY MARVEL AT HOW FORMIDABLE AN ENEMY AETHYR MUST BE...

...TO INSPIRE THOSE WHOM IT WOULD DESTROY.

EVEN BEFORE THAT THOUGHT CAN FADE...

...AETHYR CONCEIVES A WEAPON TO ELIMINATE IT!

AN OBELISK OF ENERGY... SWIRLING, SPINNING...

...TOSSING FIERY PLUMES OF ITSELF INTO THE VOID...

...UNTIL ONE FINDS IT MARK...

...AND THE BOTHERSOME NOTION IS BANISHED.

25

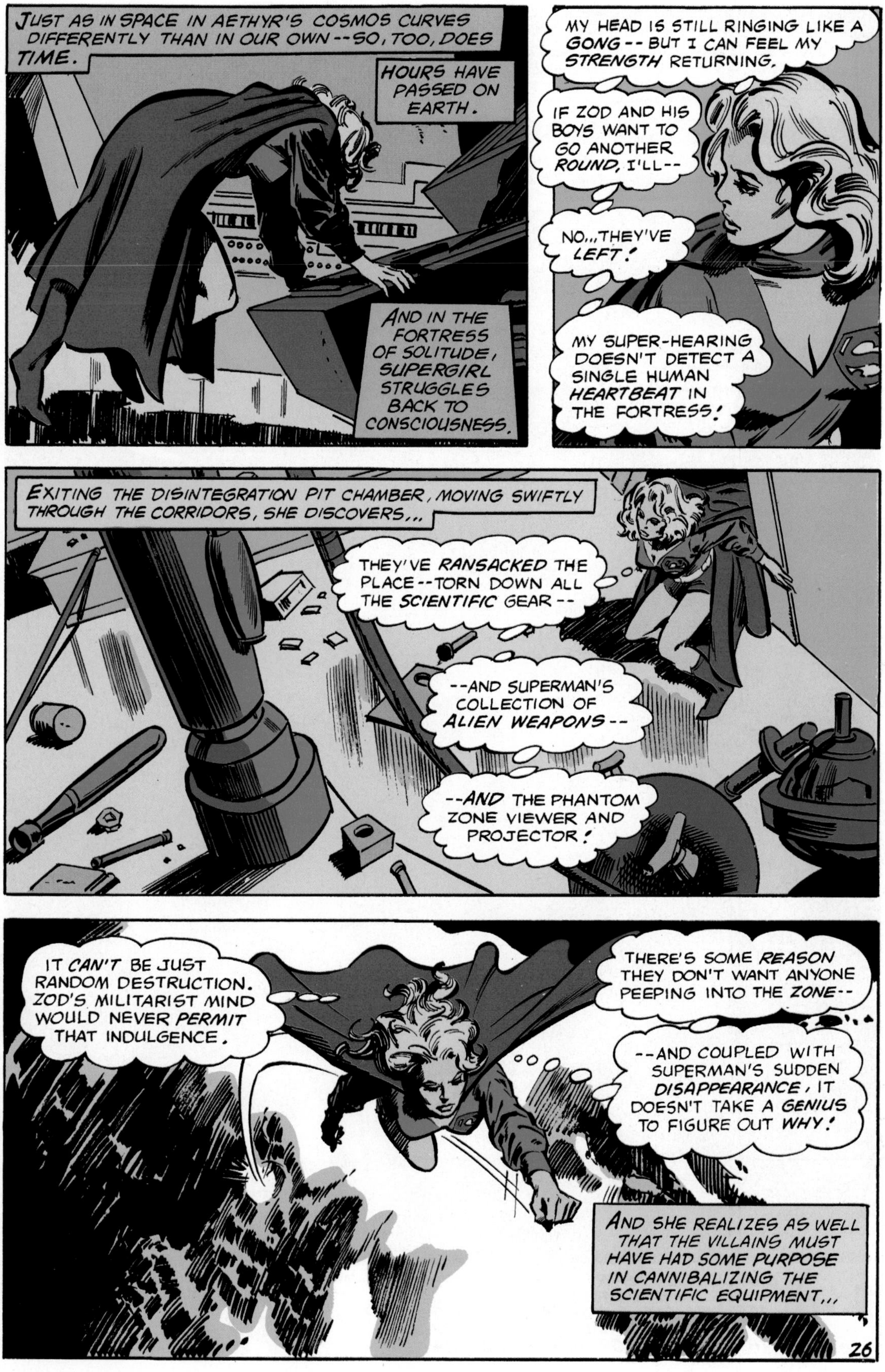
JUST AS IN SPACE IN AETHYR'S COSMOS CURVES DIFFERENTLY THAN IN OUR OWN --SO, TOO, DOES TIME.
HOURS HAVE PASSED ON EARTH.
AND IN THE FORTRESS OF SOLITUDE, SUPERGIRL STRUGGLES BACK TO CONSCIOUSNESS.
MY HEAD IS STILL RINGING LIKE A GONG -- BUT I CAN FEEL MY STRENGTH RETURNING.
IF ZOD AND HIS BOYS WANT TO GO ANOTHER ROUND, I'LL--
NO...THEY'VE LEFT!
MY SUPER-HEARING DOESN'T DETECT A SINGLE HUMAN HEARTBEAT IN THE FORTRESS!
EXITING THE DISINTEGRATION PIT CHAMBER, MOVING SWIFTLY THROUGH THE CORRIDORS, SHE DISCOVERS...
THEY'VE RANSACKED THE PLACE--TORN DOWN ALL THE SCIENTIFIC GEAR--
--AND SUPERMAN'S COLLECTION OF ALIEN WEAPONS--
--AND THE PHANTOM ZONE VIEWER AND PROJECTOR!
IT CAN'T BE JUST RANDOM DESTRUCTION. ZOD'S MILITARIST MIND WOULD NEVER PERMIT THAT INDULGENCE.
THERE'S SOME REASON THEY DON'T WANT ANYONE PEEPING INTO THE ZONE--
--AND COUPLED WITH SUPERMAN'S SUDDEN DISAPPEARANCE, IT DOESN'T TAKE A GENIUS TO FIGURE OUT WHY!
AND SHE REALIZES AS WELL THAT THE VILLAINS MUST HAVE HAD SOME PURPOSE IN CANNIBALIZING THE SCIENTIFIC EQUIPMENT...
26

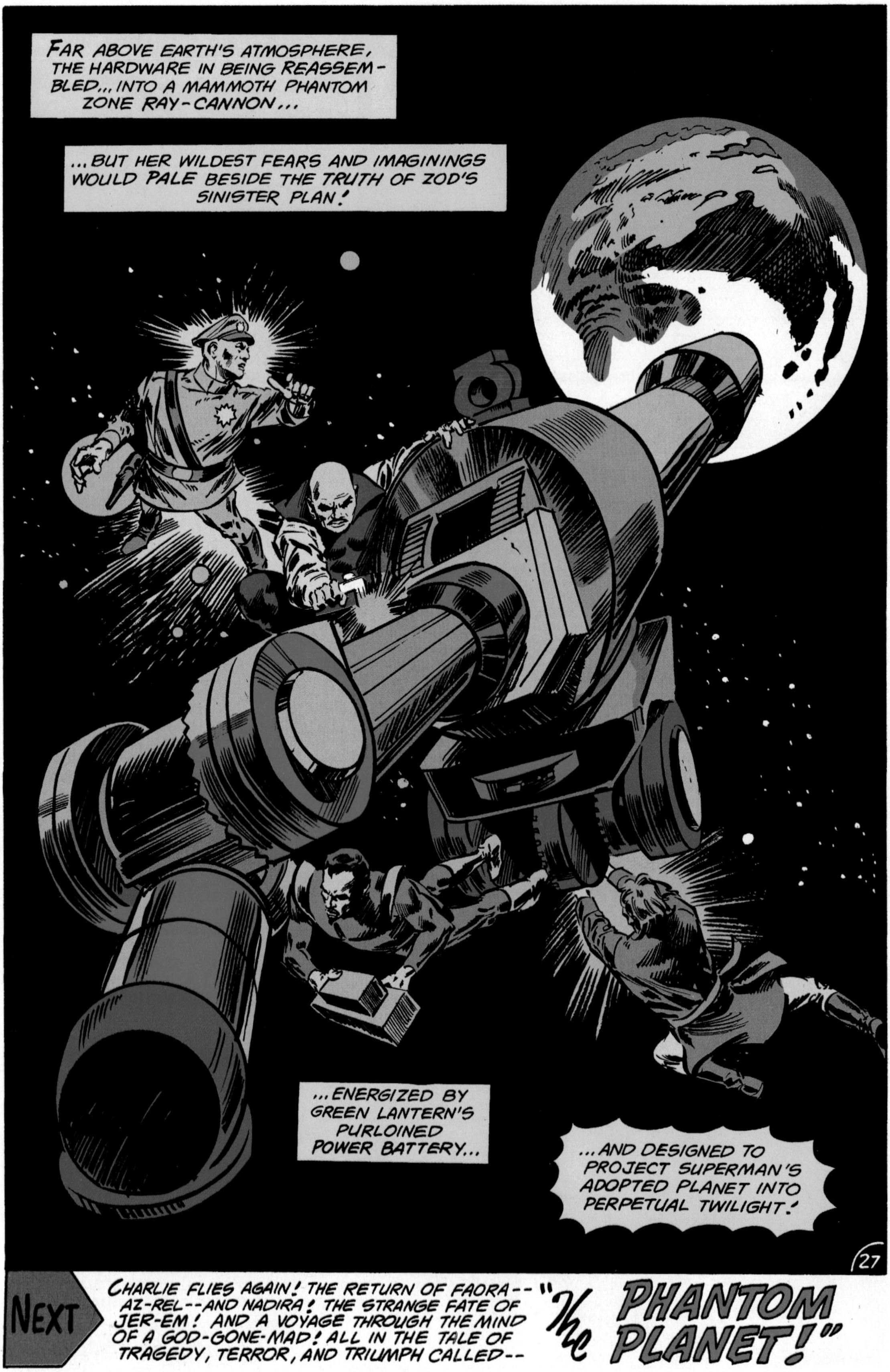
FAR ABOVE EARTH'S ATMOSPHERE, THE HARDWARE IN BEING REASSEMBLED... INTO A MAMMOTH PHANTOM ZONE RAY-CANNON...
...BUT HER WILDEST FEARS AND IMAGININGS WOULD PALE BESIDE THE TRUTH OF ZOD'S SINISTER PLAN!
...ENERGIZED BY GREEN LANTERN'S PURLOINED POWER BATTERY...
...AND DESIGNED TO PROJECT SUPERMAN'S ADOPTED PLANET INTO PERPETUAL TWILIGHT!
27
NEXT
CHARLIE FLIES AGAIN! THE RETURN OF FAORA--AZ-REL--AND NADIRA! THE STRANGE FATE OF JER-EM! AND A VOYAGE THROUGH THE MIND OF A GOD-GONE-MAD! ALL IN THE TALE OF TRAGEDY, TERROR, AND TRIUMPH CALLED--
"The PHANTOM PLANET!"

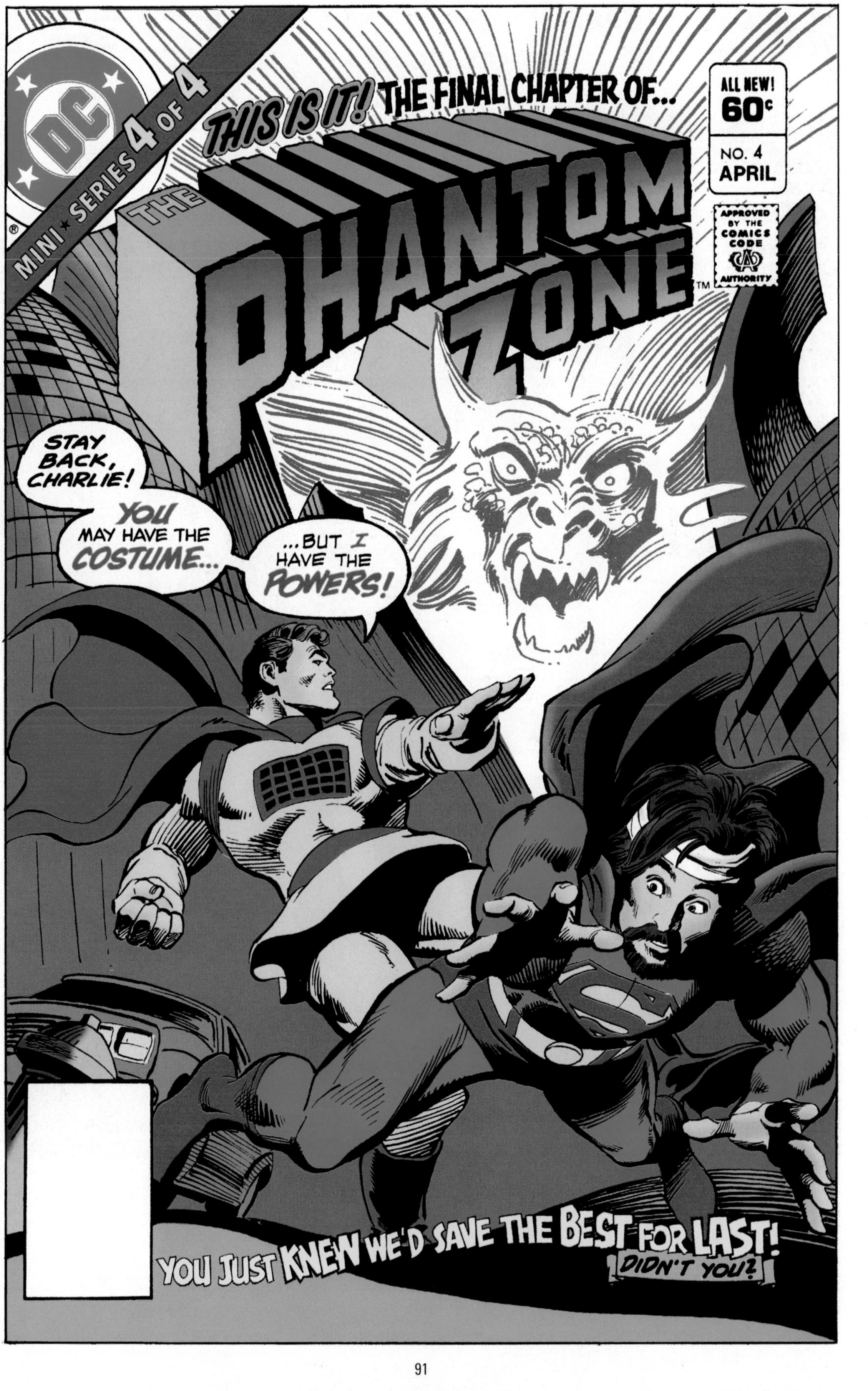
DC
MINI ★ SERIES 4 OF 4
THIS IS IT! THE FINAL CHAPTER OF...
THE PHANTOM ZONE™
ALL NEW! 60¢
NO. 4 APRIL
APPROVED BY THE COMICS CODE AUTHORITY
STAY BACK, CHARLIE!
YOU MAY HAVE THE COSTUME...
...BUT I HAVE THE POWERS!
YOU JUST KNEW WE'D SAVE THE BEST FOR LAST!
DIDN'T YOU?

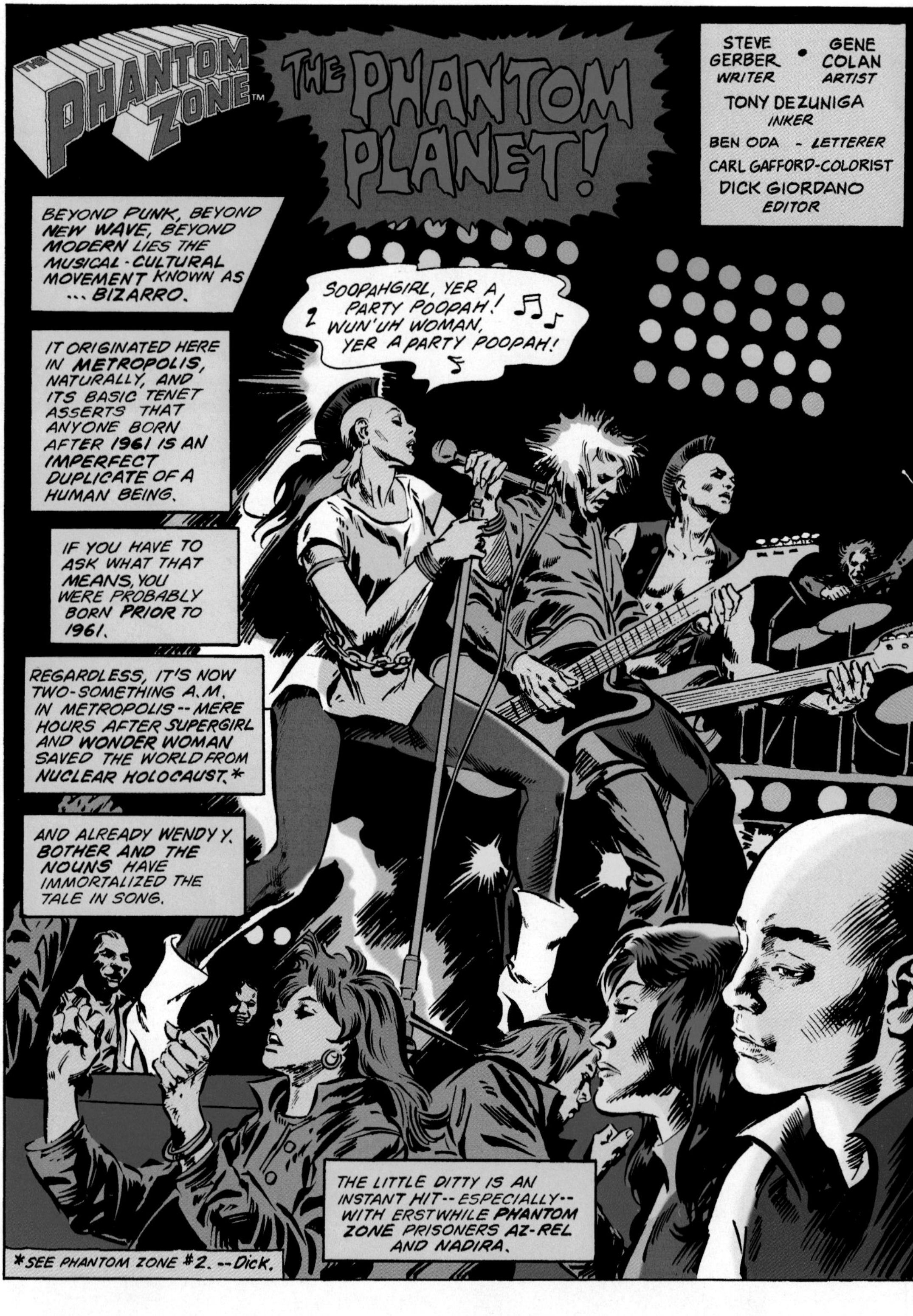
THE PHANTOM ZONE™
THE PHANTOM PLANET!
STEVE GERBER WRITER • GENE COLAN ARTIST
TONY DEZUNIGA INKER
BEN ODA - LETTERER
CARL GAFFORD-COLORIST
DICK GIORDANO EDITOR
BEYOND PUNK, BEYOND NEW WAVE, BEYOND MODERN LIES THE MUSICAL-CULTURAL MOVEMENT KNOWN AS ... BIZARRO.
SOOPAHGIRL, YER A PARTY POOPAH! WUN'UH WOMAN, YER A PARTY POOPAH!
IT ORIGINATED HERE IN METROPOLIS, NATURALLY, AND ITS BASIC TENET ASSERTS THAT ANYONE BORN AFTER 1961 IS AN IMPERFECT DUPLICATE OF A HUMAN BEING.
IF YOU HAVE TO ASK WHAT THAT MEANS, YOU WERE PROBABLY BORN PRIOR TO 1961.
REGARDLESS, IT'S NOW TWO-SOMETHING A.M. IN METROPOLIS -- MERE HOURS AFTER SUPERGIRL AND WONDER WOMAN SAVED THE WORLD FROM NUCLEAR HOLOCAUST.*
AND ALREADY WENDY Y. BOTHER AND THE NOUNS HAVE IMMORTALIZED THE TALE IN SONG.
THE LITTLE DITTY IS AN INSTANT HIT -- ESPECIALLY -- WITH ERSTWHILE PHANTOM ZONE PRISONERS AZ-REL AND NADIRA.
*SEE PHANTOM ZONE #2. --Dick.

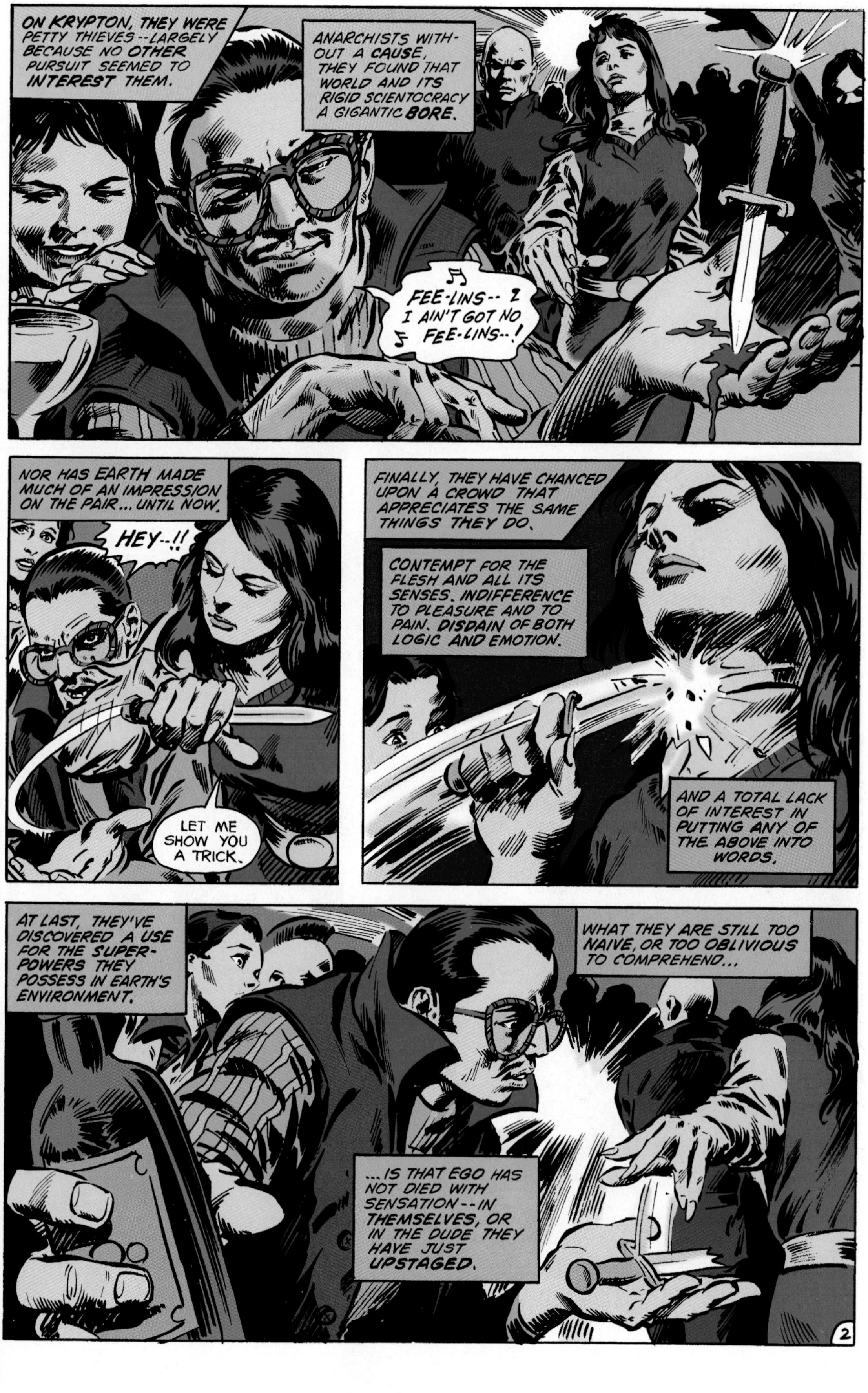
ON KRYPTON, THEY WERE PETTY THIEVES--LARGELY BECAUSE NO OTHER PURSUIT SEEMED TO INTEREST THEM.
ANARCHISTS WITH-OUT A CAUSE, THEY FOUND THAT WORLD AND ITS RIGID SCIENTOCRACY A GIGANTIC BORE.
FEE-LINS-- I AIN'T GOT NO FEE-LINS--!
NOR HAS EARTH MADE MUCH OF AN IMPRESSION ON THE PAIR... UNTIL NOW.
HEY--!!
LET ME SHOW YOU A TRICK.
FINALLY, THEY HAVE CHANCED UPON A CROWD THAT APPRECIATES THE SAME THINGS THEY DO.
CONTEMPT FOR THE FLESH AND ALL ITS SENSES. INDIFFERENCE TO PLEASURE AND TO PAIN. DISDAIN OF BOTH LOGIC AND EMOTION.
AND A TOTAL LACK OF INTEREST IN PUTTING ANY OF THE ABOVE INTO WORDS.
AT LAST, THEY'VE DISCOVERED A USE FOR THE SUPER-POWERS THEY POSSESS IN EARTH'S ENVIRONMENT.
WHAT THEY ARE STILL TOO NAIVE, OR TOO OBLIVIOUS TO COMPREHEND...
...IS THAT EGO HAS NOT DIED WITH SENSATION--IN THEMSELVES, OR IN THE DUDE THEY HAVE JUST UPSTAGED.
2

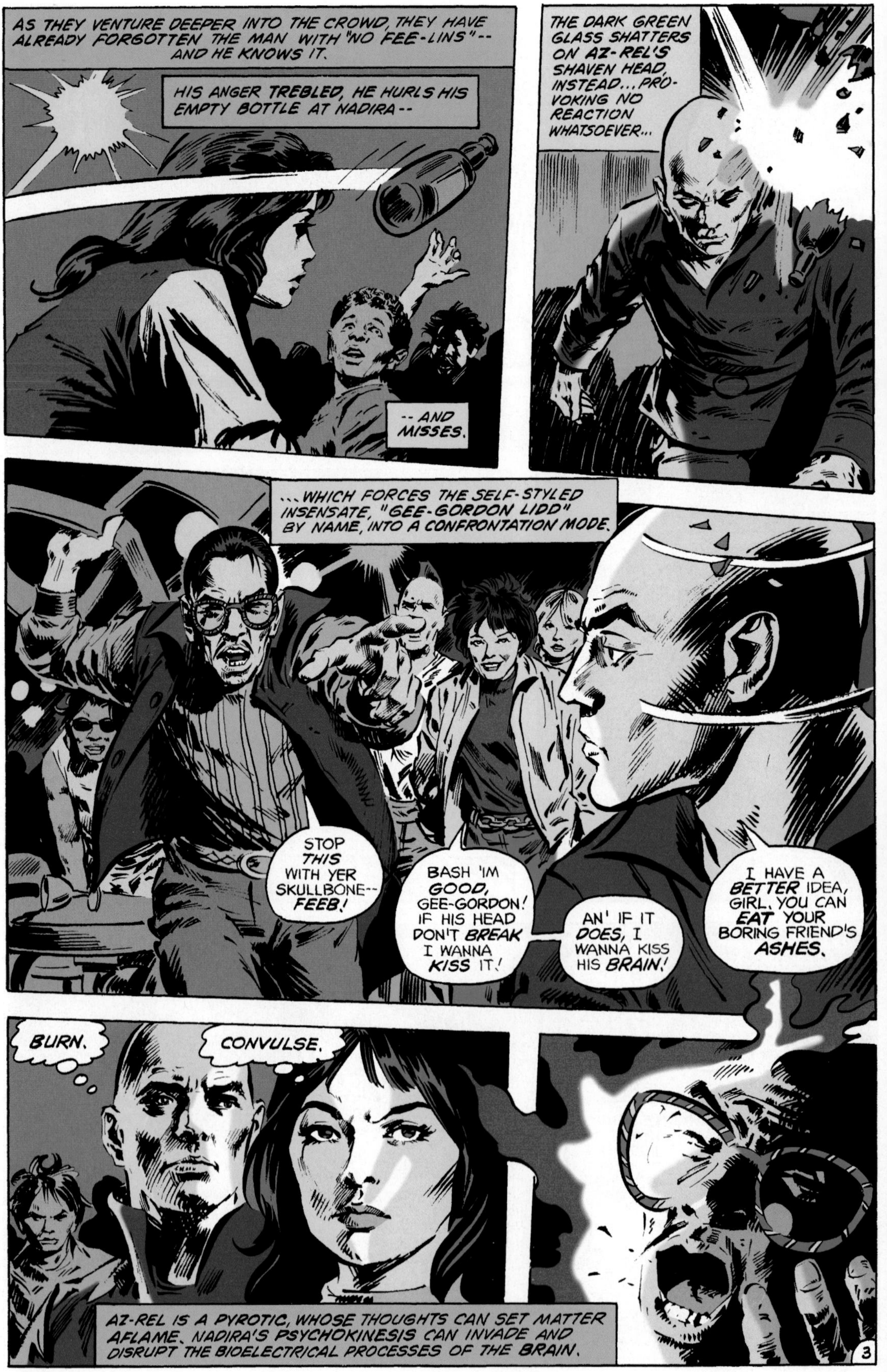
AS THEY VENTURE DEEPER INTO THE CROWD, THEY HAVE ALREADY FORGOTTEN THE MAN WITH "NO FEE-LINS" -- AND HE KNOWS IT.
HIS ANGER TREBLED, HE HURLS HIS EMPTY BOTTLE AT NADIRA --
-- AND MISSES.
THE DARK GREEN GLASS SHATTERS ON AZ-REL'S SHAVEN HEAD, INSTEAD... PROVOKING NO REACTION WHATSOEVER...
...WHICH FORCES THE SELF-STYLED INSENSATE, "GEE-GORDON LIDD" BY NAME, INTO A CONFRONTATION MODE.
STOP THIS WITH YER SKULLBONE-- FEEB!
BASH 'IM GOOD, GEE-GORDON! IF HIS HEAD DON'T BREAK I WANNA KISS IT!
AN' IF IT DOES, I WANNA KISS HIS BRAIN!
I HAVE A BETTER IDEA, GIRL. YOU CAN EAT YOUR BORING FRIEND'S ASHES.
BURN.
CONVULSE.
AZ-REL IS A PYROTIC, WHOSE THOUGHTS CAN SET MATTER AFLAME. NADIRA'S PSYCHOKINESIS CAN INVADE AND DISRUPT THE BIOELECTRICAL PROCESSES OF THE BRAIN.
3

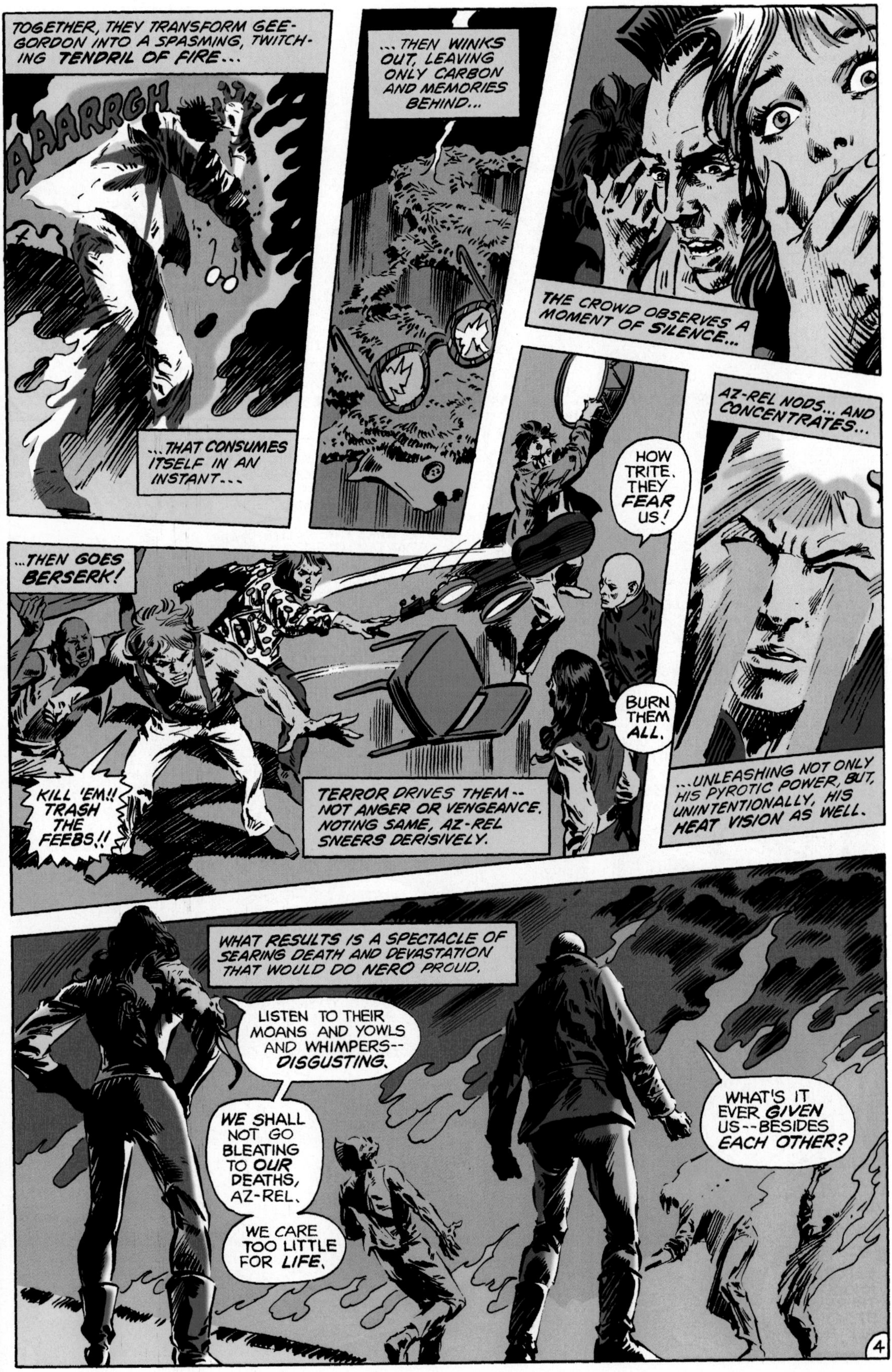
TOGETHER, THEY TRANSFORM GEE-GORDON INTO A SPASMING, TWITCHING TENDRIL OF FIRE...
AAARRGH
...THAT CONSUMES ITSELF IN AN INSTANT...
...THEN WINKS OUT, LEAVING ONLY CARBON AND MEMORIES BEHIND...
THE CROWD OBSERVES A MOMENT OF SILENCE...
...THEN GOES BERSERK!
KILL 'EM!! TRASH THE FEEBS!!
HOW TRITE. THEY FEAR US!
BURN THEM ALL.
TERROR DRIVES THEM--NOT ANGER OR VENGEANCE. NOTING SAME, AZ-REL SNEERS DERISIVELY.
AZ-REL NODS... AND CONCENTRATES...
...UNLEASHING NOT ONLY HIS PYROTIC POWER, BUT, UNINTENTIONALLY, HIS HEAT VISION AS WELL.
WHAT RESULTS IS A SPECTACLE OF SEARING DEATH AND DEVASTATION THAT WOULD DO NERO PROUD.
LISTEN TO THEIR MOANS AND YOWLS AND WHIMPERS--DISGUSTING.
WE SHALL NOT GO BLEATING TO OUR DEATHS, AZ-REL.
WE CARE TOO LITTLE FOR LIFE.
WHAT'S IT EVER GIVEN US--BESIDES EACH OTHER?
4

AM I SUCH A *TRIFLING* THING, AZ-REL?

ARE YOU SAYING YOU WOULD *HESITATE* TO LAY DOWN YOUR *LIFE* FOR ME?

NO. I AM SAYING THE THOUGHT WOULD NEVER ENTER MY *MIND.*

AH! THEN I SHALL LET *YOU* DIE, TOO!

OR PUT ME OUT OF MY *MISERY* IF YOU FEEL THE URGE.

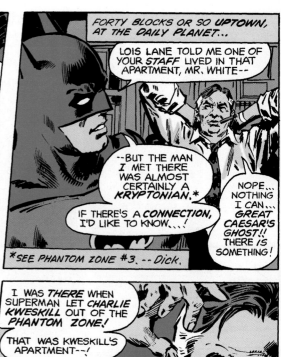

FORTY BLOCKS OR SO *UPTOWN,* AT THE *DAILY PLANET...*

LOIS LANE TOLD ME ONE OF YOUR *STAFF* LIVED IN THAT APARTMENT, MR. WHITE--

--BUT THE MAN *I* MET THERE WAS ALMOST CERTAINLY A *KRYPTONIAN.**

IF THERE'S A *CONNECTION,* I'D LIKE TO KNOW....!

NOPE... NOTHING I CAN... *GREAT CAESAR'S GHOST!!* THERE *IS* SOMETHING!

*SEE PHANTOM ZONE #3. -- Dick.

I WAS *THERE* WHEN SUPERMAN LET *CHARLIE KWESKILL* OUT OF THE *PHANTOM ZONE!*

THAT WAS KWESKILL'S APARTMENT--!

HE'S A KRYPTONIAN, TOO! HOW COULD I *FORGET* A BLASTED THING LIKE *THAT?!*

HE'S BEEN JUST PLAIN *CHARLIE* AROUND HERE FOR SO *LONG--!*

THANK YOU, MR. WHITE. I'LL BE *GOING* NOW.

OUT MY *WINDOW?!*

BEFORE I KNOW IF THERE'S A *STORY* IN ALL THIS??

THERE'S A *STORY,* ALL RIGHT....!

THE ONLY THING IN *DOUBT...* IS THE *ENDING.*

SUPERMAN *MISSING...* A MAD KRYPTONIAN LOOSE ON *EARTH....!*

AND THAT MAY BE ONLY THE *BEGINNING!*

I CAN ONLY HOPE MY *SIGNAL-DEVICE* WILL BRING THE *JUSTICE LEAGUE* RUNNING *EN MASSE!*

ZEE ZEE

NO SUCH LUCK.

5

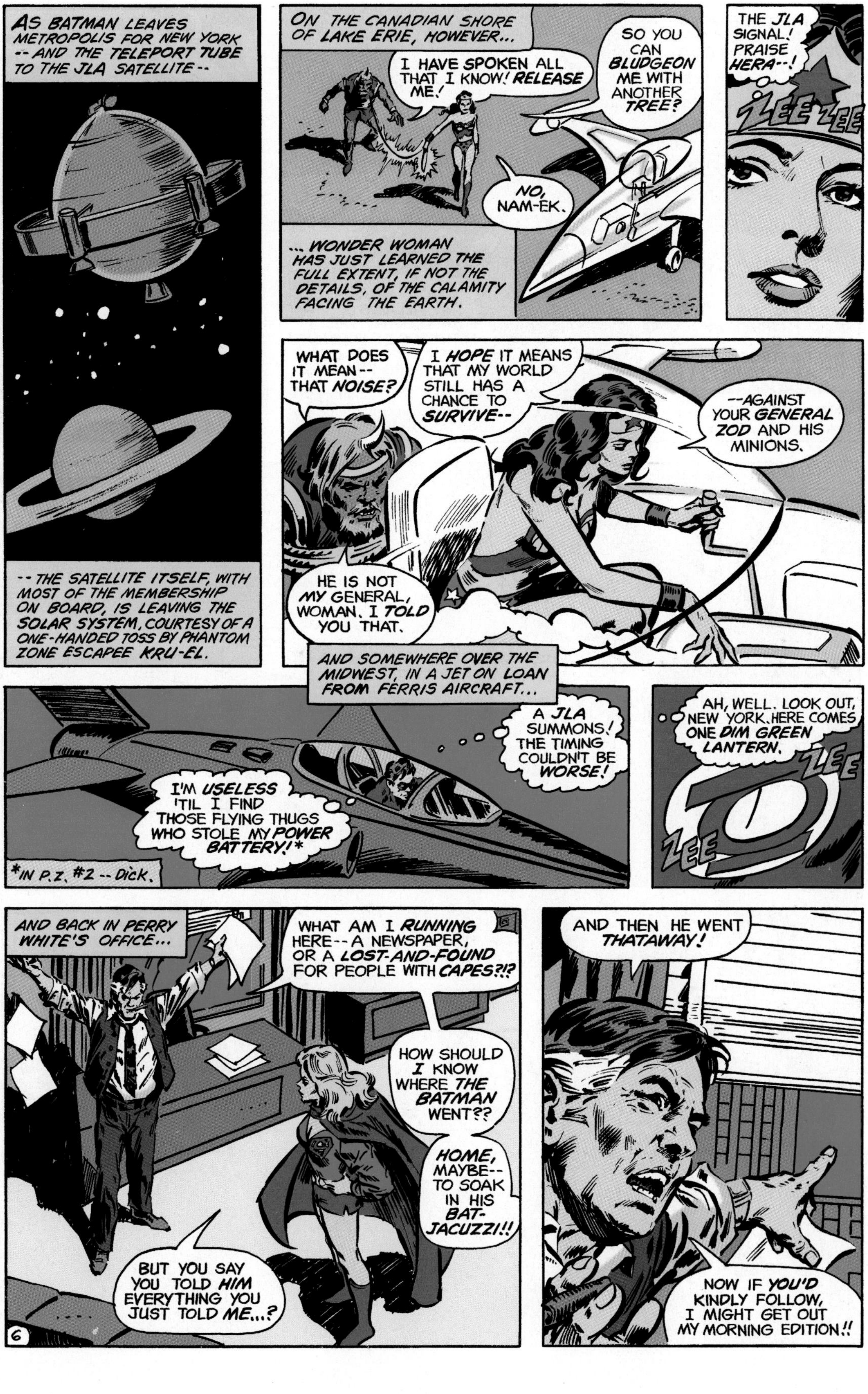
AS BATMAN LEAVES METROPOLIS FOR NEW YORK -- AND THE TELEPORT TUBE TO THE JLA SATELLITE --
-- THE SATELLITE ITSELF, WITH MOST OF THE MEMBERSHIP ON BOARD, IS LEAVING THE SOLAR SYSTEM, COURTESY OF A ONE-HANDED TOSS BY PHANTOM ZONE ESCAPEE KRU-EL.
ON THE CANADIAN SHORE OF LAKE ERIE, HOWEVER...
I HAVE SPOKEN ALL THAT I KNOW! RELEASE ME!
SO YOU CAN BLUDGEON ME WITH ANOTHER TREE?
NO, NAM-EK.
... WONDER WOMAN HAS JUST LEARNED THE FULL EXTENT, IF NOT THE DETAILS, OF THE CALAMITY FACING THE EARTH.
THE JLA SIGNAL! PRAISE HERA--!
ZEE ZEE
WHAT DOES IT MEAN -- THAT NOISE?
I HOPE IT MEANS THAT MY WORLD STILL HAS A CHANCE TO SURVIVE--
--AGAINST YOUR GENERAL ZOD AND HIS MINIONS.
HE IS NOT MY GENERAL, WOMAN. I TOLD YOU THAT.
AND SOMEWHERE OVER THE MIDWEST, IN A JET ON LOAN FROM FERRIS AIRCRAFT...
A JLA SUMMONS! THE TIMING COULDN'T BE WORSE!
I'M USELESS 'TIL I FIND THOSE FLYING THUGS WHO STOLE MY POWER BATTERY!*
*IN P.Z. #2 -- DICK.
AH, WELL. LOOK OUT, NEW YORK. HERE COMES ONE DIM GREEN LANTERN.
ZEE ZEE
AND BACK IN PERRY WHITE'S OFFICE...
WHAT AM I RUNNING HERE-- A NEWSPAPER, OR A LOST-AND-FOUND FOR PEOPLE WITH CAPES?!?
HOW SHOULD I KNOW WHERE THE BATMAN WENT??
HOME, MAYBE-- TO SOAK IN HIS BAT-JACUZZI!!
BUT YOU SAY YOU TOLD HIM EVERYTHING YOU JUST TOLD ME...?
6
AND THEN HE WENT THATAWAY!
NOW IF YOU'D KINDLY FOLLOW, I MIGHT GET OUT MY MORNING EDITION!!

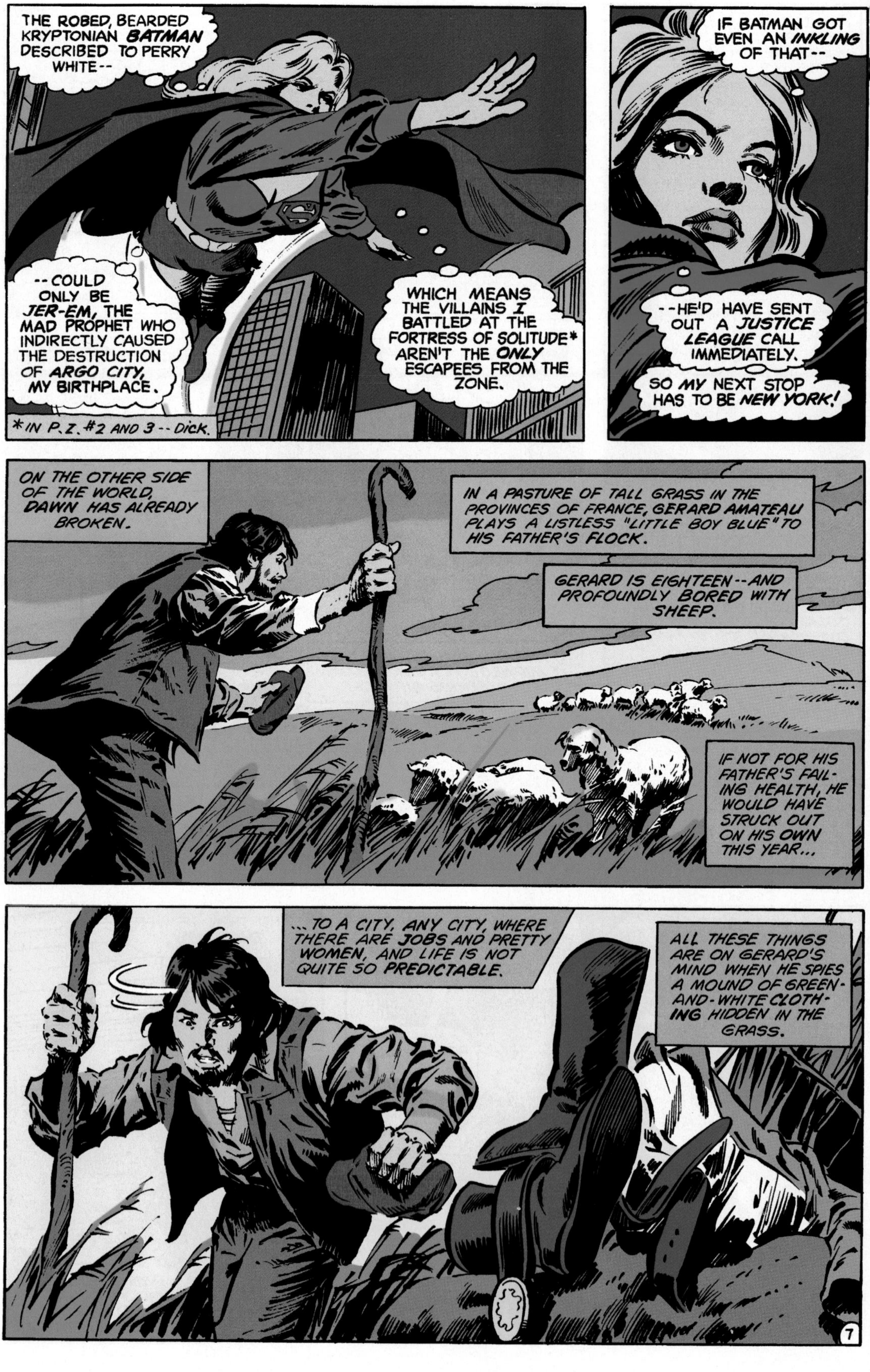
THE ROBED, BEARDED KRYPTONIAN BATMAN DESCRIBED TO PERRY WHITE--
--COULD ONLY BE JER-EM, THE MAD PROPHET WHO INDIRECTLY CAUSED THE DESTRUCTION OF ARGO CITY, MY BIRTHPLACE.
WHICH MEANS THE VILLAINS I BATTLED AT THE FORTRESS OF SOLITUDE* AREN'T THE ONLY ESCAPEES FROM THE ZONE.
*IN P.Z. #2 AND 3 -- DICK.
IF BATMAN GOT EVEN AN INKLING OF THAT--
--HE'D HAVE SENT OUT A JUSTICE LEAGUE CALL IMMEDIATELY.
SO MY NEXT STOP HAS TO BE NEW YORK!
ON THE OTHER SIDE OF THE WORLD, DAWN HAS ALREADY BROKEN.
IN A PASTURE OF TALL GRASS IN THE PROVINCES OF FRANCE, GERARD AMATEAU PLAYS A LISTLESS "LITTLE BOY BLUE" TO HIS FATHER'S FLOCK.
GERARD IS EIGHTEEN--AND PROFOUNDLY BORED WITH SHEEP.
IF NOT FOR HIS FATHER'S FAILING HEALTH, HE WOULD HAVE STRUCK OUT ON HIS OWN THIS YEAR...
...TO A CITY, ANY CITY, WHERE THERE ARE JOBS AND PRETTY WOMEN, AND LIFE IS NOT QUITE SO PREDICTABLE.
ALL THESE THINGS ARE ON GERARD'S MIND WHEN HE SPIES A MOUND OF GREEN-AND-WHITE CLOTHING HIDDEN IN THE GRASS.
7

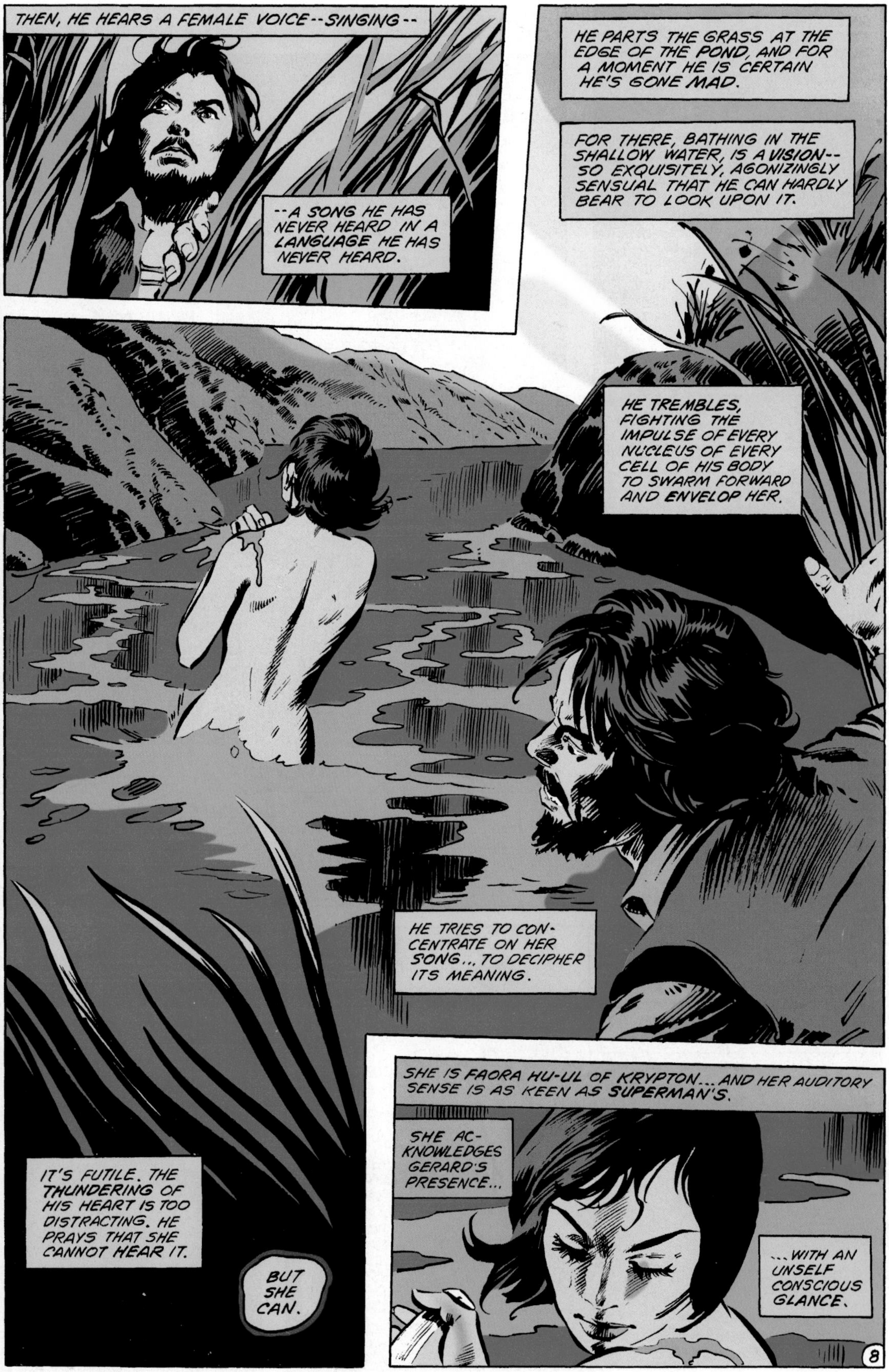
THEN, HE HEARS A FEMALE VOICE--SINGING--
--A SONG HE HAS NEVER HEARD IN A LANGUAGE HE HAS NEVER HEARD.
HE PARTS THE GRASS AT THE EDGE OF THE POND, AND FOR A MOMENT HE IS CERTAIN HE'S GONE MAD.
FOR THERE, BATHING IN THE SHALLOW WATER, IS A VISION-- SO EXQUISITELY, AGONIZINGLY SENSUAL THAT HE CAN HARDLY BEAR TO LOOK UPON IT.
HE TREMBLES, FIGHTING THE IMPULSE OF EVERY NUCLEUS OF EVERY CELL OF HIS BODY TO SWARM FORWARD AND ENVELOP HER.
HE TRIES TO CONCENTRATE ON HER SONG... TO DECIPHER ITS MEANING.
IT'S FUTILE. THE THUNDERING OF HIS HEART IS TOO DISTRACTING. HE PRAYS THAT SHE CANNOT HEAR IT.
BUT SHE CAN.
SHE IS FAORA HU-UL OF KRYPTON... AND HER AUDITORY SENSE IS AS KEEN AS SUPERMAN'S.
SHE ACKNOWLEDGES GERARD'S PRESENCE...
...WITH AN UNSELF CONSCIOUS GLANCE.
8

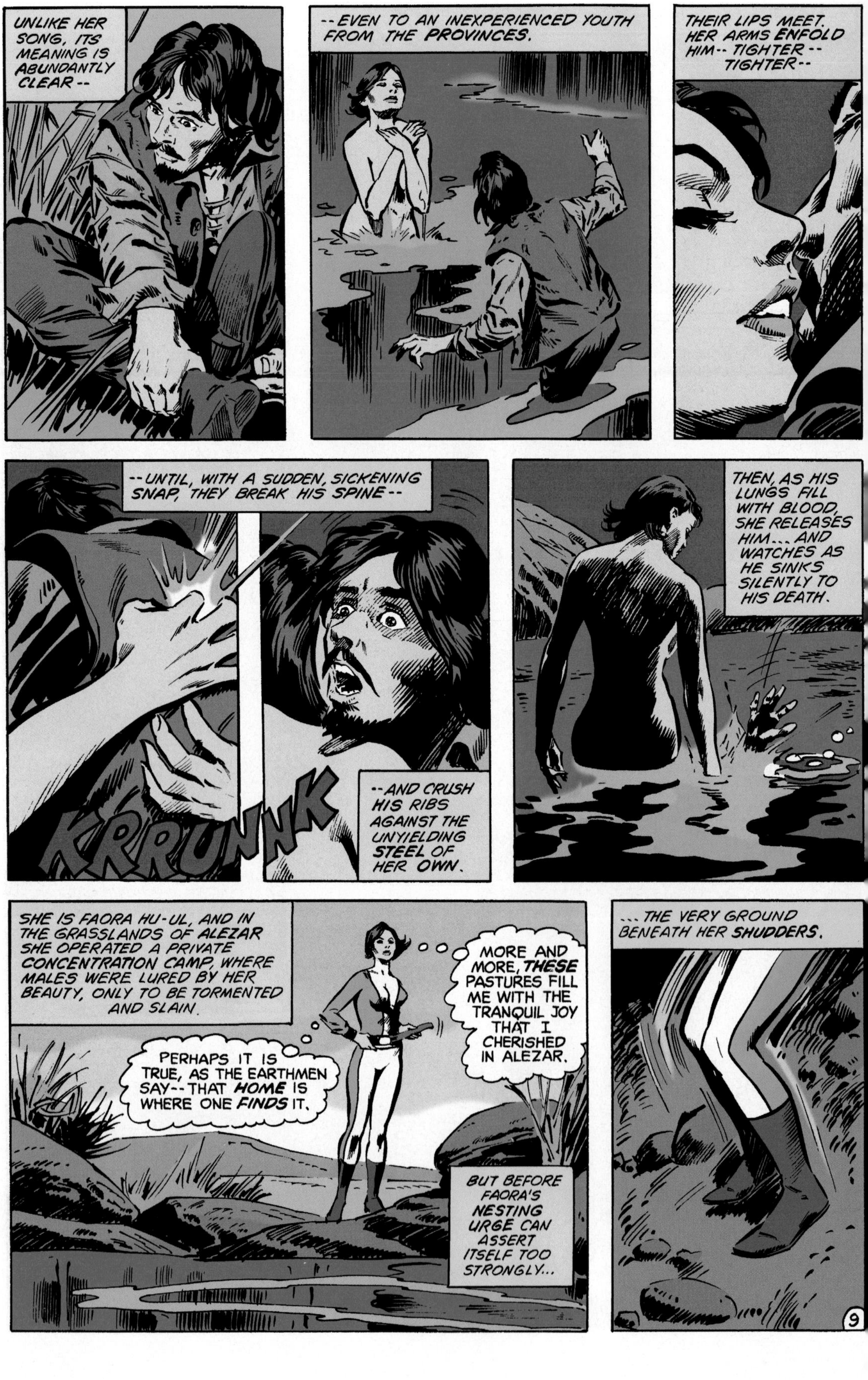
UNLIKE HER SONG, ITS MEANING IS ABUNDANTLY CLEAR --
-- EVEN TO AN INEXPERIENCED YOUTH FROM THE PROVINCES.
THEIR LIPS MEET. HER ARMS ENFOLD HIM -- TIGHTER -- TIGHTER --
-- UNTIL, WITH A SUDDEN, SICKENING SNAP, THEY BREAK HIS SPINE --
KRRUNNK
-- AND CRUSH HIS RIBS AGAINST THE UNYIELDING STEEL OF HER OWN.
THEN, AS HIS LUNGS FILL WITH BLOOD, SHE RELEASES HIM... AND WATCHES AS HE SINKS SILENTLY TO HIS DEATH.
SHE IS FAORA HU-UL, AND IN THE GRASSLANDS OF ALEZAR SHE OPERATED A PRIVATE CONCENTRATION CAMP, WHERE MALES WERE LURED BY HER BEAUTY, ONLY TO BE TORMENTED AND SLAIN.
MORE AND MORE, THESE PASTURES FILL ME WITH THE TRANQUIL JOY THAT I CHERISHED IN ALEZAR.
PERHAPS IT IS TRUE, AS THE EARTHMEN SAY -- THAT HOME IS WHERE ONE FINDS IT.
BUT BEFORE FAORA'S NESTING URGE CAN ASSERT ITSELF TOO STRONGLY...
... THE VERY GROUND BENEATH HER SHUDDERS.
9

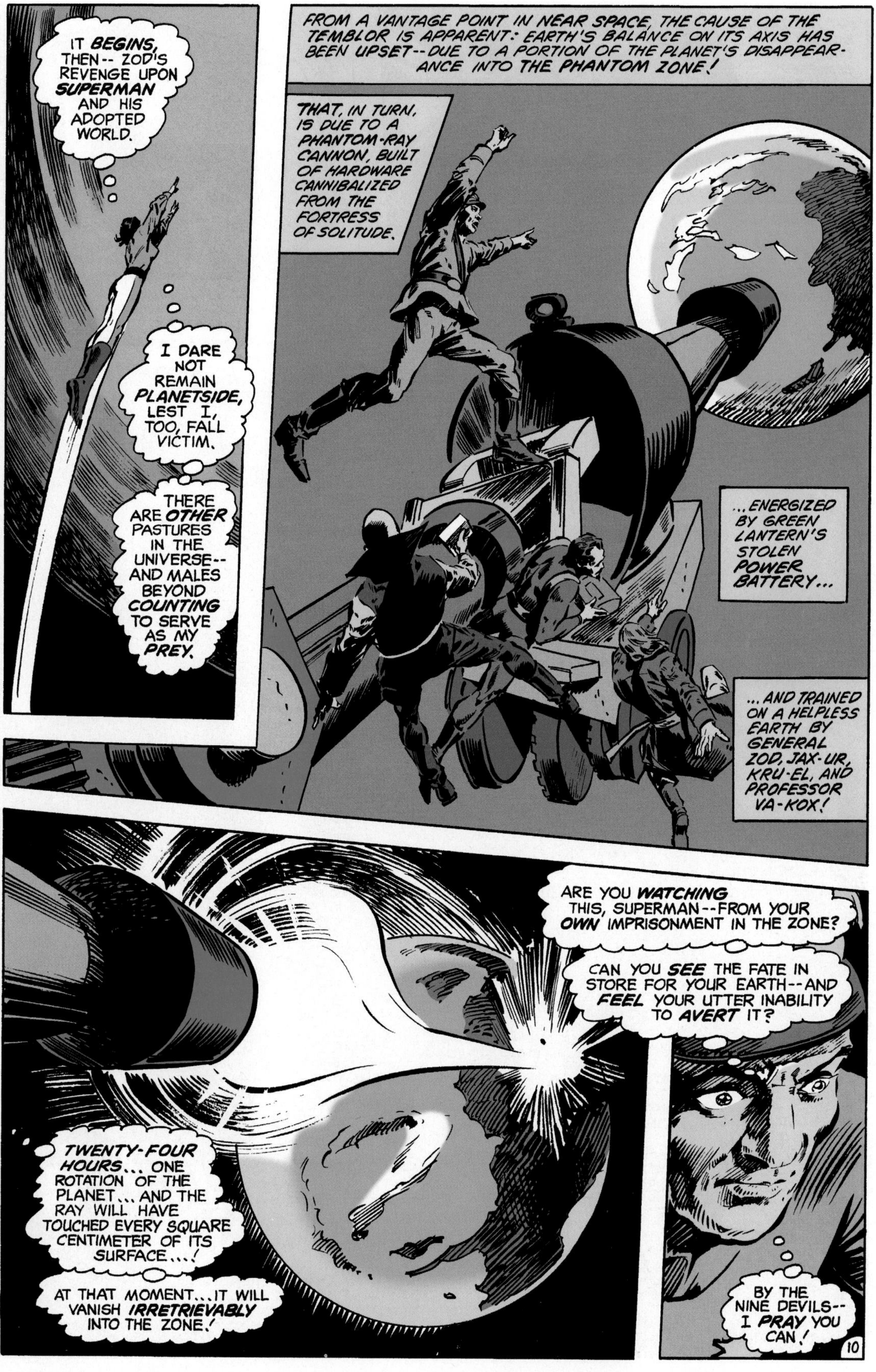

IT BEGINS, THEN-- ZOD'S REVENGE UPON SUPERMAN AND HIS ADOPTED WORLD.
I DARE NOT REMAIN PLANETSIDE, LEST I, TOO, FALL VICTIM.
THERE ARE OTHER PASTURES IN THE UNIVERSE-- AND MALES BEYOND COUNTING TO SERVE AS MY PREY.
FROM A VANTAGE POINT IN NEAR SPACE, THE CAUSE OF THE TEMBLOR IS APPARENT: EARTH'S BALANCE ON ITS AXIS HAS BEEN UPSET--DUE TO A PORTION OF THE PLANET'S DISAPPEARANCE INTO THE PHANTOM ZONE!
THAT, IN TURN, IS DUE TO A PHANTOM-RAY CANNON, BUILT OF HARDWARE CANNIBALIZED FROM THE FORTRESS OF SOLITUDE.
...ENERGIZED BY GREEN LANTERN'S STOLEN POWER BATTERY...
...AND TRAINED ON A HELPLESS EARTH BY GENERAL ZOD, JAX-UR, KRU-EL, AND PROFESSOR VA-KOX!
ARE YOU WATCHING THIS, SUPERMAN--FROM YOUR OWN IMPRISONMENT IN THE ZONE?
CAN YOU SEE THE FATE IN STORE FOR YOUR EARTH--AND FEEL YOUR UTTER INABILITY TO AVERT IT?
TWENTY-FOUR HOURS... ONE ROTATION OF THE PLANET... AND THE RAY WILL HAVE TOUCHED EVERY SQUARE CENTIMETER OF ITS SURFACE...!
AT THAT MOMENT...IT WILL VANISH IRRETRIEVABLY INTO THE ZONE!
BY THE NINE DEVILS-- I PRAY YOU CAN!
10

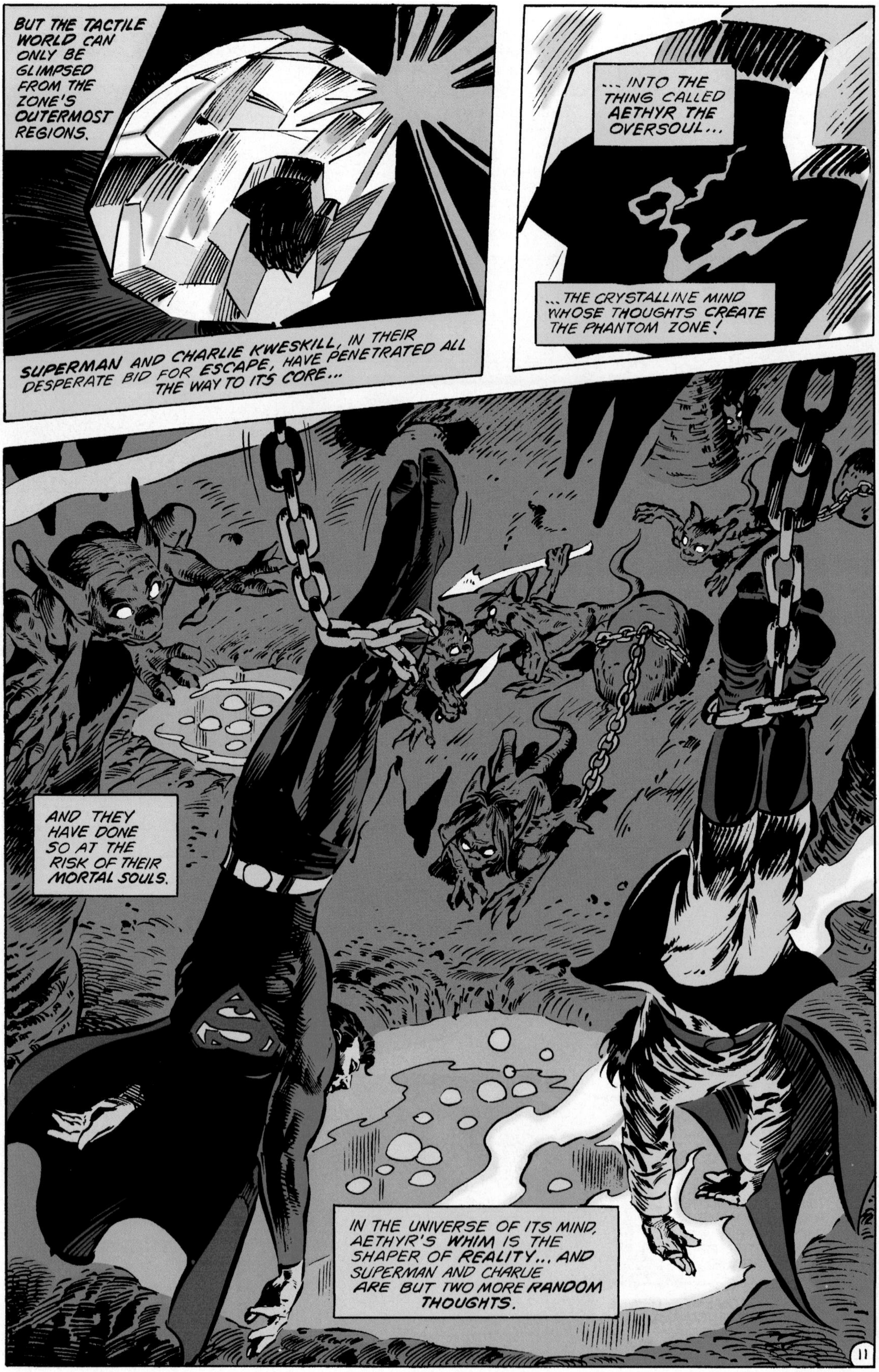

BUT THE TACTILE WORLD CAN ONLY BE GLIMPSED FROM THE ZONE'S OUTERMOST REGIONS.
SUPERMAN AND CHARLIE KWESKILL, IN THEIR DESPERATE BID FOR ESCAPE, HAVE PENETRATED ALL THE WAY TO ITS CORE...
...INTO THE THING CALLED AETHYR THE OVERSOUL...
...THE CRYSTALLINE MIND WHOSE THOUGHTS CREATE THE PHANTOM ZONE!
AND THEY HAVE DONE SO AT THE RISK OF THEIR MORTAL SOULS.
IN THE UNIVERSE OF ITS MIND, AETHYR'S WHIM IS THE SHAPER OF REALITY... AND SUPERMAN AND CHARLIE ARE BUT TWO MORE RANDOM THOUGHTS.
11

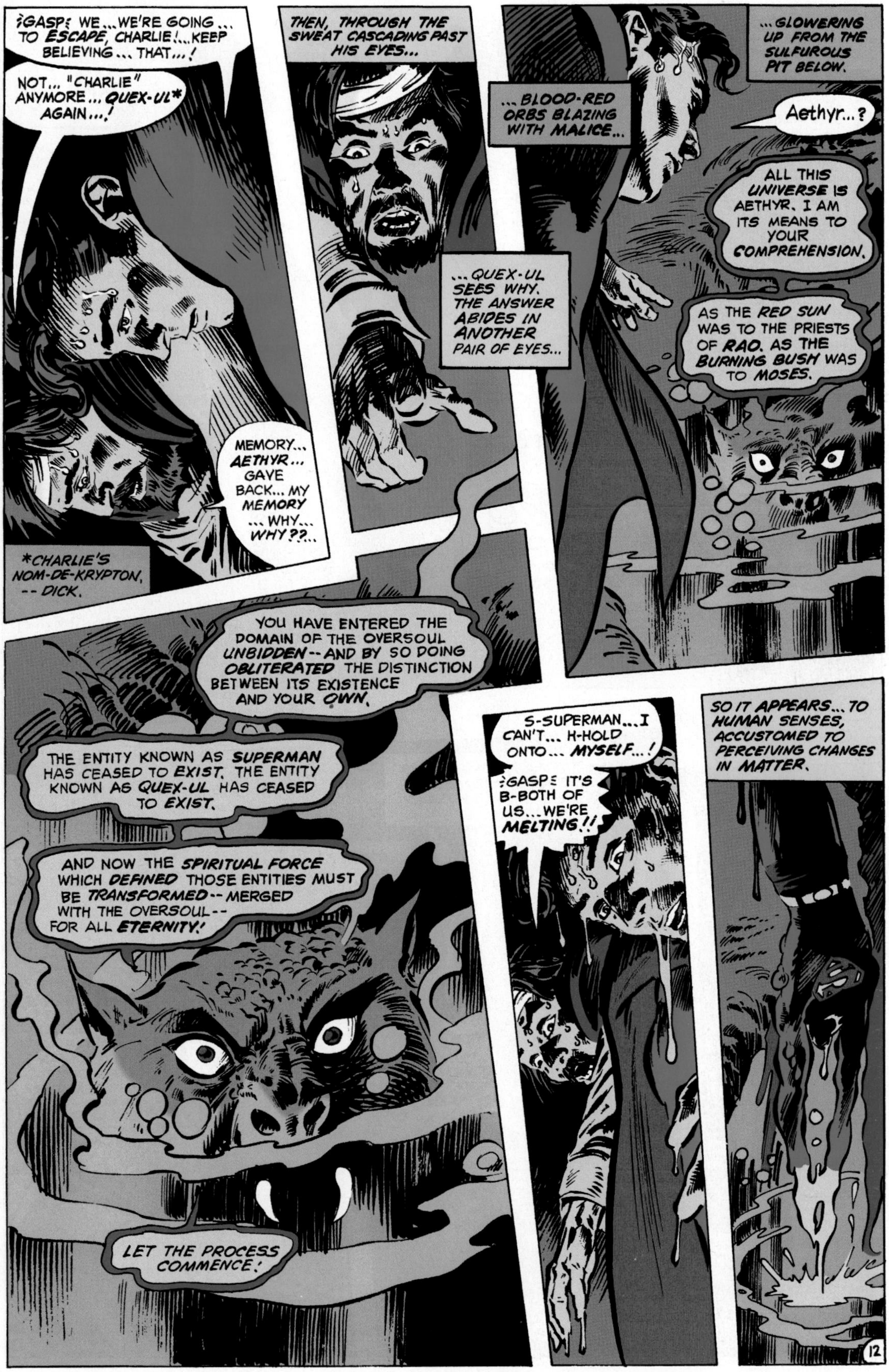

¡GASP! WE...WE'RE GOING... TO ESCAPE, CHARLIE!...KEEP BELIEVING... THAT...!
NOT... "CHARLIE" ANYMORE... QUEX-UL* AGAIN...!
MEMORY... AETHYR... GAVE BACK... MY MEMORY ...WHY... WHY??...
*CHARLIE'S NOM-DE-KRYPTON. --DICK.
THEN, THROUGH THE SWEAT CASCADING PAST HIS EYES...
...QUEX-UL SEES WHY. THE ANSWER ABIDES IN ANOTHER PAIR OF EYES...
...BLOOD-RED ORBS BLAZING WITH MALICE...
...GLOWERING UP FROM THE SULFUROUS PIT BELOW.
Aethyr...?
ALL THIS UNIVERSE IS AETHYR. I AM ITS MEANS TO YOUR COMPREHENSION.
AS THE RED SUN WAS TO THE PRIESTS OF RAO. AS THE BURNING BUSH WAS TO MOSES.
YOU HAVE ENTERED THE DOMAIN OF THE OVERSOUL UNBIDDEN--AND BY SO DOING OBLITERATED THE DISTINCTION BETWEEN ITS EXISTENCE AND YOUR OWN.
THE ENTITY KNOWN AS SUPERMAN HAS CEASED TO EXIST. THE ENTITY KNOWN AS QUEX-UL HAS CEASED TO EXIST.
AND NOW THE SPIRITUAL FORCE WHICH DEFINED THOSE ENTITIES MUST BE TRANSFORMED--MERGED WITH THE OVERSOUL-- FOR ALL ETERNITY!
LET THE PROCESS COMMENCE!
S-SUPERMAN...I CAN'T... H-HOLD ONTO... MYSELF...!
¡GASP! IT'S B-BOTH OF US...WE'RE MELTING!!
SO IT APPEARS...TO HUMAN SENSES, ACCUSTOMED TO PERCEIVING CHANGES IN MATTER.
12

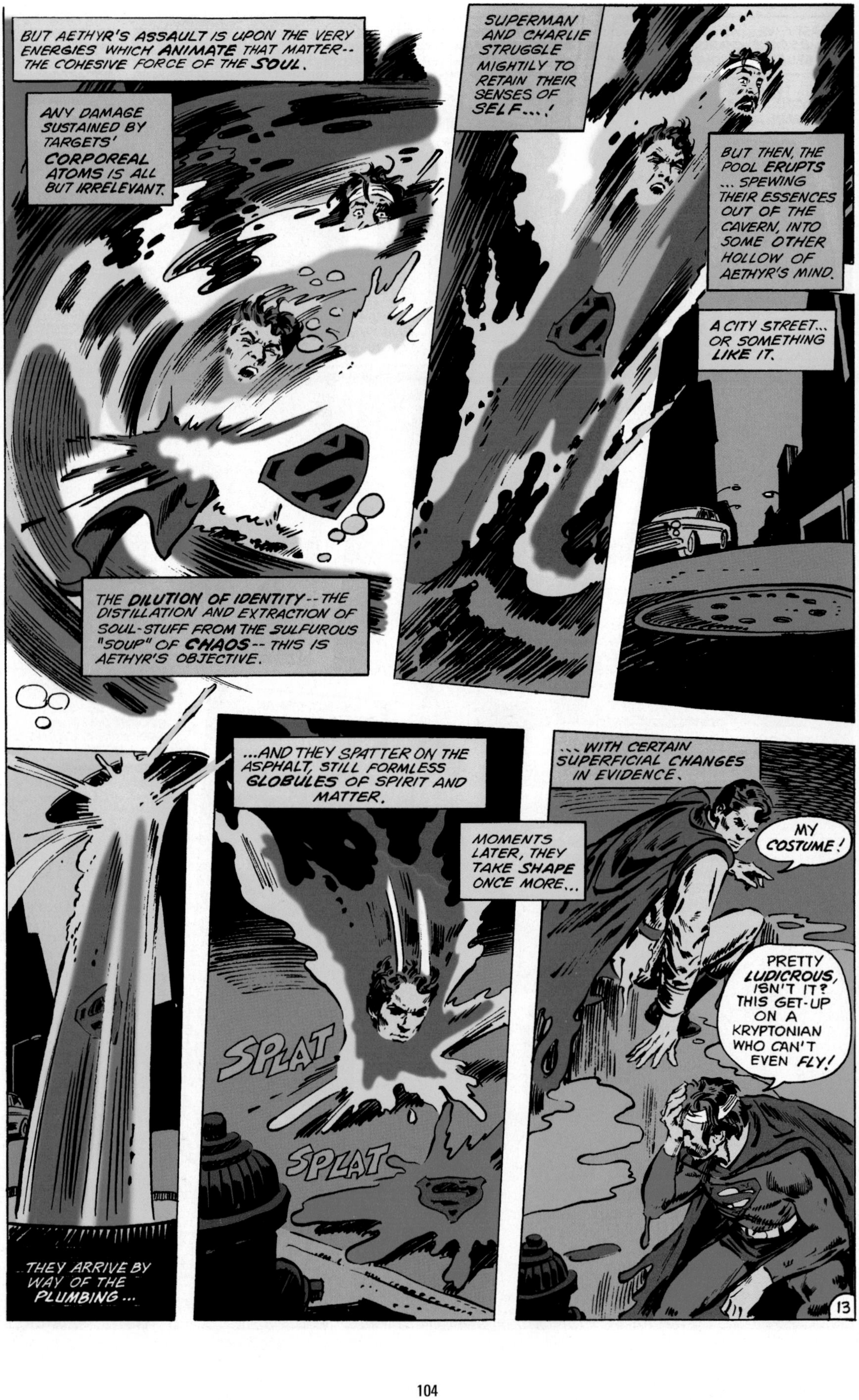
BUT AETHYR'S ASSAULT IS UPON THE VERY ENERGIES WHICH ANIMATE THAT MATTER-- THE COHESIVE FORCE OF THE SOUL.
ANY DAMAGE SUSTAINED BY TARGETS' CORPOREAL ATOMS IS ALL BUT IRRELEVANT.
THE DILUTION OF IDENTITY -- THE DISTILLATION AND EXTRACTION OF SOUL-STUFF FROM THE SULFUROUS "SOUP" OF CHAOS -- THIS IS AETHYR'S OBJECTIVE.
SUPERMAN AND CHARLIE STRUGGLE MIGHTILY TO RETAIN THEIR SENSES OF SELF...!
BUT THEN, THE POOL ERUPTS ... SPEWING THEIR ESSENCES OUT OF THE CAVERN, INTO SOME OTHER HOLLOW OF AETHYR'S MIND.
A CITY STREET... OR SOMETHING LIKE IT.
...THEY ARRIVE BY WAY OF THE PLUMBING...
...AND THEY SPATTER ON THE ASPHALT, STILL FORMLESS GLOBULES OF SPIRIT AND MATTER.
MOMENTS LATER, THEY TAKE SHAPE ONCE MORE...
SPLAT
SPLAT
...WITH CERTAIN SUPERFICIAL CHANGES IN EVIDENCE.
MY COSTUME!
PRETTY LUDICROUS, ISN'T IT? THIS GET-UP ON A KRYPTONIAN WHO CAN'T EVEN FLY!
13

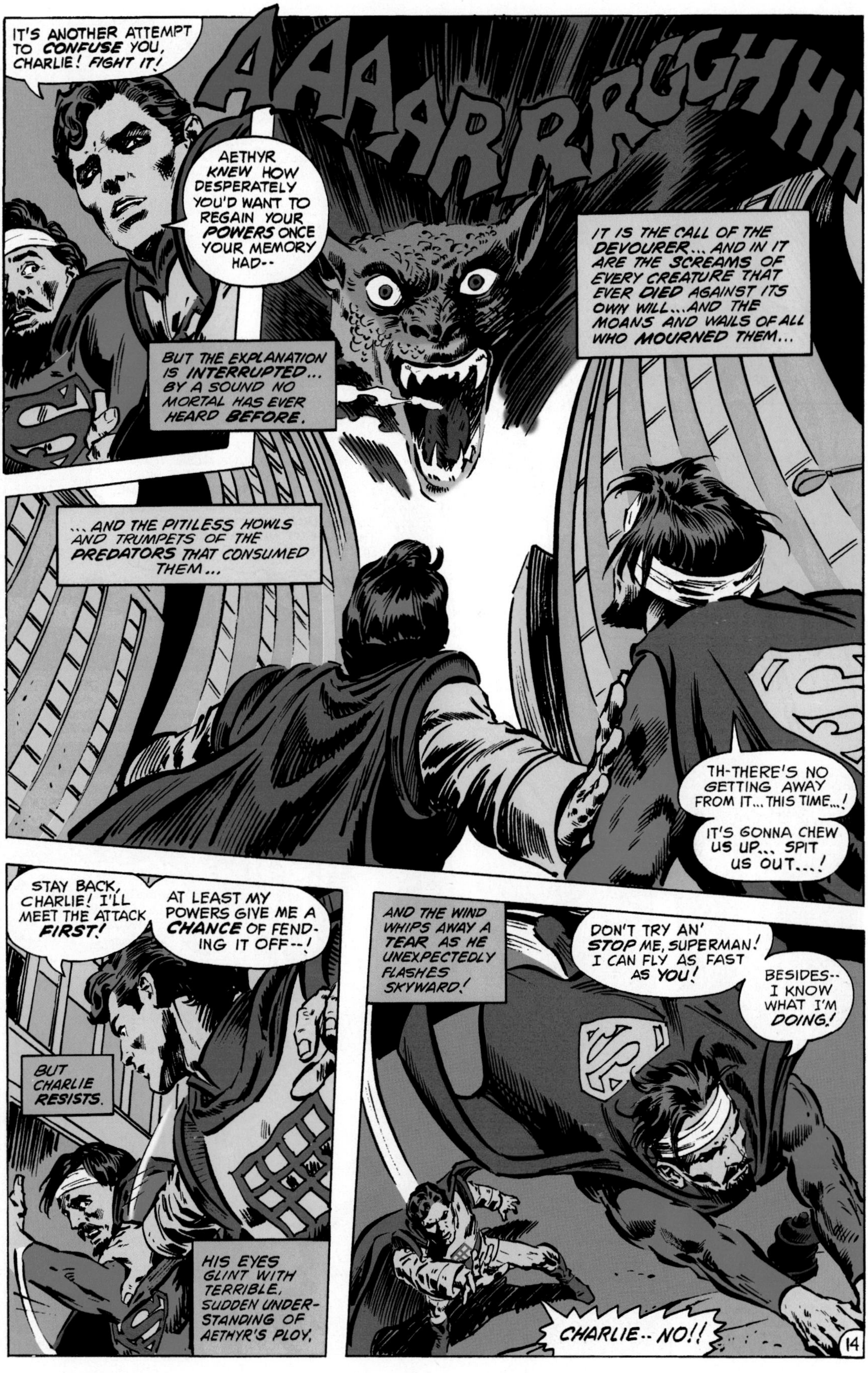
IT'S ANOTHER ATTEMPT TO CONFUSE YOU, CHARLIE! FIGHT IT!
AAAARRRRGGHHH
AETHYR KNEW HOW DESPERATELY YOU'D WANT TO REGAIN YOUR POWERS ONCE YOUR MEMORY HAD--
IT IS THE CALL OF THE DEVOURER... AND IN IT ARE THE SCREAMS OF EVERY CREATURE THAT EVER DIED AGAINST ITS OWN WILL... AND THE MOANS AND WAILS OF ALL WHO MOURNED THEM...
BUT THE EXPLANATION IS INTERRUPTED... BY A SOUND NO MORTAL HAS EVER HEARD BEFORE.
...AND THE PITILESS HOWLS AND TRUMPETS OF THE PREDATORS THAT CONSUMED THEM...
TH-THERE'S NO GETTING AWAY FROM IT... THIS TIME...!
IT'S GONNA CHEW US UP... SPIT US OUT...!
STAY BACK, CHARLIE! I'LL MEET THE ATTACK FIRST!
AT LEAST MY POWERS GIVE ME A CHANCE OF FENDING IT OFF--!
BUT CHARLIE RESISTS.
HIS EYES GLINT WITH TERRIBLE, SUDDEN UNDERSTANDING OF AETHYR'S PLOY.
AND THE WIND WHIPS AWAY A TEAR AS HE UNEXPECTEDLY FLASHES SKYWARD!
DON'T TRY AN' STOP ME, SUPERMAN! I CAN FLY AS FAST AS YOU!
BESIDES-- I KNOW WHAT I'M DOING!
CHARLIE-- NO!!
14

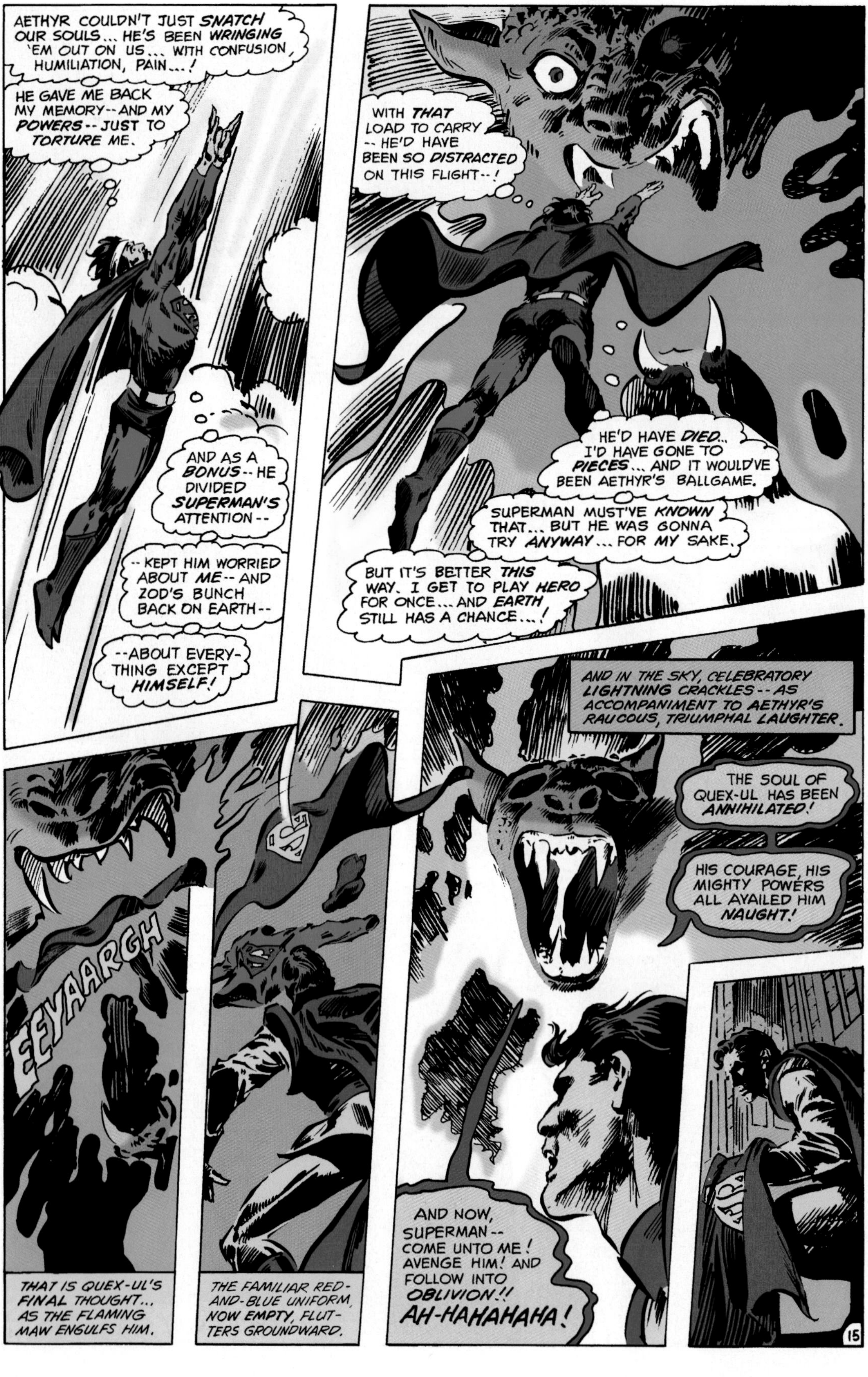
AETHYR COULDN'T JUST SNATCH OUR SOULS... HE'S BEEN WRINGING 'EM OUT ON US... WITH CONFUSION, HUMILIATION, PAIN...!
HE GAVE ME BACK MY MEMORY--AND MY POWERS--JUST TO TORTURE ME.
AND AS A BONUS--HE DIVIDED SUPERMAN'S ATTENTION--
--KEPT HIM WORRIED ABOUT ME--AND ZOD'S BUNCH BACK ON EARTH--
--ABOUT EVERYTHING EXCEPT HIMSELF!
WITH THAT LOAD TO CARRY--HE'D HAVE BEEN SO DISTRACTED ON THIS FLIGHT--!
HE'D HAVE DIED.. I'D HAVE GONE TO PIECES... AND IT WOULD'VE BEEN AETHYR'S BALLGAME.
SUPERMAN MUST'VE KNOWN THAT... BUT HE WAS GONNA TRY ANYWAY... FOR MY SAKE.
BUT IT'S BETTER THIS WAY. I GET TO PLAY HERO FOR ONCE... AND EARTH STILL HAS A CHANCE...!
EEYAARGH
THAT IS QUEX-UL'S FINAL THOUGHT... AS THE FLAMING MAW ENGULFS HIM.
THE FAMILIAR RED-AND-BLUE UNIFORM, NOW EMPTY, FLUTTERS GROUNDWARD.
AND IN THE SKY, CELEBRATORY LIGHTNING CRACKLES--AS ACCOMPANIMENT TO AETHYR'S RAUCOUS, TRIUMPHAL LAUGHTER.
THE SOUL OF QUEX-UL HAS BEEN ANNIHILATED!
HIS COURAGE, HIS MIGHTY POWERS ALL AVAILED HIM NAUGHT!
AND NOW, SUPERMAN--COME UNTO ME! AVENGE HIM! AND FOLLOW INTO OBLIVION!! AH-HAHAHAHA!
15

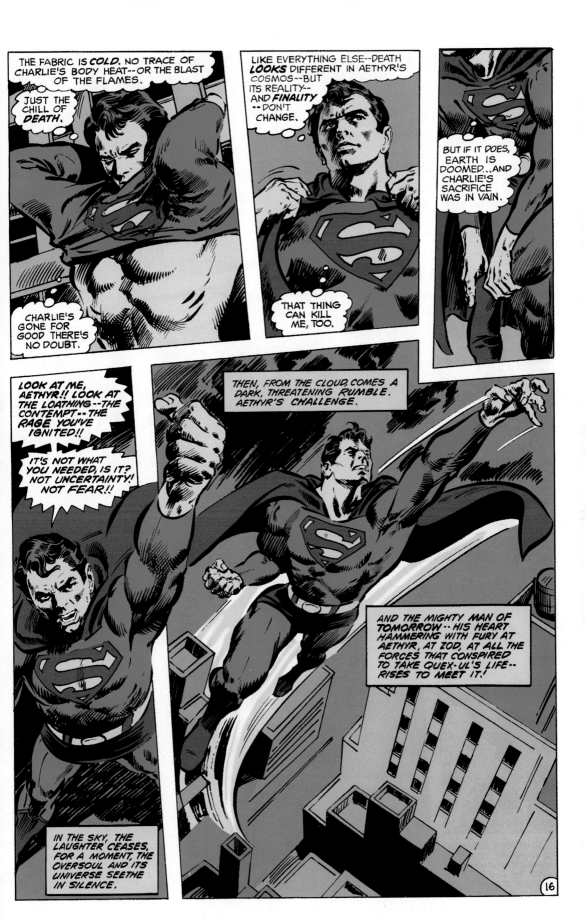

THE FABRIC IS *COLD*. NO TRACE OF CHARLIE'S BODY HEAT--OR THE BLAST OF THE FLAMES.

JUST THE CHILL OF *DEATH*.

CHARLIE'S GONE FOR GOOD, THERE'S NO DOUBT.

LIKE EVERYTHING ELSE--DEATH *LOOKS* DIFFERENT IN AETHYR'S COSMOS--BUT ITS REALITY-- AND *FINALITY* --DON'T CHANGE.

THAT THING CAN KILL ME, TOO.

BUT IF IT DOES, EARTH IS *DOOMED*...AND CHARLIE'S SACRIFICE WAS IN VAIN.

LOOK AT ME, AETHYR!! LOOK AT THE LOATHING--THE CONTEMPT--THE RAGE YOU'VE IGNITED!!

IT'S NOT WHAT YOU NEEDED, IS IT? NOT UNCERTAINTY! NOT FEAR!!

THEN, FROM THE CLOUD, COMES A DARK, THREATENING *RUMBLE*. AETHYR'S CHALLENGE.

AND THE *MIGHTY MAN OF TOMORROW* -- HIS HEART HAMMERING WITH FURY AT AETHYR, AT ZOD, AT ALL THE FORCES THAT CONSPIRED TO TAKE *QUEX-UL'S* LIFE-- RISES TO MEET IT!

IN THE SKY, THE LAUGHTER CEASES, FOR A MOMENT, THE OVERSOUL AND ITS UNIVERSE SEETHE IN SILENCE.

16

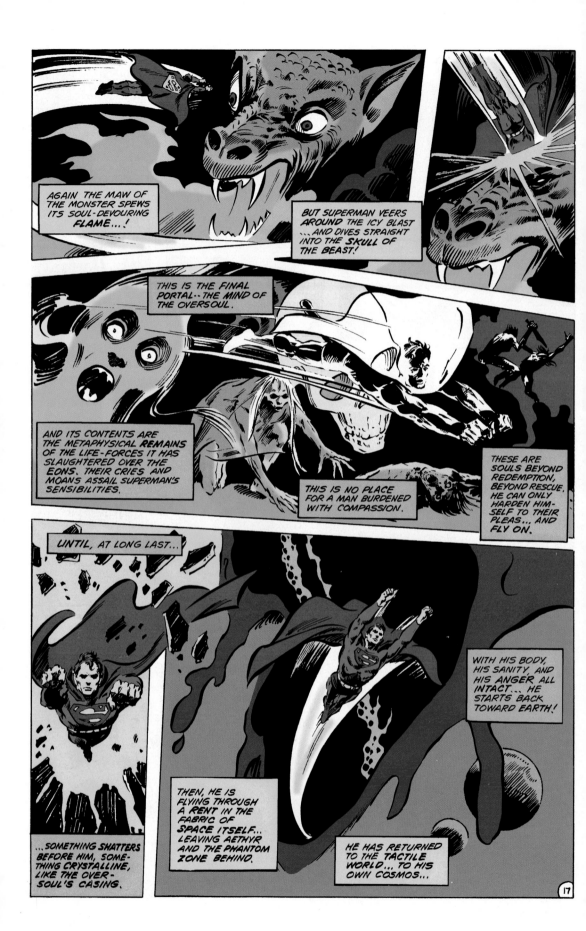

AGAIN THE MAW OF THE MONSTER SPEWS ITS SOUL-DEVOURING FLAME...!

BUT SUPERMAN VEERS AROUND THE ICY BLAST ...AND DIVES STRAIGHT INTO THE SKULL OF THE BEAST!

THIS IS THE FINAL PORTAL--THE MIND OF THE OVERSOUL.

AND ITS CONTENTS ARE THE METAPHYSICAL REMAINS OF THE LIFE-FORCES IT HAS SLAUGHTERED OVER THE EONS. THEIR CRIES AND MOANS ASSAIL SUPERMAN'S SENSIBILITIES.

THIS IS NO PLACE FOR A MAN BURDENED WITH COMPASSION.

THESE ARE SOULS BEYOND REDEMPTION, BEYOND RESCUE. HE CAN ONLY HARDEN HIM-SELF TO THEIR PLEAS... AND FLY ON.

UNTIL, AT LONG LAST...

WITH HIS BODY, HIS SANITY, AND HIS ANGER ALL INTACT... HE STARTS BACK TOWARD EARTH!

...SOMETHING SHATTERS BEFORE HIM, SOME-THING CRYSTALLINE, LIKE THE OVER-SOUL'S CASING.

THEN, HE IS FLYING THROUGH A RENT IN THE FABRIC OF SPACE ITSELF... LEAVING AETHYR AND THE PHANTOM ZONE BEHIND.

HE HAS RETURNED TO THE TACTILE WORLD... TO HIS OWN COSMOS...

17

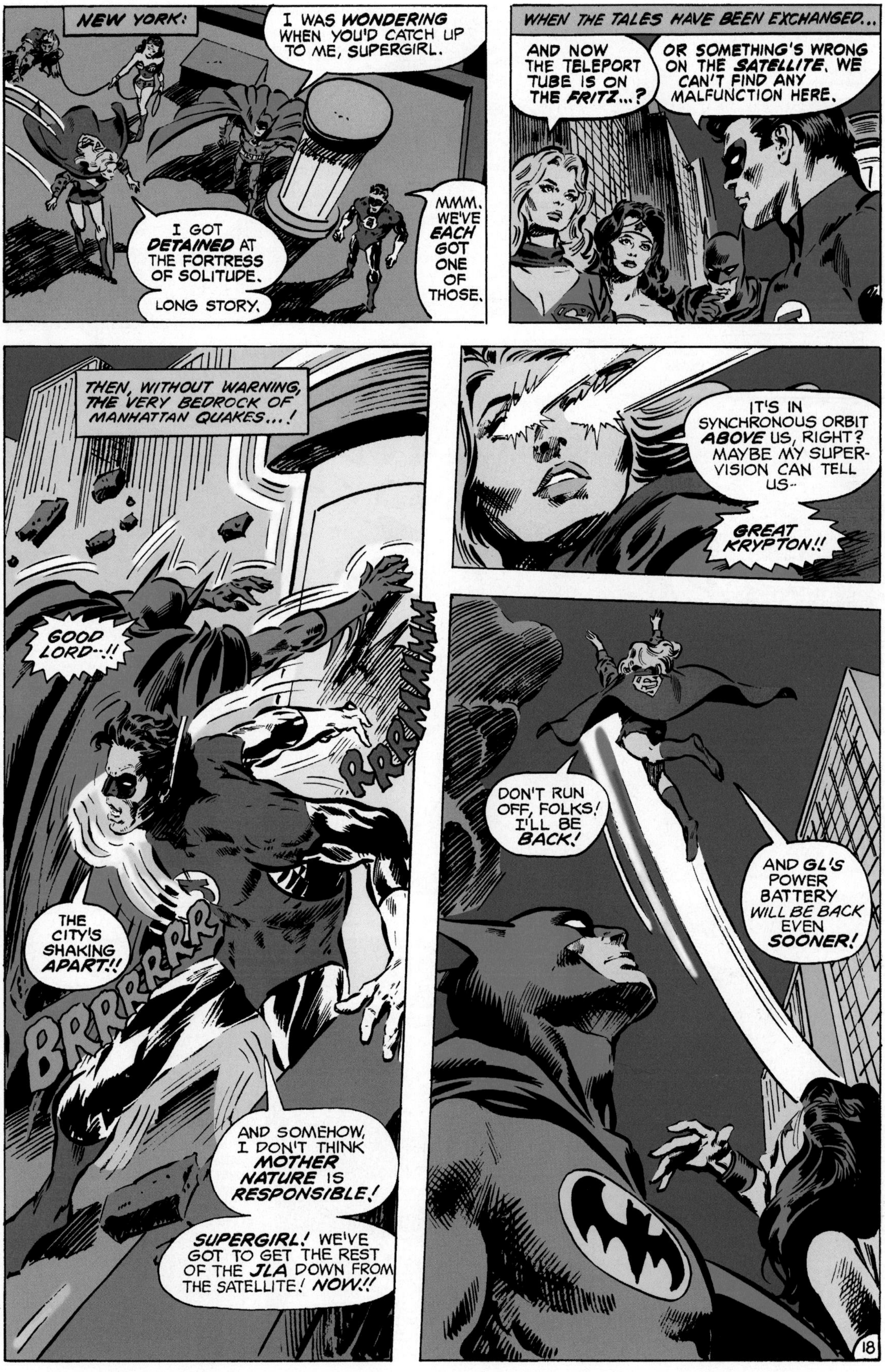
NEW YORK:
I WAS WONDERING WHEN YOU'D CATCH UP TO ME, SUPERGIRL.
I GOT DETAINED AT THE FORTRESS OF SOLITUDE.
LONG STORY.
MMM. WE'VE EACH GOT ONE OF THOSE.
WHEN THE TALES HAVE BEEN EXCHANGED...
AND NOW THE TELEPORT TUBE IS ON THE FRITZ...?
OR SOMETHING'S WRONG ON THE SATELLITE. WE CAN'T FIND ANY MALFUNCTION HERE.
THEN, WITHOUT WARNING, THE VERY BEDROCK OF MANHATTAN QUAKES...!
GOOD LORD--!!
RRRRMMMM
THE CITY'S SHAKING APART!!
BRRRRRRR
AND SOMEHOW, I DON'T THINK MOTHER NATURE IS RESPONSIBLE!
SUPERGIRL! WE'VE GOT TO GET THE REST OF THE JLA DOWN FROM THE SATELLITE! NOW!!
IT'S IN SYNCHRONOUS ORBIT ABOVE US, RIGHT? MAYBE MY SUPER-VISION CAN TELL US--
GREAT KRYPTON!!
DON'T RUN OFF, FOLKS! I'LL BE BACK!
AND GL'S POWER BATTERY WILL BE BACK EVEN SOONER!
18

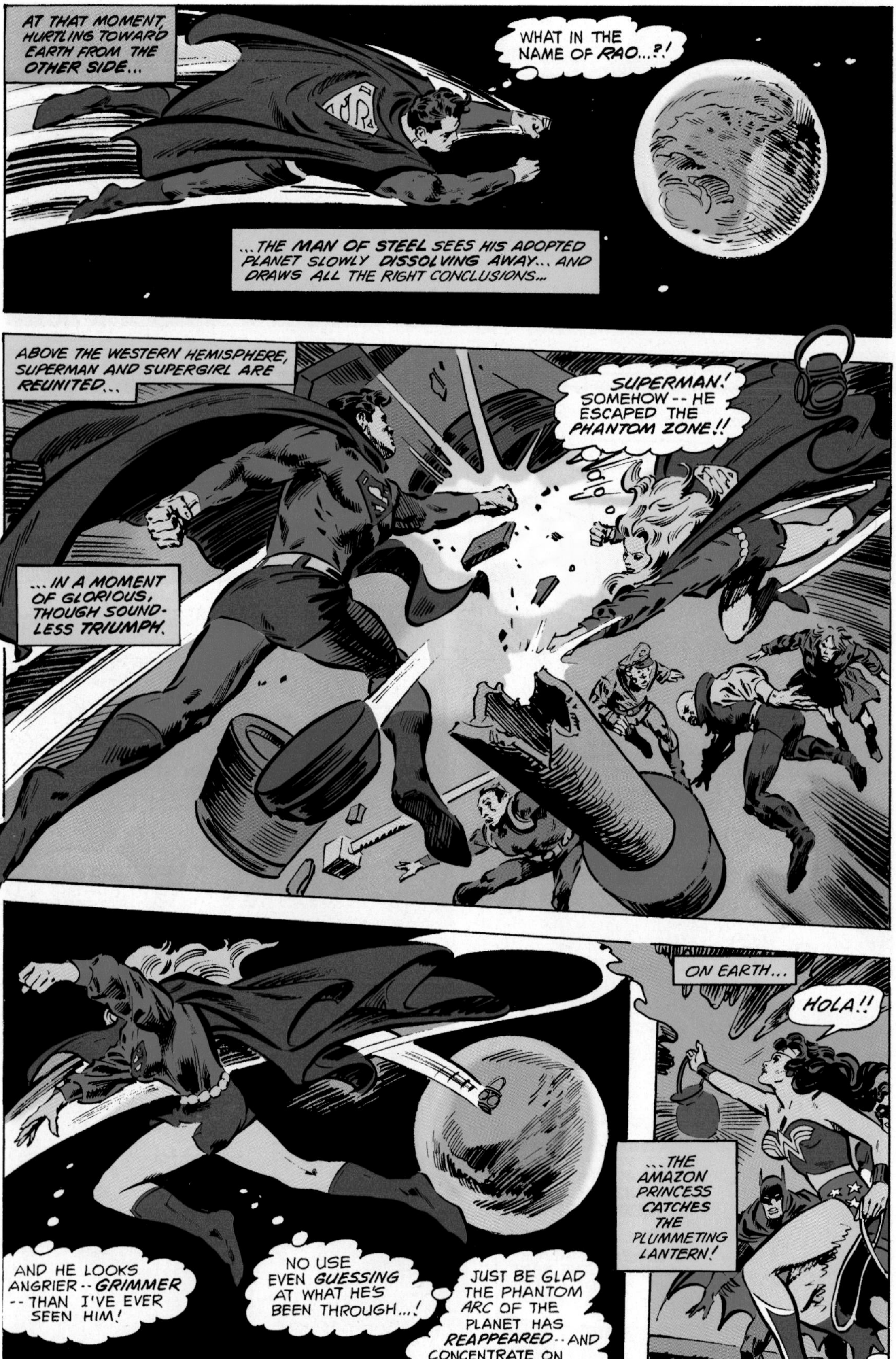
AT THAT MOMENT, HURTLING TOWARD EARTH FROM THE OTHER SIDE...
WHAT IN THE NAME OF RAO...?!
...THE MAN OF STEEL SEES HIS ADOPTED PLANET SLOWLY DISSOLVING AWAY... AND DRAWS ALL THE RIGHT CONCLUSIONS...
ABOVE THE WESTERN HEMISPHERE, SUPERMAN AND SUPERGIRL ARE REUNITED...
SUPERMAN! SOMEHOW -- HE ESCAPED THE PHANTOM ZONE!!
...IN A MOMENT OF GLORIOUS, THOUGH SOUNDLESS TRIUMPH.
AND HE LOOKS ANGRIER -- GRIMMER -- THAN I'VE EVER SEEN HIM!
NO USE EVEN GUESSING AT WHAT HE'S BEEN THROUGH...!
JUST BE GLAD THE PHANTOM ARC OF THE PLANET HAS REAPPEARED -- AND CONCENTRATE ON MAKING THIS TOSS--!
ON EARTH...
HOLA!!
...THE AMAZON PRINCESS CATCHES THE PLUMMETING LANTERN!
19

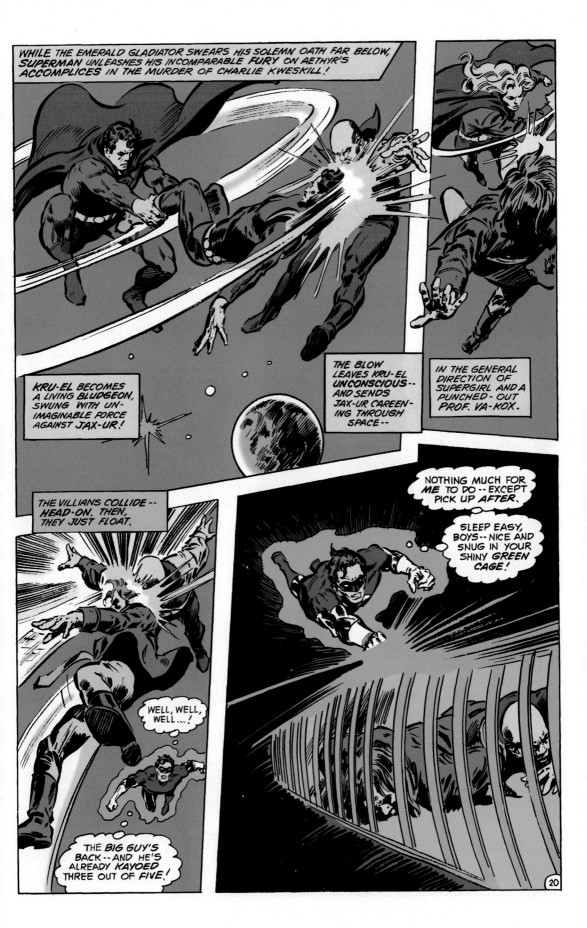

WHILE THE EMERALD GLADIATOR SWEARS HIS SOLEMN OATH FAR BELOW, SUPERMAN UNLEASHES HIS INCOMPARABLE *FURY* ON AETHYR'S ACCOMPLICES IN THE MURDER OF CHARLIE KWESKILL!

KRU-EL BECOMES A LIVING BLUDGEON, SWUNG WITH UN-IMAGINABLE FORCE AGAINST JAX-UR!

THE BLOW LEAVES KRU-EL UNCONSCIOUS-- AND SENDS JAX-UR CAREEN-ING THROUGH SPACE--

IN THE GENERAL DIRECTION OF SUPERGIRL AND A PUNCHED-OUT PROF. VA-KOX.

THE VILLIANS COLLIDE-- HEAD-ON. THEN, THEY JUST FLOAT.

NOTHING MUCH FOR ME TO DO -- EXCEPT PICK UP *AFTER*.

SLEEP EASY, BOYS-- NICE AND SNUG IN YOUR SHINY *GREEN* CAGE!

WELL, WELL, WELL....!

THE *BIG GUY'S* BACK -- AND HE'S ALREADY *KAYOED* THREE OUT OF *FIVE!*

20

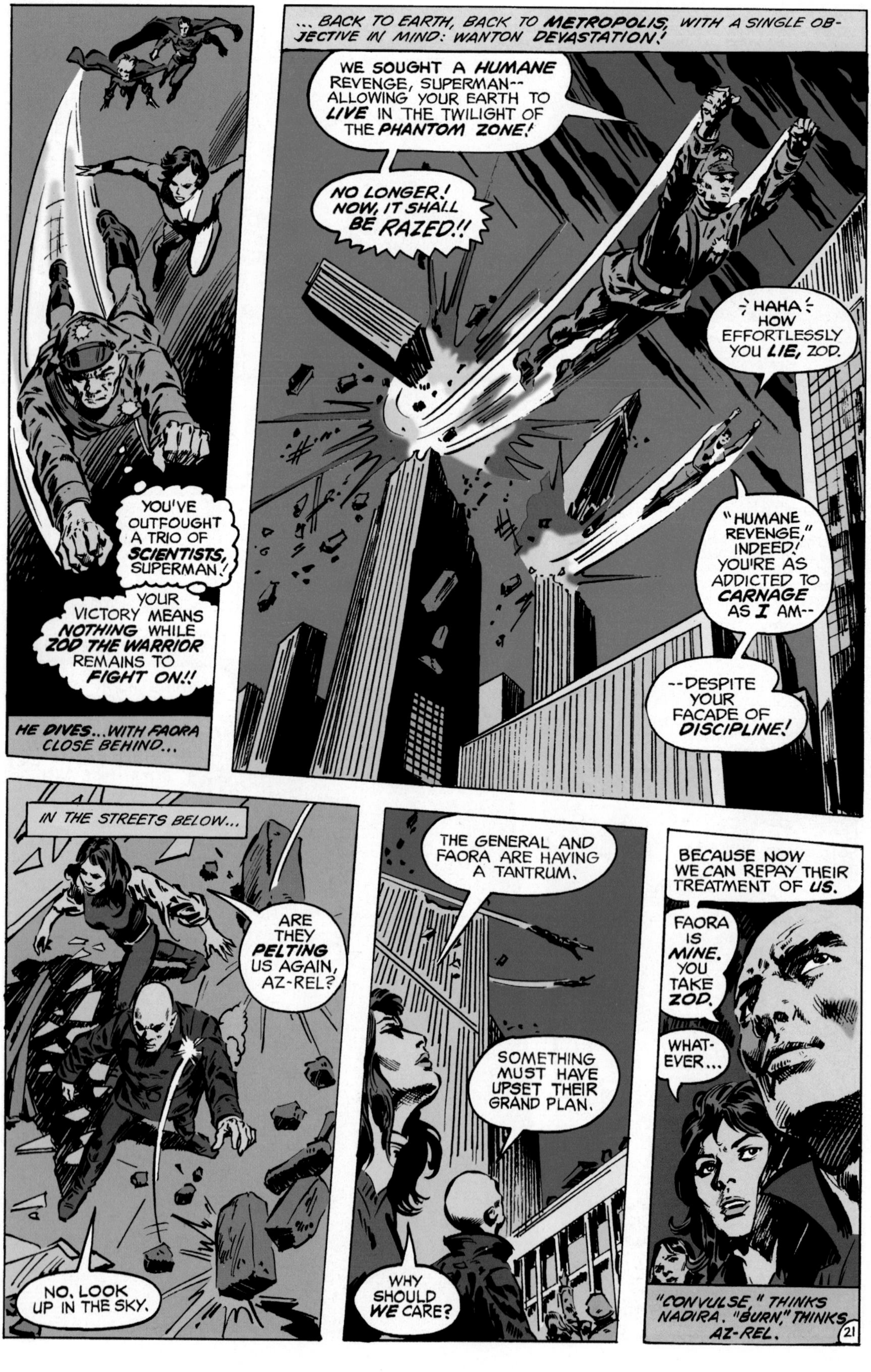
YOU'VE OUTFOUGHT A TRIO OF SCIENTISTS, SUPERMAN!
YOUR VICTORY MEANS NOTHING WHILE ZOD THE WARRIOR REMAINS TO FIGHT ON!!
HE DIVES... WITH FAORA CLOSE BEHIND...
... BACK TO EARTH, BACK TO METROPOLIS, WITH A SINGLE OBJECTIVE IN MIND: WANTON DEVASTATION!
WE SOUGHT A HUMANE REVENGE, SUPERMAN-- ALLOWING YOUR EARTH TO LIVE IN THE TWILIGHT OF THE PHANTOM ZONE!
NO LONGER! NOW, IT SHALL BE RAZED!!
HAHA HOW EFFORTLESSLY YOU LIE, ZOD.
"HUMANE REVENGE," INDEED! YOU'RE AS ADDICTED TO CARNAGE AS I AM--
--DESPITE YOUR FACADE OF DISCIPLINE!
IN THE STREETS BELOW...
ARE THEY PELTING US AGAIN, AZ-REL?
NO, LOOK UP IN THE SKY.
THE GENERAL AND FAORA ARE HAVING A TANTRUM.
SOMETHING MUST HAVE UPSET THEIR GRAND PLAN.
WHY SHOULD WE CARE?
BECAUSE NOW WE CAN REPAY THEIR TREATMENT OF US.
FAORA IS MINE. YOU TAKE ZOD.
WHAT-EVER...
"CONVULSE," THINKS NADIRA. "BURN," THINKS AZ-REL.
21

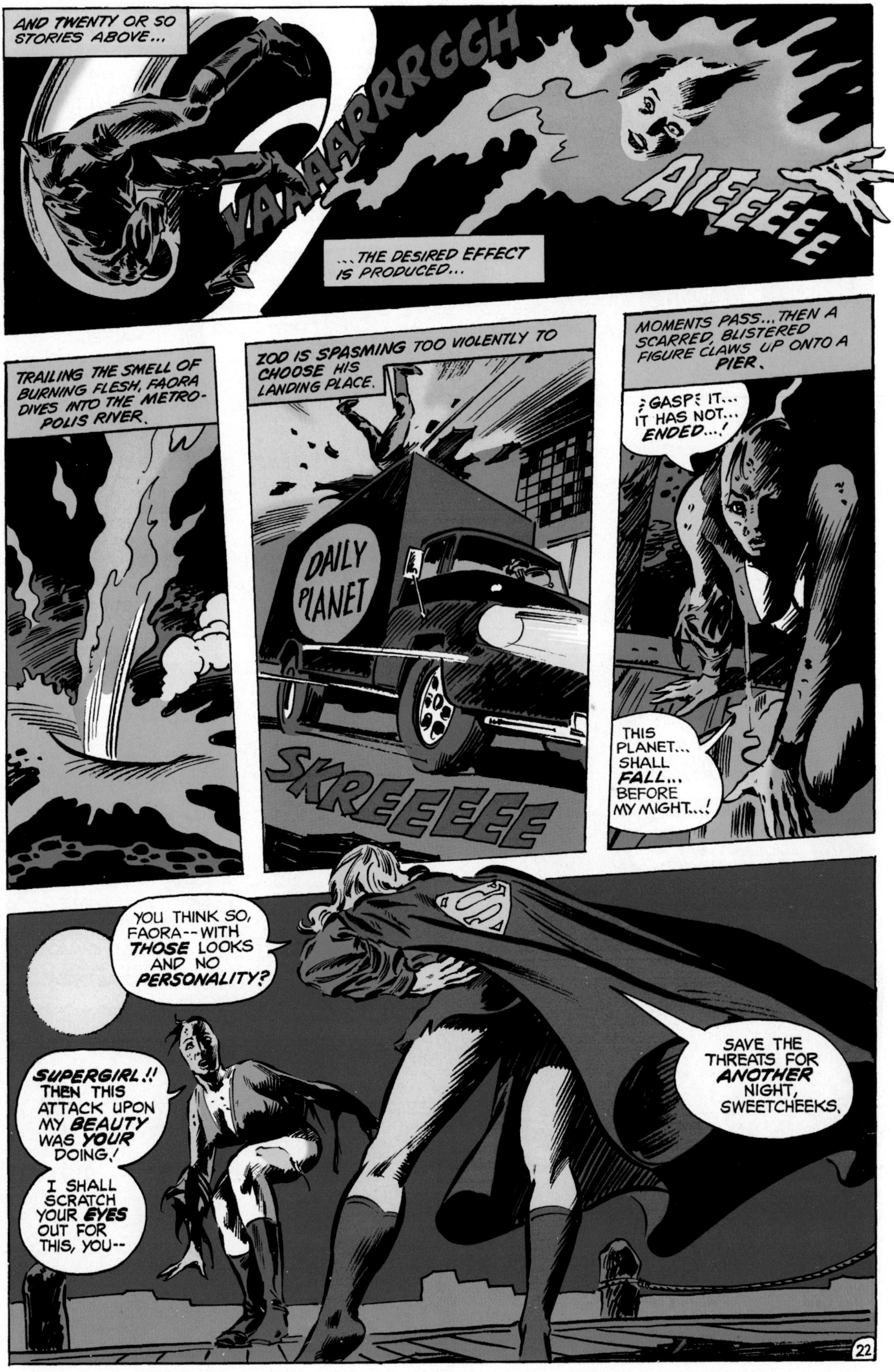
AND TWENTY OR SO STORIES ABOVE...
YAAAARRRRGGH
AIEEEEEE
...THE DESIRED EFFECT IS PRODUCED...
TRAILING THE SMELL OF BURNING FLESH, FAORA DIVES INTO THE METROPOLIS RIVER.
ZOD IS SPASMING TOO VIOLENTLY TO CHOOSE HIS LANDING PLACE.
DAILY PLANET
SKREEEEEE
MOMENTS PASS...THEN A SCARRED, BLISTERED FIGURE CLAWS UP ONTO A PIER.
GASP IT... IT HAS NOT... ENDED...!
THIS PLANET... SHALL FALL... BEFORE MY MIGHT...!
YOU THINK SO, FAORA--WITH THOSE LOOKS AND NO PERSONALITY?
SUPERGIRL!! THEN THIS ATTACK UPON MY BEAUTY WAS YOUR DOING!
I SHALL SCRATCH YOUR EYES OUT FOR THIS, YOU--
SAVE THE THREATS FOR ANOTHER NIGHT, SWEETCHEEKS.
22

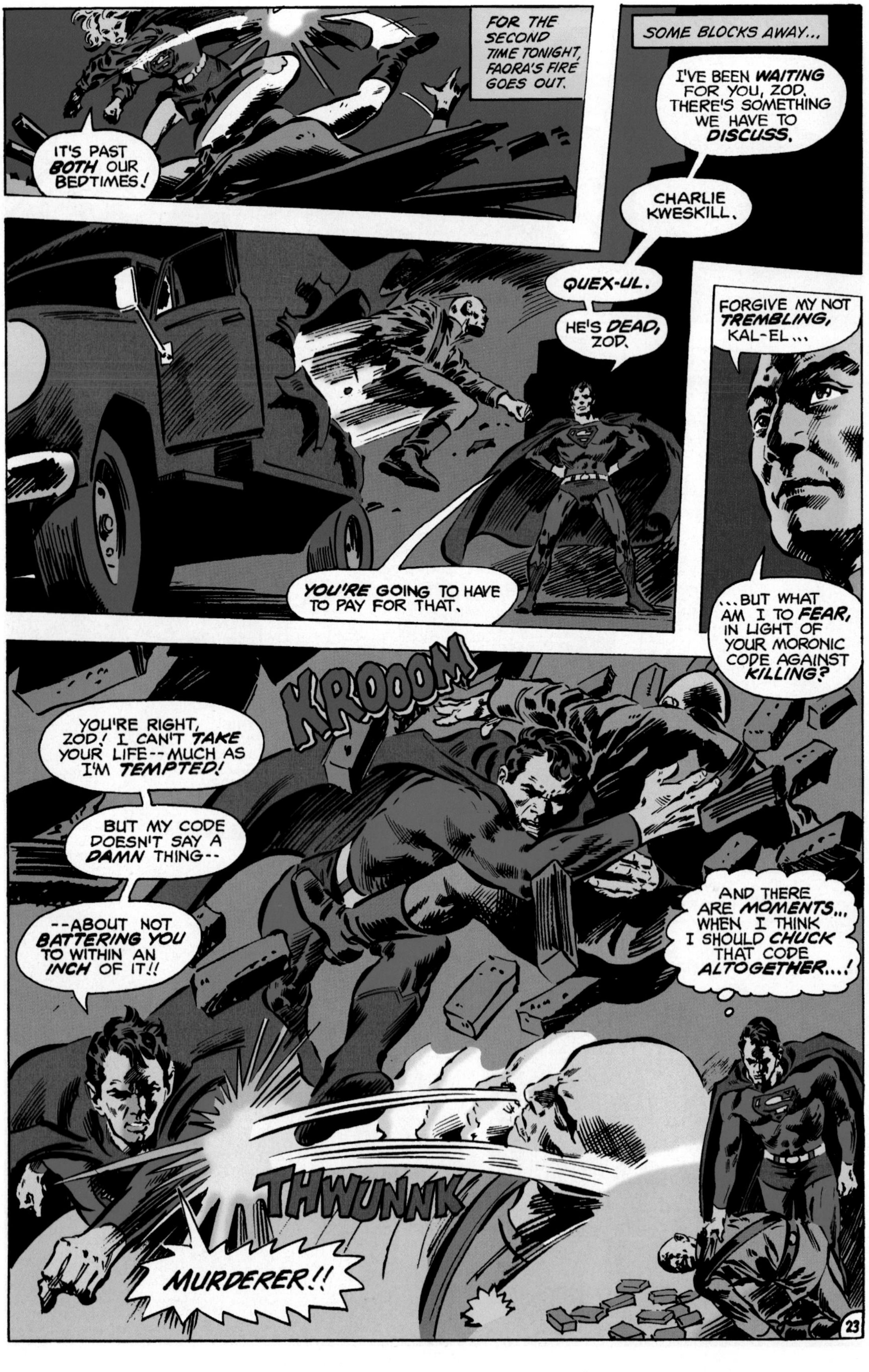

FOR THE SECOND TIME TONIGHT, FAORA'S FIRE GOES OUT.
IT'S PAST BOTH OUR BEDTIMES!
SOME BLOCKS AWAY...
I'VE BEEN WAITING FOR YOU, ZOD. THERE'S SOMETHING WE HAVE TO DISCUSS.
CHARLIE KWESKILL.
QUEX-UL.
HE'S DEAD, ZOD.
YOU'RE GOING TO HAVE TO PAY FOR THAT.
FORGIVE MY NOT TREMBLING, KAL-EL...
...BUT WHAT AM I TO FEAR, IN LIGHT OF YOUR MORONIC CODE AGAINST KILLING?
KROOOM
YOU'RE RIGHT, ZOD! I CAN'T TAKE YOUR LIFE--MUCH AS I'M TEMPTED!
BUT MY CODE DOESN'T SAY A DAMN THING--
--ABOUT NOT BATTERING YOU TO WITHIN AN INCH OF IT!!
AND THERE ARE MOMENTS... WHEN I THINK I SHOULD CHUCK THAT CODE ALTOGETHER...!
THWUNNK
MURDERER!!
23

AN ALLEYWAY ACROSS TOWN,

AZ-REL AND NADIRA, STILL SEEKING RELIEF FROM THEIR BOREDOM...

...ARE DRAWN TOWARD A WEIRD GREEN LUMINESCENCE AND THE PAINED WHIMPERING OF AN ANCIENT, CRACKING VOICE.

THEY ARE NOT EASILY REVULSED, THESE TWO -- BUT WHAT THEY FIND AT THE ALLEY'S DEAD END BRINGS THEM AS CLOSE AS THEY'LL EVER COME.

:GASP: AZ-REL... SOMETHING ...HURTS ME...!

OLD MAN...WH-WHAT... IS THAT...?

GATE...WAY...!

GATEWAY...TO RAO'S... HEAVEN...SOIL...OF HOME...

K-KRYPTONITE... ONLY WAY... FOR JER-EM...!

DO NOT BELONG...ON EARTH...IN PHANTOM ZONE...TAINTED...TAINTED!!... I GO TO RAO!...WILL YOU...JOURNEY... WITH JER-EM?...

:ecch:

HE TURNS GREEN! IT SICKENS ME --HURTS ME!

NO...I BEG...AS RAO'S... PROPHET...

COME...WITH ME...TO RAO... CHILD...!

...WITH... ME...

SHE FALLS, SCREAMING ONTO THE KRYPTONITE.

AZ-REL FLEES.

EEEEEEEEEE

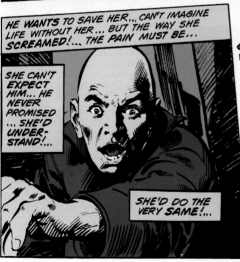

HE WANTS TO SAVE HER...CAN'T IMAGINE LIFE WITHOUT HER...BUT THE WAY SHE SCREAMED!...THE PAIN MUST BE...

SHE CAN'T EXPECT HIM...HE NEVER PROMISED ...SHE'D UNDER- STAND!...

SHE'D DO THE VERY SAME!...

BUT AS HE EMERGES FROM THE ALLEYWAY...

SWOKK

YOU SHOULD LIFT YOUR EYES FROM THE GUTTER OCCASIONALLY, SKINHEAD!

YOU MIGHT'VE SEEN ME COMING!

24

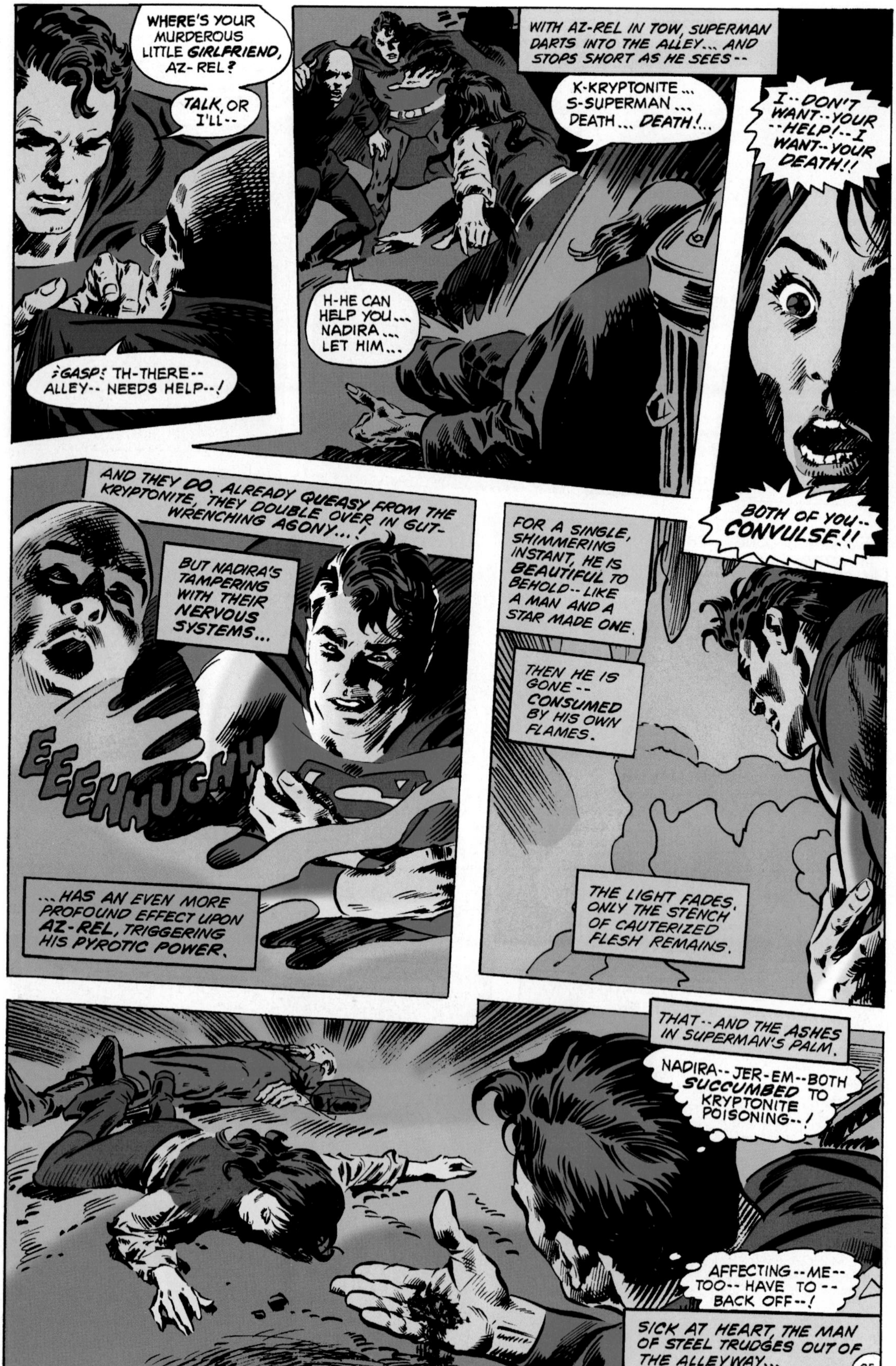

WHERE'S YOUR MURDEROUS LITTLE GIRLFRIEND, AZ-REL?
TALK, OR I'LL--
GASP! TH-THERE-- ALLEY-- NEEDS HELP--!
WITH AZ-REL IN TOW, SUPERMAN DARTS INTO THE ALLEY... AND STOPS SHORT AS HE SEES--
K-KRYPTONITE... S-SUPERMAN... DEATH... DEATH!...
H-HE CAN HELP YOU... NADIRA... LET HIM...
I--DON'T WANT--YOUR --HELP!--I WANT--YOUR DEATH!!
BOTH OF YOU-- CONVULSE!!
AND THEY DO. ALREADY QUEASY FROM THE KRYPTONITE, THEY DOUBLE OVER IN GUT-WRENCHING AGONY...!
BUT NADIRA'S TAMPERING WITH THEIR NERVOUS SYSTEMS...
EEEHHUGHH
...HAS AN EVEN MORE PROFOUND EFFECT UPON AZ-REL, TRIGGERING HIS PYROTIC POWER.
FOR A SINGLE, SHIMMERING INSTANT, HE IS BEAUTIFUL TO BEHOLD--LIKE A MAN AND A STAR MADE ONE.
THEN HE IS GONE-- CONSUMED BY HIS OWN FLAMES.
THE LIGHT FADES. ONLY THE STENCH OF CAUTERIZED FLESH REMAINS.
THAT--AND THE ASHES IN SUPERMAN'S PALM.
NADIRA-- JER-EM--BOTH SUCCUMBED TO KRYPTONITE POISONING--!
AFFECTING--ME-- TOO-- HAVE TO-- BACK OFF--!
SICK AT HEART, THE MAN OF STEEL TRUDGES OUT OF THE ALLEYWAY...
25

...AND JOINS SUPERGIRL IN THE SKY FOR A RED-EYE FLIGHT BACK TO NEW YORK.

SO THESE ARE THE *SURVIVORS*--ZOD, KRU-EL, VA-KOX, FAORA, JAX-UR, AND NAM-EK.

NOT EXACTLY AN *ADVERTISE-MENT* FOR NATURAL SELECTION, IS IT?...

NATURE DOESN'T *JUDGE*, SUPERGIRL. THAT'S WHAT *HUMANS* ARE FOR.

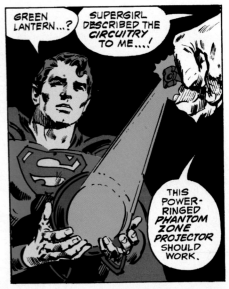

GREEN LANTERN...?

SUPERGIRL DESCRIBED THE *CIRCUITRY* TO ME....!

THIS POWER-RINGED *PHANTOM ZONE PROJECTOR* SHOULD WORK.

IT'S BACK TO THE *ZONE*, ZOD--TO THE *TWILIGHT* WHERE YOU *BELONG*.

WAS IT *WORTH* ALL THOSE *LIVES*--JUST FOR *THIS*?

TO BE *FREE*? TO *CONQUER*??

THAT WOULD BE WORTH THOSE LIVES AND A *BILLION BILLION* MORE!

AND YOURS WILL BE AMONG THEM, KAL-EL!! YOU, TOO, WILL PERISH WHEN WE--

AND NOW HE'S OFF TO RETRIEVE THE *JLA* SATELLITE...!

AND TO LOOK FOR SOME *PEACE*, I THINK, GL.

YOU NOTICED IT, TOO, THEN. HE WOULDN'T SAY A WORD--

--ABOUT WHAT HAPPENED IN THE *PHANTOM ZONE!*

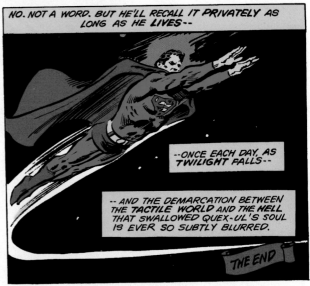

NO. NOT A WORD. BUT HE'LL RECALL IT *PRIVATELY* AS LONG AS HE *LIVES*--

--ONCE EACH DAY, AS *TWILIGHT FALLS*--

--AND THE DEMARCATION BETWEEN THE *TACTILE* WORLD AND THE *HELL* THAT SWALLOWED QUEX-UL'S SOUL IS EVER SO SUBTLY BLURRED.

THE END

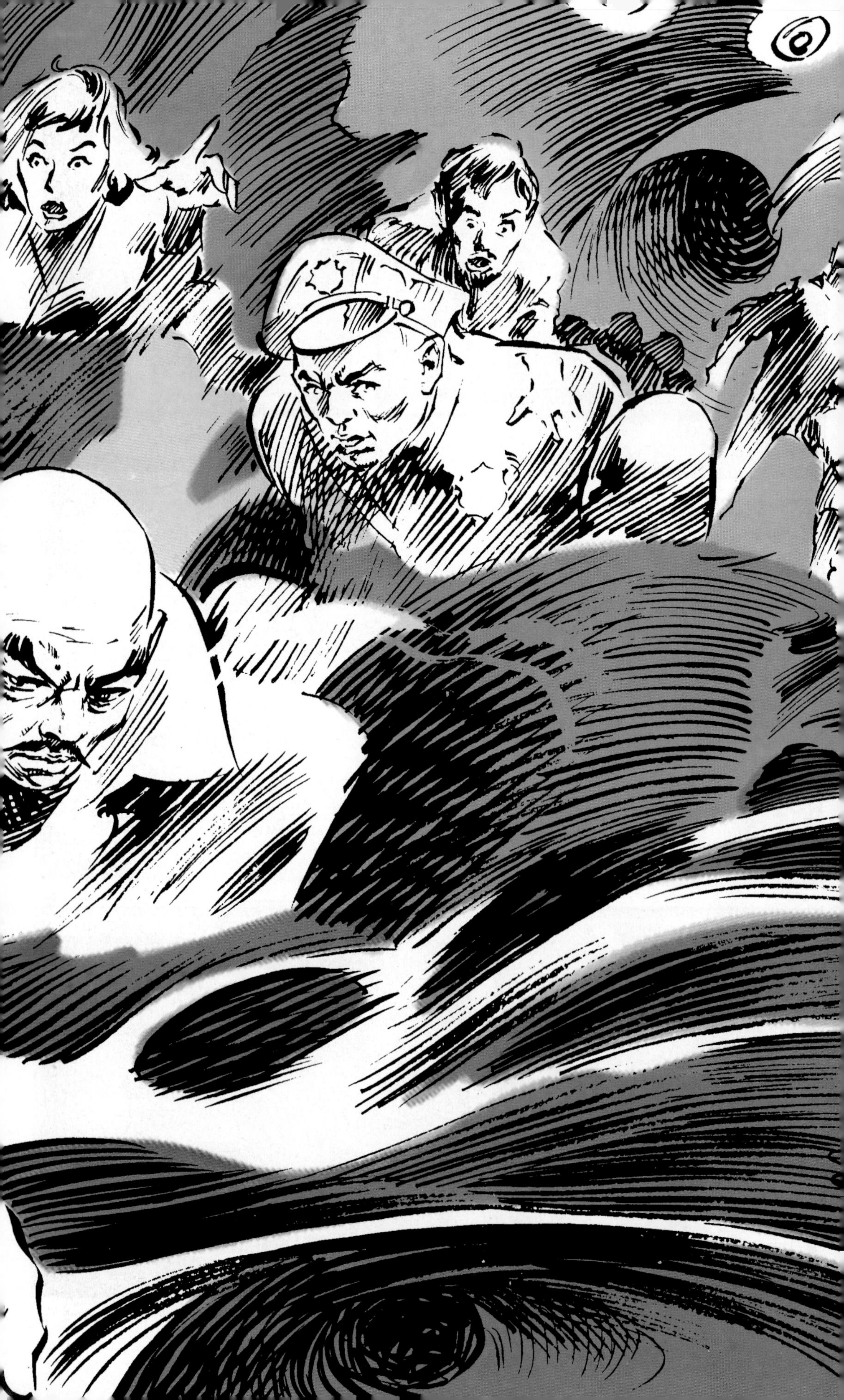

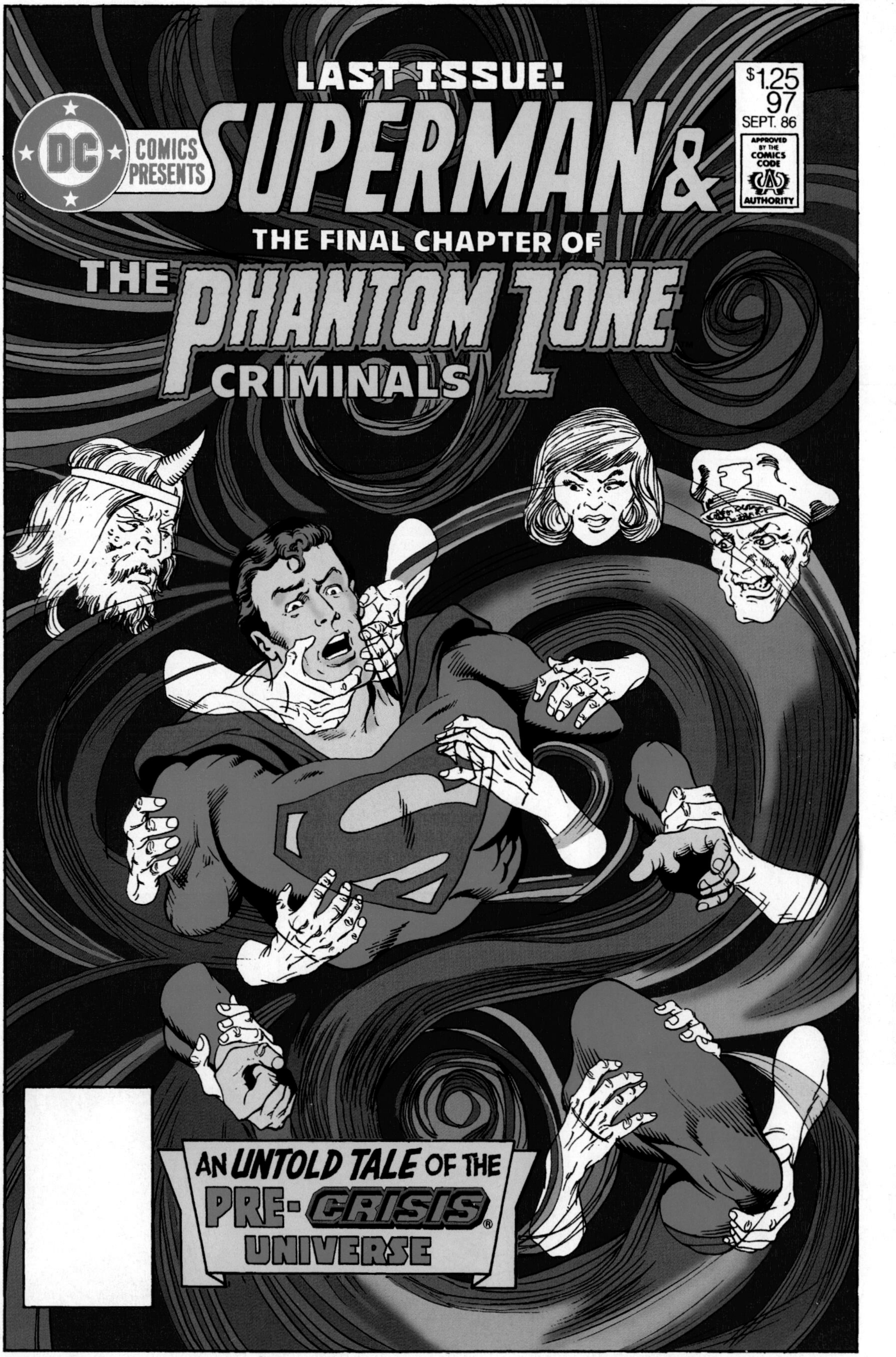
LAST ISSUE!
$1.25
97
SEPT. 86
APPROVED BY THE COMICS CODE AUTHORITY
DC
COMICS PRESENTS
SUPERMAN &
THE FINAL CHAPTER OF
THE PHANTOM ZONE CRIMINALS
AN UNTOLD TALE OF THE
PRE-CRISIS®
UNIVERSE

NIGHT THOUGHTS OF A KRYPTONIAN PHYSICIST:

WHEN I SHUT MY EYES, I FEEL THE TREMBLING... I HEAR THE GROANING AT THE CENTER OF THE WORLD.

OUR CITIES AND FARMLANDS, OUR LIBRARIES AND LABORATORIES...

...OUR TEN THOUSAND YEARS OF LEARNING TO BE CIVILIZED...

...ARE WRAPPED ABOUT A CORE OF URANIUM, A VIRTUAL ATOMIC PILE, BUILDING TOWARD CRITICAL MASS.

WILL IT BE TONIGHT...?

TOO MANY VARIABLES. IMPOSSIBLE TO PREDICT WITH ANY PRECISION.

SO I LIE AND WAIT. WITH EYES OPEN.

WE WERE WRONG TO WANT THE CHILD, LARA. ITS TIME WILL BE TOO BRIEF.

BY CHOOSING TO GIVE IT LIFE, WE'VE CONDEMNED IT TO DEATH.

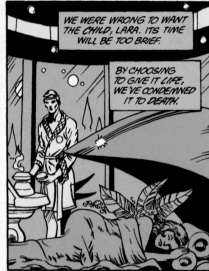

AND WITH EACH PASSING MOMENT, THE CERTAINTY OF THAT DEATH INCREASES.

IT HAS TO BE TRIED, LARA... NOW!

FOR THE CHILD'S SAKE...

...IT HAS TO BE TRIED!

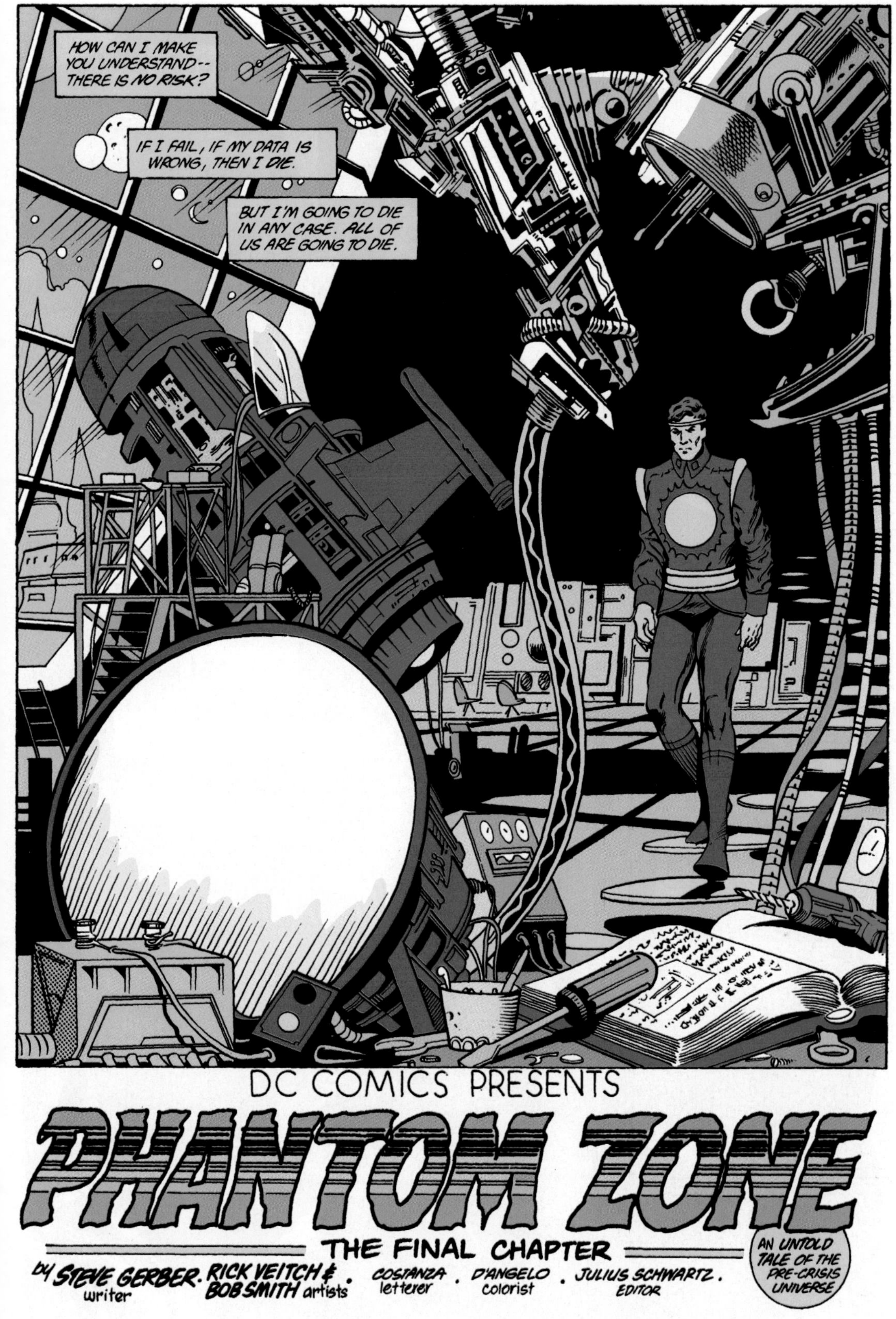
HOW CAN I MAKE YOU UNDERSTAND-- THERE IS NO RISK?
IF I FAIL, IF MY DATA IS WRONG, THEN I DIE.
BUT I'M GOING TO DIE IN ANY CASE. ALL OF US ARE GOING TO DIE.

DC COMICS PRESENTS

PHANTOM ZONE

THE FINAL CHAPTER

AN UNTOLD TALE OF THE PRE-CRISIS UNIVERSE

by STEVE GERBER, writer . RICK VEITCH & BOB SMITH artists . COSTANZA letterer . D'ANGELO colorist . JULIUS SCHWARTZ . EDITOR

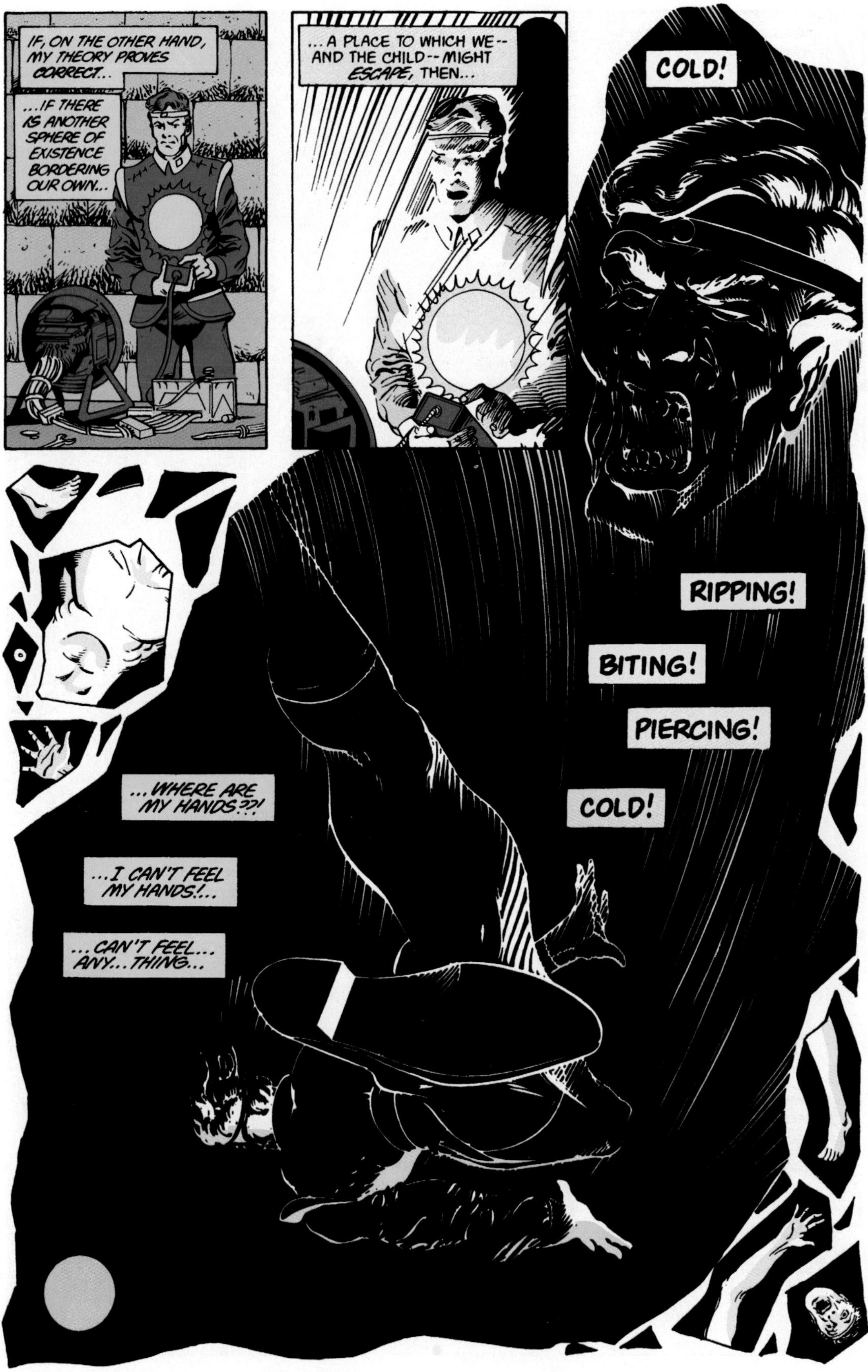
IF, ON THE OTHER HAND, MY THEORY PROVES CORRECT...
...IF THERE IS ANOTHER SPHERE OF EXISTENCE BORDERING OUR OWN...
...A PLACE TO WHICH WE-- AND THE CHILD--MIGHT ESCAPE, THEN...
COLD!
RIPPING!
BITING!
PIERCING!
COLD!
...WHERE ARE MY HANDS??!
...I CAN'T FEEL MY HANDS!...
...CAN'T FEEL... ANY...THING...

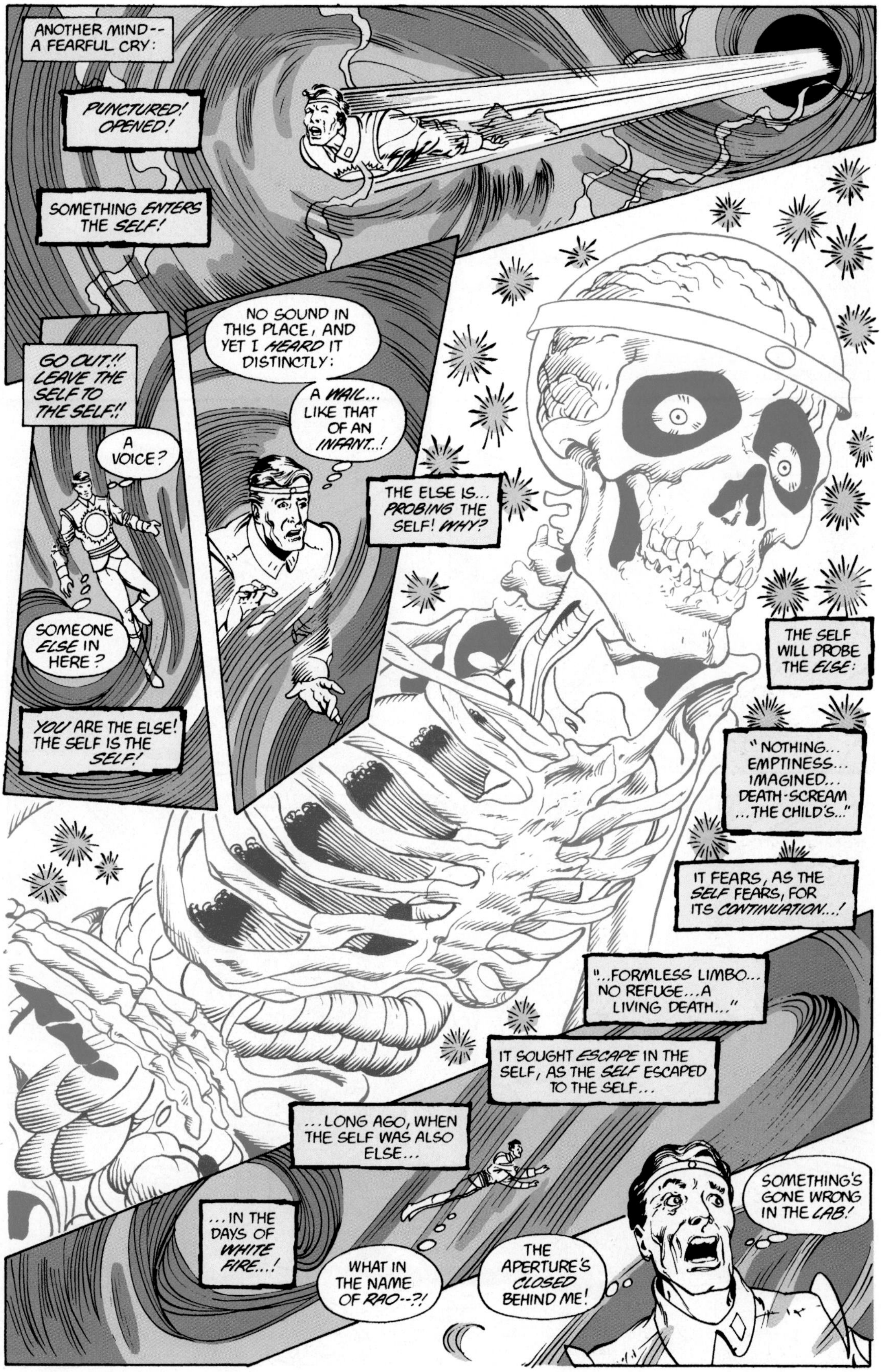
ANOTHER MIND-- A FEARFUL CRY:
PUNCTURED! OPENED!
SOMETHING ENTERS THE SELF!
GO OUT!! LEAVE THE SELF TO THE SELF!!
A VOICE?
SOMEONE ELSE IN HERE?
YOU ARE THE ELSE! THE SELF IS THE SELF!
NO SOUND IN THIS PLACE, AND YET I HEARD IT DISTINCTLY:
A WAIL... LIKE THAT OF AN INFANT...!
THE ELSE IS... PROBING THE SELF! WHY?
THE SELF WILL PROBE THE ELSE:
"NOTHING... EMPTINESS... IMAGINED... DEATH-SCREAM ...THE CHILD'S..."
IT FEARS, AS THE SELF FEARS, FOR ITS CONTINUATION...!
"...FORMLESS LIMBO... NO REFUGE...A LIVING DEATH..."
IT SOUGHT ESCAPE IN THE SELF, AS THE SELF ESCAPED TO THE SELF...
...LONG AGO, WHEN THE SELF WAS ALSO ELSE...
...IN THE DAYS OF WHITE FIRE...!
WHAT IN THE NAME OF RAO--?!
THE APERTURE'S CLOSED BEHIND ME!
SOMETHING'S GONE WRONG IN THE LAB!

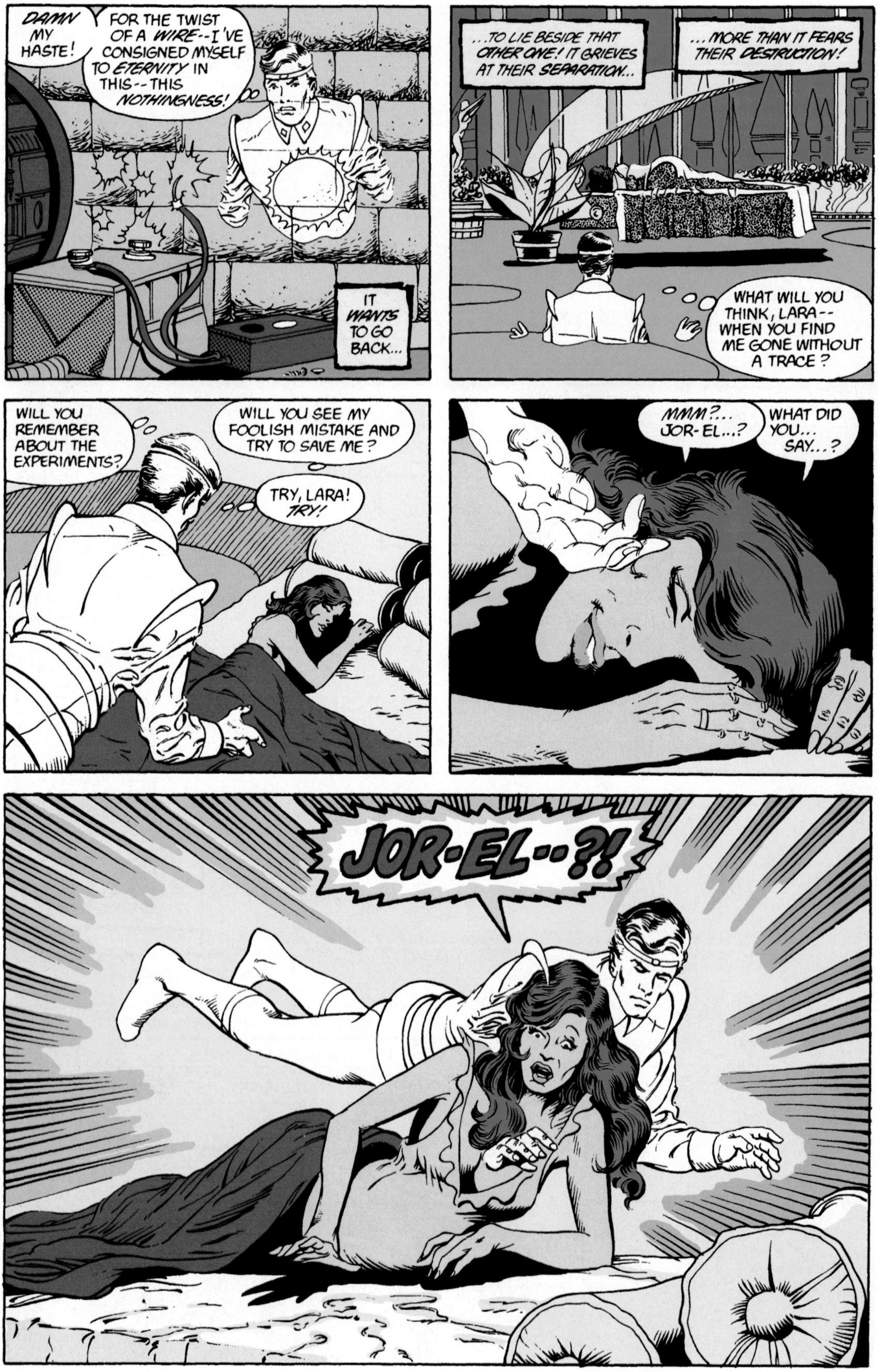
DAMN MY HASTE!
FOR THE TWIST OF A WIRE--I'VE CONSIGNED MYSELF TO ETERNITY IN THIS--THIS NOTHINGNESS!
IT WANTS TO GO BACK...
...TO LIE BESIDE THAT OTHER ONE! IT GRIEVES AT THEIR SEPARATION...
...MORE THAN IT FEARS THEIR DESTRUCTION!
WHAT WILL YOU THINK, LARA--WHEN YOU FIND ME GONE WITHOUT A TRACE?
WILL YOU REMEMBER ABOUT THE EXPERIMENTS?
WILL YOU SEE MY FOOLISH MISTAKE AND TRY TO SAVE ME?
TRY, LARA! TRY!
MMM?... JOR-EL...?
WHAT DID YOU... SAY...?
JOR-EL--?!

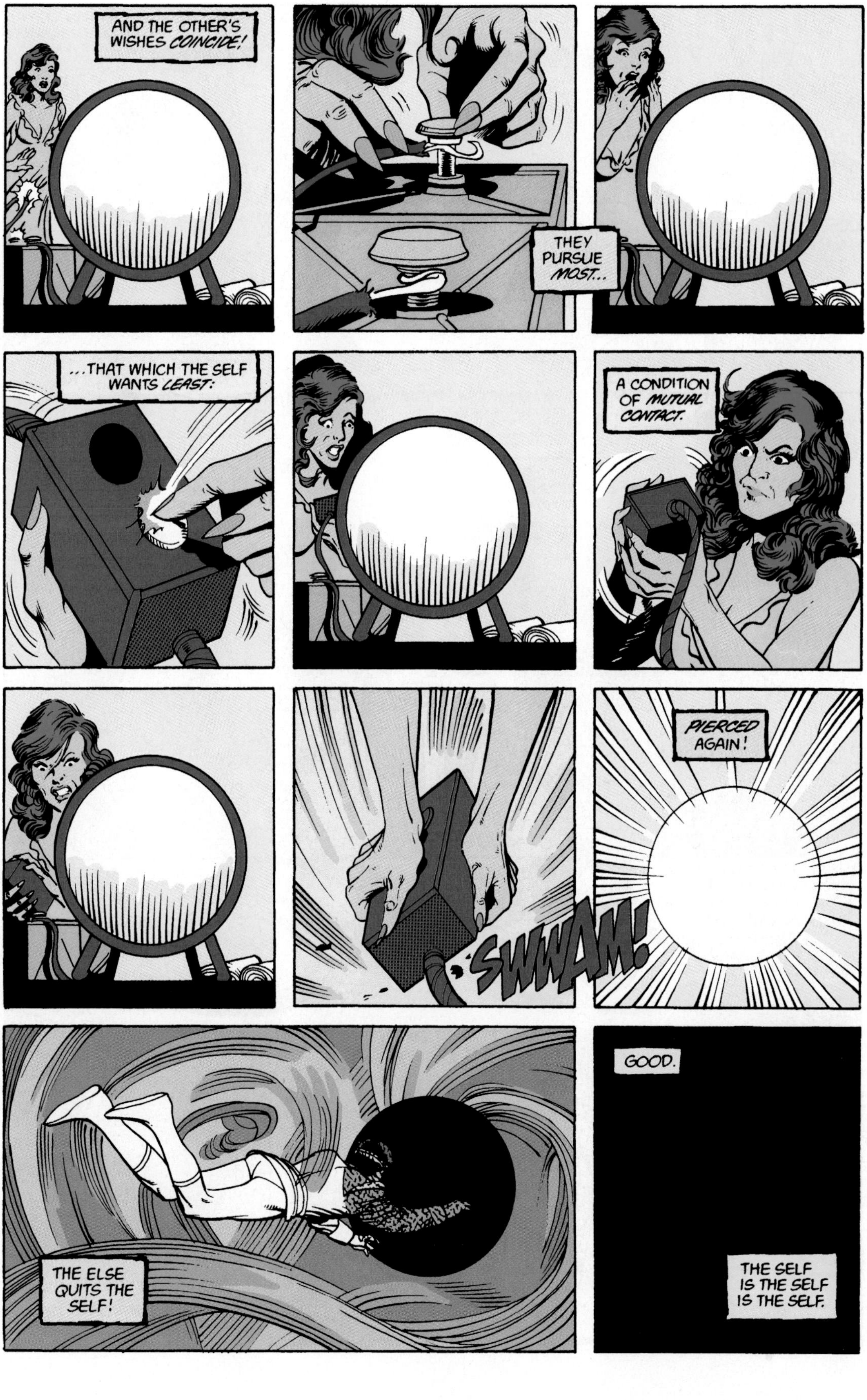

AND THE OTHER'S WISHES COINCIDE!
THEY PURSUE MOST...
...THAT WHICH THE SELF WANTS LEAST:
A CONDITION OF MUTUAL CONTACT.
PIERCED AGAIN!
SWWAM!
THE ELSE QUITS THE SELF!
GOOD.
THE SELF IS THE SELF IS THE SELF.

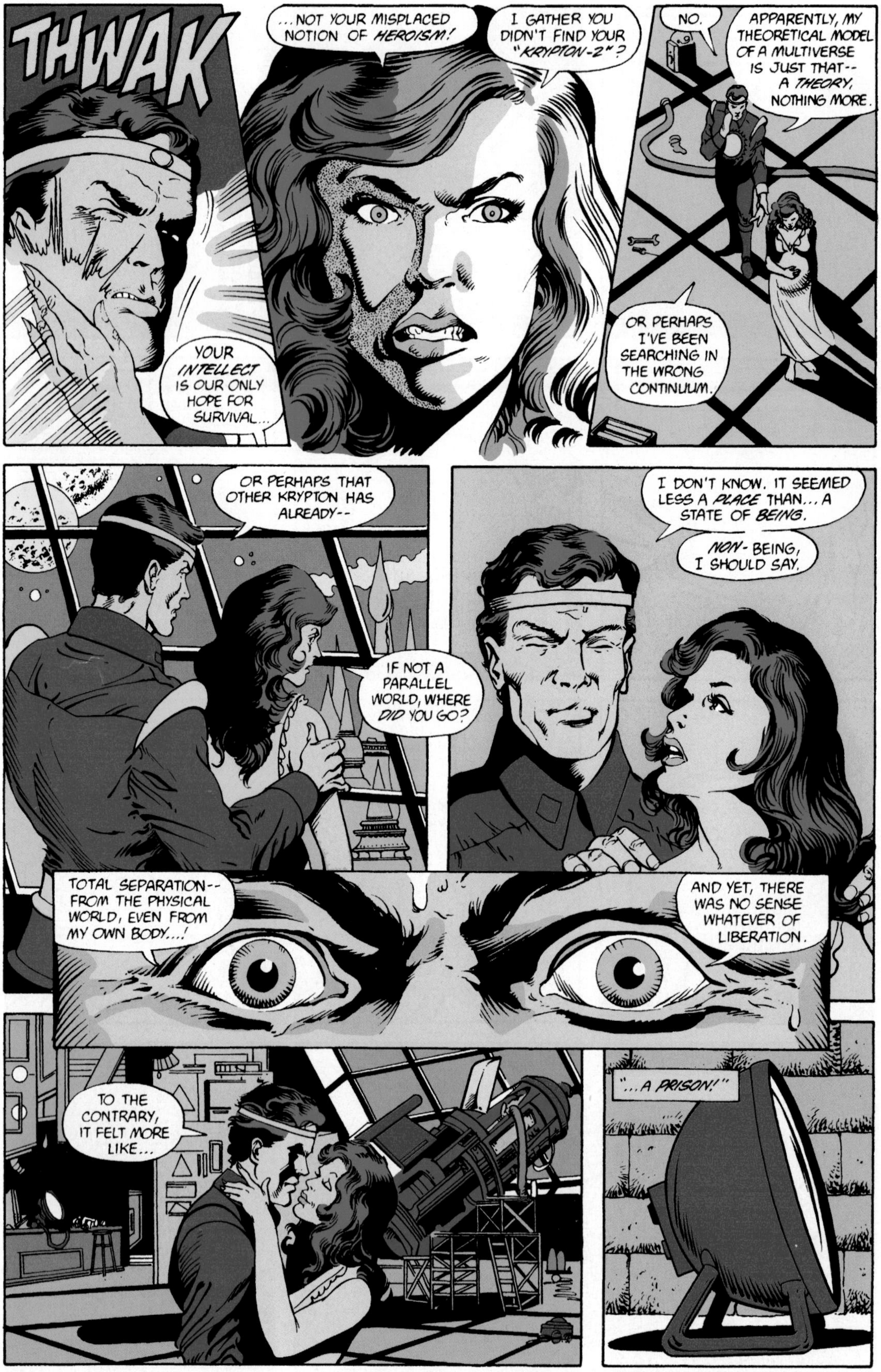
THWAK
YOUR INTELLECT IS OUR ONLY HOPE FOR SURVIVAL...
...NOT YOUR MISPLACED NOTION OF HEROISM!
I GATHER YOU DIDN'T FIND YOUR "KRYPTON-2"?
NO.
APPARENTLY, MY THEORETICAL MODEL OF A MULTIVERSE IS JUST THAT-- A THEORY, NOTHING MORE.
OR PERHAPS I'VE BEEN SEARCHING IN THE WRONG CONTINUUM.
OR PERHAPS THAT OTHER KRYPTON HAS ALREADY--
IF NOT A PARALLEL WORLD, WHERE DID YOU GO?
I DON'T KNOW. IT SEEMED LESS A PLACE THAN... A STATE OF BEING.
NON- BEING, I SHOULD SAY.
TOTAL SEPARATION-- FROM THE PHYSICAL WORLD, EVEN FROM MY OWN BODY...!
AND YET, THERE WAS NO SENSE WHATEVER OF LIBERATION.
TO THE CONTRARY, IT FELT MORE LIKE...
"...A PRISON!"

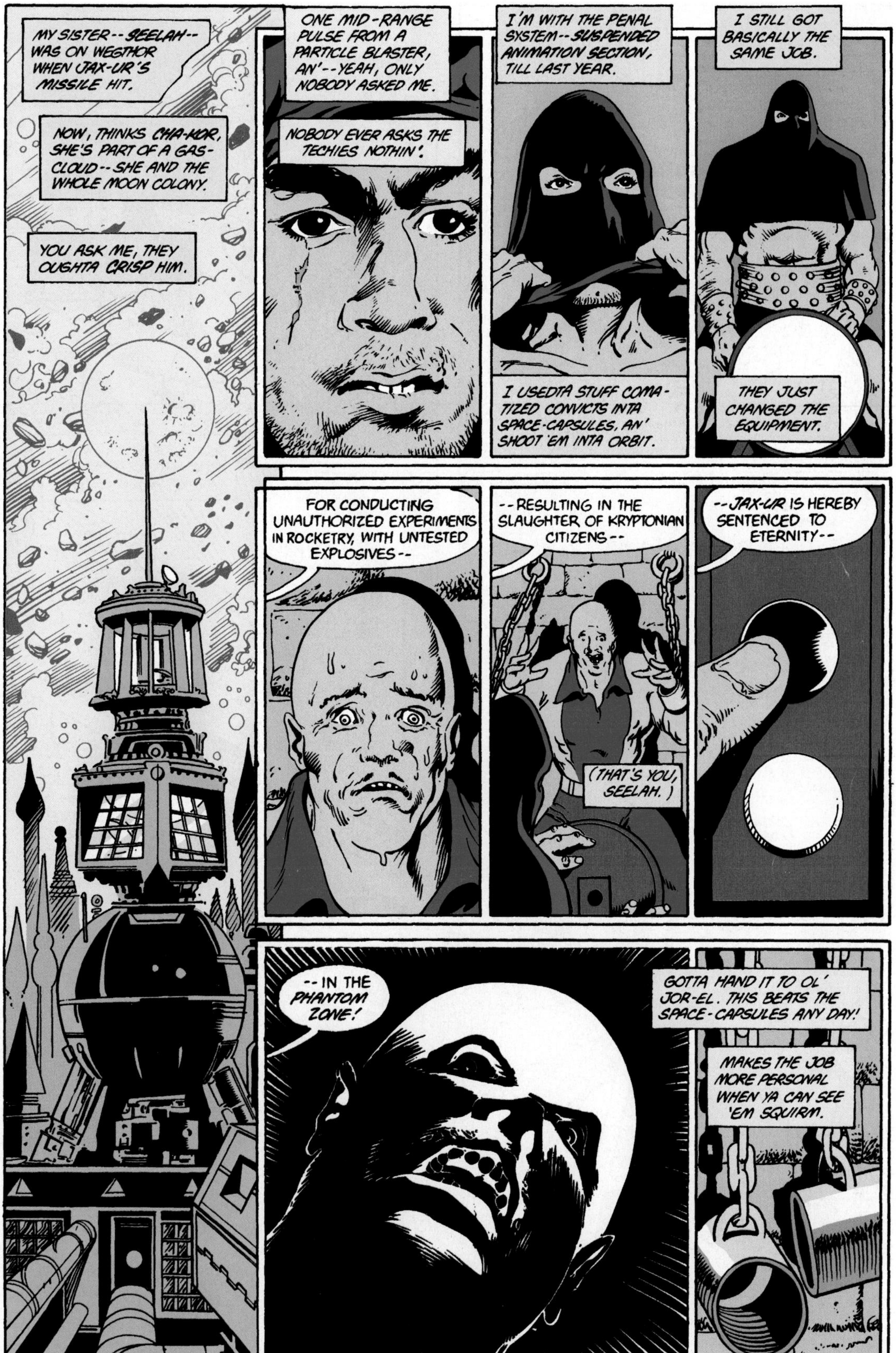
MY SISTER--SEELAH--WAS ON WEGTHOR WHEN JAX-UR'S MISSILE HIT.
NOW, THINKS CHA-KOR, SHE'S PART OF A GAS-CLOUD--SHE AND THE WHOLE MOON COLONY.
YOU ASK ME, THEY OUGHTA CRISP HIM.
ONE MID-RANGE PULSE FROM A PARTICLE BLASTER, AN'--YEAH, ONLY NOBODY ASKED ME.
NOBODY EVER ASKS THE TECHIES NOTHIN'.
I'M WITH THE PENAL SYSTEM--SUSPENDED ANIMATION SECTION, TILL LAST YEAR.
I USEDTA STUFF COMATIZED CONVICTS INTA SPACE-CAPSULES, AN' SHOOT 'EM INTA ORBIT.
I STILL GOT BASICALLY THE SAME JOB.
THEY JUST CHANGED THE EQUIPMENT.
FOR CONDUCTING UNAUTHORIZED EXPERIMENTS IN ROCKETRY, WITH UNTESTED EXPLOSIVES--
--RESULTING IN THE SLAUGHTER OF KRYPTONIAN CITIZENS--
(THAT'S YOU, SEELAH.)
--JAX-UR IS HEREBY SENTENCED TO ETERNITY--
--IN THE PHANTOM ZONE!
GOTTA HAND IT TO OL' JOR-EL. THIS BEATS THE SPACE-CAPSULES ANY DAY!
MAKES THE JOB MORE PERSONAL WHEN YA CAN SEE 'EM SQUIRM.

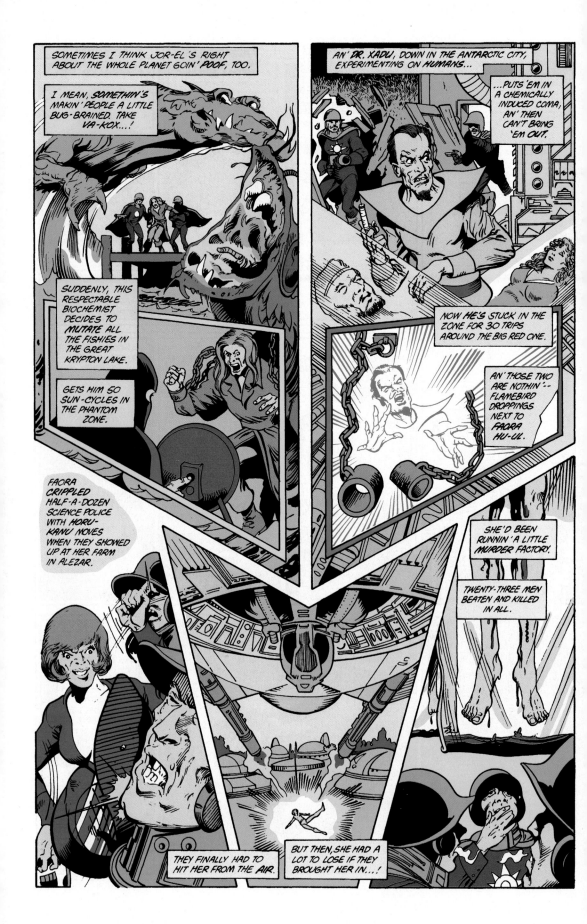

SOMETIMES I THINK JOR-EL'S RIGHT ABOUT THE WHOLE PLANET GOIN' *POOF*, TOO.

I MEAN, *SOMETHIN'S* MAKIN' PEOPLE A LITTLE BUG-BRAINED. TAKE *VA-KOX...!*

SUDDENLY, THIS RESPECTABLE BIOCHEMIST DECIDES TO *MUTATE* ALL THE FISHIES IN THE GREAT KRYPTON LAKE.

GETS HIM 50 SUN-CYCLES IN THE PHANTOM ZONE.

FAORA CRIPPLED HALF-A-DOZEN SCIENCE POLICE WITH *HORU-KANU* NOVES WHEN THEY SHOWED UP AT HER FARM IN ALEZAR.

AN' *DR. XADU*, DOWN IN THE ANTARCTIC CITY, EXPERIMENTING ON *HUMANS...*

...PUTS 'EM IN A CHEMICALLY INDUCED COMA, AN' THEN CAN'T BRING 'EM OUT.

NOW HE'S STUCK IN THE ZONE FOR 30 TRIPS AROUND THE BIG RED ONE.

AN' THOSE TWO ARE NOTHIN'-- FLAMEBIRD DROPPINGS NEXT TO *FAORA HU-UL.*

SHE'D BEEN RUNNIN' A LITTLE *MURDER FACTORY.*

TWENTY-THREE MEN BEATEN AND KILLED IN ALL.

THEY FINALLY HAD TO HIT HER FROM THE *AIR.*

BUT THEN, SHE HAD A LOT TO LOSE IF THEY BROUGHT HER IN....!

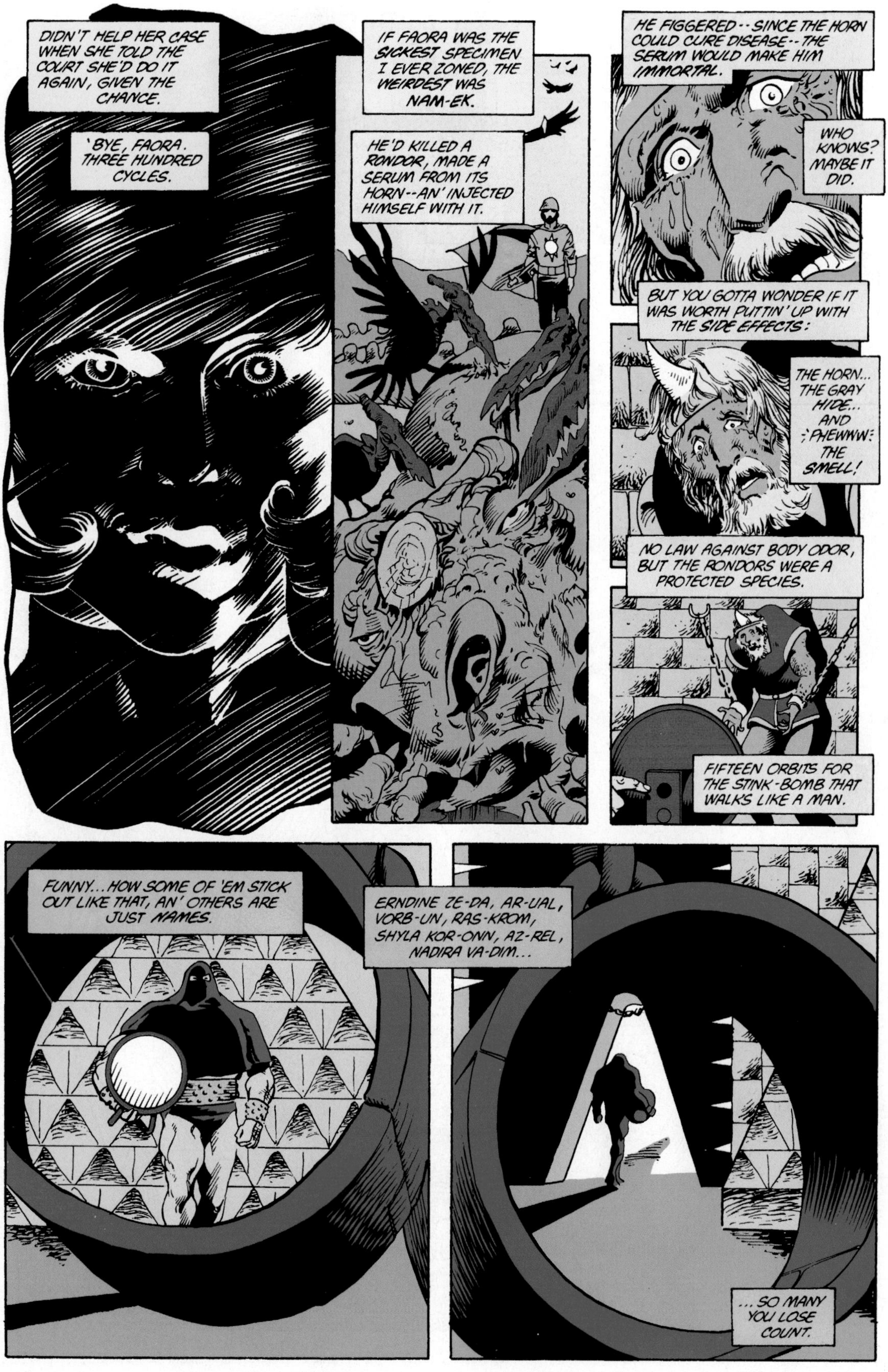

DIDN'T HELP HER CASE WHEN SHE TOLD THE COURT SHE'D DO IT AGAIN, GIVEN THE CHANCE.
'BYE, FAORA. THREE HUNDRED CYCLES.
IF FAORA WAS THE SICKEST SPECIMEN I EVER ZONED, THE WEIRDEST WAS NAM-EK.
HE'D KILLED A RONDOR, MADE A SERUM FROM ITS HORN--AN' INJECTED HIMSELF WITH IT.
HE FIGGERED--SINCE THE HORN COULD CURE DISEASE--THE SERUM WOULD MAKE HIM IMMORTAL.
WHO KNOWS? MAYBE IT DID.
BUT YOU GOTTA WONDER IF IT WAS WORTH PUTTIN' UP WITH THE SIDE EFFECTS:
THE HORN... THE GRAY HIDE... AND PHEWWW: THE SMELL!
NO LAW AGAINST BODY ODOR, BUT THE RONDORS WERE A PROTECTED SPECIES.
FIFTEEN ORBITS FOR THE STINK-BOMB THAT WALKS LIKE A MAN.
FUNNY... HOW SOME OF 'EM STICK OUT LIKE THAT, AN' OTHERS ARE JUST NAMES.
ERNDINE ZE-DA, AR-UAL, VORB-UN, RAS-KROM, SHYLA KOR-ONN, AZ-REL, NADIRA VA-DIM...
...SO MANY YOU LOSE COUNT.

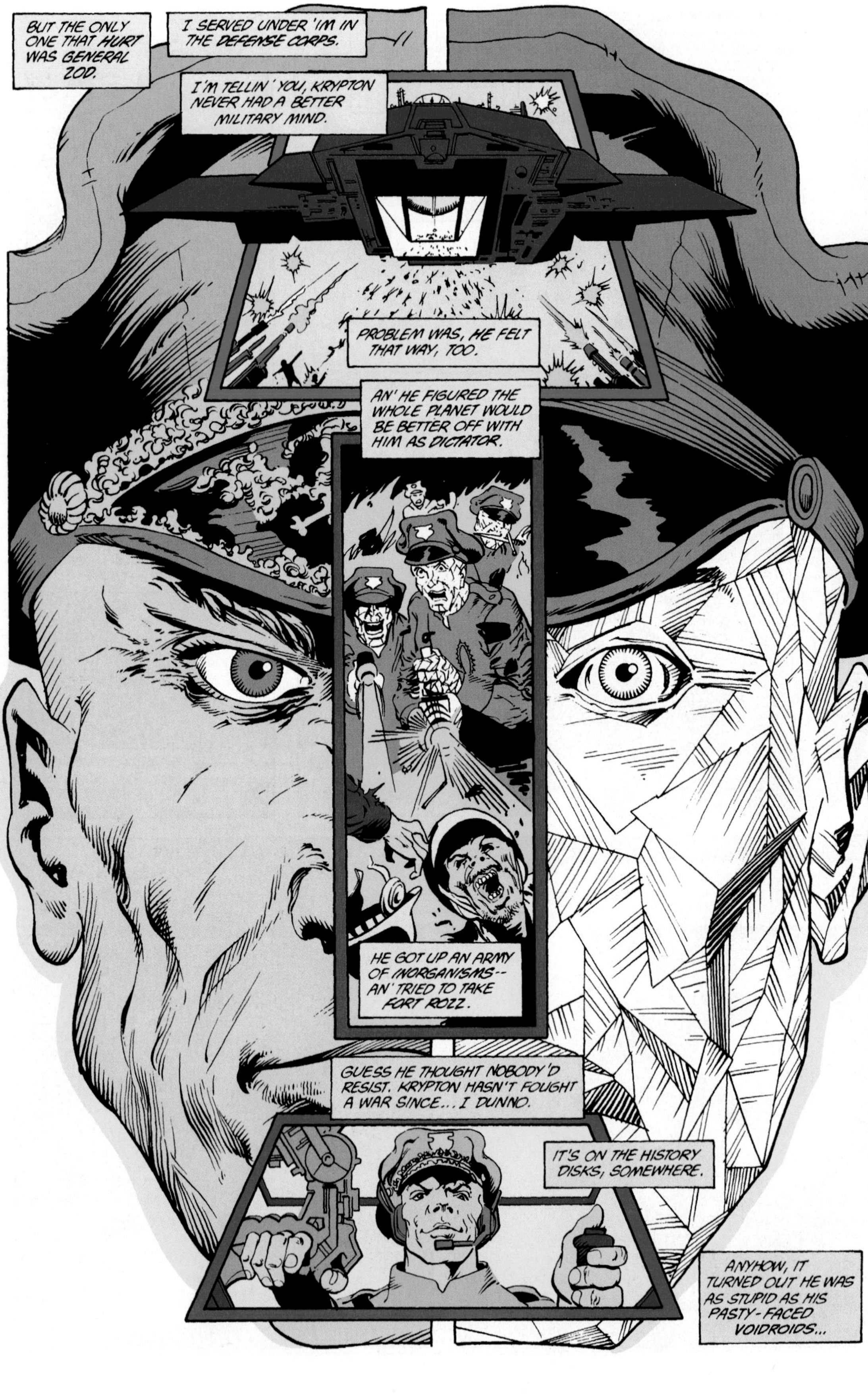
BUT THE ONLY ONE THAT HURT WAS GENERAL ZOD.
I SERVED UNDER 'IM IN THE DEFENSE CORPS.
I'M TELLIN' YOU, KRYPTON NEVER HAD A BETTER MILITARY MIND.
PROBLEM WAS, HE FELT THAT WAY, TOO.
AN' HE FIGURED THE WHOLE PLANET WOULD BE BETTER OFF WITH HIM AS DICTATOR.
HE GOT UP AN ARMY OF INORGANISMS--AN' TRIED TO TAKE FORT ROZZ.
GUESS HE THOUGHT NOBODY'D RESIST. KRYPTON HASN'T FOUGHT A WAR SINCE... I DUNNO.
IT'S ON THE HISTORY DISKS, SOMEWHERE.
ANYHOW, IT TURNED OUT HE WAS AS STUPID AS HIS PASTY-FACED VOIDROIDS...

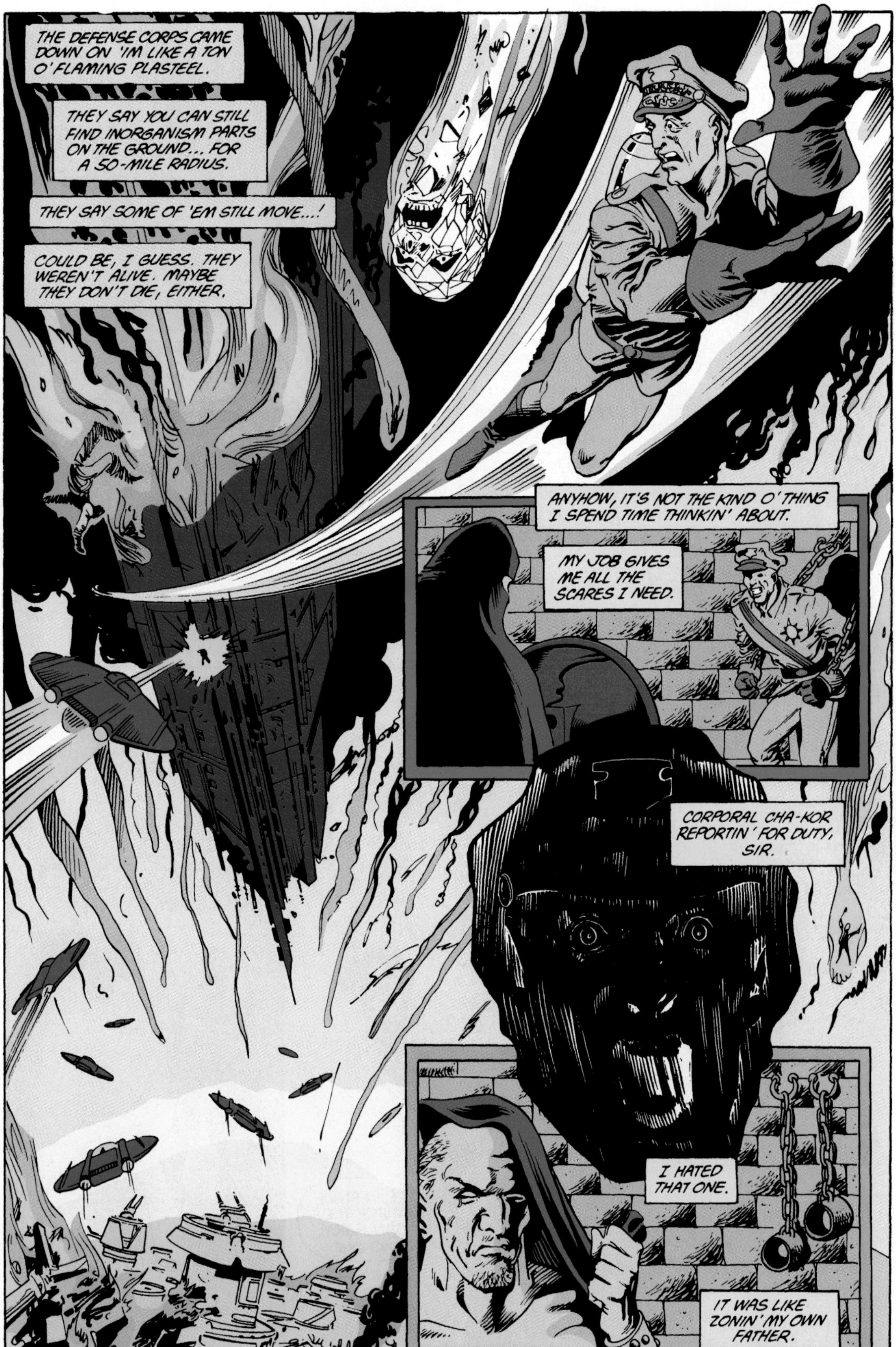
THE DEFENSE CORPS CAME DOWN ON 'IM LIKE A TON O' FLAMING PLASTEEL.
THEY SAY YOU CAN STILL FIND INORGANISM PARTS ON THE GROUND... FOR A 50-MILE RADIUS.
THEY SAY SOME OF 'EM STILL MOVE...!
COULD BE, I GUESS. THEY WEREN'T ALIVE. MAYBE THEY DON'T DIE, EITHER.
ANYHOW, IT'S NOT THE KIND O' THING I SPEND TIME THINKIN' ABOUT.
MY JOB GIVES ME ALL THE SCARES I NEED.
CORPORAL CHA-KOR REPORTIN' FOR DUTY, SIR.
I HATED THAT ONE.
IT WAS LIKE ZONIN' MY OWN FATHER.

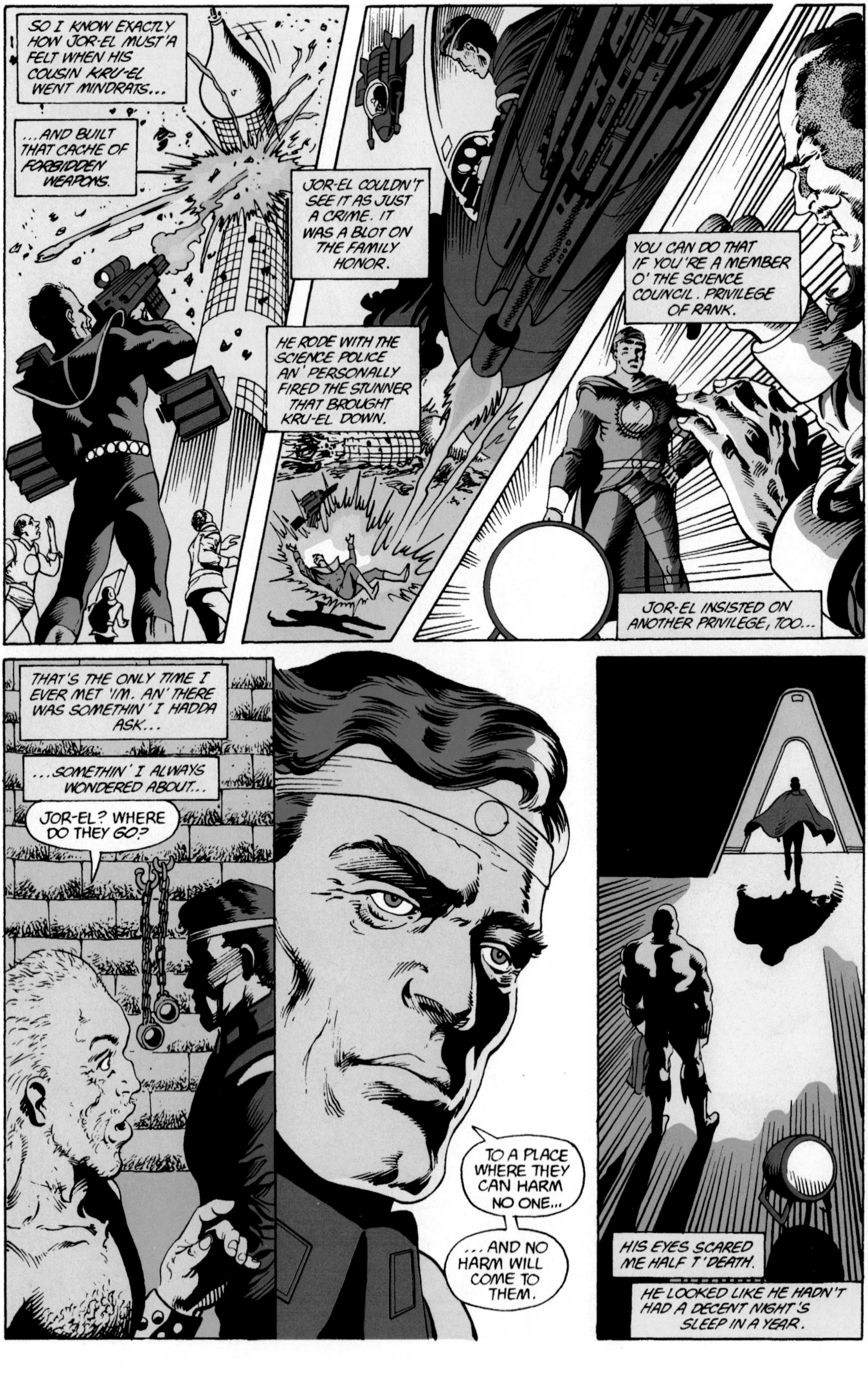
SO I KNOW EXACTLY HOW JOR-EL MUST'A FELT WHEN HIS COUSIN KRU-EL WENT MINDRATS...
...AND BUILT THAT CACHE OF FORBIDDEN WEAPONS.
JOR-EL COULDN'T SEE IT AS JUST A CRIME. IT WAS A BLOT ON THE FAMILY HONOR.
HE RODE WITH THE SCIENCE POLICE AN' PERSONALLY FIRED THE STUNNER THAT BROUGHT KRU-EL DOWN.
YOU CAN DO THAT IF YOU'RE A MEMBER O' THE SCIENCE COUNCIL. PRIVILEGE OF RANK.
JOR-EL INSISTED ON ANOTHER PRIVILEGE, TOO...
THAT'S THE ONLY TIME I EVER MET 'IM. AN' THERE WAS SOMETHIN' I HADDA ASK...
...SOMETHIN' I ALWAYS WONDERED ABOUT...
JOR-EL? WHERE DO THEY GO?
TO A PLACE WHERE THEY CAN HARM NO ONE...
...AND NO HARM WILL COME TO THEM.
HIS EYES SCARED ME HALF T'DEATH.
HE LOOKED LIKE HE HADN'T HAD A DECENT NIGHT'S SLEEP IN A YEAR.

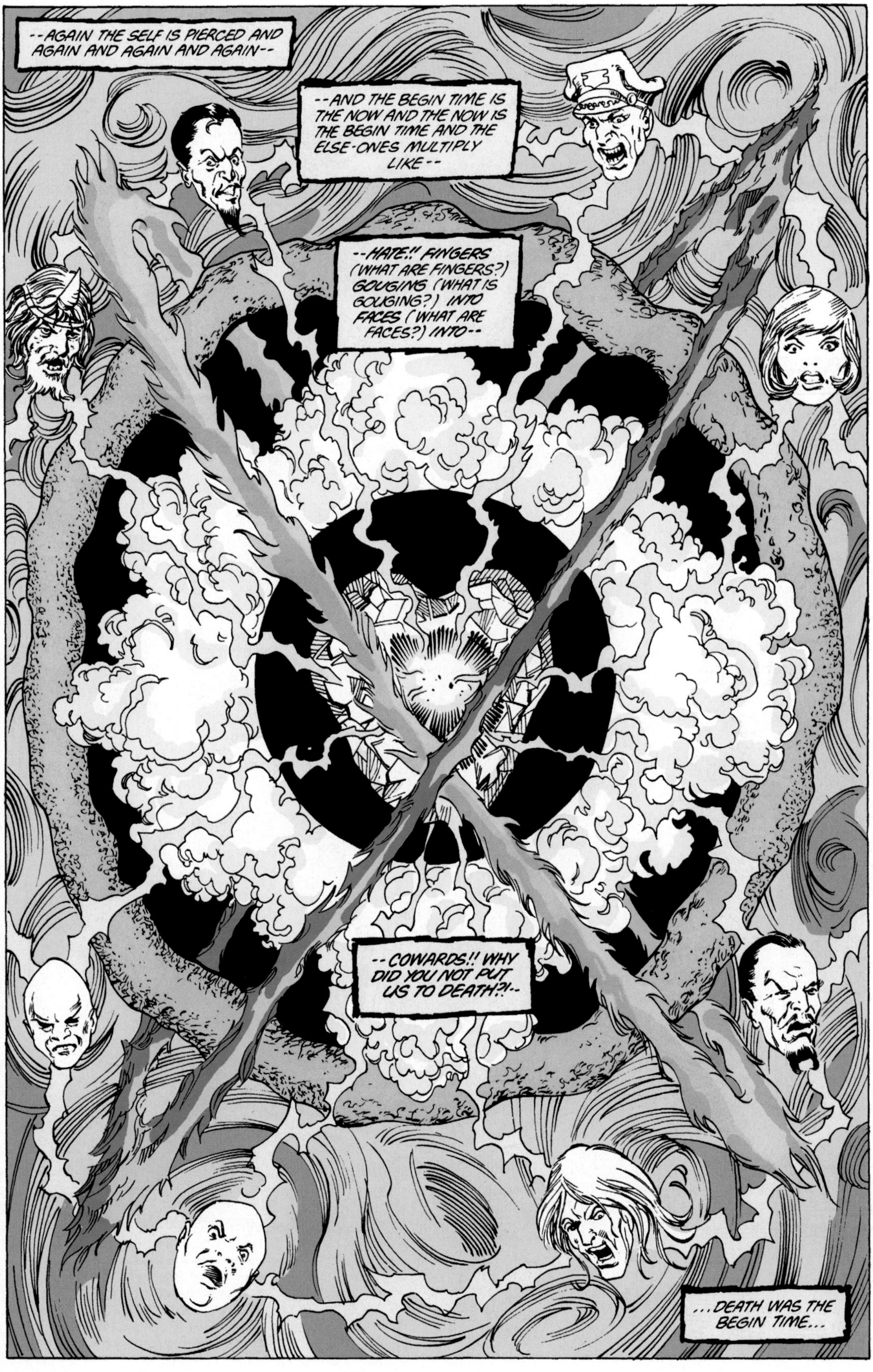
--AGAIN THE SELF IS PIERCED AND AGAIN AND AGAIN AND AGAIN--
--AND THE BEGIN TIME IS THE NOW AND THE NOW IS THE BEGIN TIME AND THE ELSE-ONES MULTIPLY LIKE--
--HATE!! FINGERS (WHAT ARE FINGERS?) GOUGING (WHAT IS GOUGING?) INTO FACES (WHAT ARE FACES?) INTO--
--COWARDS!! WHY DID YOU NOT PUT US TO DEATH?!-
...DEATH WAS THE BEGIN TIME...

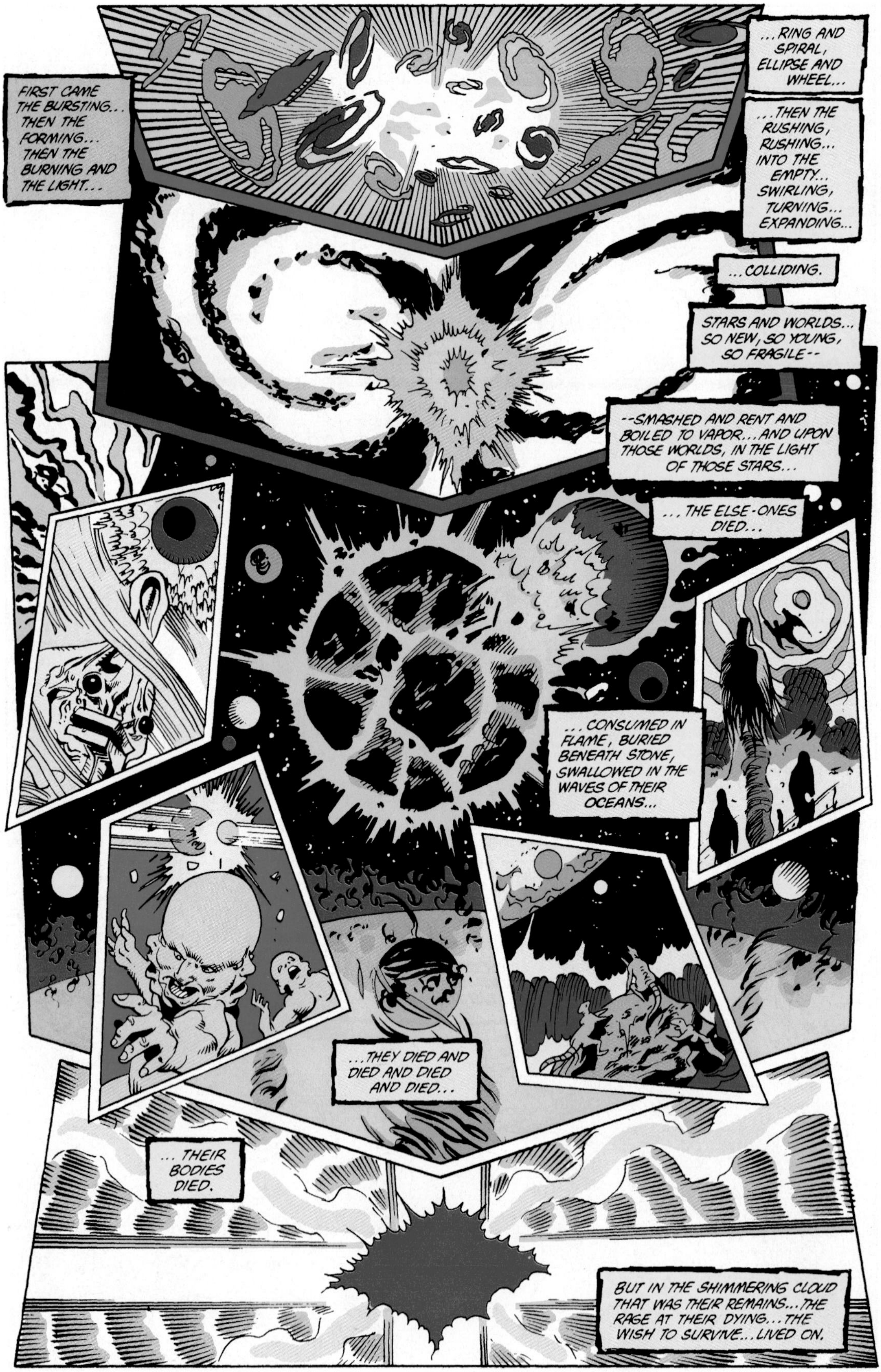
FIRST CAME THE BURSTING... THEN THE FORMING... THEN THE BURNING AND THE LIGHT...
...RING AND SPIRAL, ELLIPSE AND WHEEL...
...THEN THE RUSHING, RUSHING... INTO THE EMPTY... SWIRLING, TURNING... EXPANDING...
...COLLIDING.
STARS AND WORLDS... SO NEW, SO YOUNG, SO FRAGILE--
--SMASHED AND RENT AND BOILED TO VAPOR... AND UPON THOSE WORLDS, IN THE LIGHT OF THOSE STARS...
...THE ELSE-ONES DIED...
...CONSUMED IN FLAME, BURIED BENEATH STONE, SWALLOWED IN THE WAVES OF THEIR OCEANS...
...THEY DIED AND DIED AND DIED AND DIED...
...THEIR BODIES DIED.
BUT IN THE SHIMMERING CLOUD THAT WAS THEIR REMAINS... THE RAGE AT THEIR DYING... THE WISH TO SURVIVE... LIVED ON.

AND SO, THE INTERFUSION...
A BILLION-BILLION SOULS...
MERGED TO FORM A
SINGLE WILL...

...A SINGLE SELF...

...FROM THE GASEOUS
REMNANTS OF THEIR
GALAXIES...

MY GALAXIES.

THE SELF IS ONE.

AND THE SELF
SHALL NOT BE
TOUCHED.

AND THE SELF SHALL
NOT BE HARMED.

THE SELF SHALL BE APART
FROM ALL BUT THE SELF.

APART FROM THE
FORCES THAT CAUSE
BILLIONS TO PERISH.

FAR
APART.

...THE BEGIN
TIME...WAS
DEATH...

...DEATH AND
THE ELSE-
ONES...

...CHAOS
AND
PAIN...

...THE SELF HAD
FORGOTTEN...

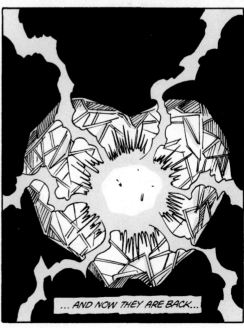

...AND NOW THEY ARE BACK...

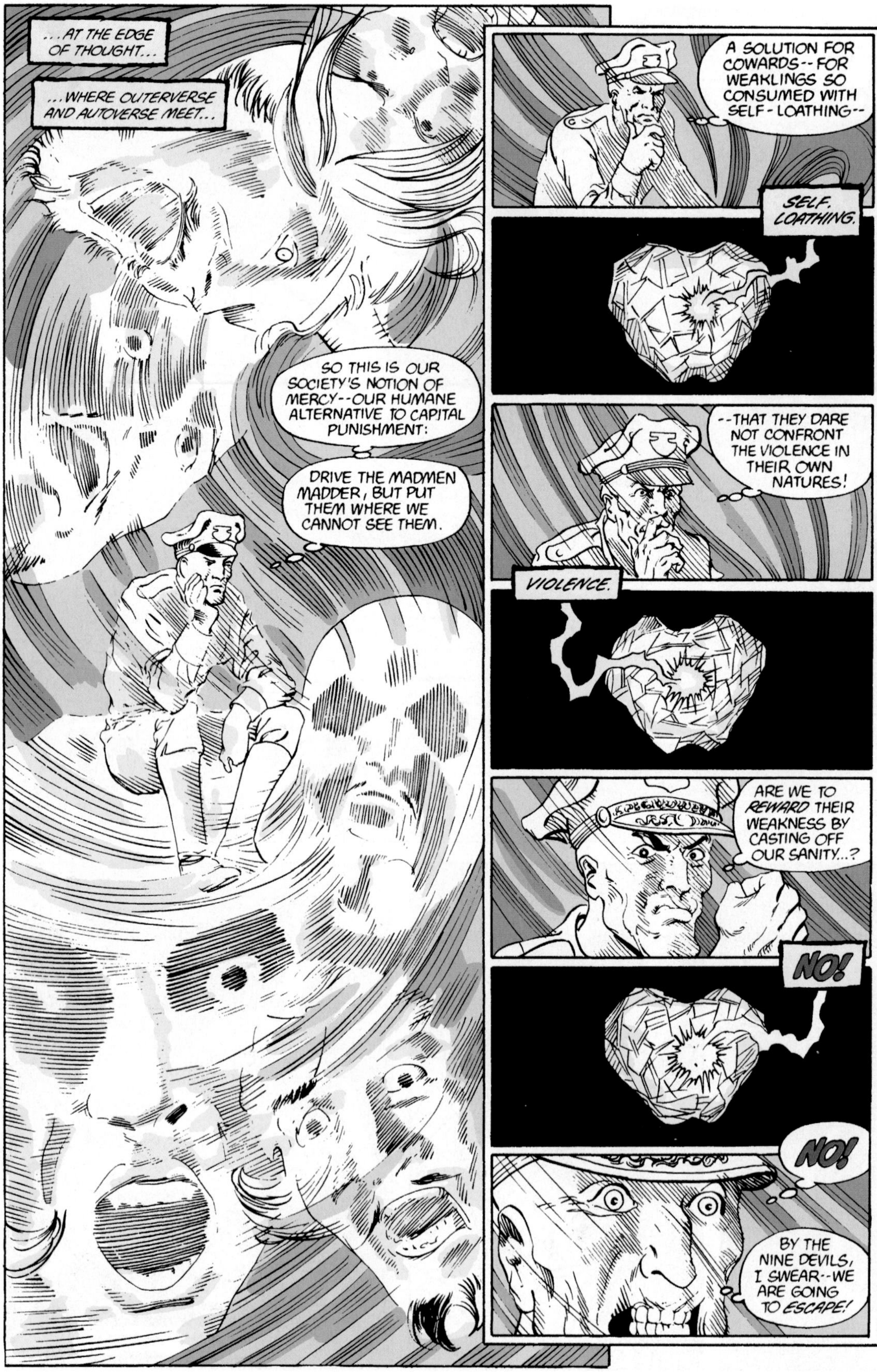
...AT THE EDGE OF THOUGHT...
...WHERE OUTERVERSE AND AUTOVERSE MEET...
SO THIS IS OUR SOCIETY'S NOTION OF MERCY--OUR HUMANE ALTERNATIVE TO CAPITAL PUNISHMENT:
DRIVE THE MADMEN MADDER, BUT PUT THEM WHERE WE CANNOT SEE THEM.
A SOLUTION FOR COWARDS--FOR WEAKLINGS SO CONSUMED WITH SELF-LOATHING--
SELF. LOATHING.
--THAT THEY DARE NOT CONFRONT THE VIOLENCE IN THEIR OWN NATURES!
VIOLENCE.
ARE WE TO REWARD THEIR WEAKNESS BY CASTING OFF OUR SANITY...?
NO!
NO!
BY THE NINE DEVILS, I SWEAR--WE ARE GOING TO ESCAPE!

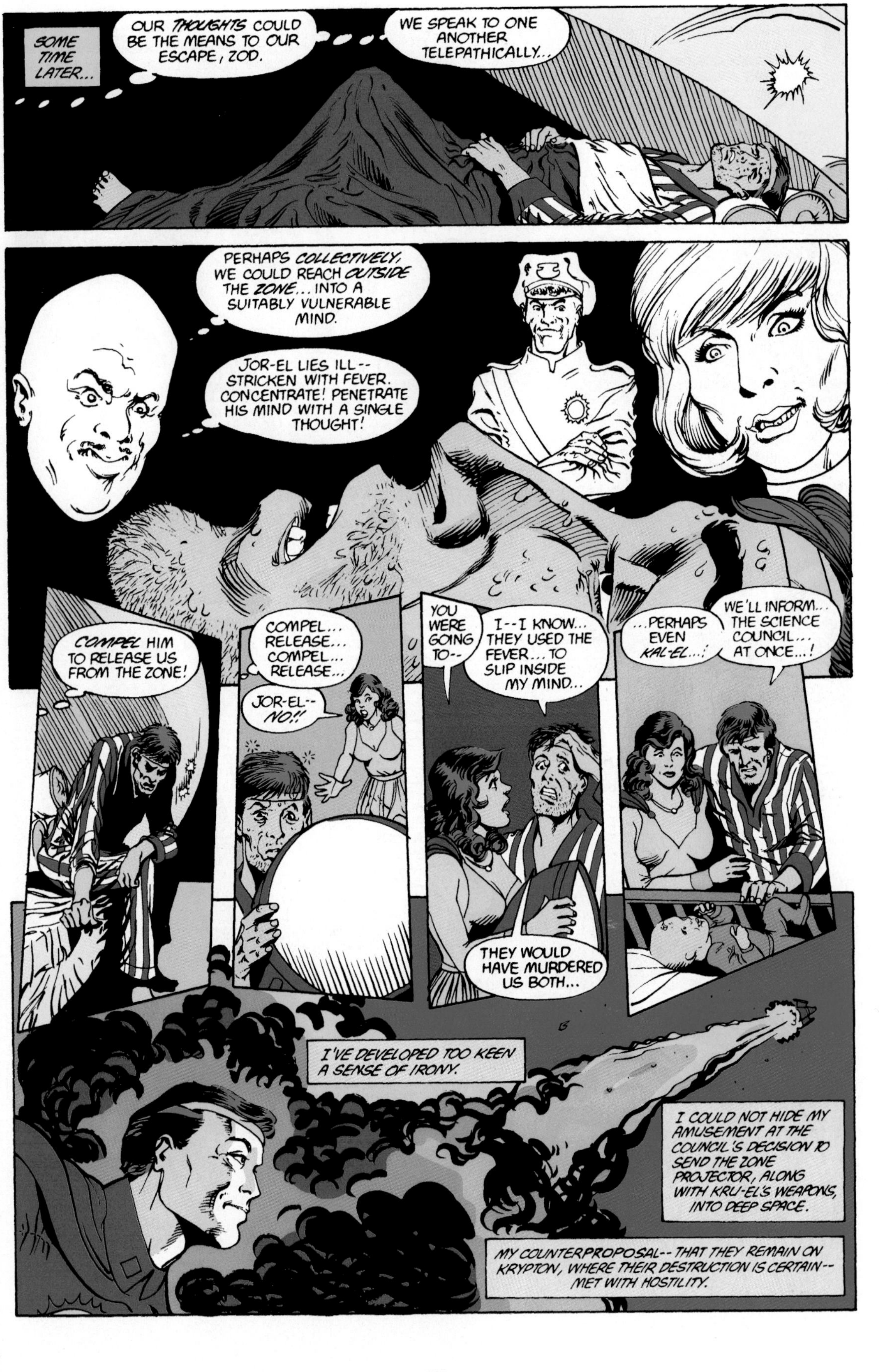
SOME TIME LATER...
OUR THOUGHTS COULD BE THE MEANS TO OUR ESCAPE, ZOD.
WE SPEAK TO ONE ANOTHER TELEPATHICALLY...
PERHAPS COLLECTIVELY, WE COULD REACH OUTSIDE THE ZONE... INTO A SUITABLY VULNERABLE MIND.
JOR-EL LIES ILL-- STRICKEN WITH FEVER. CONCENTRATE! PENETRATE HIS MIND WITH A SINGLE THOUGHT!
COMPEL HIM TO RELEASE US FROM THE ZONE!
COMPEL... RELEASE... COMPEL... RELEASE...
JOR-EL-- NO!!
YOU WERE GOING TO--
I--I KNOW... THEY USED THE FEVER... TO SLIP INSIDE MY MIND...
THEY WOULD HAVE MURDERED US BOTH...
...PERHAPS EVEN KAL-EL...!
WE'LL INFORM... THE SCIENCE COUNCIL... AT ONCE...!
I'VE DEVELOPED TOO KEEN A SENSE OF IRONY.
I COULD NOT HIDE MY AMUSEMENT AT THE COUNCIL'S DECISION TO SEND THE ZONE PROJECTOR, ALONG WITH KRU-EL'S WEAPONS, INTO DEEP SPACE.
MY COUNTERPROPOSAL-- THAT THEY REMAIN ON KRYPTON, WHERE THEIR DESTRUCTION IS CERTAIN-- MET WITH HOSTILITY.

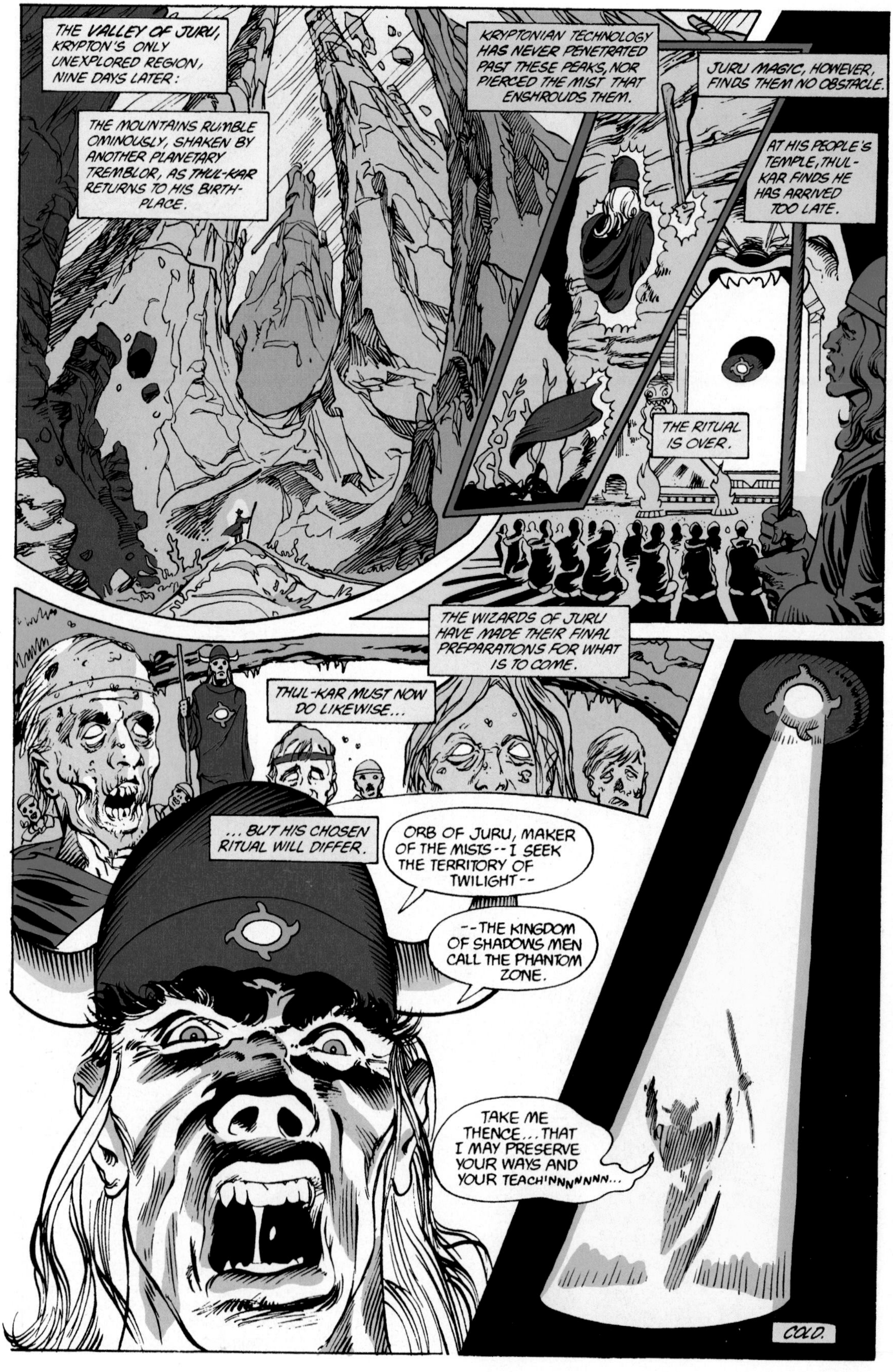
THE VALLEY OF JURU, KRYPTON'S ONLY UNEXPLORED REGION, NINE DAYS LATER:
THE MOUNTAINS RUMBLE OMINOUSLY, SHAKEN BY ANOTHER PLANETARY TREMBLOR, AS THUL-KAR RETURNS TO HIS BIRTH-PLACE.
KRYPTONIAN TECHNOLOGY HAS NEVER PENETRATED PAST THESE PEAKS, NOR PIERCED THE MIST THAT ENSHROUDS THEM.
JURU MAGIC, HOWEVER, FINDS THEM NO OBSTACLE.
AT HIS PEOPLE'S TEMPLE, THUL-KAR FINDS HE HAS ARRIVED TOO LATE.
THE RITUAL IS OVER.
THE WIZARDS OF JURU HAVE MADE THEIR FINAL PREPARATIONS FOR WHAT IS TO COME.
THUL-KAR MUST NOW DO LIKEWISE...
...BUT HIS CHOSEN RITUAL WILL DIFFER.
ORB OF JURU, MAKER OF THE MISTS--I SEEK THE TERRITORY OF TWILIGHT--
--THE KINGDOM OF SHADOWS MEN CALL THE PHANTOM ZONE.
TAKE ME THENCE...THAT I MAY PRESERVE YOUR WAYS AND YOUR TEACHINNNNNNN...
COLD.

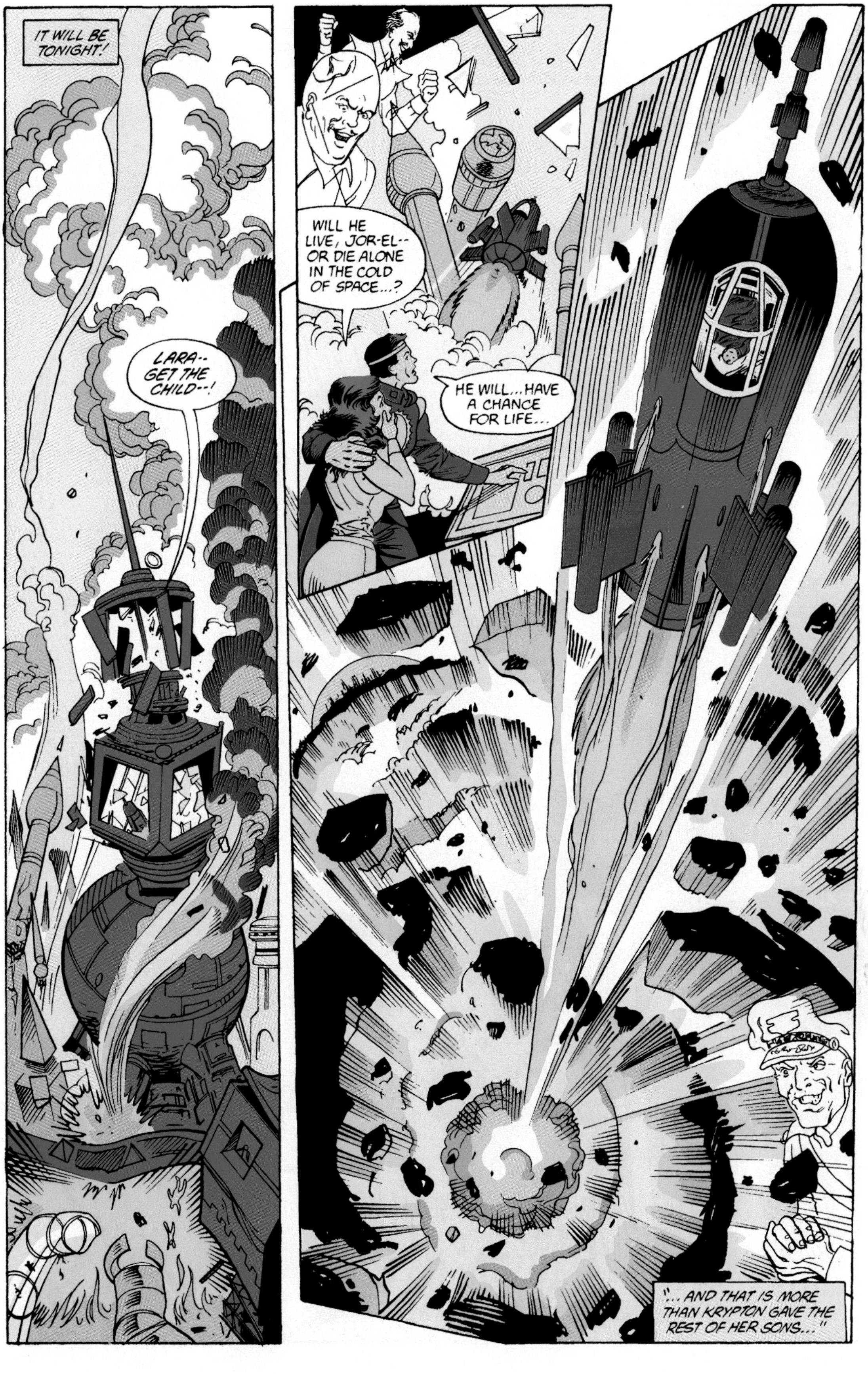
IT WILL BE TONIGHT!
LARA-- GET THE CHILD--!
WILL HE LIVE, JOR-EL-- OR DIE ALONE IN THE COLD OF SPACE...?
HE WILL...HAVE A CHANCE FOR LIFE...
"...AND THAT IS MORE THAN KRYPTON GAVE THE REST OF HER SONS..."

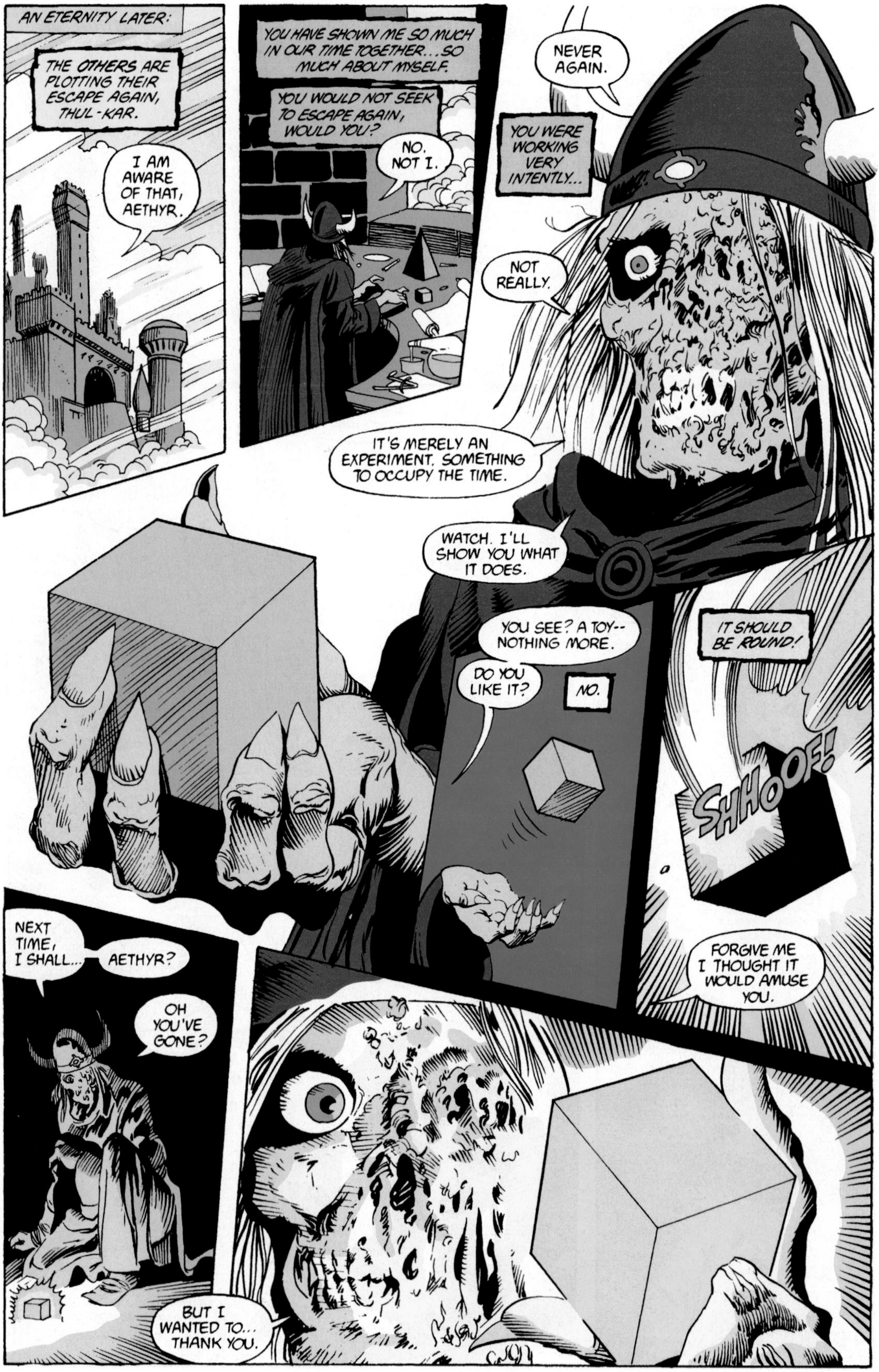
AN ETERNITY LATER:
THE OTHERS ARE PLOTTING THEIR ESCAPE AGAIN, THUL-KAR.
I AM AWARE OF THAT, AETHYR.
YOU HAVE SHOWN ME SO MUCH IN OUR TIME TOGETHER... SO MUCH ABOUT MYSELF.
YOU WOULD NOT SEEK TO ESCAPE AGAIN, WOULD YOU?
NO. NOT I.
NEVER AGAIN.
YOU WERE WORKING VERY INTENTLY...
NOT REALLY.
IT'S MERELY AN EXPERIMENT. SOMETHING TO OCCUPY THE TIME.
WATCH. I'LL SHOW YOU WHAT IT DOES.
YOU SEE? A TOY-- NOTHING MORE.
DO YOU LIKE IT?
NO.
IT SHOULD BE ROUND!
SHHOOF!
FORGIVE ME I THOUGHT IT WOULD AMUSE YOU.
NEXT TIME, I SHALL...
AETHYR?
OH YOU'VE GONE?
BUT I WANTED TO... THANK YOU.

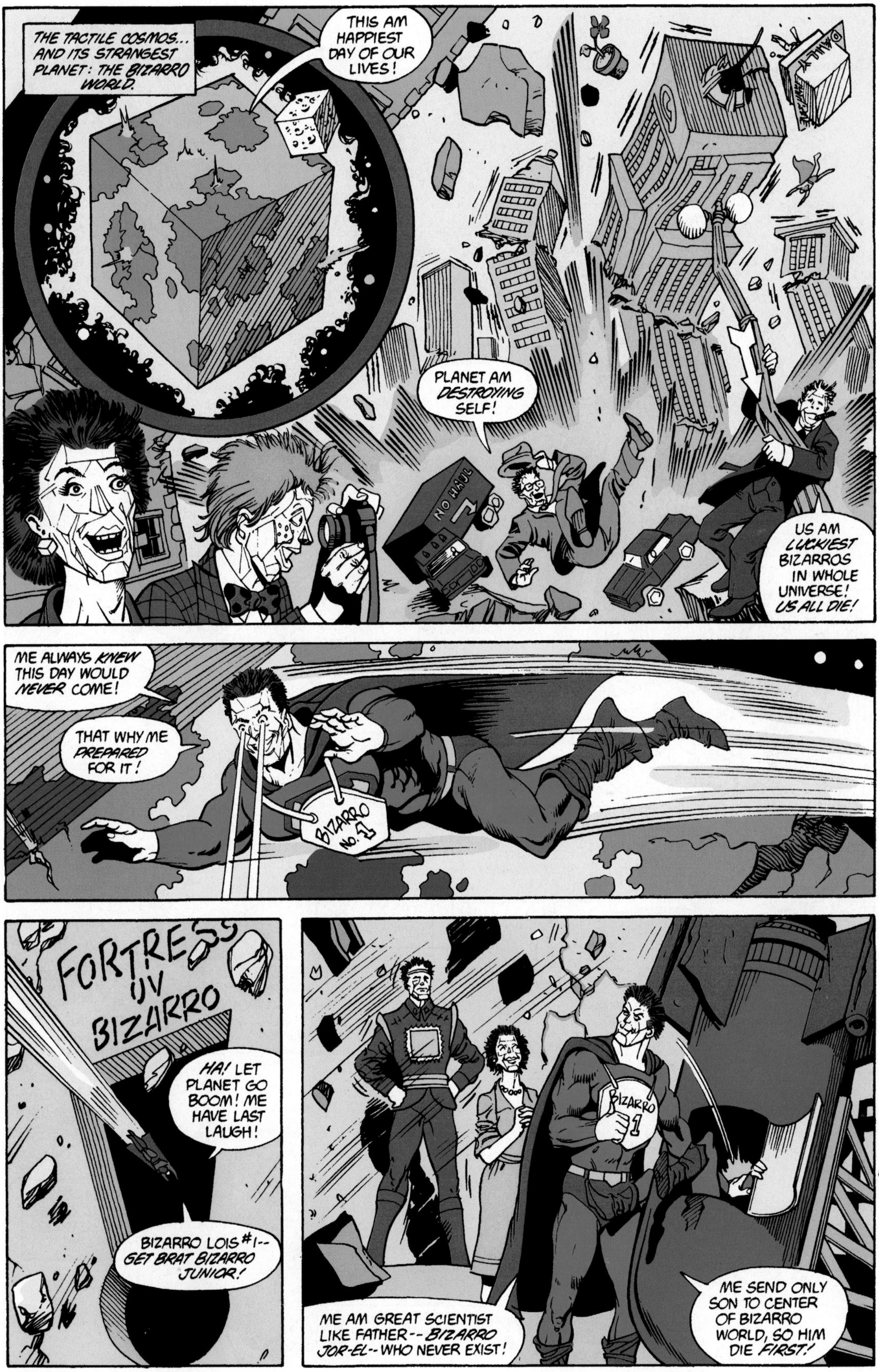
THE TACTILE COSMOS... AND ITS STRANGEST PLANET: THE BIZARRO WORLD.
THIS AM HAPPIEST DAY OF OUR LIVES!
PLANET AM DESTROYING SELF!
NO HAUL
US AM LUCKIEST BIZARROS IN WHOLE UNIVERSE! US ALL DIE!
ME ALWAYS KNEW THIS DAY WOULD NEVER COME!
THAT WHY ME PREPARED FOR IT!
BIZARRO NO. 1
FORTRESS UV BIZARRO
HA! LET PLANET GO BOOM! ME HAVE LAST LAUGH!
BIZARRO LOIS #1-- GET BRAT BIZARRO JUNIOR!
BIZARRO 1
ME AM GREAT SCIENTIST LIKE FATHER-- BIZARRO JOR-EL-- WHO NEVER EXIST!
ME SEND ONLY SON TO CENTER OF BIZARRO WORLD, SO HIM DIE FIRST!

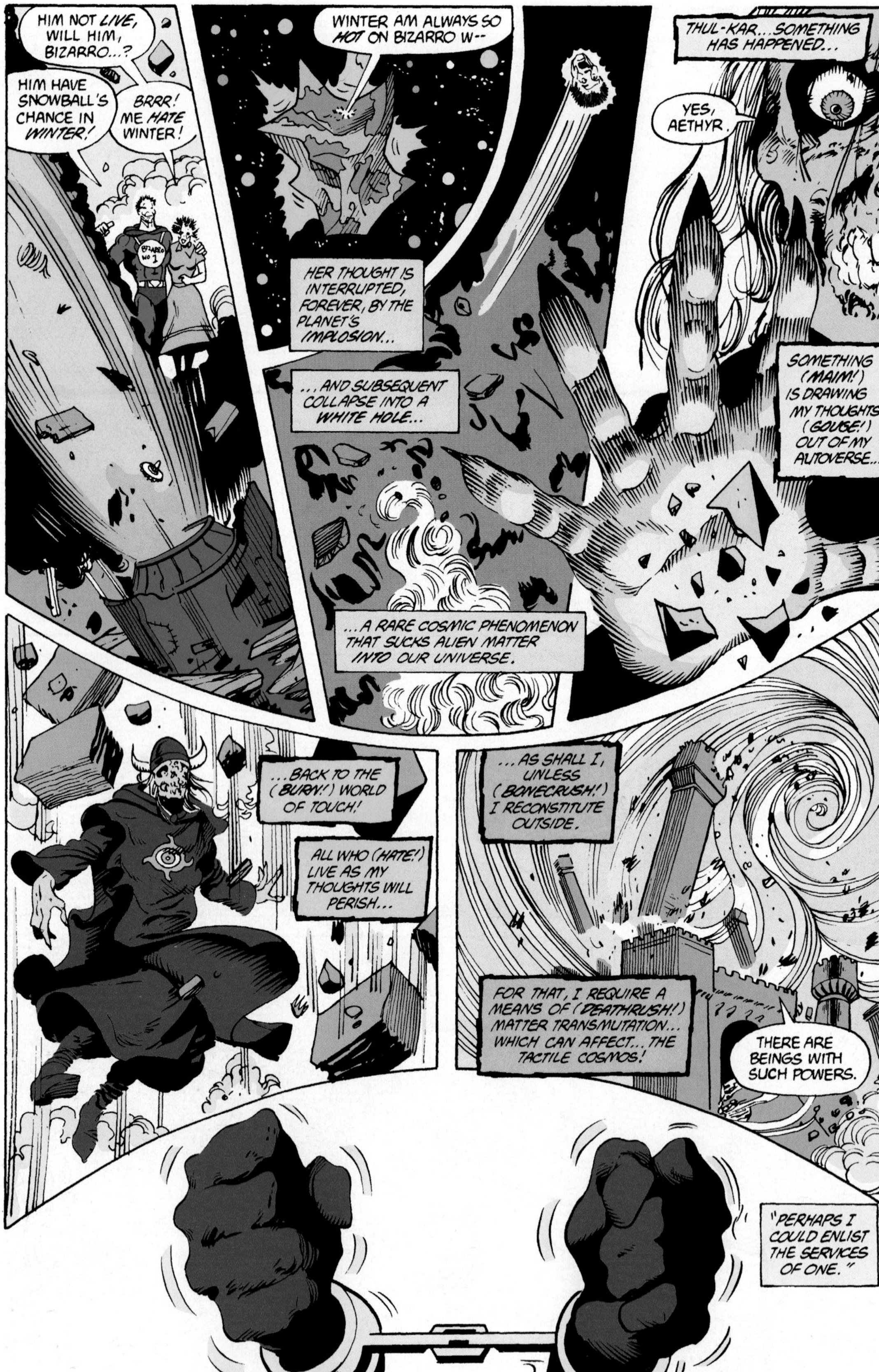
HIM NOT LIVE, WILL HIM, BIZARRO...?
HIM HAVE SNOWBALL'S CHANCE IN WINTER!
BRRR! ME HATE WINTER!
BIZARRO NO 1
WINTER AM ALWAYS SO HOT ON BIZARRO W--
HER THOUGHT IS INTERRUPTED, FOREVER, BY THE PLANET'S IMPLOSION...
...AND SUBSEQUENT COLLAPSE INTO A WHITE HOLE...
...A RARE COSMIC PHENOMENON THAT SUCKS ALIEN MATTER INTO OUR UNIVERSE.
THUL-KAR... SOMETHING HAS HAPPENED...
YES, AETHYR.
SOMETHING (MAIM!) IS DRAWING MY THOUGHTS (GOUGE!) OUT OF MY AUTOVERSE...
...BACK TO THE (BURN!) WORLD OF TOUCH!
ALL WHO (HATE!) LIVE AS MY THOUGHTS WILL PERISH...
...AS SHALL I, UNLESS (BONECRUSH!) I RECONSTITUTE OUTSIDE.
FOR THAT, I REQUIRE A MEANS OF (DEATHRUSH!) MATTER TRANSMUTATION... WHICH CAN AFFECT... THE TACTILE COSMOS!
THERE ARE BEINGS WITH SUCH POWERS.
"PERHAPS I COULD ENLIST THE SERVICES OF ONE."

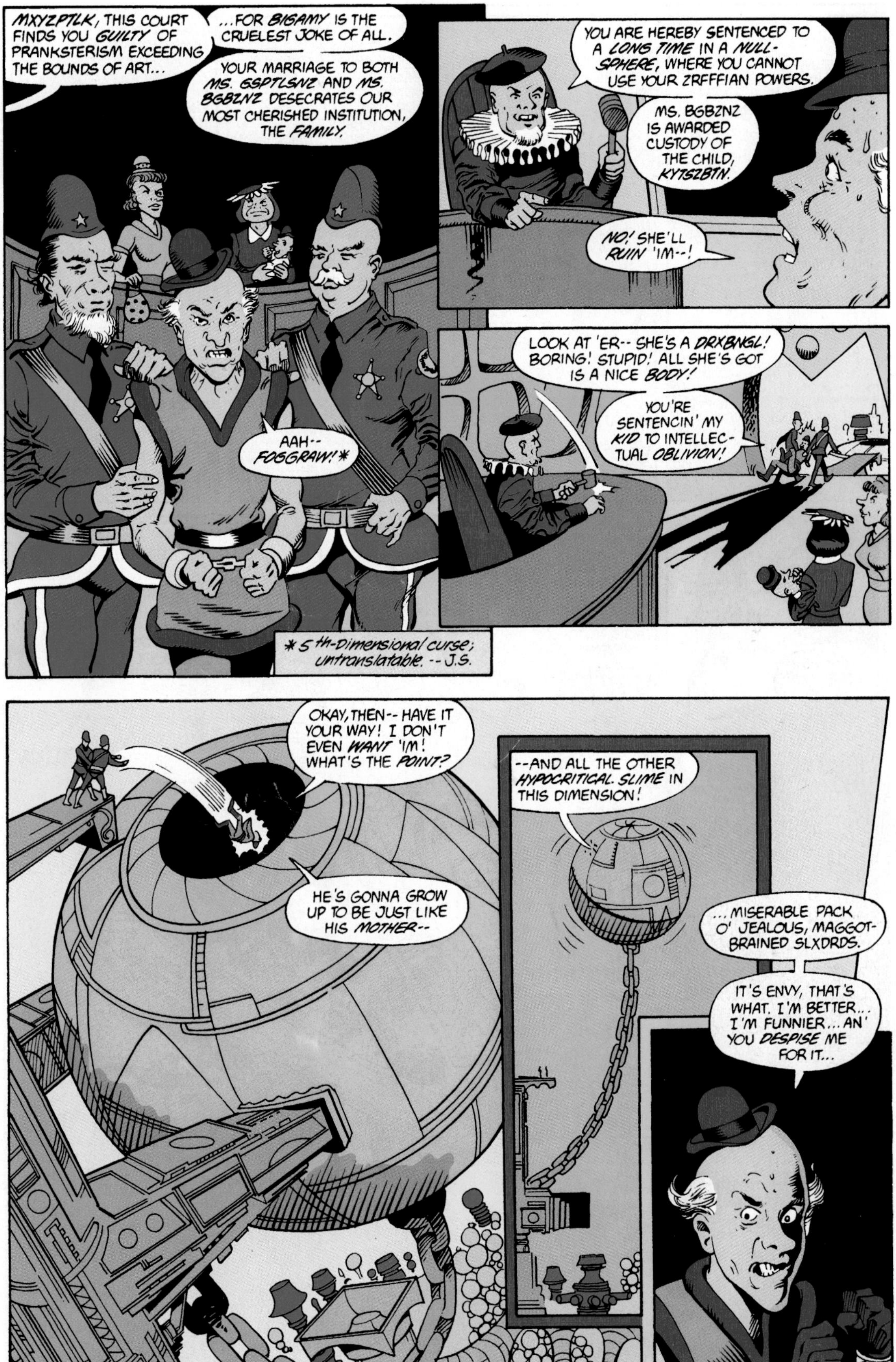
MXYZPTLK, THIS COURT FINDS YOU GUILTY OF PRANKSTERISM EXCEEDING THE BOUNDS OF ART...
...FOR BIGAMY IS THE CRUELEST JOKE OF ALL.
YOUR MARRIAGE TO BOTH MS. GSPTLSNZ AND MS. BGBZNZ DESECRATES OUR MOST CHERISHED INSTITUTION, THE FAMILY.
AAH--FOGGRAW!*
*5th-Dimensional curse; untranslatable. --J.S.
YOU ARE HEREBY SENTENCED TO A LONG TIME IN A NULL-SPHERE, WHERE YOU CANNOT USE YOUR ZRFFIAN POWERS.
MS. BGBZNZ IS AWARDED CUSTODY OF THE CHILD, KYTSZBTN.
NO! SHE'LL RUIN 'IM--!
LOOK AT 'ER-- SHE'S A DRXBNGL! BORING! STUPID! ALL SHE'S GOT IS A NICE BODY!
YOU'RE SENTENCIN' MY KID TO INTELLECTUAL OBLIVION!
OKAY, THEN-- HAVE IT YOUR WAY! I DON'T EVEN WANT 'IM! WHAT'S THE POINT?
HE'S GONNA GROW UP TO BE JUST LIKE HIS MOTHER--
--AND ALL THE OTHER HYPOCRITICAL SLIME IN THIS DIMENSION!
...MISERABLE PACK O' JEALOUS, MAGGOT-BRAINED SLXDRDS.
IT'S ENVY, THAT'S WHAT. I'M BETTER... I'M FUNNIER... AN' YOU DESPISE ME FOR IT...

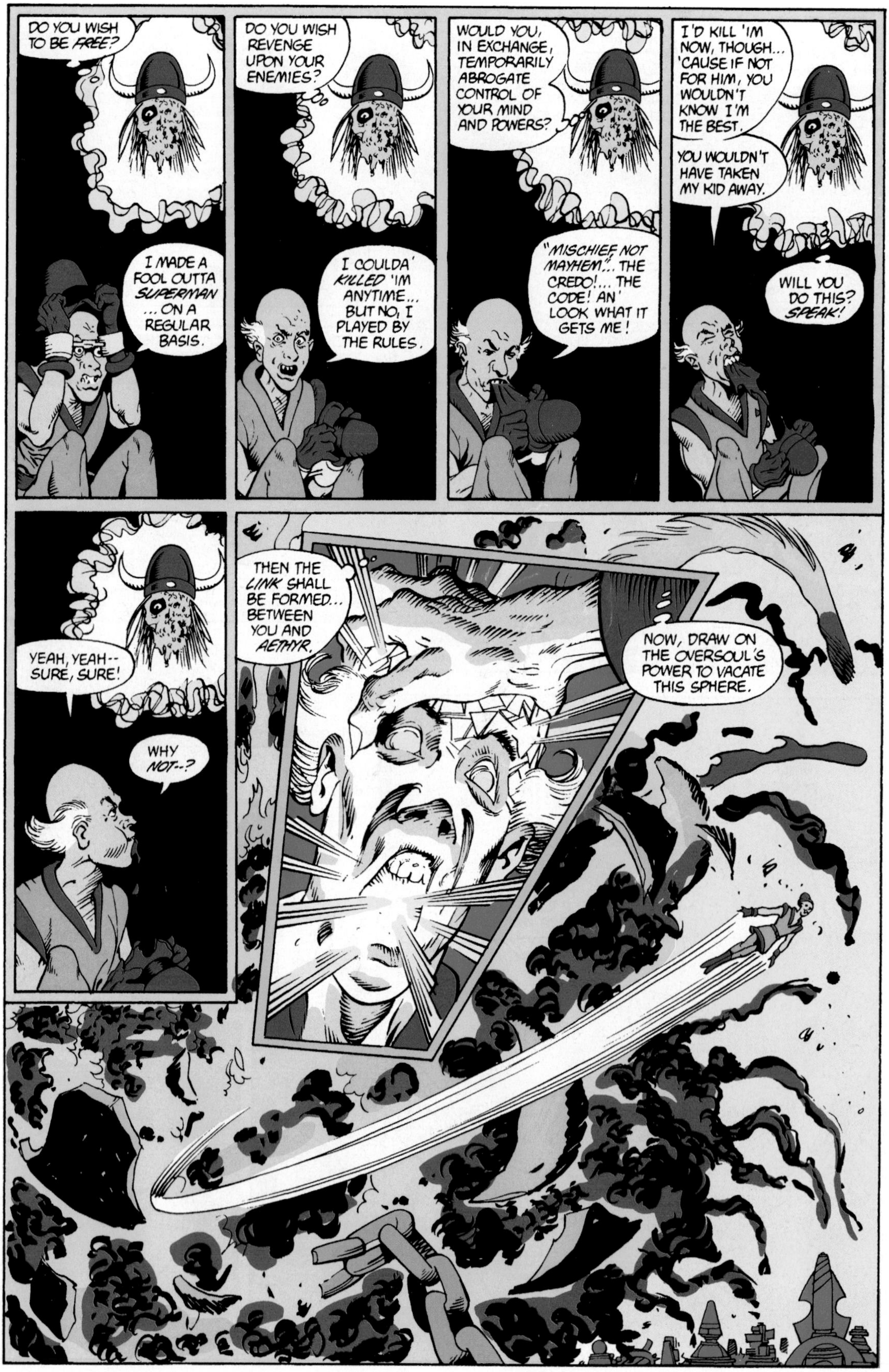
DO YOU WISH TO BE *FREE*?
I MADE A FOOL OUTTA *SUPERMAN* ...ON A REGULAR BASIS.
DO YOU WISH REVENGE UPON YOUR ENEMIES?
I COULDA' *KILLED* 'IM ANYTIME... BUT NO, I PLAYED BY THE RULES.
WOULD YOU, IN EXCHANGE, TEMPORARILY ABROGATE CONTROL OF YOUR MIND AND POWERS?
"*MISCHIEF, NOT MAYHEM*"... THE CREDO!... THE CODE! AN' LOOK WHAT IT GETS ME!
I'D KILL 'IM NOW, THOUGH... 'CAUSE IF NOT FOR HIM, YOU WOULDN'T KNOW I'M THE BEST.
YOU WOULDN'T HAVE TAKEN MY KID AWAY.
WILL YOU DO THIS? *SPEAK!*
YEAH, YEAH-- SURE, SURE!
WHY *NOT*--?
THEN THE *LINK* SHALL BE FORMED... BETWEEN YOU AND *AETHYR*.
NOW, DRAW ON THE OVERSOUL'S POWER TO VACATE THIS SPHERE.

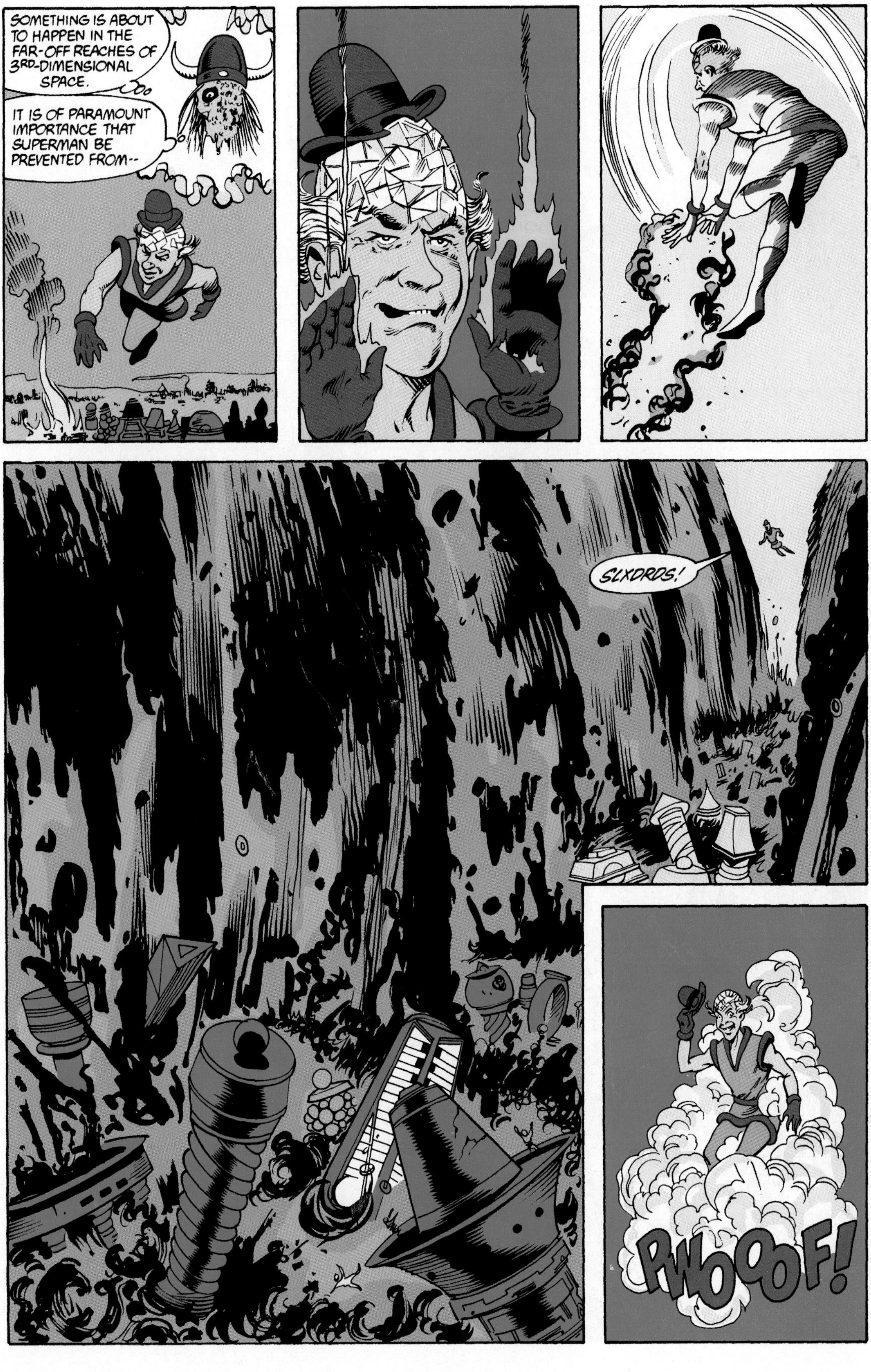
SOMETHING IS ABOUT TO HAPPEN IN THE FAR-OFF REACHES OF 3RD-DIMENSIONAL SPACE.
IT IS OF PARAMOUNT IMPORTANCE THAT SUPERMAN BE PREVENTED FROM--
SLXDRDS!
PWOOOOF!

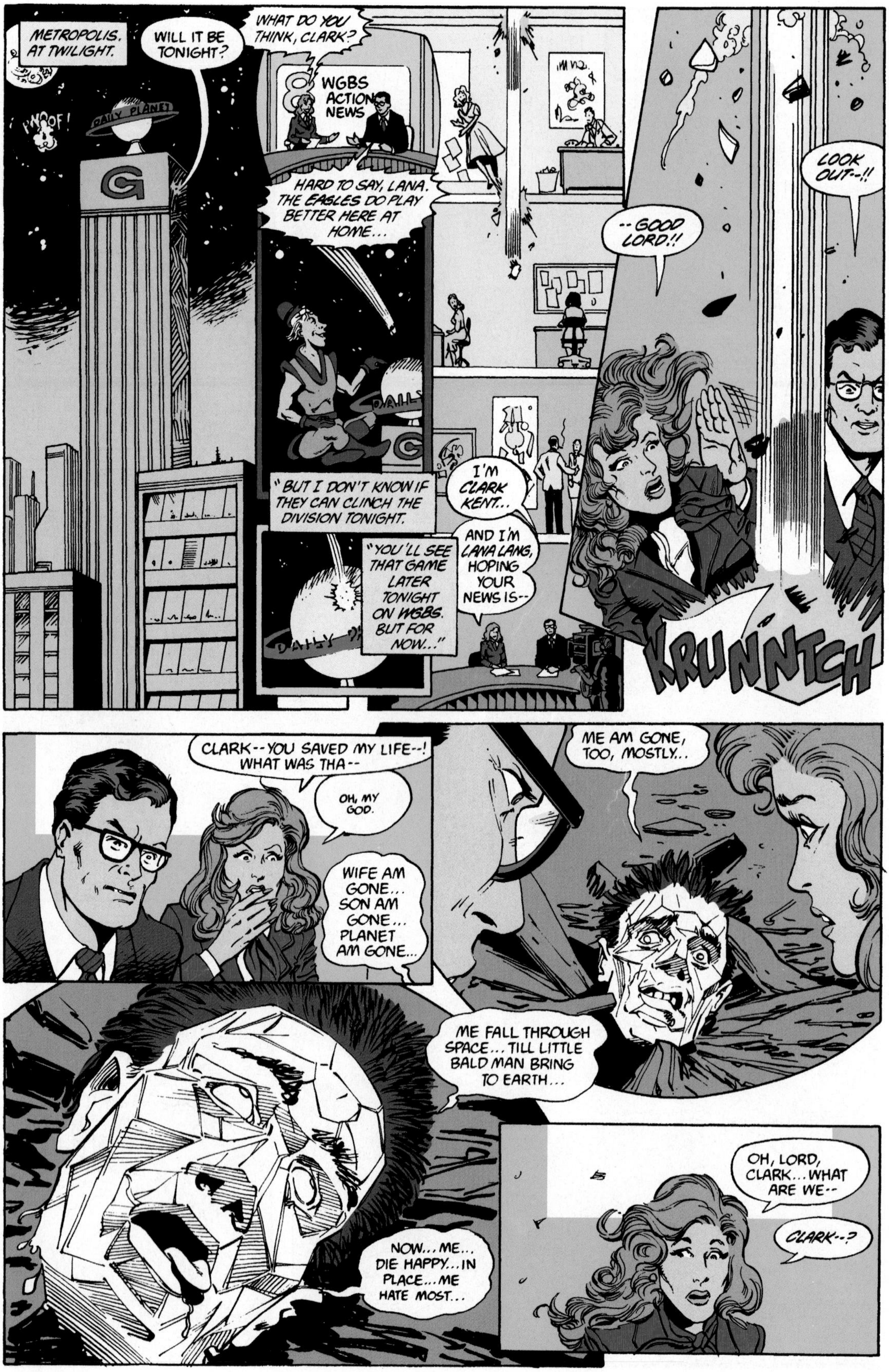
METROPOLIS. AT TWILIGHT.
WILL IT BE TONIGHT?
WHAT DO YOU THINK, CLARK?
WGBS ACTION NEWS
HARD TO SAY, LANA. THE EAGLES DO PLAY BETTER HERE AT HOME...
"BUT I DON'T KNOW IF THEY CAN CLINCH THE DIVISION TONIGHT.
"YOU'LL SEE THAT GAME LATER TONIGHT ON WGBS. BUT FOR NOW..."
I'M CLARK KENT...
AND I'M LANA LANG, HOPING YOUR NEWS IS--
--GOOD LORD!!
LOOK OUT--!!
KRUNNTCH
CLARK--YOU SAVED MY LIFE--! WHAT WAS THA--
OH, MY GOD.
WIFE AM GONE... SON AM GONE... PLANET AM GONE...
ME AM GONE, TOO, MOSTLY...
ME FALL THROUGH SPACE... TILL LITTLE BALD MAN BRING TO EARTH...
NOW... ME... DIE HAPPY... IN PLACE... ME HATE MOST...
OH, LORD, CLARK... WHAT ARE WE--
CLARK--?

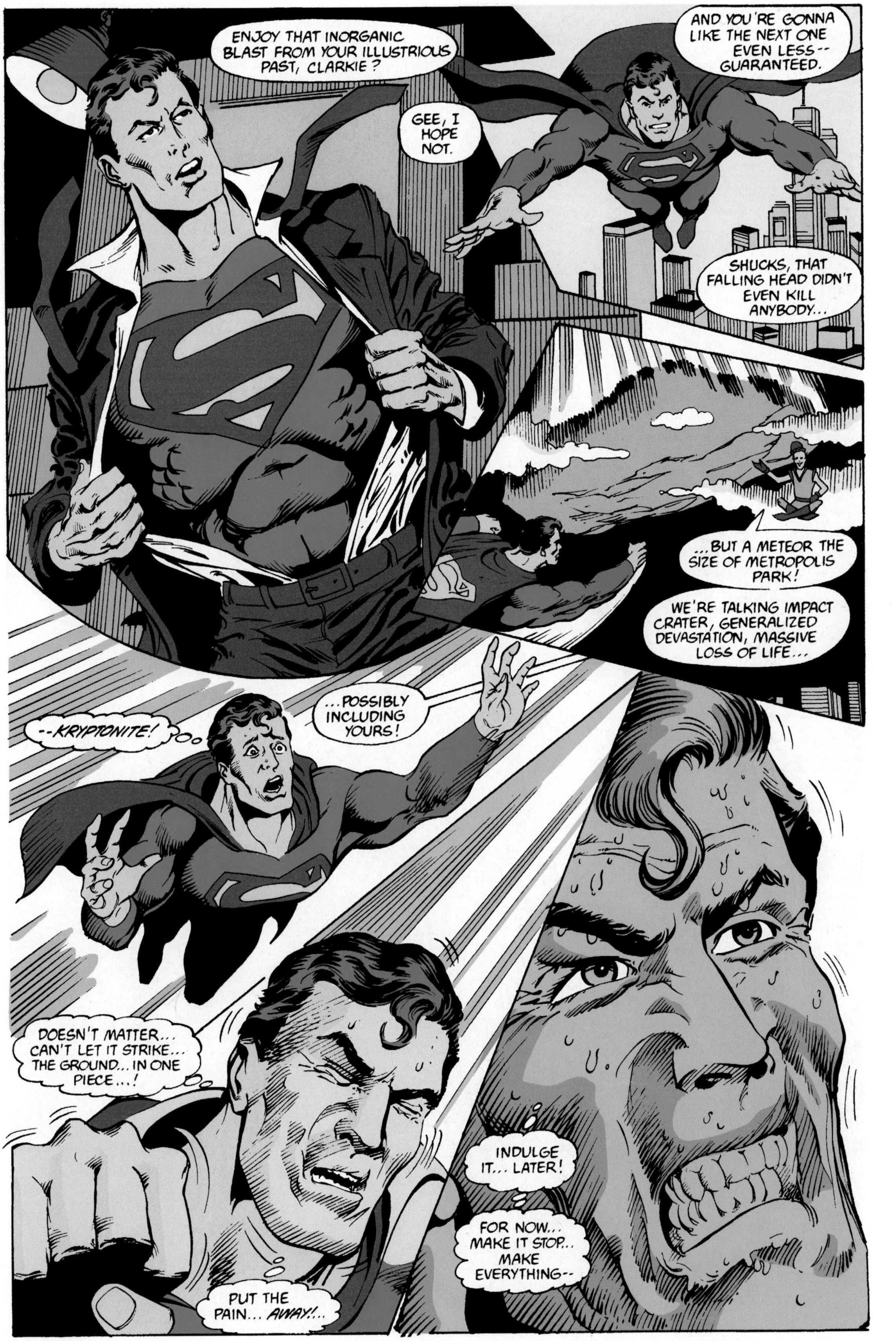
ENJOY THAT INORGANIC BLAST FROM YOUR ILLUSTRIOUS PAST, CLARKIE?
GEE, I HOPE NOT.
AND YOU'RE GONNA LIKE THE NEXT ONE EVEN LESS-- GUARANTEED.
SHUCKS, THAT FALLING HEAD DIDN'T EVEN KILL ANYBODY...
...BUT A METEOR THE SIZE OF METROPOLIS PARK!
WE'RE TALKING IMPACT CRATER, GENERALIZED DEVASTATION, MASSIVE LOSS OF LIFE...
...POSSIBLY INCLUDING YOURS!
--KRYPTONITE!
DOESN'T MATTER... CAN'T LET IT STRIKE... THE GROUND... IN ONE PIECE...!
INDULGE IT... LATER!
FOR NOW... MAKE IT STOP... MAKE EVERYTHING--
PUT THE PAIN... AWAY!...

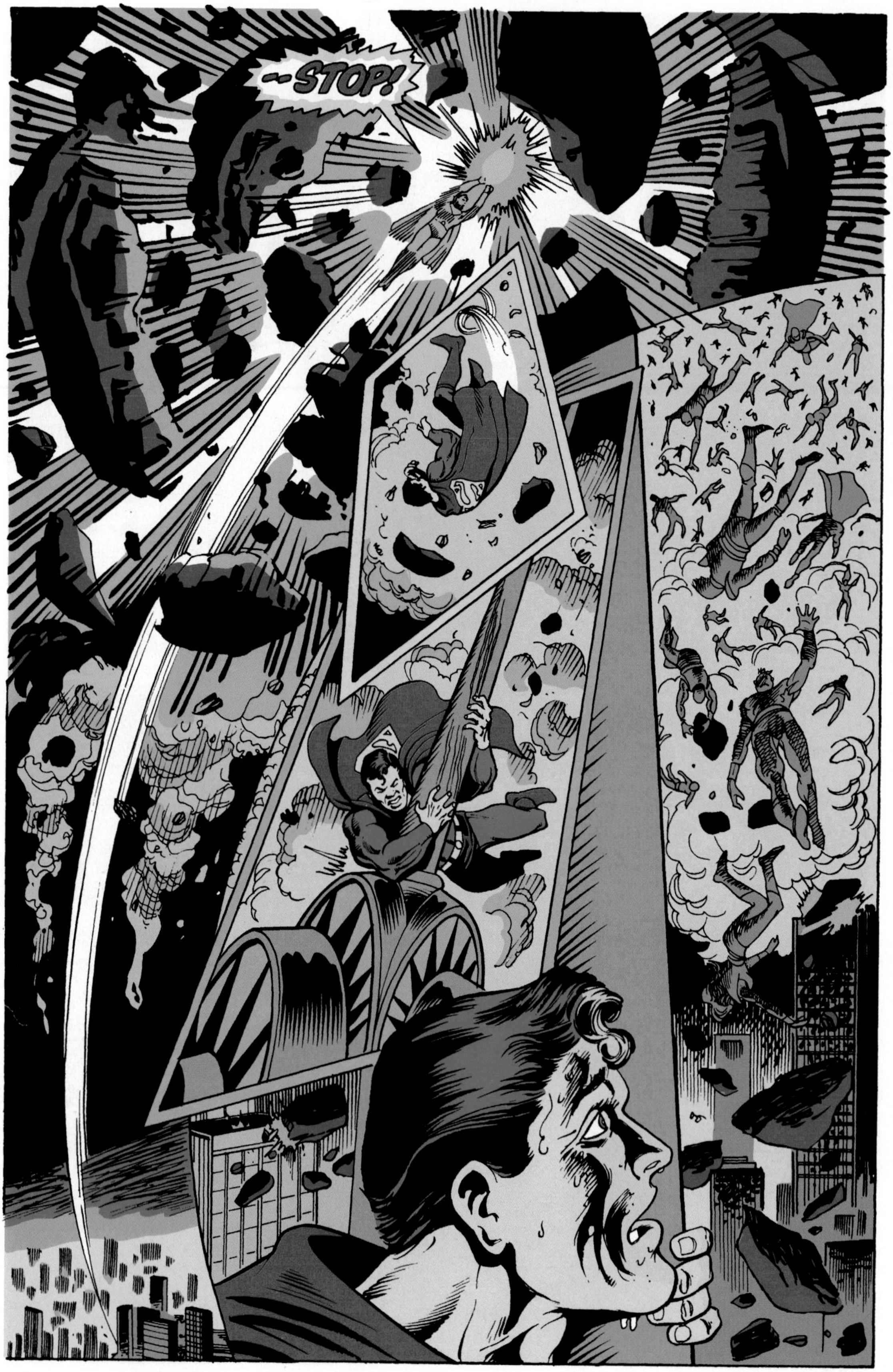
--STOP!

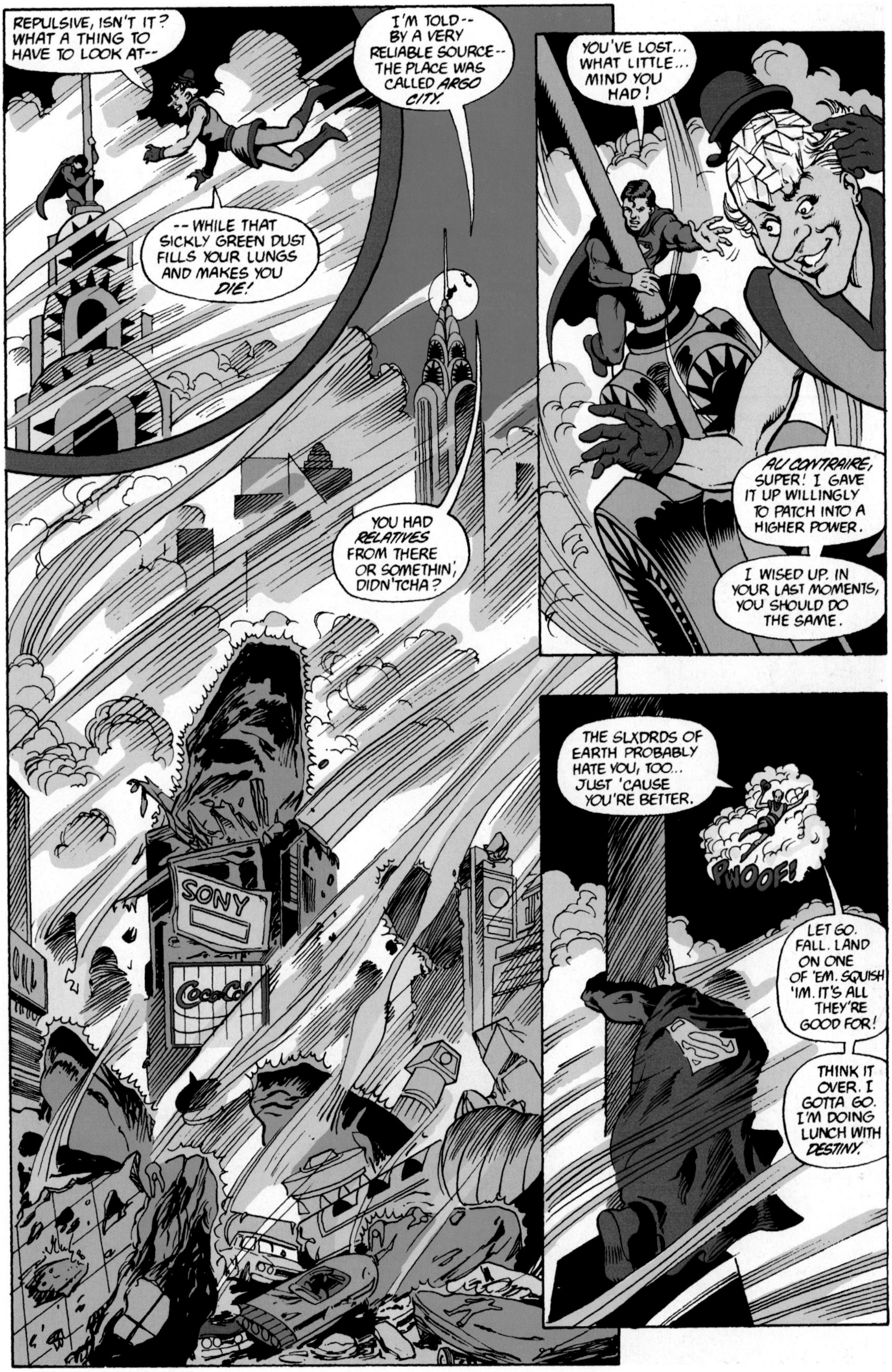
REPULSIVE, ISN'T IT? WHAT A THING TO HAVE TO LOOK AT--
--WHILE THAT SICKLY GREEN DUST FILLS YOUR LUNGS AND MAKES YOU *DIE!*
I'M TOLD-- BY A VERY RELIABLE SOURCE-- THE PLACE WAS CALLED *ARGO CITY.*
YOU HAD *RELATIVES* FROM THERE OR SOMETHIN', DIDN'TCHA?
SONY
Coca-Co
YOU'VE LOST... WHAT LITTLE... MIND YOU HAD!
AU CONTRAIRE, SUPER! I GAVE IT UP WILLINGLY TO PATCH INTO A HIGHER POWER.
I WISED UP. IN YOUR LAST MOMENTS, YOU SHOULD DO THE SAME.
THE SLXDRDS OF EARTH PROBABLY HATE YOU, TOO... JUST 'CAUSE YOU'RE BETTER.
PWOOF!
LET GO. FALL. LAND ON ONE OF 'EM. SQUISH 'IM. IT'S ALL THEY'RE GOOD FOR!
THINK IT OVER. I GOTTA GO. I'M DOING LUNCH WITH *DESTINY.*

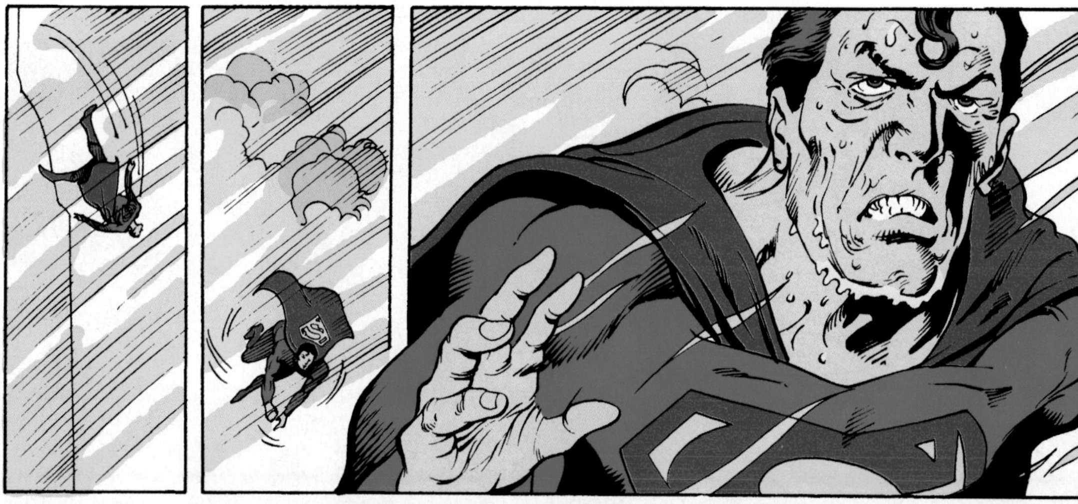

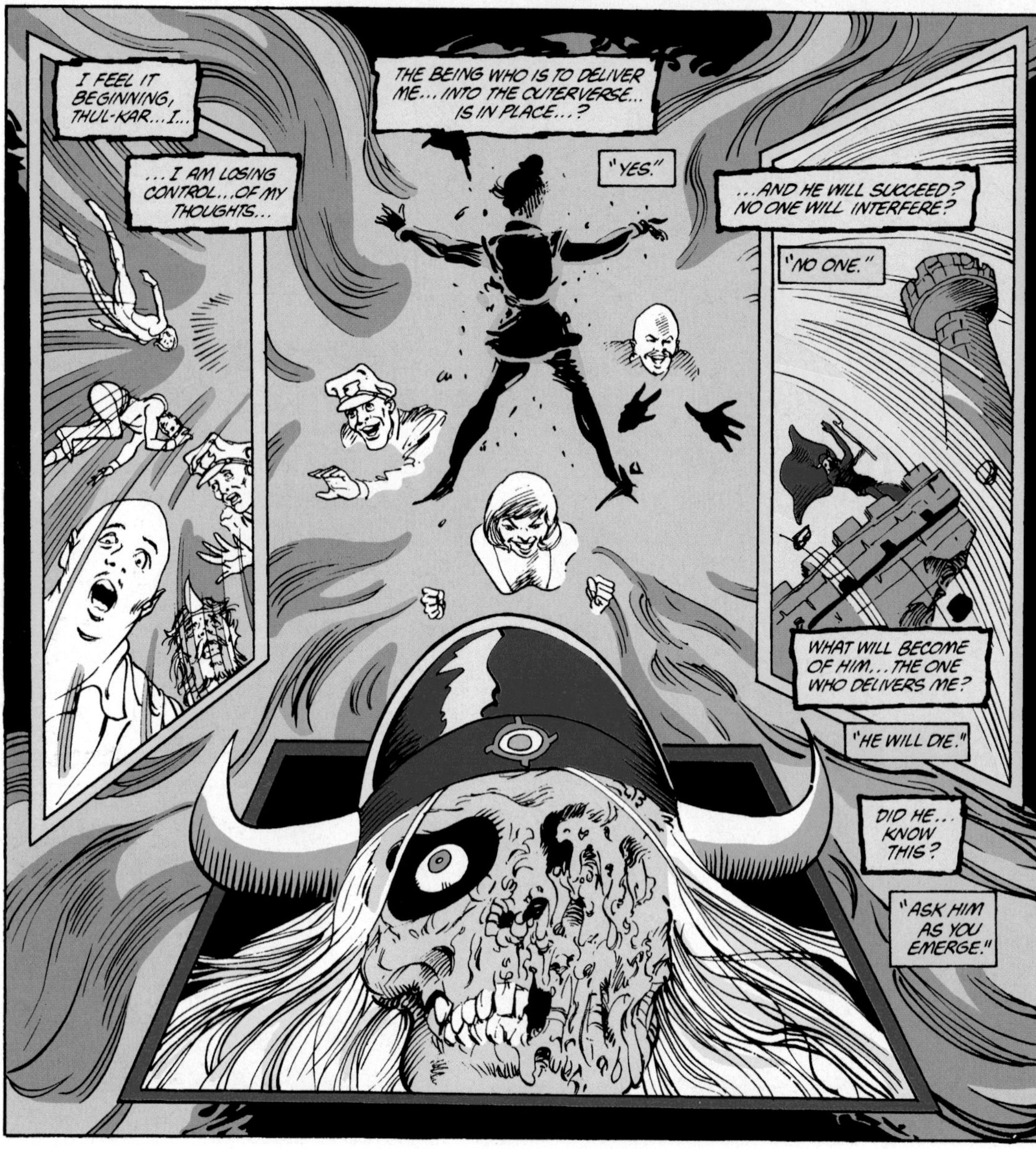

I FEEL IT BEGINNING, THUL-KAR...I...
...I AM LOSING CONTROL...OF MY THOUGHTS...
THE BEING WHO IS TO DELIVER ME...INTO THE OUTERVERSE... IS IN PLACE...?
"YES."
...AND HE WILL SUCCEED? NO ONE WILL INTERFERE?
"NO ONE."
WHAT WILL BECOME OF HIM...THE ONE WHO DELIVERS ME?
"HE WILL DIE."
DID HE... KNOW THIS?
"ASK HIM AS YOU EMERGE."

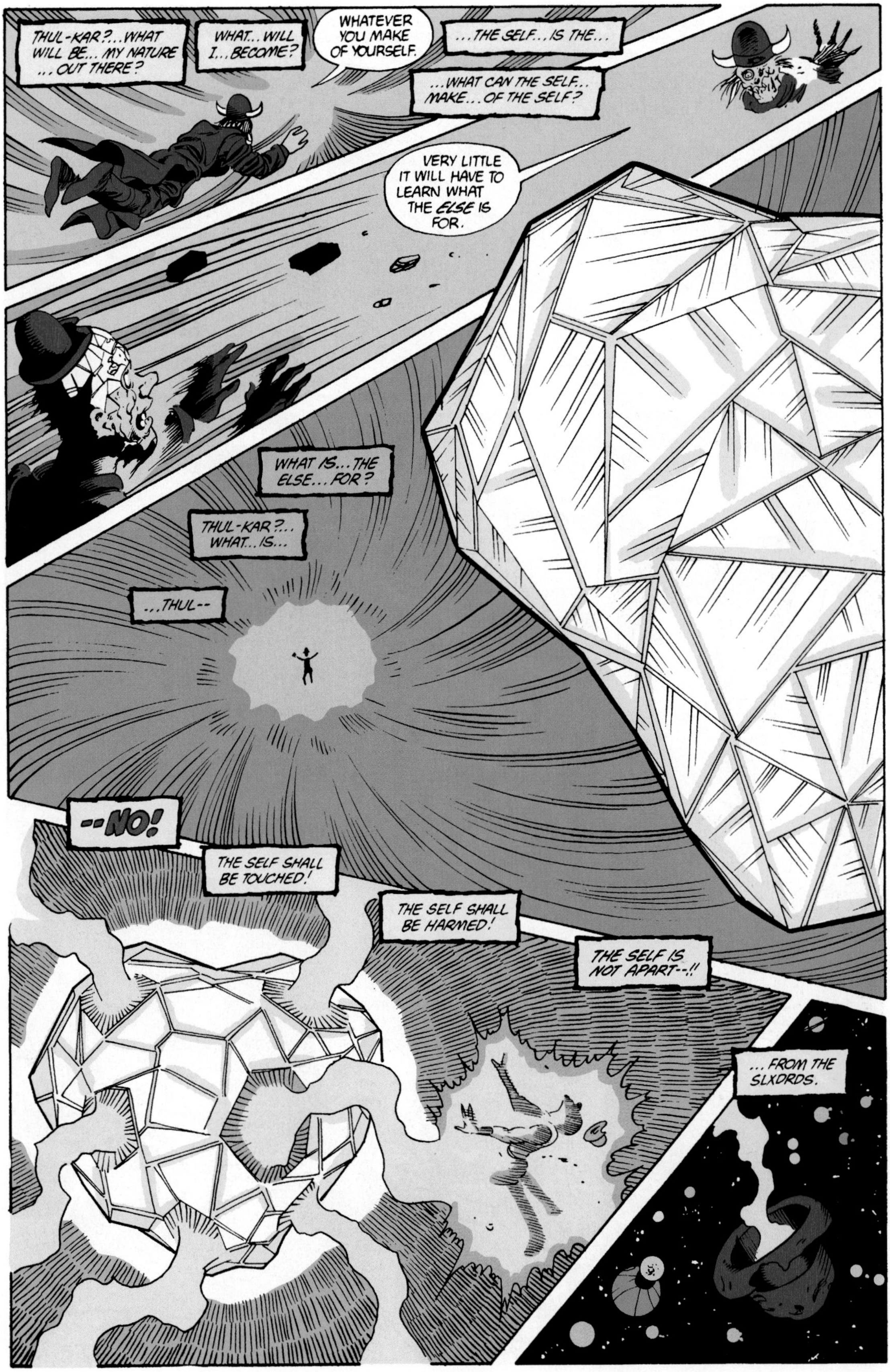
THUL-KAR?...WHAT WILL BE... MY NATURE ...OUT THERE?
WHAT... WILL I...BECOME?
WHATEVER YOU MAKE OF YOURSELF.
...THE SELF...IS THE...
...WHAT CAN THE SELF... MAKE... OF THE SELF?
VERY LITTLE IT WILL HAVE TO LEARN WHAT THE ELSE IS FOR.
WHAT IS...THE ELSE...FOR?
THUL-KAR?... WHAT...IS...
...THUL--
--NO!
THE SELF SHALL BE TOUCHED!
THE SELF SHALL BE HARMED!
THE SELF IS NOT APART--!!
...FROM THE SLXDRDS.

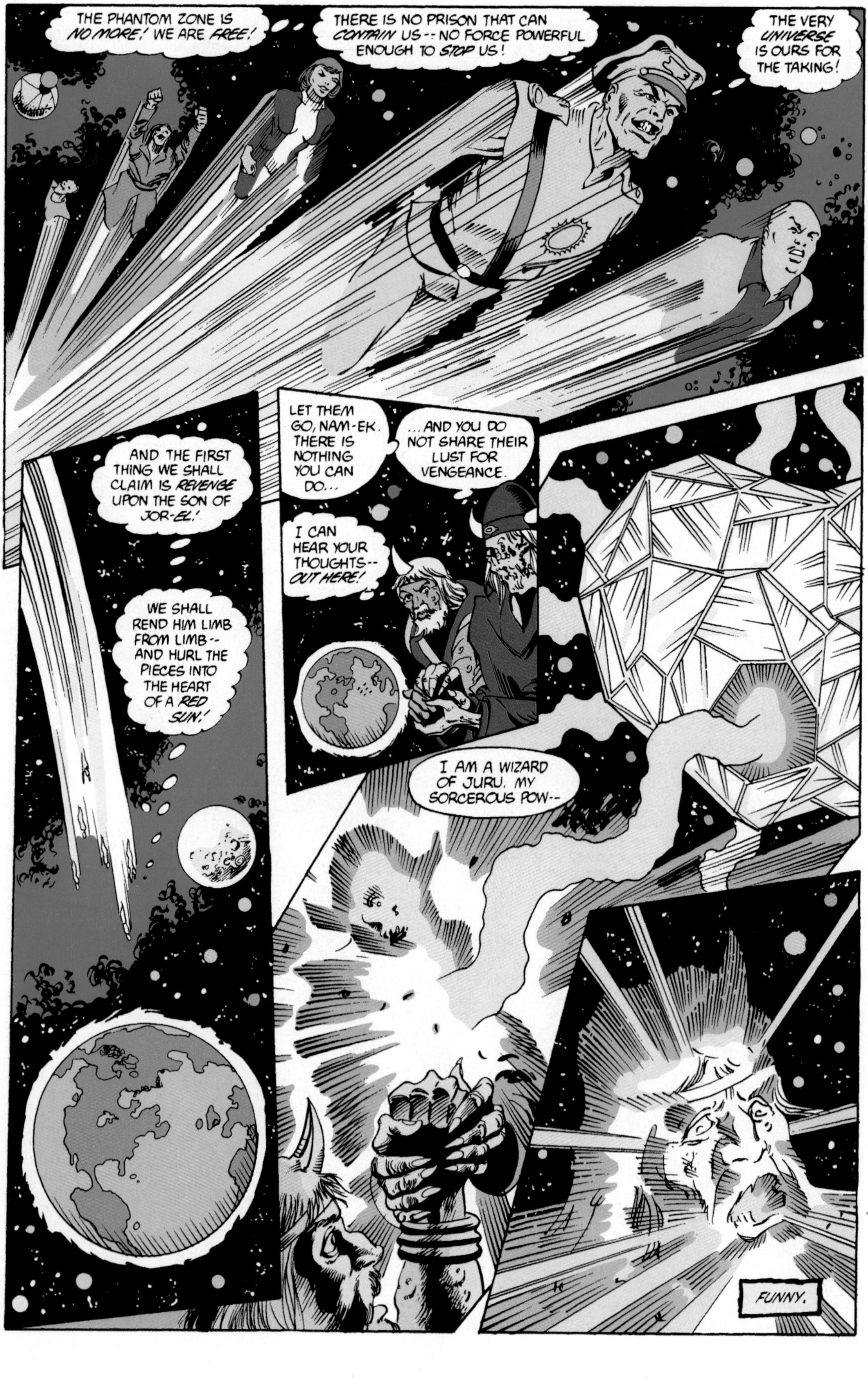
THE PHANTOM ZONE IS NO MORE! WE ARE FREE!
THERE IS NO PRISON THAT CAN CONTAIN US-- NO FORCE POWERFUL ENOUGH TO STOP US!
THE VERY UNIVERSE IS OURS FOR THE TAKING!
AND THE FIRST THING WE SHALL CLAIM IS REVENGE UPON THE SON OF JOR-EL!
WE SHALL REND HIM LIMB FROM LIMB-- AND HURL THE PIECES INTO THE HEART OF A RED SUN!
LET THEM GO, NAM-EK. THERE IS NOTHING YOU CAN DO...
...AND YOU DO NOT SHARE THEIR LUST FOR VENGEANCE.
I CAN HEAR YOUR THOUGHTS-- OUT HERE!
I AM A WIZARD OF JURU. MY SORCEROUS POW--
FUNNY.

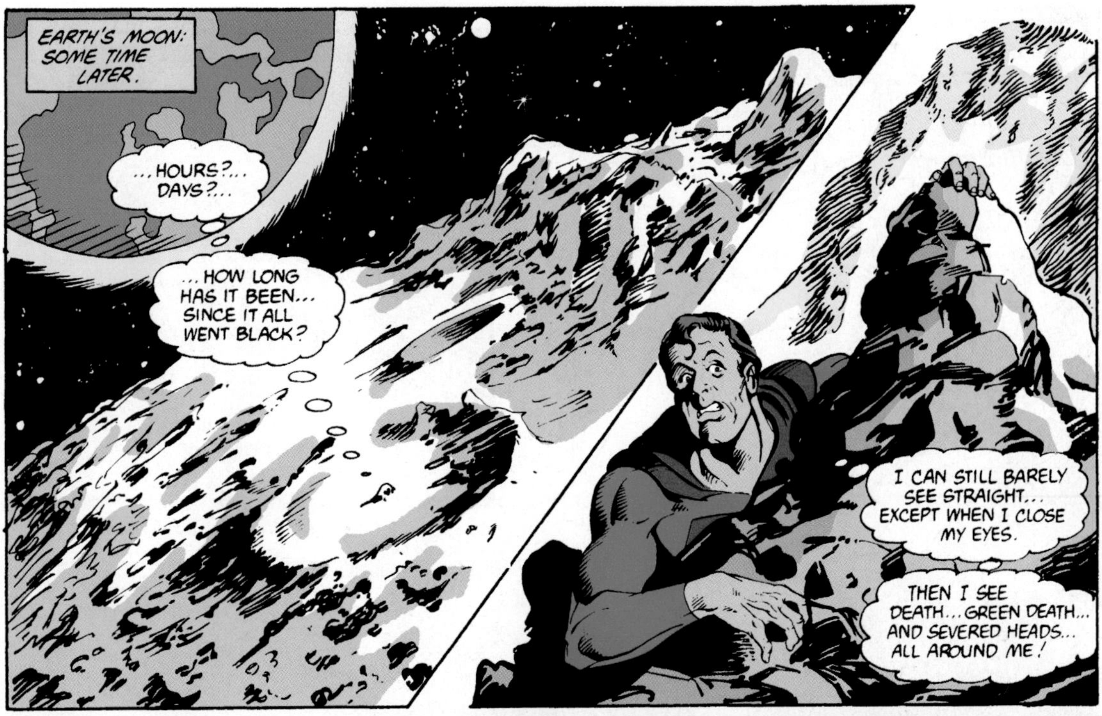
EARTH'S MOON: SOME TIME LATER.
...HOURS?... DAYS?...
...HOW LONG HAS IT BEEN... SINCE IT ALL WENT BLACK?
I CAN STILL BARELY SEE STRAIGHT... EXCEPT WHEN I CLOSE MY EYES.
THEN I SEE DEATH... GREEN DEATH... AND SEVERED HEADS... ALL AROUND ME!

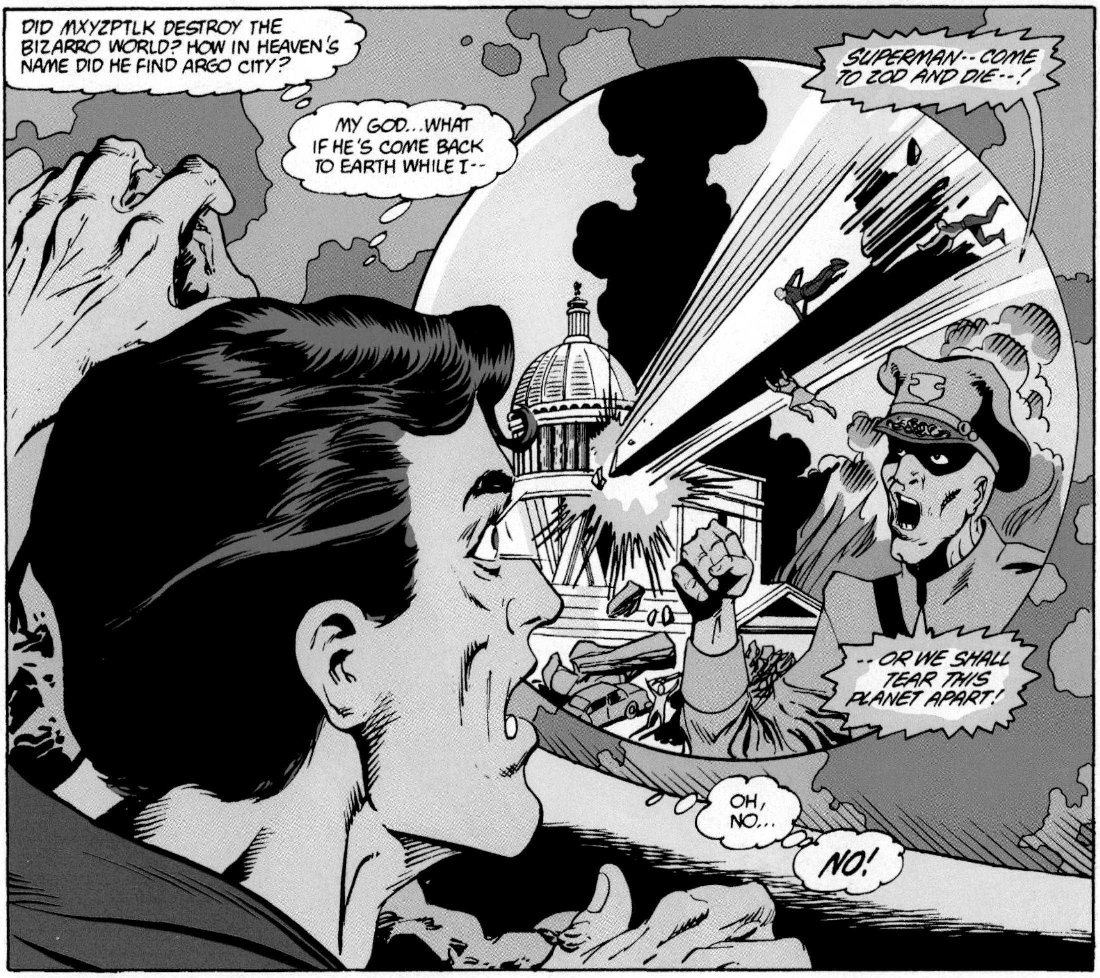
DID MXYZPTLK DESTROY THE BIZARRO WORLD? HOW IN HEAVEN'S NAME DID HE FIND ARGO CITY?
MY GOD...WHAT IF HE'S COME BACK TO EARTH WHILE I--
SUPERMAN--COME TO ZOD AND DIE--!
--OR WE SHALL TEAR THIS PLANET APART!
OH, NO...
NO!

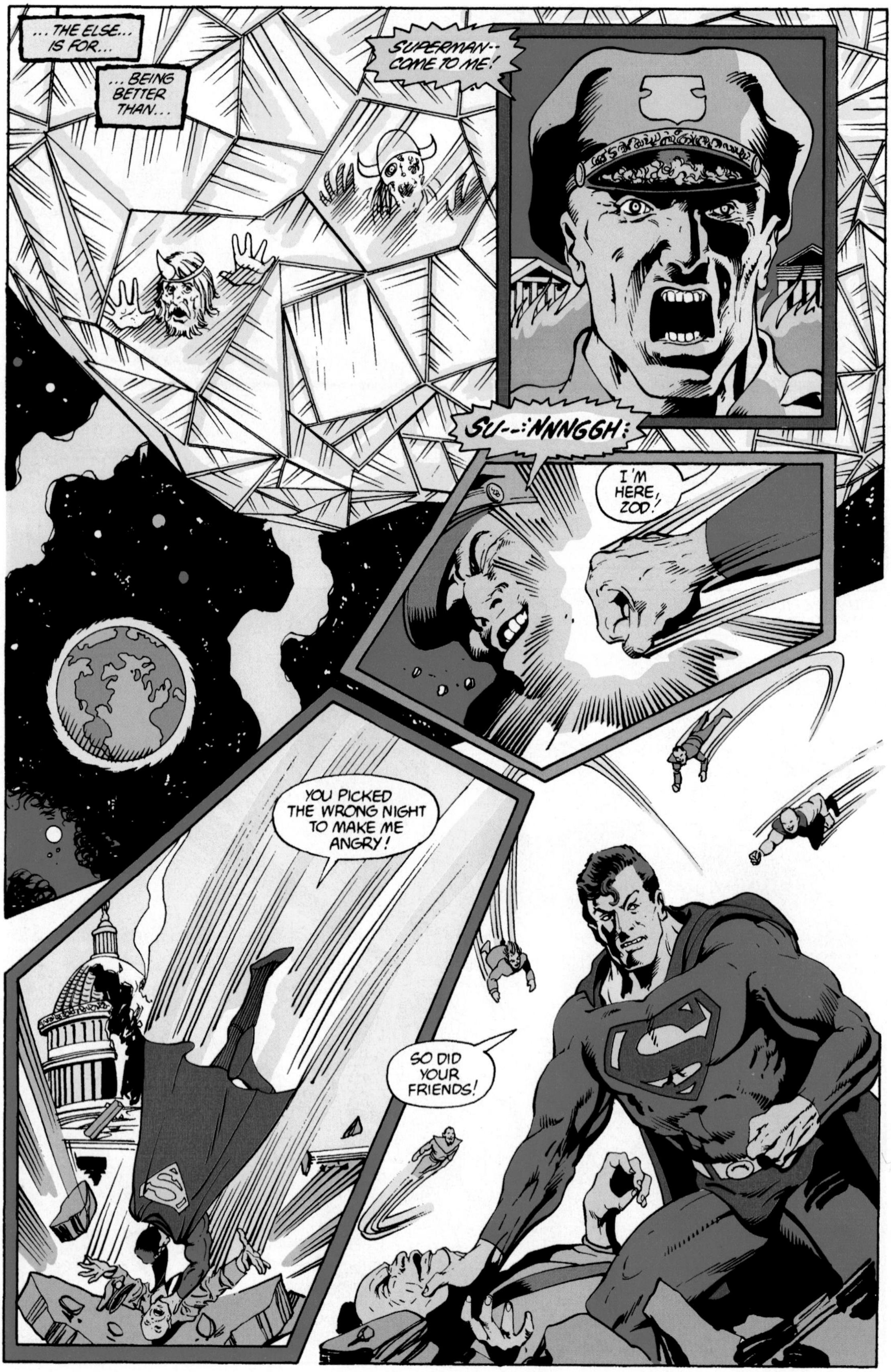
...THE ELSE... IS FOR...
...BEING BETTER THAN...
SUPERMAN-- COME TO ME!
SU--NNNGGH!
I'M HERE, ZOD!
YOU PICKED THE WRONG NIGHT TO MAKE ME ANGRY!
SO DID YOUR FRIENDS!

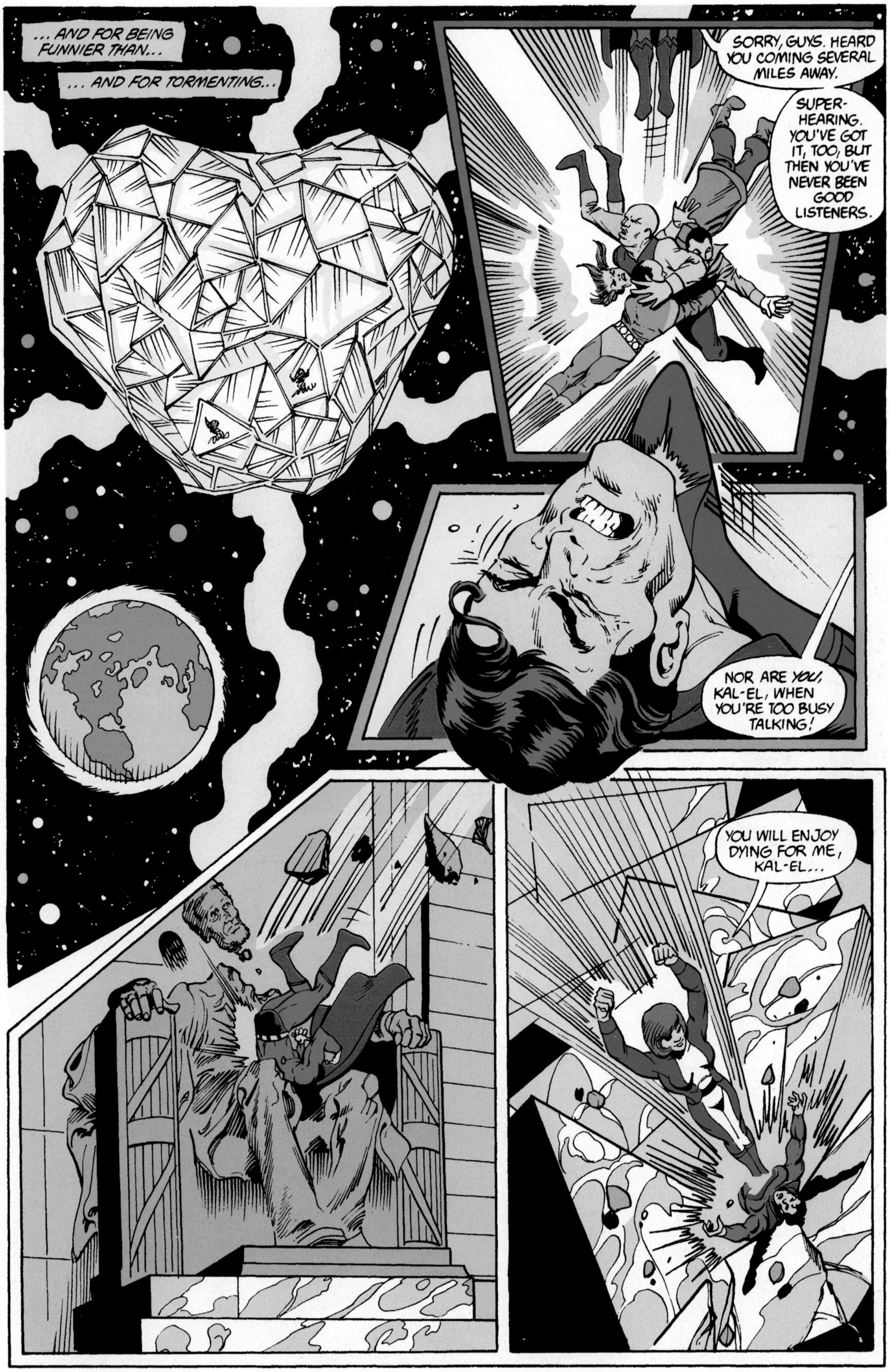
...AND FOR BEING FUNNIER THAN...
...AND FOR TORMENTING...
SORRY, GUYS. HEARD YOU COMING SEVERAL MILES AWAY.
SUPER-HEARING. YOU'VE GOT IT, TOO, BUT THEN YOU'VE NEVER BEEN GOOD LISTENERS.
NOR ARE YOU, KAL-EL, WHEN YOU'RE TOO BUSY TALKING!
YOU WILL ENJOY DYING FOR ME, KAL-EL...

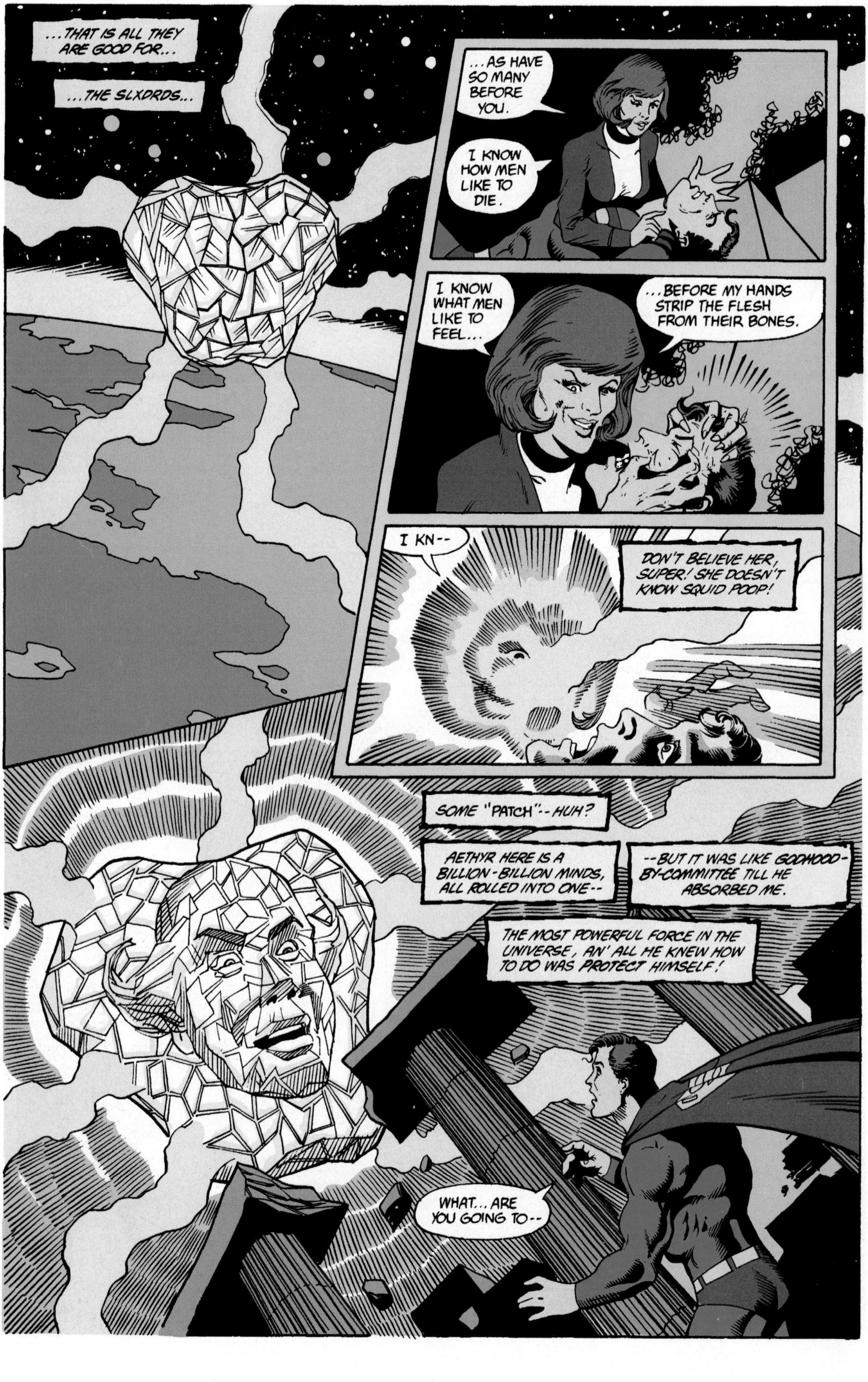
...THAT IS ALL THEY ARE GOOD FOR...
...THE SLXDRDS...
...AS HAVE SO MANY BEFORE YOU.
I KNOW HOW MEN LIKE TO DIE.
I KNOW WHAT MEN LIKE TO FEEL...
...BEFORE MY HANDS STRIP THE FLESH FROM THEIR BONES.
I KN--
DON'T BELIEVE HER, SUPER! SHE DOESN'T KNOW SQUID POOP!
SOME "PATCH"--HUH?
AETHYR HERE IS A BILLION-BILLION MINDS, ALL ROLLED INTO ONE--
--BUT IT WAS LIKE GODHOOD-BY-COMMITTEE TILL HE ABSORBED ME.
THE MOST POWERFUL FORCE IN THE UNIVERSE, AN' ALL HE KNEW HOW TO DO WAS PROTECT HIMSELF!
WHAT... ARE YOU GOING TO--

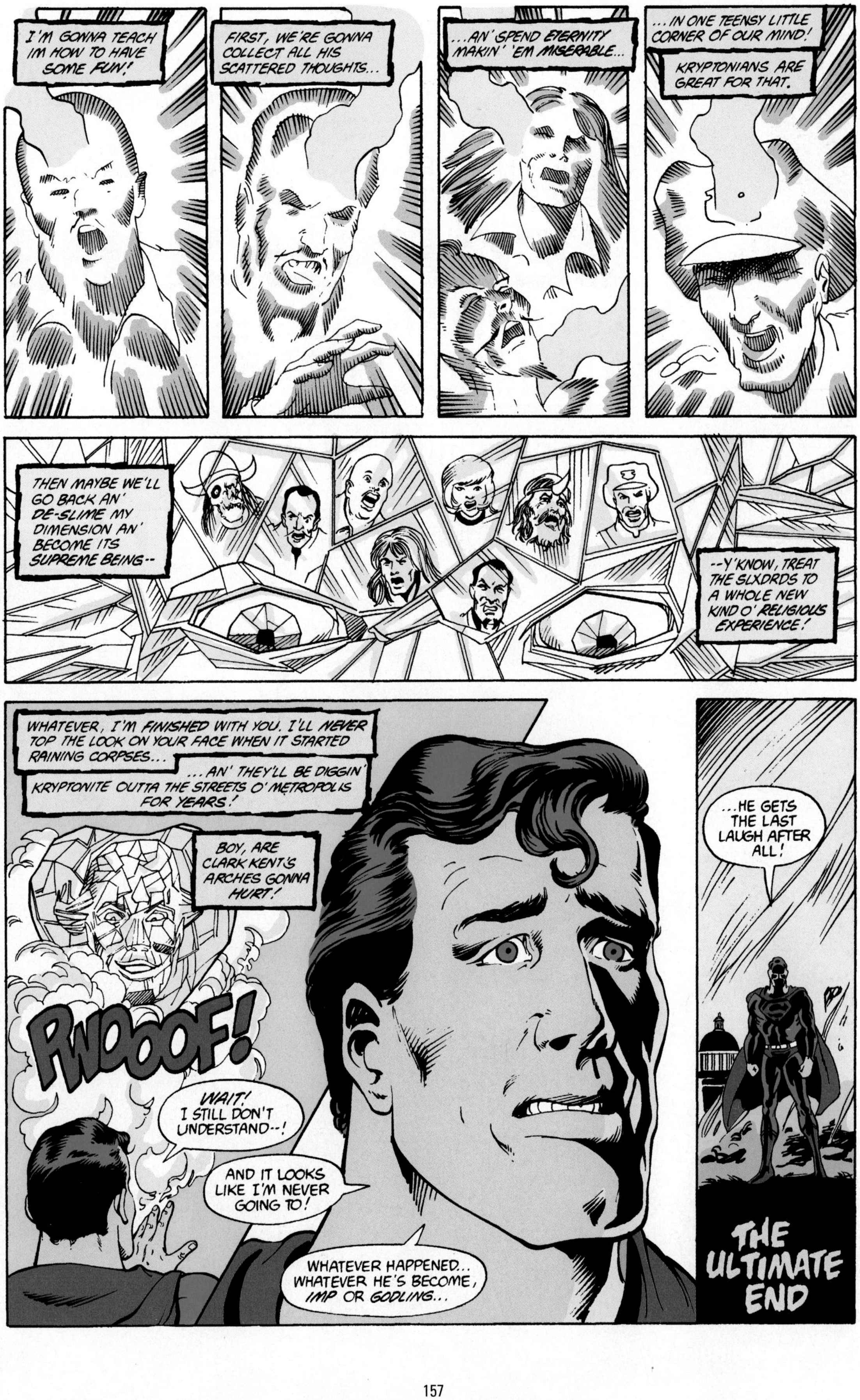
I'M GONNA TEACH IM HOW TO HAVE SOME FUN!
FIRST, WE'RE GONNA COLLECT ALL HIS SCATTERED THOUGHTS...
...AN' SPEND ETERNITY MAKIN' 'EM MISERABLE...
...IN ONE TEENSY LITTLE CORNER OF OUR MIND!
KRYPTONIANS ARE GREAT FOR THAT.
THEN MAYBE WE'LL GO BACK AN' DE-SLIME MY DIMENSION AN' BECOME ITS SUPREME BEING--
--Y'KNOW, TREAT THE SLXDRDS TO A WHOLE NEW KIND O' RELIGIOUS EXPERIENCE!
WHATEVER, I'M FINISHED WITH YOU. I'LL NEVER TOP THE LOOK ON YOUR FACE WHEN IT STARTED RAINING CORPSES...
...AN' THEY'LL BE DIGGIN' KRYPTONITE OUTTA THE STREETS O' METROPOLIS FOR YEARS!
BOY, ARE CLARK KENT'S ARCHES GONNA HURT!
PWOOOF!
WAIT! I STILL DON'T UNDERSTAND--!
AND IT LOOKS LIKE I'M NEVER GOING TO!
WHATEVER HAPPENED... WHATEVER HE'S BECOME, IMP OR GODLING...
...HE GETS THE LAST LAUGH AFTER ALL!
THE ULTIMATE END

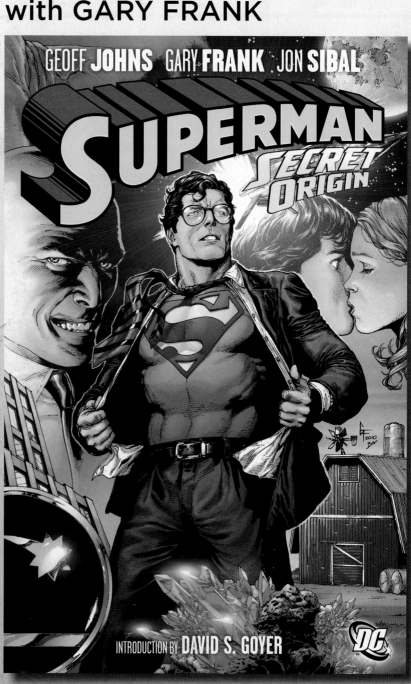

"It's fresh air. I like this all-too-human Superman, and I think a lot of you will, too."
—SCRIPPS HOWARD NEWS SERVICE

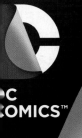

START AT THE BEGINNING!

SUPERMAN: ACTION COMICS VOLUME 1: SUPERMAN AND THE MEN OF STEEL

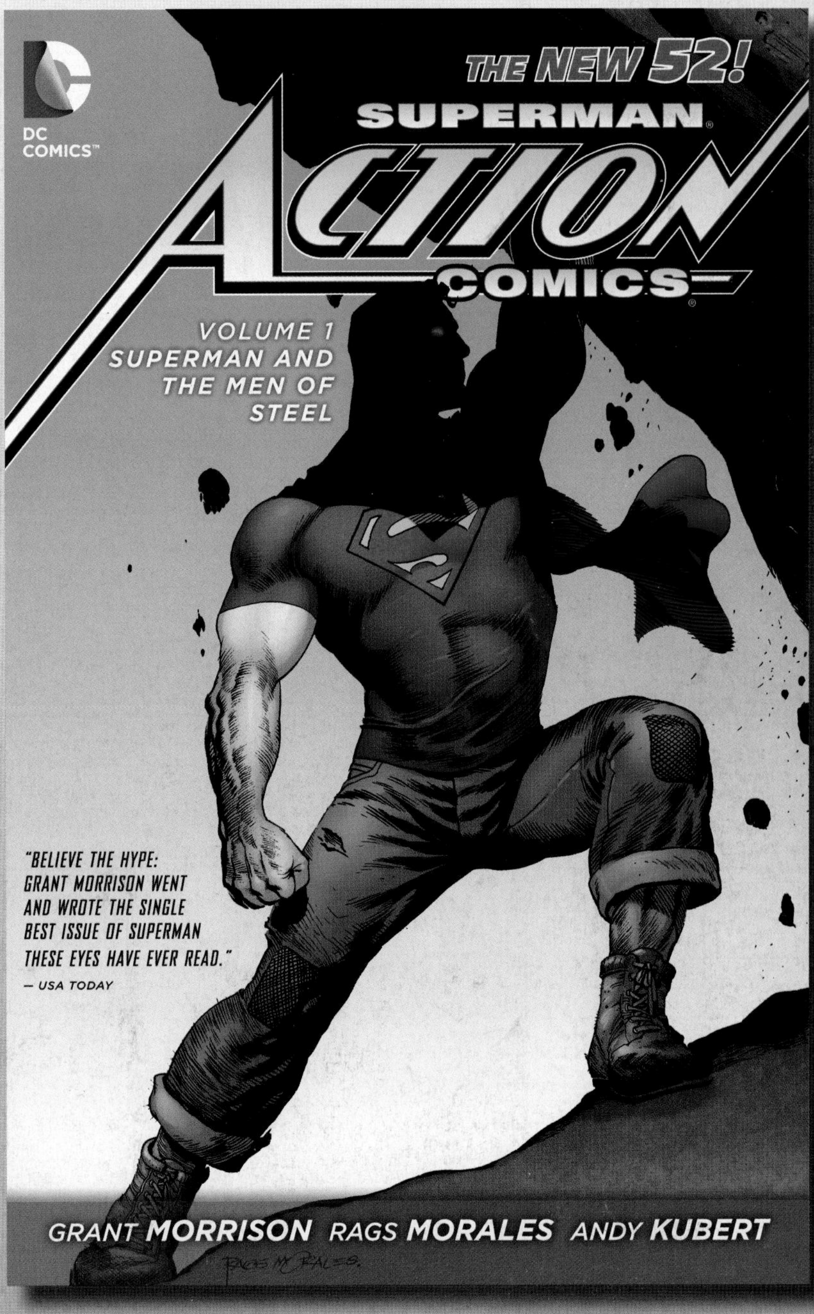

DC COMICS
THE NEW 52!
SUPERMAN
ACTION COMICS
VOLUME 1
SUPERMAN AND THE MEN OF STEEL
"BELIEVE THE HYPE: GRANT MORRISON WENT AND WROTE THE SINGLE BEST ISSUE OF SUPERMAN THESE EYES HAVE EVER READ."
— USA TODAY
GRANT MORRISON RAGS MORALES ANDY KUBERT

SUPERMAN VOLUME 1: WHAT PRICE TOMORROW?

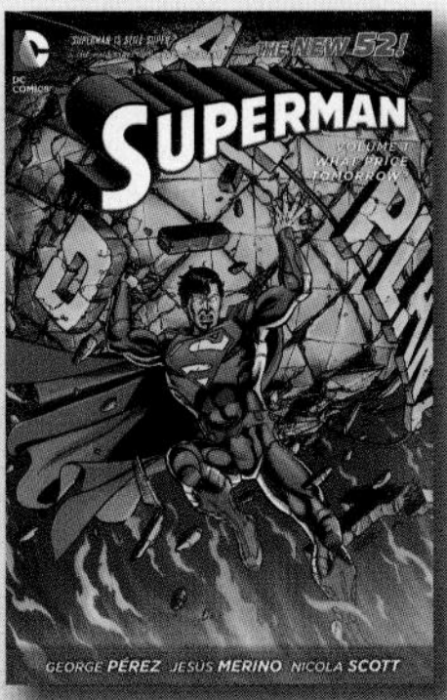

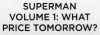

THE NEW 52!
SUPERMAN
GEORGE PÉREZ JESUS MERINO NICOLA SCOTT

SUPERGIRL VOLUME 1: THE LAST DAUGHTER OF KRYPTON

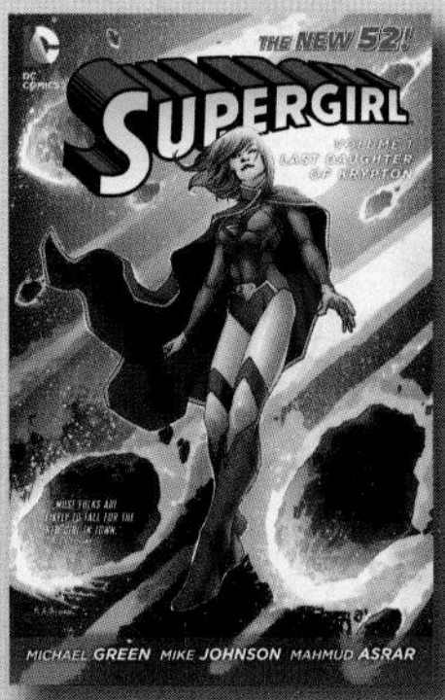

THE NEW 52!
SUPERGIRL
MICHAEL GREEN MIKE JOHNSON MAHMUD ASRAR

SUPERBOY VOLUME 1: INCUBATION

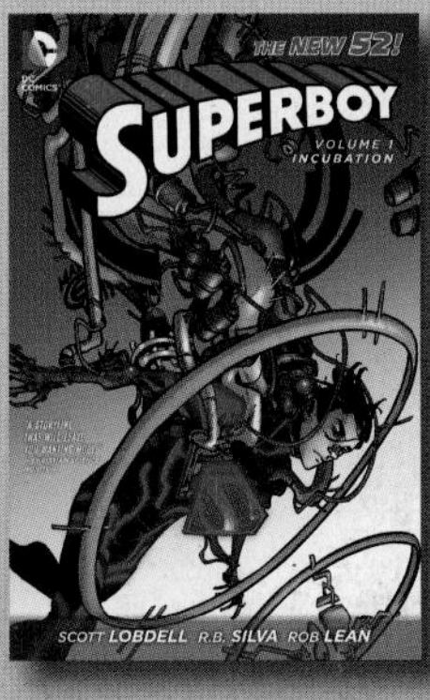

THE NEW 52!
SUPERBOY
VOLUME 1 INCUBATION
SCOTT LOBDELL R.B. SILVA ROB LEAN